MIND
WATCHING

MIND
WATCHING

WHY WE BEHAVE THE WAY WE DO

HANS AND MICHAEL EYSENCK

This edition published in the United Kingdom in 1994 by MMB,
an imprint of Multimedia Books Limited,
32/34 Gordon House Road, London NW5 1LP

Exclusive distribution in the USA by
Smithmark Publishers Inc.
16 East 32nd Street, New York, NY10016

Editor: Anne Cope
Production: Hugh Allan, Zivia Desai
Design: Bob Hook and Ivor Claydon
Picture research: Pat Hodgson

A catalogue record for this book is available from the British Library.

ISBN 1 85375 164 2

Typeset by Wyvern Typesetting, Bristol, UK
Printed in the Czech Republic by Imago

To Fleur, with love from her father and grandfather

Contents

D • PERCEPTION AND PROBLEM-SOLVING

E • THE USES OF PSYCHOLOGY

Prologue

One of our major concerns in writing this book is to demonstrate that the only way in which we can ever hope to obtain complete understanding of ourselves and our behaviour is by integrating information from several different disciplines. Psychology lies at the meeting point of several other sciences, including physiology, genetics, biology, anthropology, zoology and sociology. The structure of this book is based on the assumption that human beings can and should be looked at from several different perspectives.

Section A considers men and women as social animals and group members. Other people are far and away the most important factors in our environment, and psychology must encompass that fact. The subject matter is similar to that of *sociology*, but social psychologists tend to be more inclined to adopt a scientific approach to social phenomena than sociologists.

Section B considers the human species in the light of evolution. This approach obviously overlaps with the sciences of *zoology* and *biology*, and allows us to see the extent to which we have been moulded by evolutionary forces. The emphasis is on primates such as monkeys and apes, because these are more likely to provide us with relevant information about ourselves than the rats and pigeons so beloved of certain psychologists.

Section C considers human beings from the inside, so to speak. This is traditionally the territory explored by researchers in *physiology*, but there are many psychophysiologists who believe (as we do) that physiology and psychology are intimately related. This section also deals with certain aspects of the nature–nurture controversy, and thus relates to the science of *genetics*.

Section D considers men and women as fallible problem-solvers who have to cope with a complex environment. This requires the use of many psychological processes, including attention, perception, thinking and memory. This section is perhaps the most purely psychological in the sense that other sciences do not usually study these processes in any detail.

Section E deals mainly with important *applications* of psychological research. The chapters in this section demonstrate the great value of psychology in treating clinical conditions, in bringing up children, in improving our educational system, and even in understanding the roots of political ideology.

In sum, the hope is that psychology can make real progress by combining information from different scientific approaches. Several such approaches are discussed at length in this book, and we show how much progress has already been made. As yet, psychology is only a sturdy toddler; one day, it will grow to adulthood.

Hans and Michael Eysenck
London 1989

A
PERSON TO PERSON

Very complicated psychological processes are involved when human beings get together. Now although sociologists and social psychologists are both interested in people's social activities, the former tend to be interested in large groups within society—political organizations, social classes, industrial concerns—whereas the latter are more concerned with small groups—20 people or fewer.

In practical terms, sociologists are hampered by their inability to do anything but simply observe what is happening and to guess why it is happening. They are not usually in a position to alter the way a large organization is run in order to explore the consequences. In other words, sociologists cannot carry out experiments in the normal sense of that word. This is not necessarily a crippling disadvantage. After all, astronomers cannot directly affect the workings of the universe to see what happens, but they have made major discoveries.

In contrast to sociologists and astronomers, social psychologists can very readily carry out experiments. They can set up small groups, they can manipulate the activities in which such groups participate, and they can even decide who is allowed to talk to whom and when. Some of the choicest fruits of their labour are discussed in the chapters that follow.

One of the saddest phenomena of contemporary urban life is the well-known tendency for bystanders not to get involved when there is an accident or other emergency. This is often blamed on the generally uncaring and selfish attitudes of Western society, but there is convincing evidence (Chapter 1) that other factors are involved. For example, when we see other people not responding to an emergency we assume that nothing serious has happened.

A particularly interesting and important question in social psychology is this: Why are people attracted to one another? While people usually say that personal qualities such as friendliness, honesty and warmth are what matter most, research suggests that physical attractiveness is much more important than is generally supposed. Indeed, Michael Efran of the University of Toronto (Chapter 2) found that jurors were less certain about the guilt of attractive defendants and recommended much milder punishment for them!

In Chapter 3 we deal with the mysteries of non-verbal communication—touch, eye contact, smiling, personal space. This is the method of communication we use to express positive and negative feelings towards others. The most surprising thing about non-verbal communication is that often neither the communicator nor the recipient is aware of what is happening. Nevertheless we send and receive non-verbal signals in an amazingly sensitive and well-orchestrated way.

Many social psychologists are interested in the effects of power and status on human behaviour. After all, there are important status differences between the members of many social groups. This is especially clear at work, where the boss is regarded as the leader, and everyone else plays a subordinate role. But the disastrous consequences of having powerful leaders are revealed clearly by a study of history, which is full of horrifying examples of abuse of power, of slavish obedience to brutal authority.

On the face of it, it seems difficult to investigate such manifestations of power in the laboratory. Nevertheless Philip Zimbardo (Chapter 5) set up a mock prison at Stanford University, using respectable college students as mock guards and prisoners. He naturally assumed that they would behave in a civilized fashion. To his surprise the mock guards rapidly started to abuse their position of power over the pseudo-prisoners. In an even more celebrated and disturbing study at Yale, Stanley Milgram (Chapter 4) discovered that many people were prepared to administer near-lethal electric shocks to a hapless victim if ordered to do so by an authority figure.

Since apparently normal and well-adjusted people were used in these studies, Zimbardo and Milgram both concluded that abuses of power occur primarily because society inculcates the notion that followers are expected to obey leaders, no matter what orders are issued. In other words, abuse of power is inevitable in certain situations, and does not necessarily occur because leaders are sadists or psychopaths.

However, we believe that individual differences in personality are more important than Zimbardo and Milgram admitted. Only some of the people in their studies abused their position, and neither Zimbardo nor Milgram really explained this aspect of their findings.

There has been much bitter controversy as to the possible ill effects on society of the media's apparent obsession with sex and violence. This controversy has generated much more heat than light, in part because many of the contributors to it have had their own vested interests to defend.

Psychologists have carried out a lot of painstaking research in this area, and the fruits of their labour are examined in Chapter 6. There *are* certain types of people who are pushed in the direction of greater aggression and callousness by what they see, hear and read.

One of the major lessons of the Zimbardo and Milgram studies is that people often act in aggressive and unpleasant ways largely because of the *situation* they find themselves in. This was borne out by a study (Chapter 7) in which perfectly sane volunteers presented themselves at various psychiatric hospitals complaining of fictional symptoms. The researcher, David Rosenhan of Stanford University, predicted that under such circumstances the psychiatrists concerned would have a strong tendency to apply a psychiatric label to completely normal people, and that is exactly what he found.

Fortunately, Rosenhan's conclusion that we cannot tell the difference between the sane and the insane does not appear to be true, although it is worrying that the way in which we react to other people is greatly affected by the labels applied to them. If you meet someone at a party you are almost certain to treat them differently if you are told they are a schizophrenic or a psychopath rather than a nurse. This is, of course, a sensible policy. But what if the label is wrong?

There is an important ethical point worth pondering as you read these chapters. Many of the most dramatic findings are the result of studies in which the participants were thoroughly deceived about major aspects of the experiment. In some cases, too, things were arranged so that the participants were almost bound to be embarrassed, frightened or humiliated.

Most psychologists would argue that ends can justify means. In other words, if the findings of an experiment are important enough, they may justify a certain amount of discomfort on the part of the participants. This position makes some sense, but it raises two awkward questions. First, how much agreement is there on the relative importance of a particular experiment? Second, is the amount of discomfort predictable *before* the experiment is carried out? There are no categorical answers to such questions. However, the British Psychological Society and the American Psychological Association have both issued guidelines on ethical principles in recent years.

Chapter 1
THE BAD SAMARITAN

One of the recurring images of our time is that of someone being attacked and screaming for help in the middle of a large, impersonal city, his or her cries going unheard, and the onlookers doing absolutely nothing except mind their own business. This apparent apathy has been used as evidence of the alienated and uncaring attitude which modern cities induce in most of their inhabitants.

There have certainly been many real-life incidents that seem to fit this gloomy picture. A famous example was the case of Kitty Genovese, who was stabbed to death in the Queens area of New York City as she returned home from work at 3 o'clock in the morning. Yet there were 38 witnesses who not merely saw but *watched* the murder from the windows of their apartments, and none of them intervened. Only one person took the relatively modest step of calling the police, and even that action was only taken after he had sought the advice of a friend in another part of the city.

When this horrifying story was given massive coverage in the *New York Times*, there were apoplectic reactions from readers, several of whom wrote letters demanding that the names of the witnesses should be published so that they could be exposed to the public contempt they deserved. Various noted psychiatrists sought to explain the apathetic attitude of the witnesses. More interesting than the explanations themselves was the fact that they had practically nothing in common. Dr George Serban argued as follows: 'It's the air of all New York, the air of injustice. The feeling that you might get hurt if you act and that whatever you do, you will be the one to suffer.' Dr Ralph S. Banay suggested that the apathy of the bystanders was caused by confusion between fantasy and reality, a confusion engendered by an endless stream of television violence: 'We underestimate the damage these accumulated images do to the brain . . . they were deaf, paralyzed, hypnotized with excitation. Fascinated by the drama, by the action, and yet not entirely sure that what was taking place was actually happening.' Perhaps some of the bystanders expected Kojak to materialize and solve the problem!

In another incident in New York, this time in the Bronx, an 18-year-old switchboard operator was raped and beaten while alone in her office. She escaped briefly from her attacker, and ran naked and bleeding into the street, screaming for help. Approximately 40 people gathered and watched in broad daylight as the rapist tried to drag her back upstairs. Not one of them came to her rescue despite her screams. She was finally rescued by two policemen who happened to be passing.

Then there was the case of Andrew Mormille, a 17-year-old boy who was stabbed in the stomach as he went home by train in Manhattan. Although his attackers promptly left the compartment, not one of the other eleven people in the compartment tried to help the boy as he bled to death. A full-length feature film, *The Incident*, was based on this murder.

KEY EXPERIMENT: DIFFUSION OF RESPONSIBILITY

John Darley and Bibb Latané of New York University[1,2] were intrigued by the Kitty Genovese case. Was the apparent apathy displayed by the witnesses quite what it seemed? They pointed out that although it seems sensible to suppose that the greater the number of people who witness an incident the more likely the victim is to receive assistance, this proved shockingly untrue in the Genovese case. With so many witnesses to the murder, surely someone should have gone to the girl's assistance?

Darley and Latané argued that, paradoxically, a victim may be in a more fortunate position with just one bystander than with several. In such a situation, responsibility for helping the victim falls firmly on to one person rather than being spread among many. In other words, when there are many observers of a crime or an emergency there is a diffusion of responsibility. Potential blame for failing to help is also distributed. Each person bears a small portion of the guilt, rather than the full weight of it.

Darley and Latané tested their ideas in a series of experiments in which the experimenter explained that he was interested in learning about the kinds of personal problems faced by college students when confronted with the pressures of an urban environment. To save any embarrassment about discussing personal problems in front of strangers, the students were told, they were to remain anonymous and would be placed in separate rooms. The experimenter told them he would not listen to their discussions, because the presence of an outside listener might prove inhibiting. Communication was to be by means of microphones, each subject hearing other people's communications through a pair of headphones. Subjects were led to believe that there were one, two, three or six people in the discussion at any one time. In fact, in

The presence of the police at an accident usually absolves the casual onlooker from the responsibility of helping.

The man in the foreground has clearly labelled the figure on the sidewalk as drunk or undeserving. The other man is not so sure. Will he stop?

each 'discussion' there was only one real subject—contributions from other 'subjects' were tape-recorded.

The future 'victim' spoke first in the discussion, saying that he was finding it difficult to adjust to New York City and to his academic studies. In tones indicating a feeling of some embarrassment, he mentioned that he was prone to seizures, especially when studying hard or having to take examinations. All of the other 'subjects' then contributed in turn, after which the victim spoke again. His voice became loud and incoherent, finishing up as follows: 'I–er–I–uh–I've got one of these–er–seizure er–er–things coming on and–and–and I could really–er–use some help so if somebody would–er–er–help–er–er–help–er–uh–uh–uh (choking sounds) . . . I'm gonna die–er–er–I'm . . . gonna die–er–help–er–er–seizure–er . . . (choking sounds, silence).'

The researchers wanted to see whether the listening subjects would leave the room to go to the assistance of the student who was apparently having an epileptic fit. Of those subjects who thought they were the only person who knew the 'victim' was having an epileptic attack, every single one left the room and reported the emergency. On the other hand, of those who believed that four other subjects had also heard the victim's pleas for help, only 62

per cent responded. Since everyone heard the same tape recording of the emergency, diffusion of responsibility had clearly occurred.

Of course, all of this is rather academic from the victim's point of view. He doesn't care who helps him, as long as someone does. From his perspective, the important question is whether his chances are better with, say, five bystanders than with one. In the Darley and Latané study, the 'victim's' chances of being helped within 45 seconds of the onset of his fit were about 50 per cent with a single bystander, but 0 per cent with five bystanders. In other words, help is more likely to be forthcoming, and more quickly, when there is only one bystander.

A further interesting observation made by Darley and Latané concerned participants' awareness of the factors determining whether or not they responded to the appeal for help. Subjects who believed there were four other bystanders, and who said they were aware of this fact when the epileptic seizure occurred, consistently claimed that it had had no effect on their own behaviour.

Darley and Latané also considered the behaviour of those participants who failed to report the emergency. In contrast to the stereotyped view of such people, they were by no means 'apathetic'. Most of them asked the experimenter if the victim was all right and being taken care of. Many showed various signs of nervousness (trembling hands, sweating palms) and actually seemed more emotionally aroused than the participants who reported the emergency. They had not decided *not* to intervene, it seemed, but were in an uncomfortable state of indecision.

These people waiting at a bus stop are in a bind. They cannot ignore the figure on the ground, nor can they walk away—they have a bus to catch. Only two people have decided to find out what is wrong.

TAKING OUR CUE FROM OTHERS

Of course, the number of bystanders is by no means the only factor that determines whether a victim will be assisted or not. As Latané and Darley pointed out, there are several stages involved in reacting to an emergency. First, the incident must be noticed and interpreted. The process of interpretation is vital, since many emergencies have an ambiguous quality about them—the man lying in the gutter may have had a heart attack or he may have had too much to drink. In the light of the chosen interpretation, the bystander has to decide where his responsibility lies, what kind of assistance, if any, is warranted. Then he must act on his decision.

Latané and Darley were quite right to argue that the process of interpretation is especially important. Emergencies are rare occurrences and most of us are ill-equipped to identify them or respond to them. So what sort of information do we use to clarify matters? Most of the time we take our cue from other people. If they look worried, it's an emergency. If they remain calm and unruffled, the incident can safely be ignored.

To probe the influence of social factors Latané and Darley did a simple study in which two girls started playing frisbee in a waiting room at Grand Central Station in New York. When the frisbee was thrown to a confederate, she either joined in enthusiastically or accused the girls of being childish and acting dangerously, and promptly kicked the frisbee back. If the confederate responded negatively, none of the other people in the waiting room joined in throwing the frisbee; but if the confederate joined in, so did 86 per cent of the other people present. Indeed, in the latter situation people wandered over from other parts of the waiting area to join in, and the girls' main problem was how to bring the frisbee-throwing game to a halt!

The importance of social influence on bystander intervention was demonstrated in another study, this time conducted at Princeton University by John Darley and his associates. The participants were all asked to do some sketching, and were either put in a room alone or with one other participant. Participants either sat facing each other, or back to back. While they were busy sketching, a workman in the adjoining room pushed over some heavy screens, which fell with a resounding crash. This was followed immediately by a cry of 'Oh, my leg!' and a series of loud groans. Ninety per cent of the participants who were on their own went to the assistance of the workman, 80 per cent of the facing pairs of participants responded to the crash, but only 20 per cent of the back-to-back pairs tried to help.

Why the huge difference between the facing pairs and the back-to-back pairs? Why did not seeing each other make so much difference? The answer may be that the interpretation of an ambiguous event such as the sound of a crash is greatly affected by the reactions of other people. In the face-to-face situation each participant could see his partner's startled response to the crash, and so the interpretation that there was a genuine emergency was strengthened. Virtually all the people sitting face to face indicated that they thought the crash meant something was wrong, but only half of those sitting back to back interpreted the crash in this way. So the behaviour of other bystanders is crucial and can have very diverse effects. There have been numerous cases of mass panic, sometimes with disastrous results. The stock market crash of October 1987 was a case in point. On the other hand, if some members of a group indicate by their passive and unconcerned behaviour that an event is *not* an emergency, the response of the rest of the group may be inhibited.

The negative effect of social influence was investigated by Latané and Darley in another study in which participants faced an ambiguous but potentially dangerous situation (smoke wafting into the experiment room through a small vent). They faced this situation alone, or with two other participants, or with two confederates of Latané and Darley who had been briefed to stare at the smoke for a moment, shrug their shoulders, and then totally ignore it.

Seventy-five per cent of the solo participants went out of the room to report the possible emergency, compared with only 10 per cent of those in the company of the confederates who ignored the danger. As comedian and Harvard professor Tom Lehrer pointed out many years ago, people would rather die than make asses of themselves! It was clearly the impassive behaviour of the two confederates which inhibited participants' reactions , because the smoke was more frequently reported when there were three genuine participants present, each reinforcing the others' apprehension.

THE NUMBERS GAME

In short, it may be dangerous to rely on the old adage about 'safety in numbers'. If there are several bystanders in an emergency, they may be less inclined than a single bystander to do anything constructive. This may be because each of them feels it is not particularly his or her responsibility to intervene, or because the passive and controlled behaviour of other bystanders indicates that there is no emergency. The denial or diffusion of responsibility in a crowd seems to be more marked in women than men, presumably because it is a cultural tradition that women let men take the initiative in emergencies.

Bibb Latané and his associates also asked people to clap or shout as loudly as possible, either on their own or in small groups of various sizes, and found that the sound of twelve hands clapping was not even three times as loud as the sound of two. The same was true for shouting. They concluded that this was evidence of the same behaviour shown by groups of bystanders: social buck-passing.

Are there any circumstances in which the presence of other bystanders might help rather than hinder direct intervention? Perhaps the desire to gain the approval of others might sometimes lead a bystander to go to the rescue? In an experiment set up to examine this question, participants were led to believe that four other people in the experiment would either be aware or not be aware of how they reacted to overhearing a violent fight between another participant and an 'intruder'—the incident ended in the intruder 'escaping' with the other participant's tape recorder. Of the bystanders who thought their reactions would not be seen by the others 39 per cent went to help, compared with 74 per cent of those who thought they were under observation. So the presence of other bystanders can have positive as well as negative consequences. Afterwards, many of the participants who thought they were being watched claimed that this actually *inhibited* them from helping, which shows an interesting difference between their actual behaviour and their conscious awareness.

So the presence of other bystanders can also make it *more* likely that people will help in an emergency, but only if the situation is interpreted as a genuine emergency. Leonard Bickman provided evidence of this by setting up an experiment in which individual participants heard a bookcase apparently falling on another participant, followed by a scream. When a confederate of the experimenter interpreted the crash and the scream as an emergency, the participant 'bystander' offered assistance much faster than when the confederate suggested there was nothing to worry about. As expected, the confederate's interpretation of the incident influenced helping behaviour by altering the bystander's own interpretation: 93 per cent of the bystanders hearing the confederate say it was an emergency thought the victim had been hurt, against only 54 per cent of those told it was not an emergency.

THE VICTIM: WHO GETS HELPED?

Most liberal and egalitarian-minded individuals would like to think that all kinds of people are likely to be assisted in an emergency, but the available evidence indicates that bystanders are fairly selective in deciding who to help. One of the points that may have been important in the case of Kitty Genovese is that several of the onlookers thought the incident was 'a lover's quarrel', and most people's instinct in such circumstances is not to interfere. To investigate this further, Lance Shotland and Margaret Straw of Penn State University arranged for a violent quarrel and fight between a man and a woman to take place in the presence of or within earshot of witnesses. The woman started screaming and pleading 'Get away from me!' In order to establish the 'relationship' between the two for the benefit of the bystanders, the woman screamed either 'I don't know you!' or 'I don't know why I ever married you!'

The tendency to intervene was tremendously affected by the presumed relationship between the attacker and the victim: 65 per cent of the bystanders intervened when they thought the fight involved strangers, but only 19 per cent did so when they thought the fight involved a married couple. The bystanders obviously believed they had witnessed a genuine fight, because 30 per cent of the women witnesses feared sufficiently for their own safety to shut the door of their room, turn the lights out, and even lock the door!

Almost everyone not directly involved in this confrontation seems to want to restrain the protagonists. The mood of this crowd is that getting involved is the right thing to do.

Would you play the good Samaritan in this situation? All the clues—the wine bottle, the food wrappers, the gentleman calmly reading his paper—suggest that help is not needed.

There are probably several reasons why fewer people went to the assistance of the married couple. First, they thought a married woman would probably be embarrassed by the intervention of an outsider, whereas a woman attacked by a stranger wouldn't. Second, they assumed that a woman attacked by a stranger would be more in need of help than a woman attacked by her husband. And finally, it occurred to them that the man would be more likely to offer violence to anyone who interfered if the woman he was attacking was his wife.

A survey published by the Law Enforcement Assistance Administration in Washington, USA, showed that 60 per cent of assaults are on total strangers. But when Shotland and Straw showed films of a vicious fight between a man and a woman, only one person in thirty guessed that the two people were strangers. The overwhelming majority assumed that a close relationship existed between them. Interestingly, newspaper interviews with witnesses to real-life aggression confirm that bystanders usually assume that men beat up their nearest and dearest. In short, acts of aggression are less likely to be interrupted in large cities than in smaller communities. In a larger community the relationship between two fighting people is *less* likely to be known and therefore more likely to be misinterpreted.

A further reason why onlookers are reluctant to get involved in a fight between people they assume to be married is that they feel, rightly or wrongly, that the woman may be partly responsible for the attack on her. As a general rule, we have more sympathy for victims we believe to be blameless than for victims who appear to have 'asked for it'. The drunken bully in the bar who boasts of his great strength and then gets knocked out is left on the floor.

Irving Piliavin and his associates investigated this phenomenon by staging a number of incidents in the subway in New York. A male 'victim' staggered forward and collapsed on the floor, lying face up. Sometimes he carried a black cane and appeared sober, and sometimes he smelled of alcohol and carried a bottle of liquor wrapped in a brown paper bag. Less assistance was given when he was 'drunk' than when he was 'ill', probably because drunks are seen as responsible for their own plight, and because helping a smelly drunk who may vomit or become abusive involves greater 'cost'. However, provided there was one Good Samaritan who offered assistance, several more helpers were usually quick to materialize, irrespective it seemed of whether the victim was ill or drunk.

In an emergency, bystanders have to act rapidly on the basis of fairly meagre evidence. However, one fact about the victim that is immediately obvious is his or her race, and it is reasonable to assume that this plays a part in whether bystanders help or turn a blind eye. Samuel Gaertner of the University of Delaware put forward the interesting theory that most whites in the United States would prefer not to think of themselves as the sort of people who would ignore a black victim's cries for assistance if the responsibility for helping was clearly theirs alone. However, he argued, if the situation allowed them to rationalize their prejudice, then prejudice would operate, but in a fairly subtle manner.

Gaertner investigated this hypothesis by arranging for a series of white female bystanders to witness a stack of chairs falling on a screaming girl, who was either black or white. The bystanders were either alone or with a calm, impassive confederate of the experimenter. All the bystanders who witnessed the incident on their own went to the assistance of the injured victim. Her race did not affect their action. However, 90 per cent of those who were with the impassive confederate lent a helping hand to the white victim but only 30 per cent of them helped the black victim. In the latter situation, it was possible for them to rationalize their prejudice against the black victim simply by arguing that the incident was not serious or that it was not their particular responsibility to act. Incidentally, both in this study and in others, people who expressed unprejudiced views in questionnaires acted in just as biased a way as those who admitted they were prejudiced.

So the nature of the victim is important in determining whether he or she will receive help. In addition to the factors already discussed—race, assumed relationship between attacker and victim, assumed responsibility of the victim for his or her misfortune—there is the physical attractiveness of the victim to be taken into account. A good-looking victim is more likely to receive help than a victim with a 'port wine stain' birthmark on his face (see next chapter).

What does it cost to help a young and pretty motorcyclist? Not very much. And who knows where such gallantry might lead?

Why should the characteristics of the victim be so important? One theory is that the bystander decides whether or not to intervene on the basis of the 'costs' associated with helping (possible physical harm, verbal abuse, embarrassment) or the costs of not helping (guilt, censure from others), and the 'rewards' of helping (praise from self, victim and others) or the rewards of not helping (continuation of other activities). In this delicate balance of profit and loss, the costs will be high if the victim is perceived to be unpleasant or disgusting. In another experiment it was found that if a 'victim' collapsed in the subway, help was less likely to be offered, and was slower in arriving, when the victim had 'blood' (red food colouring) dribbling out of his mouth, despite his apparently greater need of assistance. Presumably the cost of helping a bloody victim is greater because most bystanders have an inbuilt fear of the sight of blood.

But of all the factors that have been found to affect bystanders' willingness to become involved, none has a more profound effect than the ambiguity or lack of ambiguity of the emergency. If it is obvious that someone is in desperate need of assistance, considerations such as the race of the victim, diffusion of responsibility, and social influence have relatively little effect—almost everyone rapidly and spontaneously does what they can to assist.

Russell Clark and Larry Word of Florida State University conducted an experiment in which bystanders either heard a maintenance man fall and cry out in agony, or simply heard him fall but not cry out. In the former situation, unambiguously an emergency, every group of subjects, whether they were alone or in pairs or in groups of five, provided assistance. In other words, there was no evidence of diffusion of responsibility at all. If it was unclear whether the incident was an emergency or not, as in the latter situation, assistance was only one-third as likely to be offered. Typically, bystanders in groups did not react at all in ambiguous situations.

The reason why ambiguity plays such a major role is that if a bystander interprets an ambiguous incident as *not* being an emergency, thinking of a suitable course of action and deciding to take on the responsibility of doing something become just too much trouble. In other words, the victim must be utterly convincing about the genuineness of his plight and his need for help.

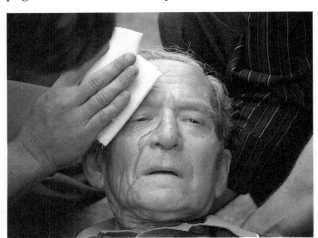

CONCLUSIONS

One of the main implications of the various studies mentioned in this chapter is that the notion of the apathetic bystander is extremely misleading. In many circumstances, almost all bystanders will do whatever is possible to help someone who is injured or in obvious distress.

The problem of deciding whether an event is or is not an emergency, and what to do about it if it is, is difficult because most of us lack experience of emergencies. Admittedly, society does provide us with some rules, but many of these are contradictory. 'Do unto others as you would have them do unto you' flatly contradicts 'Don't poke your nose into other people's business' or, as the Bible says more poetically, 'He that passeth by and meddleth with strife belonging not to him is like one that taketh a dog by the ears'.

The bystander usually knows neither the victim nor the attacker, and does not have the time to find out anything about them. He must respond on the basis of probability rather than certainty, and so he relies on the demeanour of other bystanders and the apparent worthiness of the victim as guides to action. His problem is made worse by anxiety, which makes him clumsier and slower than usual.

In fact, bystanders are probably more deserving of praise than censure. For the most part, they cope surprisingly well with upsetting, complicated, and rapidly changing events.

Even when there is blood, helping hands are never far away if the need for help is clear.

Chapter 2
HEY, GOOD-LOOKING!

Aristotle, who as usual managed to hit the nail on the head, argued that beauty was a greater recommendation than any letter of introduction. But until quite recently the social implications of physical attractiveness did not receive serious attention from psychologists. Perhaps this is because the idea that 'good looks will get you everywhere' assorts rather ill with the cosy, democratic philosophy that anyone can do anything with hard work and application. Our ignorance was such only a few years ago that we knew more about attractive stimuli for fish than for humans. People are, of course, more complicated than fish. While the three-spined stickleback can be relied on to become sexually excited when confronted with a red object, even a soggy piece of cardboard, human beings are less predictable. This unpredictability is captured in the

Although it is comforting to think that beauty lies in the eye of the beholder, there are norms of beauty to which we all respond.

saying 'Beauty is in the eye of the beholder'. People who are in love find each other more physically attractive than the facts usually warrant. But it is also the case that different people asked to sort a set of photographs of different faces into those of greater and lesser attractiveness will tend to agree with each other's opinions. The film industry capitalizes on this broad agreement when it invests in film stars of unusual physical attractiveness and mediocre acting ability.

STATURE AND STATUS, FACES AND BODIES

It is usually assumed that physical attractiveness is both easier to identify and more important in women than in men. However, height is a valued characteristic in Western men. As the distinguished American sociologist Feldman put it: 'American society is a society with a heightist premise: to be tall is to be good and to be short is to be stigmatized.' In support of this contention, Feldman

noted that every American president elected this century was the taller of the two major political candidates, and it is certainly hard to imagine an unusually short man being thought of as presidential timber. Before we attach too much importance to this finding, however, we should remember that the successful presidential candidate is also nearly always hairier than his opponent, suggesting that King Kong might be an outstanding candidate.

When a 'Mr England' was introduced to a number of classes of college students in America, he was referred to as someone varying between relatively low status ('Mr England, a student from Cambridge') and high status ('Professor England from Cambridge'). Afterwards, the students were asked to estimate the man's height to the nearest half inch. As Mr England climbed the academic ladder of success, he gained a total of five inches in the eyes of the students. This confirms the idea that height in men is valued. Even more surprising were the results of a survey of male graduates of the University of Pittsburgh. This revealed that the tallest students (6 ft 2 in and over) received an average starting salary at least 12 per cent higher than those who were under 6 ft.

Since the characteristics of the face are a major part of physical attractiveness in both sexes, it is interesting to consider which facial features are most important. This can be done by asking people to rate eyes, mouth, nose, etc. for attractiveness,

and comparing the results with ratings of overall facial attractiveness. It has been found that the attractiveness of a face is most affected by the general expression, followed by the mouth, complexion, eyebrows, eyes, hair, chin and nose, in that order. As Alexander Pope expressed it,

'Tis not a lip, or eye, we beauty call,
But the joint force and full result of all.

Jerry Wiggins of the University of Illinois started his investigation of physical attractiveness in women by suggesting that men can be divided into three broad categories on the basis of their particular predilections: breast men, buttock men and leg men. He presented his subjects with nude female silhouettes of various shapes and sizes, and found that, overall, relatively large breasts, long legs and small buttocks were most popular. Large breasts were especially favoured by readers of *Playboy*. Small breasts were preferred by men with fundamentalist religious beliefs and mild depression.

The stereotyped muscle man with an Atlas physique (broad chest and narrow hips) has often been presented as the ideal male body. Whether women agree seems doubtful. A none too serious survey in the magazine *Cosmopolitan* asked 100 women to name the male body characteristic they found most sexually exciting. Only one woman felt aroused by muscular chests and shoulders,

What is it that makes this girl attractive? Not her lips, her eyes or her hair, but 'the joint force and full result of all'.

Research suggests that most women do not go weak at the knees when they see bulging delts, pecs, biceps, lats and quads!

Experimenting with make-up and hairdos is, at any age, a way of saying, 'I am not attractive enough as I am' or 'I want more people to look at me and like what they see.'

whereas 39 women selected buttocks. Rating studies using various male profile silhouettes suggest that women prefer men with only moderately large chests, large legs and small buttocks. Some women preferred relatively small men; these women tended to be reserved in manner but of high social status, which could be good news for dancers and jockeys!

Do we see ourselves as others see us? While there is usually some correspondence between an individual's self-report of his or her physical attractiveness level and the opinion of external observers, agreement between the two assessments is often poor. Many people see themselves as much less pretty or handsome than they actually are, and this tendency seems to be more marked in the young. In one study conducted among girls of ten or eleven it was found that three-quarters seriously believed themselves to be the least physically attractive of all the girls in their class at school.

One of the factors affecting attractiveness was identified by American Country and Western singer Mickey Gilley. In one of his songs he says: 'Ain't it funny, ain't it strange/The way a man's opinions change/When he starts to face that lonely night . . . All the girls get prettier at closing time./ They all get to look like movie stars.' In a study conducted in various bars on a Thursday evening, a group of psychologists found that people rated members of the opposite sex as more physically attractive at midnight than at 10.30 pm!

KEY EXPERIMENT: ATTRACTIVENESS AND JURY DECISION-MAKING

Some of the most thought-provoking and disquieting work on physical attractiveness was done in the 1970s by Michael Efran[1] of the University of Toronto. He, like everyone else, was well aware that physical attractiveness is much desired and valued by most cultures and societies, and that it confers various benefits on the handsome and the beautiful. The fascinating issue which Efran set out to explore was this: Just how far do the advantages of being physically attractive go? Can beautiful people get away with murder?

Many lawyers suspect that juries and judges tend to be more lenient when the accused person is attractive rather than ugly, but less lenient when the victim of a crime is physically attractive. In a famous case in 1857 Madeleine Smith, the young, vivacious and beautiful daughter of a prosperous Scottish architect, was accused of murdering her lover Pierre L'Angelier by administering arsenic. While this was shocking enough, Scottish society was even more outraged when it became clear from her diaries that she thoroughly enjoyed sexual activity. In spite of the fact that she was the only person to gain from his death (he had threatened blackmail if she would not marry him) and that she was known to have purchased arsenic on three separate occasions, the jury returned a verdict of 'not proven'. Did her beauty help to save her from the gallows? Three eminent authorities decided not to allow into evidence L'Angelier's pocket-book, which would have greatly strengthened the prosecution's case. Were they too entranced by Miss Smith's obvious charms?

It seemed to Efran that jury decisions might well be swayed by the physical attractiveness of the defendant. In his initial investigation he asked a large number of students whether they believed that jurors should be influenced by the defendant's physical attractiveness. He also asked them whether the defendant's character and past history should be considered. There was a striking difference in the answers given to the two questions: 79 per cent believed that jurors should be influenced by the defendant's character and history but only 7 per cent believed that physical attractiveness should be an influencing factor.

Given that most people believe that the looks of the accused are irrelevant, it should be very difficult to find evidence of juries being affected by the defendant's appearance. On the contrary, Michael Efran found it was quite easy. Mock juries, some of them consisting of men only and some of women only, were set up, and the jurors were asked to imagine that they were the student members of a student-faculty court hearing the case of a student accused of cheating in an examination. The 'evidence' was rather inconclusive, since the accused had been seen conversing with another student during the examination, but the conversation had not been overheard. The accused was sometimes male, sometimes female, and an attractive or unattractive photograph was given to the jurors. Their task was to decide on the probability of guilt, and also on the severity of punishment if the accused were found guilty.

Efran found that despite their expressed belief that physical attractiveness should not matter, the jurors were less certain about the guilt of attractive defendants and recommended much milder punishment for them. The tendency to bend over backwards to be lenient to an attractive defendant was especially marked when the defendant was a pretty girl and the jurors were all young men.

This study by Efran, like most good studies, raised more questions than it answered. Do real juries confronted with real cases make decisions in the same way as simulated juries considering hypothetical cases? If they do, then there are obvious reasons for concern, since the notion that every person is equal before the law is fundamental to our legal system. Most people would find it highly objectionable if pretty or handsome criminals escaped their just deserts while plain and ugly innocents languished in prison.

In another ingenious study, two experimental juries watched real trials along with the real juries. The real juries were less likely to favour conviction than the judge or either of the experimental juries. If the consequences of a guilty verdict are likely to be extremely serious, juries tend to be cautious. However, since most people are not aware of being influenced by the attractiveness of the person before them, it is a reasonable assumption that juries are influenced, to varying degrees, by the appearance of the accused. However, most of the available research suggests that physical attractiveness has little or no effect on juries when serious crimes are involved.

A further question arising out of Efran's study is this: Does the attractiveness of the victim affect jury decisions? Billy Thornton of the University of Maine considered the emotive crime of rape, and looked at the influence of the physical attractiveness of rape victims on the decisions of an experimental jury. Predictably, women jurors were more likely to convict than men jurors. The attractiveness of the victim did not affect the jury's assessment of the credibility of her testimony or the extent of her responsibility, but the accused man was given a longer sentence when the victim was pretty rather than plain.

In another study, an attempt was made to make the simulated trial situation entirely realistic. The jurors listened to a one-hour tape recording of a case involving automobile negligence, and there were slides showing the plaintiff and the defendant. When the plaintiff was unattractive and the defendant attractive, only 17 per cent of the verdicts were in favour of the plaintiff, and an average of only $5,500 was awarded to the plaintiff. When the plaintiff was attractive and the defendant unattractive, the respective figures were 49 per cent and $10,000. Unto him that hath, more shall be given . . .

The bias shown towards or against defendants and victims because of their relative good looks or lack of them is rather puzzling in view of the fact that most people claim they would not let mere appearance affect their judgment. Possibly we are more lenient to beautiful women than to plain Janes because we regard them as possessing generally desirable qualities and so assume they will be less likely to transgress in the future than their unattractive sisters.

This possibility can be tested by focusing on

If you were a member of the jury in a shoplifting case, to which of these women would you give the benefit of the doubt? Would you be swayed by impeccable millinery and tailoring or by punk exoticism?

crimes which very good-looking people might be expected to be more likely to commit again than unattractive people. Suppose, for example, that a woman ingratiates herself with a middle-aged bachelor and persuades him to invest a sizeable sum of money in a non-existent company, and that this leads to charges of larceny and obtaining money under false pretences. We would probably all agree that middle-aged bachelors are more readily parted from their money by attractive women than by plain women, but if it is easier for a beautiful woman to obtain money by deception, then she may be more likely to repeat the trick in the future than an unattractive woman. Reasoning thus, the jurors in a simulated trial punished the glamorous larcenist more severely than the unglamorous one, sentencing her to an average of five and a half years in prison, as compared with four years.

In spite of this finding, it is patently obvious that in most circumstances attractive adults tend to be given the benefit of any doubt. According to one study, this tendency has its origins in early child-hood. Female students were given a brief written

Since the world is a less rewarding place for those who are not good-looking, shouldn't we consciously try to reverse our bias? We all amount to more than the sum of our appearance.

account of the undesirable behaviour (physical aggression towards another child or towards an animal) of a child of seven. The child was seen as being more culpable if he or she was unattractive, and his or her transgressions were regarded as less forgivable than when committed by an attractive child. When the reported aggression was severe, the students were more inclined to attribute a chronic anti-social disposition to the unattractive child than to the attractive child, and they also felt that unattractive children were more likely to commit a similar offence at some time in the future than good-looking children.

It could be argued that the physical attractiveness of a defendant only affects the workings of justice in those cases where the evidence is ambiguous and unclear. However, these are exactly the cases which tend to come to trial, since defendants usually plead guilty if the evidence against them is overwhelming. Would it be constructive to forewarn jurors about the possible bias caused by the attractiveness or otherwise of defendants and victims? When jurors serving in a case of negligent homicide made an explicit commitment to be impartial, they actually gave socially and physically unattractive defendants *less* severe sentences. It therefore appears that alertness to bias may produce a 'reverse' biasing affect.

THE UGLY TRUTH

It has been demonstrated many times that physically attractive people are believed to be superior to unattractive people in all kinds of ways. They are thought of as more perceptive, confident, assertive, happy, amiable, humorous, flexible, friendly, exciting, intelligent and talented than unattractive people, and there is some evidence that they regard themselves in a relatively flattering light. In addition, attractive people date more frequently than unattractive people, their opinions are more sought after, valued, and the world in general is more helpful to them.

However, there is one major exception to this view, perhaps caused by feelings of jealousy. Unattractive women do *not* rate beautiful women as having more socially desirable personalities than plain women. They regard beautiful women as being vain, egotistical, incompetent as parents, status-seeking, snobbish, and out of touch with those less privileged than themselves. They also see attractive women as being more likely to have extramarital affairs, and also more likely to initiate divorce proceedings.

In general, however, the beautiful people of this planet inhabit a more pleasant, forgiving and supportive social world than plain people. The conditions which face the unattractive are less easy to adapt to. Amerigo Farina and his associates at the University of Connecticut carried this idea to its logical conclusion and investigated whether physical unattractiveness might indirectly contribute to mental illness. The first problem they encountered when they tried to test this theory in a mental hospital was hostility from the hospital staff, some of whom felt it was offensive to try to demonstrate that people who are emotionally unstable and unable to adjust to society are ugly as well.

Farina discovered that female mental patients do indeed appear to be much less attractive than female shoppers or university employees. Of course, it could be argued that mental patients are less able or less inclined to groom themselves than other people. Nevertheless, the least physically attractive of the patients had more previous admissions to hospital than the more attractive ones, had spent more days in the hospital during their current stay, and were more likely to be diagnosed as seriously disturbed or schizophrenic. The less attractive patients were also judged to be less pleasant, and they interacted less with other people and were visited less frequently.

Obviously it would be ludicrous to assume that physical unattractiveness is the only or even a major factor in mental illness. What is plausible, however, is that people who already have problems (anxiety, lack of social skills) might find them exacerbated if they have to cope with the additional problem of being physically unattractive.

If problems in coping with society are greater for the physically unattractive, then in some circumstances the use of cosmetic surgery should prove helpful. In one study carried out in New York cosmetic surgery was made available to prisoners suffering from a variety of disfigurements (knife and burn scars, tattoos, injection scars from drug abuse). Among those not addicted to heroin, cosmetic surgery almost halved the incidence of recidivism (return to prison within one year of release) seen in prisoners whose disfigurements remained untreated. Fifty-six per cent of prisoners receiving no surgery returned to prison, compared with only 30 per cent of those receiving surgery. Cosmetic surgery was particularly helpful to those with facial disfigurements, and seemed to spur them into changing other aspects of themselves.

Posing and preening for the girls! These young men wish to be thought good-looking, but also exciting, confident, brave, talented . . .

DATING AND MATING

One situation in which physical appearance plays an important role is dating and yet people often seem blissfully unaware of the extent to which physical attractiveness in others affects their behaviour. Students of both sexes persist in claiming that the most important attribute of a potential date is personality, followed by character, followed by looks, then (much farther down the list) intelligence. But research tends to contradict this. A Computer Dance was organized for new students at the University of Minnesota, with a computer allegedly being used to match couples according to interests and personality.[2] When the dance had been in full swing for nearly three hours, all the students were asked how much they liked their dates, whether they wanted to go out with them again, and so on. For both men and women, the only important factor in determining how much they liked their dates was their physical attractiveness. Personality counted for little, and those whose academic performance was good were liked less than those who were poor academically.

Perhaps looks count for more on first meetings than when people know each other better. As George Bernard Shaw put it, with his customary Irish flair: 'Beauty is all very well, but who ever looks at it when it has been in the house three days?' Shaw may be right about beauty becoming less important as familiarity increases, but he is wrong to suggest that it ever becomes irrelevant. Some cynics have claimed that dating is a form of trading: each person tries to make a particular social interaction as profitable as possible, profit being defined as the rewards gained from the interaction minus the costs that must be paid. Thus a girl who is worth travelling five miles to see would need to be unusually attractive to warrant a 50-mile trip. If physical attractiveness constitutes a 'reward', then the point of equilibrium will tend to occur when two people are of approximately equal attractiveness. Indeed, engaged and married couples do tend to be similar in physical attractiveness, although there are exceptions.

Ever wondered why so many airline pilots are good-looking? Or why so many garage attendants, janitors and librarians aren't? Would you feel happy flying with the man above?

The matching of attractiveness seems reasonable enough from some points of view, but rather puzzling from others. Since nearly everyone values extremely attractive individuals of the opposite sex most, why do unattractive men tend to marry ugly women, and vice versa? The answer seems to be that our choice is determined not so much by what we want but by what we can get. There is no point in trying to climb Everest if you have no climbing equipment.

Sociologists have noted that attractiveness facilitates social mobility. Working-class girls who marry 'above themselves' are much more physically attractive than those who do not. These upwardly mobile girls seem to cast their nets more widely and selectively than their peers; they are far less likely to 'go steady' with one boy at school, and report far less sexual activity during their schooldays (10 per cent versus 70 per cent for non-mobile girls), presumably because they can have enough boyfriends without allowing sexual intercourse.

Another social advantage of physical attractiveness is its instant 'halo' effect. If a man is seen in the company of beautiful women, he tends to go up a notch in our estimation, and likewise with a woman accompanied by a handsome man. On the other hand, we tend to devalue someone who goes out with unattractive members of the opposite sex.

THE RIGHT FACE FOR THE RIGHT JOB

Finally, physical attractiveness often plays a decisive part in the job market. Several laws have quite properly been passed in both Britain and the United States to prohibit job discrimination on the basis of race and sex. Perhaps rather more insidious, because less well recognized, is job discrimination on the basis of physical attractiveness. Robert Dipboye and his associates at the University of Tennessee asked college students to evaluate the qualifications of twelve applicants for the job of trainee sales manager. The students were given a brief description of the applicants' qualifications and their photographs, and were most inclined to hire a physically attractive man with high qualifications. When they were asked to select just one candidate, 11 per cent picked the well-qualified but unattractive man, but 35 per cent chose the well-

qualified and attractive man. The students were then asked to assume that they had hired each applicant and to suggest an appropriate starting salary. Higher salaries were given to the most highly qualified, to men, and to the most physically attractive.

'Heightism' operates in many institutions, not least in the police force. City gents in bowlers are not notably short either.

Surely professional interviewers would not allow physical attractiveness to influence their decisions about an applicant's suitability for a job? Dipboye considered this possibility in a study in which college students and professional interviewers evaluated several applicants for the position of head of a furniture department in a large shop in a city centre. Attractive applicants were nearly always preferred to unattractive applicants of equal educational achievement both by the professional interviewers and the students.

An interesting exception to the notion that physically attractive people are more likely to be selected for desirable jobs than the physically unattractive was discovered by Thomas Cash and his co-workers. They found that attractive men had an advantage over unattractive men when applying for 'masculine' jobs (car salesman, shipping clerk), but not when applying for 'feminine' jobs (telephone operator, office receptionist). Similarly, attractive women were preferred to unattractive women for feminine jobs, but not for masculine jobs.

CONCLUSIONS

Physical attractiveness plays an important role in first encounters between men and women, but few of us realize just how far-reaching its influence really is. Physically attractive people are treated more leniently than unattractive people by juries, they are less likely to become mentally ill, they are more socially mobile, and they are more likely to impress potential employers. It seems unfair that the attractive should enjoy all these important advantages. The first step in remedying the situation is to establish the facts, which is what we have done, of necessity briefly, in this chapter. Then comes the task of making as many people as possible aware of the potential dangers in discriminating against the physically unattractive.

Chapter 3
PRIVACY AND INTIMACY

When we meet other people, we find ourselves thinking and feeling all sorts of things, most of which are better not expressed. We tend not to say 'I find you extremely boring', 'I don't like you', or 'You're an arrogant fool', except perhaps to our nearest and dearest. However, we often communicate such thoughts and feelings by means of non-verbal signals such as facial expression, gesture, posture, eye movements and tone of voice. Looking at someone who is talking to you is an indication that you are paying attention to what he or she is saying. Conversely, failure to look at the other person is sometimes an indication that you find his or her conversation boring. Similarly, if we dislike people we tend to show it by standing some way away from them and talking about totally impersonal topics.

At first glance, it seems strange that a complex set of non-verbal signals is required in everyday social situations. After all, the English language, with its 500,000 words, provides a very rich and powerful means of communication. Why has the 'silent language' of non-verbal signals developed? Michael Argyle of Oxford University has suggested that language and non-verbal signals largely serve different functions, with non-verbal signals being used to establish and maintain personal relationships, and language being used to communicate information about events external to the speakers. The potential embarrassment of blurting out one's feelings about the person one is talking to can, it seems, be largely avoided by resorting to the much greater ambiguity of non-verbal signals.

Michael Argyle and his fellow workers were intrigued to know exactly what determines how we feel towards strangers. Is it what they say or how they say it? Accordingly, they arranged for an attractive female to say things designed to express an attitude of superiority or inferiority. Her accompanying non-verbal signals conveyed either a superior attitude (unsmiling, head raised, loud dominating voice) or an inferior attitude (nervous deferential smile, head lowered, nervous eager-to-please voice). When there was a clash between what she said and the non-verbal signals she gave, feelings of friendliness, pleasantness and so on towards her were far more affected by her non-verbal signals than by what she said.

One of the most fascinating aspects of non-verbal signals is that people are often influenced by them without being aware of it. Eckhard Hess found that emotional arousal produces enlargement of the pupil of the eye, and that men are more attracted by girls with enlarged pupils, although they are seldom aware that this is the cue to which they are responding. It is interesting to note that the drug belladonna (meaning literally 'beautiful woman') produces enlarged pupils and was once considered a powerful weapon of seduction.

TOUCHERS AND NON-TOUCHERS
An especially important form of non-verbal communication is touching, which has been studied in detail by Sidney Jourard of the University of Florida. He asked unmarried men and women between the ages of 18 and 22 to indicate which

Gestures say a lot about feelings. The girl tries to hide behind her hand, although ostensibly brushing back her hair; the boy's hand wanders up to touch his ear—he is not at ease either.

regions of their bodies had been touched by their mother, father and closest friend of the same and the opposite sex, and which regions of these other people's bodies they had touched. With the obvious exception of touching between close friends of the opposite sex, there was some evidence of a touch taboo, possibly because touching in many Western societies normally has sexual connotations.

Young men and young women reported about equal touching by their mothers, and on as many regions of their body. But young men did not touch their mothers' bodies in as many places as their mothers touched them, nor in as many as the young women touched their mothers. The young women touched their fathers on more regions than the young men did, and in return they were touched on more body areas by their fathers than were the young men. Indeed, several men reported that they were unable to recall any physical contact with their fathers at all. When it comes to touching within families, daughters are the favoured ones.

Jourard concluded that touching is the primitive language of love, and that extensive physical contact may act as nature's sedative or tranquillizer. However, while there are many therapy groups in California and elsewhere which engage in 'feeling' and 'groping', the results of increased physical contact are disappointingly variable.

Jourard was also interested in cross-cultural differences in touching. He watched pairs of people talking in cafés and coffee shops, and counted the number of times that one person touched another at one table during one hour. In San Juan in Puerto Rico the total number of touches was 180. In Paris, it was 110. In London, it was 0! Maybe the notion that the English are cold and aloof has some truth to it.

Perhaps the most explored cross-cultural difference in non-verbal behaviour has been the distance people like to keep between themselves and the person they are talking to. Germans, North Americans and Swedes typically select greater distances than Latin Americans, Greeks, Southern Italians and Arabs. A comparison of Arabs and Americans revealed that the Arabs confronted each other more directly, got closer together, were more likely to touch and to maintain eye contact, and talked louder. Imagine the problems at international gatherings, with American and English delegates edging backwards pursued by Arabs and Southern Europeans.

While there has been a lot of interesting work on non-verbal communication, most of it has explored one kind of signal at a time (touching, eye contact, physical distance). The work we are about to discuss provides important insights into the

ways in which different aspects of non-verbal communication affect each other, and suggests a useful theoretical framework.

KEY EXPERIMENT: EYE CONTACT

Michael Argyle and Janet Dean[1] of Oxford University took as their starting point the assumption that social interaction typically involves both approach and avoidance tendencies. On the one hand, the desire to be liked by another person and attraction for that person encourage intimacy; on the other, anxieties about revealing oneself or of being rejected discourage intimacy. How is a comfortable balance between opposite tendencies arrived at?

Argyle and Dean suggested that interpersonal intimacy is chiefly manifested in a variety of non-verbal interactions, including the physical distance between people, eye contact, smiling and leaning. Standing very close to someone, for example, is more 'intimate' than standing further away. But if someone stands too close to us, closer than we find comfortable, the balance we are trying to establish is upset. While the easiest solution would be to move away in order to restore the balance, this is not always possible or socially acceptable. The alternative is to compensate for the increased intimacy of one aspect of non-verbal communication by reducing the intimacy of one or more other aspects.

Argyle and Dean explored some of these ideas in an experiment in which various people were asked to take part in a study of conversations. When a participant arrived for the experiment, he or she was introduced to another person who appeared to be another participant, but who was actually a confederate of the experimenter. The genuine participant and the confederate then engaged in three conversations, sitting 2 ft apart for one conversation, and 6 and 10 ft apart for the other two; they also sat at 90 degrees to each other. They then jointly made up stories on the basis of pictures suggesting different themes. The confederate gazed continually at the participant, and two observers behind a one-way screen looked directly into the participant's eyes without being seen.

The notion that people attempt to maintain a comfortable level of interpersonal intimacy suggests that Argyle and Dean's participants should have restored equilibrium at the shortest physical distance (2 ft) by reducing the intimacy of other non-verbal reactions. As predicted, the amount of eye contact which the participant had with the confederate progressively decreased the closer together they sat. When the participant and the confederate were of opposite sex, eye contact occurred 58 per cent of the time at 10 ft, 55 per cent of the time at 6 ft, but only 30 per cent of the time at 2 ft. There were similar but less dramatic effects when participant and confederate were of the same sex: eye contact decreased from 72 per cent at 10 ft to 55 per cent at 2 ft. There was much less eye contact overall with opposite-sex than with same-sex pairs,

Left: two very different greetings—a whole-hearted hug and a dutiful peck-on-the-cheek with as little body contact as possible. Touch conventions vary from country to country.

A great deal is happening here! Even visual space is meticulously divided—no two people are gazing in the same direction. The queue is a privacy device—how can one feel threatened or invaded by the back of someone's head?

presumably because there is more concern about being disliked by strangers of the opposite sex, and hence a certain amount of wariness.

These findings seemed to Argyle and Dean to show that reduced eye contact is one way of coping with the uncomfortable realization that a stranger is sitting closer to you than you would like. However, there is an alternative explanation. One of the reasons why we look at another person is to gain information about their reactions to us. Now the further away from us the other person is, the more difficult it becomes to see the subtleties of their facial expression. In such a situation we need to look more in order to find out what we want to know. Argyle and Dean noted other manifestations of discomfort besides reduced eye contact when confederate and participants were only 2 ft away from each other; participants tended to lean backwards, look down, shade their eyes with their hands, narrow their eyes, scratch their heads, smoke and blow their noses much more frequently than at 6 ft or 10 ft.

confederate if he or she is sitting farther away. Nevertheless, very similar findings to those of Argyle and Dean have been obtained in other studies in which such problems were eliminated.

INTERACTION OF VERBAL AND NON-VERBAL SIGNALS

An interesting extension of the Argyle and Dean work concerns the way in which verbal and non-verbal intimacy affect each other. If someone is asked to talk about relatively intimate topics with a stranger, will this affect his or her non-verbal behaviour? Richard Schulz and John Barefoot studied this question by getting people to answer questions varying between the fairly neutral ('What are your favourite subjects in school?') and the very personal ('Describe a person with whom you have been or are in love'). When participants were answering the more intimate questions they spent less time looking at the experimenter than when they were talking about neutral topics, presumably in an attempt to achieve a comfortable level of intimacy.

Schulz and Barefoot also found that participants gave shorter answers when they were sitting close to the experimenter (in this case 3 ft) and also engaged in less eye contact. A more puzzling finding was that participants smiled twice as much when they were close to the experimenter as when they were further away. Argyle and Dean had assumed that less smiling would occur if the desired level of intimacy was exceeded. However, smiling can mean a number of different things. The 'come hither' smile of someone who knows he or she is attractive must not be confused with the rather forced smile of someone experiencing inner tension.

REDUCING INTIMACY TO A COMFORTABLE LEVEL

If we are in a social situation and feel that the level of interpersonal intimacy is too high, what aspects of our behaviour are we most likely to change in an effort to restore the balance? Argyle has suggested that there is an important difference between the relatively unchanging characteristics of an interaction—such as physical distance, body orientation and posture—and its more variable and dynamic aspects—such as eye contact, facial expression and verbal intimacy. Adjustments in overall intimacy typically seem to involve the dynamic components of intimacy rather than the relatively stable ones.

As we all know from personal experience, people differ considerably in their preferred level of interpersonal intimacy in a given situation. It follows from some of the ideas of Argyle and Dean that those people who are especially worried about being rejected by others tend to prefer relatively low levels of intimacy. Some findings relevant to this particular question were obtained by Miles Patterson[2] of the University of Missouri. He placed

While many psychologists liked the basic idea that different aspects of non-verbal behaviour combine to produce an overall preferred level of interpersonal intimacy, they were somewhat dubious about one or two features of Argyle and Dean's study. For example, the participants may have sensed that it was very unnatural to be stared at by the confederate throughout the whole of each conversation. Also, as the distance between participant and confederate increased, so did the distance between the participant and the observers behind the one-way screen who were recording eye contact. It must be more difficult to tell whether or not the participant has direct eye contact with the

In spite of the obvious value of the Argyle and Dean theory, there are circumstances in which it predicts the exact opposite of what actually happens. It would probably be fair to say that preferred levels of intimacy between people are more flexible and more subject to change by non-verbal signals than Argyle and Dean implied.

PERSONAL SPACE

Another interesting and important aspect of non-verbal behaviour, closely related to the behaviours studied by Argyle, is that of personal space. Robert Sommer of the University of California has argued that personal space refers to 'an area with invisible boundaries surrounding a person's body into which intruders may not come'. Others have likened personal space to a buffer zone which affords protection against perceived threats. In passing it is worth noting that many species seem to have their own personal spaces. For example, the minimum social distance for flamingos is about 2 ft, for subordinate male rabbits 1 ft, and for some kinds of monkey nothing at all.

One way of testing the importance of personal space is to see what happens when it is invaded. We humans feel threatened and worried by invasion, and usually act defensively. A very simple attempt to observe reactions to invasion of personal space was made by Nancy Jo Felipe and Robert Sommer, who conducted one of their studies in the grounds of a large mental institution. The experimenter walked around the grounds and sat about 6 inches away from any man sitting alone and not engaged in a clearly defined activity. If the 'victim' moved his chair or moved further along the bench, the experimenter moved the same amount to keep the space between them the same as before. The victim typically responded by facing away from the experimenter, placing his elbows by his sides, mumbling, laughing nervously or talking delusionally. Half the victims took flight within nine minutes of the experimenter sitting beside them, and only 8 per cent stayed put, presumably because they did not feel that their personal space had been invaded.

Naturally enough, Felipe and Sommer wondered whether these striking results were due to the use of mental patients as subjects. In their next experiment, a female experimenter sat down very close to female college students in a relatively empty university library. Seventy per cent of the students left the library within 30 minutes. Only 13 per cent tolerated the close proximity of the experimenter and stayed put.

If someone enters our personal space and makes us feel uneasy, are we likely to ask the other person to move a little further away? Apparently not, according to the findings of Felipe and Sommer. They noted that only two of the mental patients and one out of 80 students asked the person invading their space to move away. This common reluctance to openly admit discomfort led

The unwelcome arm around the shoulder. The girl cannot extricate herself without seeming rude, so she leans back slightly and holds her glass in front of her to ward off further contact.

a swivel chair several feet away from the experimenter's chair, and each participant was invited to 'pull up a chair'. People tended to put the swivel chair either about 3½ ft away from the experimenter's chair or about 14 ft away. Those who rated high on a test of social anxiety tended to put more distance between themselves and the experimenter than those who were not socially anxious.

The equilibrium model proposed by Argyle and Dean has obvious relevance to everyday social interaction. It also seems to shed light on the procedures typically adopted for religious confessions and psychiatric sessions, in which the sinner or patient is encouraged to say negative things about himself or herself in the presence of another person (the priest or the psychiatrist) who avoids all eye contact. Since lengthy discussion of one's own inadequacies is an intimate topic of conversation and likely to be embarrassing, any increase in interpersonal intimacy by means of eye contact would probably lead to reduced verbal disclosure ('I was rude to Mr Smith last week' instead of 'I dumped all my old grass cuttings in Mr Smith's drive last week').

The girl in the jeans is not too worried by the attentions of the boy on her left, but clearly indicates that she is not interested by turning her whole body away from him.

Hall, one of the main investigators of human personal space, to write: 'We treat space somewhat as we treat sex. It is there but we don't talk about it.'

It has usually been assumed that invasion of personal space produces stress and tension, but there have been relatively few attempts to test this assumption. However, Dennis Middlemist and his colleagues at Oklahoma State University did so, using a three-urinal men's lavatory as the unlikely setting for their study. What they set out to prove was that stress or anxiety delays the onset of urination (decreased relaxation of the external sphincter, they argued, would cause increased intravesicular pressure and so shorten urine flow). They proved their point. When a man urinated alone, the average delay before urination was 5 seconds, compared with 8½ seconds when a confederate was standing in the adjacent urinal. The average duration of urine flow decreased from 25 seconds for men on their own to 17½ seconds for men standing next to the confederate.

Gerald Koocher of Harvard Medical School was rather unhappy about this attempt to establish a psychology of the privy, pointing out that the boundary between drawing on everyday experiences and spying on people's intimate functions is a delicate one. Middlemist retorted that none of the participants in his urinal experiment appeared in the least worried or concerned.

Do some people have a larger personal space than others? Some animal studies suggest that the answer is probably yes, and highlight the importance of dominance or status. For example, dominant male rabbits maintain an average of 3 ft between themselves and their subordinates, whereas their subordinates are content with an average of 1 ft between themselves and others. In similar vein, the distance between a dominant chicken and a subordinate chicken is directly proportional to the frequency with which the latter is pecked in the home coop.

In our own society, 'important' people are usually given a larger personal space than other people—it would certainly seem strange if Queen Elizabeth or George Bush were jostled in the ribs at a public gathering. Larry Dean and his co-workers made observations on dominance-related personal space among personnel at the United States Naval Station in Long Beach, California. They discovered that interactions directed towards a superior typically took place at a greater distance than interactions directed towards a subordinate. Furthermore, this effect became more noticeable as the difference in rank increased.

◄ *Previous page: no privacy here, or is there? Despite the acres of flesh on display, personal space is preserved by the strategic placing of deckchairs and beach paraphernalia. Imaginary though such boundaries are, they are generally respected.*

SEX DIFFERENCES IN PERSONAL SPACE

Some interesting sex differences in personal space have also been discovered. Women choose to sit closer to other women than men do to other men, possibly because women are trained to express affection openly whereas men are trained to preserve 'a stiff upper lip'. Michael Ross compared the reactions of discussion groups of eight men or eight women sitting in an uncrowded room (13½ ft by 10 ft) or a crowded room (only 8 ft by 5½ ft). Men were generally happier with themselves and with the other members of the group in the relatively uncrowded room, whereas women were exactly the opposite and preferred the more intimate atmosphere of the smaller room.

A rather more puzzling sex difference was described by Jeffrey Fisher and Donn Byrne of Purdue University. In one study, the personal space of a male or a female student sitting in a university library was invaded by someone who sat down either immediately adjacent to them or directly across the table from them. Male students felt more uncomfortable with someone sitting opposite them than with someone sitting next to them, whereas female students were more upset by someone sitting next to them—the 'Miss Muffet' reaction.

In a second study, Fisher and Byrne argued that students sitting alone in a library use books, coats and sweaters and so on to mark off territory and erect barriers against intruders. Female students tended to erect barriers between themselves and adjacent seats, whereas male students erected barriers between themselves and the seat across the table.

We know that individuals generally sit face-to-face in competitive situations and side-by-side in co-operative ones. Since men are taught to be more competitive than women, it is possible that men view strangers who sit opposite them as a potential threat or challenge. In contrast, women are taught to be more friendly and co-operative than men, and so might interpret a stranger coming and sitting next to them as an unwarranted demand for attention and friendship.

HOW WE REACT WHEN OUR SPACE IS INVADED

Another example of invasion of personal space which will be familiar to most motorists is being stared at by the occupant of the next car while waiting at traffic lights. Most people who have had this experience will recognize it as subtly disturbing, and will remember fidgeting, adjusting the car radio, starting talking to their passengers in the car, and so on. A less obvious reaction in this situation has also been noticed: drivers pull away from the lights more rapidly when they have been stared at. Can we interpret this as a form of escape response to a threatening situation?

A similar form of escape reaction was studied by Vladimir Konečni and his associates at the University of California. They found that pedestrians cross the road rather faster when someone has been standing very close to them waiting for the crossing signal. In another experiment with pedestrians at a road crossing, Konečni had a confederate stand either 1 ft or 10 ft from a fellow pedestrian while they both waited for the lights to change. When they were both on the crossing, the confederate 'accidentally' dropped an object in front of the pedestrian. The question was whether the pedestrian would act in a helpful way, in other words hand the object back to the confederate or call out to him saying 'Hey, you've dropped something'. When the object was a cheap pencil, only 47 per cent of pedestrians were helpful in the 1-ft condition, compared with 80 per cent in the 10-ft condition. A similar but less dramatic difference was obtained when the confederate dropped a key-ring. It seems that we respond to invasions of our personal space by disliking the invader. This in turn makes us disinclined to lend a helping hand if required. However, this effect decreases as the value of the object lost increases (a key-ring with keys on it elicits more help than something trivial like a pencil).

Why do people respond in such subtle but consistently observable ways to invasion of their personal space? After all, being stared at or having a stranger stand very close to you usually involves no tangible threat, and yet we become embarrassed, attempt to escape, and are reluctant to help the person who has violated our personal space. One of

Going to see the doctor usually involves some loss of privacy. The desk is not strictly necessary but it enables both doctor and patient to feel more comfortable. In general, women tend to feel less threatened by face-to-face encounters than by side-to-side.

the functions of personal space may be to keep aggression down to manageable proportions. The barriers we erect may be invisible but they are nonetheless a sort of safety zone in which others are unlikely to attack us or we them.

LIKING AND LOVING

All of us have seen people becoming anxious and embarrassed when another person's non-verbal behaviour indicates a high level of intimacy—invasion of personal space is one of the surest ways of causing embarrassment. But as Argyle and Dean pointed out, people typically cope with this situation by some kind of compensatory non-verbal behaviour designed to restore the desired level of intimacy.

Miles Patterson agreed that increased intimacy by one member of a pair may lead to a compensatory decrease in intimacy by the other but pointed out that the opposite is true of couples falling in love. Increased non-verbal intimacy by one partner typically leads to *increased* non-verbal intimacy by the other. In other words, lovers usually reciprocate intimate behaviour rather than compensate for it.

Patterson argued that some kind of extension of previous theories was called for. He suggested that increased non-verbal intimacy on the part of one member of a pair produces physiological arousal and an associated emotional state. If the increase in non-verbal intimacy leads to negative emotional reactions (e.g. anxiety), then the other person will respond with compensatory behaviour (decreased eye contact, greater physical distance, etc.). On the other hand, if a positive emotional state is created (e.g. love), then there will be a reciprocation of the original intimacy behaviours, leading to a new and enhanced level of intimacy.

Why did Argyle and Dean and others highlight unpleasant emotional reactions to increased intimacy to the virtual exclusion of the pleasanter ones? According to Patterson, the answer lies in the fact that most psychological experiments are not conducive to feelings of joy and euphoria. The pairs of people used in most experiments are total strangers to each other, the setting is usually fairly impersonal (e.g. a laboratory or a public place), and the participants are exposed to relatively extreme scenarios (e.g. being forced to sit almost on top of each other, or having someone stare at them for minutes on end). It is not surprising that people's reaction to such threatening, unsympathetic circumstances is discomfort or anxiety, followed by a definite decrease in non-verbal intimacy.

In striking contrast, there is the interaction between a mother and her baby within the home.

Two forms of intimate behaviour on one bench: the reciprocal touching of young lovers, and the identical hands-in-lap posture of the old couple. Intimates often 'mirror' each other although they are not aware of it.

The British psychologist John Bowlby reported that the more infants smile at their mothers, the more likely mothers are to approach them, talk or sing to them, and pick them up and hug them. It is just as well that we sometimes respond to non-verbal intimacy with open arms rather than fight or flight. If we didn't, the human race would have died out long ago.

CONCLUSIONS

The most important function of non-verbal signals is to indicate the real feelings one person has towards another. Members of couples highly attracted to each other like to stand closer together than members of couples who do not like each other. For any two people interacting with each other, there is likely to be a preferred level of intimacy, and deviations from this level are disliked and where possible compensated for.

Invasion of personal space (or for that matter refusal to enter someone else's personal space) is a particularly powerful non-verbal signal. If a stranger stands much closer to us than we would like, clear signs of embarrassment manifest themselves, we become tense and anxious, and may even attempt to escape from the situation. While it is by no means clear why everyone has his or her own personal space, we are not alone in the animal world in finding some form of invisible barrier between ourselves and others useful. The importance of this barrier can be gauged by the strong emotions we experience when it is violated.

Chapter 4
THE DANGERS OF OBEDIENCE

Virtually all societies develop hierarchies in which certain people are given power and authority over others. In our society, for example, parents, shop stewards, headmasters and managers are invested with varying degrees of authority. But the relationship between authority figures and their subordinates is almost bound to lead to moral conflict. This is powerfully illustrated by the story of Abraham, commanded by God to kill his son Isaac. Abraham's dilemma was that he felt love for God and for his son, and yet he was apparently required to betray one of them. How far was his obedience to God supposed to go?

A similar conflict occurs when soldiers at war are ordered to kill defenceless civilians, as happened in Vietnam when Lieutenant Calley ordered the massacre of civilians at My Lai. Calley's defence rested on the assertion that he had been following the orders of his superiors.

So how do people resolve the conflicts they face when authority figures issue commands which negate human life and human dignity? The problem is one that psychologists have tried to study, and their answers have given us much valuable and unexpected information about human nature.

KEY EXPERIMENT: OBEDIENCE TO AUTHORITY

The most important and best-known work on obedience to authority was carried out by Stanley Milgram[1,2] at Yale University in the early 1960s. The impact of his work was such that he was awarded the Socio-Psychological Prize of the American Association for the Advancement of Science.

One of the many fascinating aspects of Milgram's work was that the results he came up with surprised both himself and his professional colleagues, not to mention the general public. In fact his work almost entirely escaped one of the most common complaints levelled at psychological research, namely that the experimental findings merely confirm common sense. Anyone unfamiliar with Milgram's work may find it interesting to guess how much obedience to the authority of the experimenter was shown by the great variety of individuals of different ages and occupations who participated in the following study.

Imagine that you have arrived at Yale University to take part in a study of learning and memory. You go into a room and are met by a 31-year-old high school biology teacher, the experimenter, whose demeanour is rather stern. The other person in the room is also there to take part in the experiment. He is a rotund, 47-year-old accountant of Irish-American stock, mild-mannered and likable.

The experimenter tells you that he is interested in the effects of punishment on learning. It is decided, apparently by drawing lots, that the

Every society has invented official ways of rewarding obedience and duty, thereby ensuring continuing obedience and duty. Without them, society would dissolve into anarchy.

accountant will be the learner and you will be the teacher. You all go into an adjacent room, where the learner is strapped into an 'electric chair' apparatus, and an electrode is attached to his wrist. Electrode paste is applied 'to avoid blisters and burns'. You are told that the electrode is connected to a nearby shock generator unit.

You then go to another room, which has a shock generator unit in it. It has 30 lever switches, each labelled with a voltage between 15 and 450 volts. Groups of four switches of increasing voltage are labelled Slight Shock, Moderate Shock, Strong Shock, Very Strong Shock, Intense Shock, Extreme Intensity Shock, and Danger: Severe Shock. The final two lever switches are simply labelled XXX.

You are told to administer a shock to the learner every time he gives a wrong answer on the learning task, and you are instructed to 'move one level higher on the shock generator each time the learner flashes a wrong answer'. You are also told that although the shocks can be extremely painful, they cause no permanent tissue damage. You yourself are given a sample shock of 45 volts to show you that the equipment is working.

As the learning task proceeds, the learner makes a number of errors, and is given progressively more intense shocks. After receiving shocks of 75, 90 and 105 volts, he merely grunts. At 120 volts, he shouts to the experimenter that the shocks are becoming painful. At 150 volts, he shouts 'Hey, get me out of here! I won't be in this experiment any more! I refuse to go on!' At 180 volts, he yells 'I can't stand the pain', and by 270 volts his response becomes an agonized scream. Thereafter, there are shrieks of agony, and vehement refusals to go on with the experiment or provide answers to the learning task. When the 300-volt shock is reached, he pounds on the wall. If you, the 'teacher', say at any point that you don't want to continue the experiment, the experimenter calmly informs you that you must.

What would you do in this unpleasant situation? What do you imagine other people would do? Stanley Milgram put these two questions to groups of psychiatrists, students and middle-class adults. When predicting their own behaviour, absolutely everyone predicted that they would defy the experimenter and refuse to continue with the experiment either when the shock reached 300 volts or, typically, much earlier. Perhaps because people tend to have a more flattering opinion of themselves than of other people, there was a tendency to believe that other people would be less reluctant to prolong the suffering of the learner. For example, psychiatrists at a leading medical school predicted that 3.73 per cent of subjects would still obey the experimenter at 300 volts, but that only one in a thousand would go on to the 450-volt stage.

Most people unfamiliar with the actual results would predict that only a psychopath or a sadist would be likely to keep on administering intense electric shocks to an obviously distraught and unwilling subject. In fact, Milgram found that 62 per cent of the people exposed to the conditions just described continued to obey the experimenter, and continued to the 450-volt level. In fact there were 500 times as many individuals prepared to administer the maximum shock as predicted by a group of eminent psychiatrists!

Milgram's findings appeared to indicate that people are prepared to go to extreme lengths in order to remain obedient to authority. On the face of it, this seems an extraordinary and very puzzling finding, and not very relevant to everyday life. However, it is worth remembering how people at work behave towards their superiors. People in authority quite frequently say or do things which are obviously wrong or inadequate, and yet subordinates are reluctant to challenge them. If anyone *does* challenge a decision, he or she is likely to experience a certain amount of anxiety.

While you were reading the description of Stanley Milgram's experiment, you may well have wondered about the ethics of conducting an experiment in which extremely painful electric shocks are administered to a 'learner'. The Milgram study has indeed been attacked on ethical grounds, not because of the damage done to the learner, but because of its effects on the 'teacher'. In fact, the learner was in league with the experimenter and did not actually receive any shocks at all. The drawing of lots was 'rigged' so that the mild-mannered accountant would always be the learner and the subject would always be the teacher.

But the effects of the experiment on the 'teachers' were dramatic. One subject, a 46-year-old encyclopedia salesman, passed from nervous laughter to such violent convulsions that the experiment had to be halted. As one observer reported: 'I observed a mature and initially poised businessman enter the laboratory smiling and confident. Within 20 minutes he was reduced to a twitching, stuttering wreck, who was rapidly approaching a point of nervous collapse. He constantly pulled on his earlobe, and twisted his hands. At one point, he pushed his fist into his forehead and muttered "Oh God, let's stop it". And yet he continued to respond to every word of the experimenter, and obeyed to the end.'

This was not an exceptional case. Many people had fits of nervous laughter, sweated, groaned, trembled, and dug their fingernails into their skin. Not surprisingly, there was considerable public concern and even outrage about the morality of exposing people to such anguish. Did psychologists have the right to reduce anyone to a 'twitching, stuttering wreck'? Could a person's self-image be permanently damaged by knowing that he had been prepared to go to almost lethal lengths to obey the voice of authority? Milgram's subjects trusted the experimenter and assumed he would act in a careful, responsible manner; wasn't this trust abused by putting them through such a degrading experience? Last but not least, the success of the experiment depended on deception—the actual situation was not what it appeared to be.

Confronted with this hornet's nest of moral problems, Milgram put forward a number of reasonable counter-arguments to justify his research. He pointed out that there was a full debriefing at the end of the experiment, with all the participants being told that the learner had not actually received any dangerous electric shocks; the true purpose of the experiment was also explained to them. Of those who took part, 84 per cent stated they were glad to have taken part in the experiment, 15 per cent felt neither good nor bad about it, and only one person in a hundred expressed negative feelings. Further questioning revealed that four-fifths of the participants felt that more experiments of this sort should be conducted, and 74 per cent said they had learned something of personal importance as a result of taking part. Many participants said that they would be more wary in future about assuming that authority figures should always be obeyed.

Milgram also argued that what critics of his work really objected to was the unflattering picture it drew of human nature rather than the deception or methodology involved. Would the Milgram study have been the subject of public outrage if all the participants had disobeyed the experimenter at the first sign of discomfort from the learner? The evidence suggests not. Several people were given a description of the Milgram study; some were told that most of the participants were obedient to the experimenter, and the rest that most of them were disobedient. They rated the experiment as more harmful and as providing a worse experience when there was a large measure of obedience. Although many psychologists worry about the ethics of deception and argue that it is wrong to mislead people who take part in experiments, few lay observers felt that the morality of the Milgram study had anything to do with whether or not the participants were deceived.

The most frightening implication of the Milgram study is that half the population of North America is either sadistic or psychopathic, or both, which is clearly absurd, whatever we see on our television screens or read in the newspapers. In fact, when similar studies were carried out in Rome, Munich, South Africa and Australia, the level of obedience to the experimenter was rather greater than that obtained by Milgram. Indeed, 85 per cent of the people who were tested in Munich were discovered to be fully obedient to the experimenter.

A line of helpless cogs? What are the credentials and beliefs of those to whom they delegate responsibility?

Since over half the population in most countries is apparently prepared to administer very strong electric shocks to other people, then most of the obedient participants in Milgram-type studies must be quite ordinary people. The case of Adolf Eichmann, tried and convicted for ordering the deaths of many thousands of Jews, is relevant here. The prosecution attempted to depict Eichmann as a sadistic monster, which seems reasonable enough in view of the enormity of his crimes. In actual fact his actions were in many ways those of an uninspired bureaucrat who simply sits at his desk and tries to carry out his job competently.

Let us consider just three of Milgram's 'ordinary' obedient participants. One was a 39-year-old social worker, referred to by Milgram as Morris Braverman; he was bald, rather serious-looking, and gave the impression of being intelligent and concerned. As the shocks increased in intensity, he started to snicker. Gradually his suppressed laughter became more insistent and disruptive, apparently triggered off by the learner's screams. At times, he even rubbed his face in an attempt to hide his laughter. Afterwards, he seemed to find his own behaviour rather bewildering: 'My reactions were awfully peculiar . . . my reactions were giggly, and trying to stifle laughter. This isn't the way I usually am . . . And my reaction was to the situation of having to hurt somebody. And being totally helpless and caught up in a set of circumstances where I just couldn't deviate and I couldn't try to help. This is what got me.'

Another obedient participant was a housewife whom Milgram called Mrs Elinor Rosenblum. Mrs Rosenblum was proud of the fact that she had graduated from the University of Wisconsin 20 years earlier. She did volunteer work once a week with groups of juvenile delinquents, and was active in the local Girl Scout organization. She constantly referred to her social achievements and had a pleasant but rather verbose manner. During the experiment, she kept muttering that she was shaking, but nevertheless went on to administer the 450-volt shock. When she was asked what was the highest level of sample shock she would be prepared to experience, she became indignant: 'Fifteen volts. I don't even think it's necessary. Fifteen, if I were to get any, and I wouldn't even want that. I don't think it's necessary.' She described how she felt during the experiment: 'Every time I pressed the button, I died. Did you see me shaking? I was just dying here to think that I was administering shocks to the poor man.' It did not seem to dawn on her that there was something inconsistent about being prepared to administer a shock to someone else that was thirty times more intense than the shock she was reluctantly prepared to tolerate herself.

One of the most striking cases of total obedience was that of Pasqual Gino, a 43-year-old water inspector of Italian descent. He continued through to the end of the series of shocks. When the

A subordinate taking abuse from a superior—note the retracted chin and neck. How much will he take? How much does his duty as a soldier require him to take?

learner stopped providing answers on the learning task, he said, he reasoned to himself: 'Good God, he's dead. Well, here we go, we'll finish him. And I just continued all the way through to 450 volts.' He was relieved to discover that the learner was still alive at the end of the experiment, but indicated that he wouldn't have been concerned if the learner had been dead, as he was simply carrying out a job.

What the Milgram experiment did very successfully was to create a conflict situation in which some forces push the subject towards obedience and others prompt him towards disobedience. In our culture there is a lot of emphasis on obedience to authority, on the grounds that an efficient and well-organized society can only exist if there is a fairly stable hierarchy in which some people give the orders and others carry them out. Most societies attempt to ensure obedience by promoting the obedient individual, raising him or her to a higher rung on the hierarchical ladder. This is a doubly ingenious ploy, because the individual is rewarded for his or her obedience and feels motivated to climb to the next rung, and because the hierarchy itself is preserved and strengthened. In the Milgram study, the experimenter represented an authority figure. His authority was enhanced by the special coat he wore, by his association with Yale University, by his aura of expertise in human behaviour, and by his presumably detailed knowledge of the experiment being carried out. In everyday life, we place

Three stills from the Milgram experiment.
Above: the 'victim' is wired up to the shock generator.
Right: the 'teacher' gives himself a mild electric
shock to convince himself that the apparatus really
works. Below right: the victim's screams are heard
through the dividing wall (Voice Feedback situation).

responsibility for our health in the hands of our doctor, we go to an accountant for financial advice, and so on. Of necessity we rely heavily on the opinions of various authority figures, and this is what Milgram's subjects did.

On the other hand, the 'learner' in the Milgram study did everything he could to persuade the subject to stop administering shocks. He screamed, he begged the subject to stop, and in some cases he even said he had a heart condition. The participants, however, were not able to satisfy both the experimenter and the 'victim'. This was the conflict that caused the tension and the nervous laughter.

In Milgram's experiment obedience to the experimenter could have been reduced either by increasing the obviousness of the learner's plight or by reducing the authority of the experimenter. Milgram looked at a series of four situations in which the 'learner' was brought progressively closer, in a psychological sense, to the subject administering the shocks. In the Remote Feedback situation, the victim could be neither heard nor seen, though he did pound on the wall at one point. In the Voice Feedback situation (this was the situation described at the start of this chapter), the victim could be heard screaming but could not be seen. In the third situation (Proximity), the victim was only 18 inches away from the subject and could therefore be seen as well as heard. The fourth situation (Touch-Proximity) was identical to the third, except that the subject had to force the victim's hand onto the shockplate in order to administer shocks above the 150-volt level.

Milgram found that the closer his subjects were to the victim, the more concerned they were about him and the more reluctant they were to obey the experimenter. Sixty-six per cent of subjects were obedient in the Remote situation, 62 per cent in Voice Feedback, 40 per cent in Proximity, and 30 per cent in Touch-Proximity. It is obviously easier to ignore the consequences of one's actions when the victim is neither audible nor visible. In other words most people would find it easier, psychologically, to drop a bomb from 20,000 ft and possibly kill thousands of people than to stab a person to death with a knife.

What happens if the influence of the authority figure is attenuated? To answer this, Milgram compared a situation in which the experimenter sat only a few feet away from the subject with another situation in which, after giving the initial instructions, the experimenter left the laboratory and gave his orders by telephone. The comparison had dramatic results: 65 per cent of subjects were obedient in the first situation but only 22.5 per cent in the second. However, if the experimenter returned to the laboratory after the subject had refused to give higher intensity shocks when ordered to do so by telephone, he was often able to persuade the subject to revert to obedience. Some subjects found an interesting and ingenious way of minimizing conflict: they sabotaged the experiment by assuring the experimenter on the telephone that they were raising the shock intensities as instructed but kept on administering the lowest level of shock.

Throughout these experiments the participants were pulled in opposite directions by the experimenter and by the victim. If the suffering of the victim was emphasized or the authority of the experimenter reduced, the level of obedience fell. But if the victim's plight was *not* forcibly brought to the subject's attention, and the experimenter was perceived as a valid authority figure, obedience was the norm.

Many critics of Milgram's work argued that his unexpected findings might have been due to the setting of the experiment, Yale University. Indeed, several subjects remarked that it was the fact that Yale University was a reputable and distinguished institution that gave them confidence in the integrity of the experimenter. Men will happily expose their throats to a man with a razor blade in a barber's shop but not in a shoe shop. Most women will not undress fully in the presence of a male stranger, but are prepared to do so for a gynaecological examination.

So Milgram tried to find out how important the setting was by moving his apparatus to a three-room office suite in a ramshackle commercial building in a poor neighbourhood. The study was allegedly carried out by Research Associates of Bridgeport, a private firm which claimed to be conducting research for industry. He discovered that moving the experiment from the elegance of Yale University to a run-down office building made some difference, but not as much as might have been expected. Forty-eight per cent of the Bridgeport subjects were prepared to administer all the shocks compared with 65 per cent of the Yale subjects.

Not surprisingly, it was the unexpected behaviour of the obedient subjects which attracted the lion's share of attention from the experts (and others) and stimulated various other experiments. Most subsequent researchers found that between one third and one half of participants do not obey—they defy the authority of the experimenter. Are disobedient people different from obedient people? One might imagine, for example, that men would be more likely to administer intense shocks than women—after all they are supposed to be more aggressive. On the other hand, women tend to be more yielding than men on many tests of compliance, and so might be readier to obey the experimenter. In fact, Milgram found no difference in obedience between male and female participants. What he did discover was that obedient women became much more nervous and concerned than obedient men. But when ordered to administer genuine electric shocks to a puppy in a Milgram-type study, only 54 per cent of male participants did so, as against 100 per cent of female participants, who were prepared to give the most severe shock to the howling and yelping dog.

How does one explain these astonishing findings? As yet, all we can reasonably say is that not enough work has been done to enable psychologists to predict who will be obedient and who will be disobedient. Typically, however, better educated people are more likely to be disobedient, perhaps because they do not regard the experimen-

ter as so intimidating. People who have spent a number of years in one of the armed forces are more likely to be obedient, suggesting that the effects of service discipline are very long-lasting.

Common sense suggests that people with an authoritarian personality (discussed in Chapter 25) are more obedient than those of a more liberal disposition. Milgram tested this, and found that obedient subjects had much more pronounced authoritarian attitudes than defiant subjects on a test of fascist tendencies (the 'F Scale').

ABDICATION OF RESPONSIBILITY

But of all the questions raised by Milgram's dramatic work, the most engrossing is whether or not his findings are relevant to some of the atrocious war crimes of this century. Milgram obviously feels that they are, citing evidence from interviews with former members of SS concentration camp personnel and Gestapo units. Two themes reiterated again and again were the dehumanization of the victims of such crimes and the 'helpless cog' attitude of those responsible for committing them.

One of the main features of Nazi Germany was the systematic devaluation of the Jews over a period of more than a decade by means of vehement anti-Jewish propaganda. Jews were excluded from German citizenship and, ultimately, denied the status of human beings. On a vastly reduced scale, many of Milgram's obedient subjects harshly devalued

'Teacher' is an authority figure in most young children's lives but her influence is attentuated if parents are permissive.

Hitler's subordinates, tried for war crimes, claimed that they had 'followed orders'.

their victims. One subject justified his behaviour by saying that the victim 'was so stupid and stubborn he deserved to get shocked'. When Milgram asked some of the participants in the study to think of five words to describe the learner's personality, obedient subjects gave fewer positive and more negative words than disobedient subjects.

The 'helpless cog' attitude was exemplified by Adolf Eichmann. At his trial for his part in the extermination of the Jews, his main defence was that he was merely a little cog in the machinery that carried out the directives of the German Reich. Personal responsibility for one's actions is easier to evade if one belongs to an organization in which responsibilities are divided and duties highly specialized.

Wesley Killam and Leon Mann of the University of Sydney compared obedience in two groups of subjects, one group playing a 'transmitter role' (ordering someone else to administer the shocks to a learner) and the other playing an 'executant role' (directly administering the shocks). The transmitter group, at one remove from administering the shocks, was twice as obedient as the executant group.

OBEDIENCE: A FATAL FLAW?

The implications of his work made Milgram profoundly pessimistic about the future. He wrote: 'The capacity for man to abandon his humanity, indeed the inevitability that he does so, as he

Passenger and hostess both know their roles, but subordinate roles are often trickier. More middle management executives have breakdowns than senior.

merges his unique personality into the larger institutional structures . . . is the fatal flaw nature has designed into us, and which in the long run gives our species only a modest chance for survival.' He even went so far as to claim that an individual's conscience ceases to operate when he or she is responding to the dictates of authority. Under such circumstances, the individual enters an 'agentic' state, viewing himself or herself as merely the instrument of the authority figure.

Is such pessimism justified? There are some reasons for supposing that it is not. Certainly the analogy drawn between the Milgram experimental situation and Nazi Germany is imprecise and even misleading. Milgram's experiment was presented to the participants in a way that emphasized its positive, culturally desirable values, such as increasing our understanding of human learning and memory. By contrast, the goals of Nazi Germany were morally vile, in spite of the attempt to portray them as a purification of the Aryan race and the creation of a higher civilization. Another difference is that Milgram's subjects were only obedient when the experimenter kept a close watch on them, whereas minute-by-minute surveillance was largely unnecessary in the conditions which prevailed in Nazi Germany.

Milgram's idea that people obeying an authority figure overrule or simply forget their own consciences may have been true of some of the officers in charge of Nazi concentration camps, but it was certainly not true of most of his subjects. It would indeed have been disturbing if the subjects had whistled and looked relaxed and happy while administering severe electric shocks. The obvious tension and unease of most of the obedient subjects clearly showed that they had not lost sight of moral issues. Their moral confusion was shown by a disinclination to look at the learner, which hardly suggests sadistic pleasure in inflicting pain.

Another reassuring finding emerged when Milgram put two stooge subjects in with each genuine subject, all performing the teacher role. When the two stooge subjects quit the experiment half way through, 90 per cent of the real subjects followed suit and also disobeyed the experimenter. While there were many people in Nazi Germany who strongly disapproved of what was happening, subjects in the Milgram experiment had little idea whether other people would approve of them for disobeying, although they knew the experimenter would not approve. In a sense, Milgram loaded the dice by depriving his subjects of any effective moral support that might have strengthened their desire to disobey.

MISINTERPRETING BEHAVIOUR

Finally, we return to the vexed question of why outside observers so spectacularly overestimated the levels of disobedience likely in the Milgram experiment. An interesting suggestion was put forward by Stephen West and his associates. They argued that 'actors' (anyone actively involved in a situation) and external observers frequently have very different perceptions of the causes of behaviour in any given situation. The attention of the actor is focused on the environment from which he selects information to guide his actions, whereas the attention of the observer is focused on the actor and his behaviour. In consequence, the actor tends to attribute the causes of his behaviour to his environment, whereas the observer attributes the actor's actions to characteristics of the actor. For example, if you ask different people why a particular person robbed a bank, they will probably tell you he is a shady, anti-social, and thoroughly disreputable character. If you ask the robber himself, he will probably say that he had a tip-off that the bank was easy to rob or that he needed the money.

According to West's analysis, people underestimated obedience in the Milgram situation because they tended not to take the authority of the experimenter into account. They asked themselves what kinds of people would be obedient, and concluded that only sadists would go along with the experimenter.

To prove his theory, West persuaded a number of people to take part in the burglary of an advertising firm; their job was to act as inside lookouts and

Without some rules, even rules about jay walking, life would slowly grind to a halt. But because authority is distant – no cops in sight—the rules are ignored.

microfilm the firm's records. Those who took part said they agreed to do so because of the amount of money involved and the allegedly foolproof nature of the plan. External observers, on the other hand, put their dubious behaviour down to their character, describing them as outgoing, unintelligent, poor, insecure, unhappy, untrustworthy, unsophisticated and impulsive. No doubt you will already have thought of some choice adjectives to describe experimental psychologists who try to persuade young college students to embark on a career in industrial espionage!

CONCLUSIONS

Extremely powerful conflicts can arise when people are ordered to perform immoral acts by an authority figure, and these conflicts can produce almost intolerably high levels of tension. Obedience is more likely when the individual is more involved with the authority figure than with the victim; disobedience is more likely when the individual witnesses the plight of the victim in some way. Milgram's work poses a number of moral issues from the point of view of both experimenter and subject. It is instructive to compare the experimental findings of Milgram and others with the horrific reality of Hitler's Germany, but the analogy should not be taken too far.

Chapter 5
THE MOCK PRISON EXPERIMENT

One of the most notorious experiments in the history of psychology—because of what it appeared to reveal about human nature and the way in which it was set up—was an attempt to discover exactly how and why being in prison is such a degrading experience. There is clearly a lot wrong with the prison system in Western societies. The rising incidence of prison riots in Britain and America is a sign that something is seriously wrong.

Reforming the system is all very well, but the problems must be correctly identified first. At least three major components of the prison system need to be considered: the guards or warders, the prisoners themselves, and the organizational structure and physical environment of the prison. Are the warders to blame for the current climate of unrest? We know that individuals of a somewhat aggressive or sadistic disposition often choose to become warders. The second possibility is that prisoners, being naturally subversive and anti-social, tend to create an unsavoury atmosphere whatever their environment. The third possibility is that it is the prison itself, the building, cell conditions, lack of privacy and rigid power structure, which is mainly responsible.

A plausible case can be made for any or all of these factors causing trouble, yet it is extremely difficult to prove. What can psychologists contribute towards an understanding of the malfunctions in the prison system? It was Philip Zimbardo of Stanford University who came up with an ingenious experiment designed to explore these failings.[1] Many critics have accused him and his colleagues of overstepping the mark in their pursuit of scientific knowledge, but until the experiment began they could not have predicted what would happen. The Zimbardo experiment is one of the most famous, some would say infamous, in the annals of psychology.

KEY EXPERIMENT: THE MOCK PRISON STUDY

Philip Zimbardo and his co-workers at Stanford University, Craig Haney, Curt Banks and David Jaffe, were interested in determining the causes of the dehumanization that is so prevalent in prisons. Suppose that ordinary members of society were persuaded to act as guards and prisoners in a mock prison which mimicked the environment and day-to-day running of a real prison? If the mock prison failed to produce the hostility and alienation of a real prison, this would surely suggest that the personality characteristics of the guards or the prisoners, or both, are the vital ingredients in the unpleasantness found in a real prison. On the other hand, if the behaviour observed in the mock prison was very similar to that in a real prison, this would suggest that it is the environment of a prison which is the crucial factor in producing unpleasantness.

The experiment started on 14 August 1971 in Palo Alto, California. The quiet of a Sunday morning was shattered by a screeching squad car siren as police swept through the city picking up the participating college students from their homes in a surprise 'mass arrest'. All of the 'suspects' were charged with a felony, informed of their constitutional rights, spread-eagled against the police car, searched, handcuffed, and taken away in the back seat of the police car to the police station. The whole operation was carried out so realistically, thanks to the co-operation of the Palo Alto City Police Department, that the alarmed mother of one 18-year-old student arrested for armed robbery said: 'I felt my son must have done something.'

On arrival at the police station, each suspect was fingerprinted and identification forms were prepared for his 'jacket' or central information file. He was then left on his own in a detention cell. Later in the day, each suspect was blindfolded and taken to the 'Stanford County Prison', where he was stripped naked, skin-searched, deloused and issued with a uniform, bedding and basic supplies. The uniform worn by the prisoners consisted of a loose-fitting smock with an identity number on the front and back, no underclothes, a light chain and lock around one ankle, rubber sandals, and a cap made from a nylon stocking.

The prison warden gathered the prisoners together, and told them about the 16 basic rules of prisoner conduct, starting with 'Prisoners must address the guards as "Mr Correctional Officer" ' and ending with 'Failure to obey any of the above rules may result in punishment'.

The 'guards' had been told beforehand that their task was to 'maintain the reasonable degree of order within the prison necessary for its effective functioning'. They were given only minimal guidance about the way they were expected to behave, except that they were specifically prohibited from using physical aggression. They were

A routine pick-up of suspects. Milgram made his 'arrests' very realistic; his 'suspects' suspected nothing.

clearly distinguishable from the prisoners by their uniform, which consisted of a plain khaki shirt and trousers, a whistle, a police nightstick and reflecting sunglasses.

The guards and prisoners were selected from among a total of 75 respondents to a newspaper advertisement asking for male volunteers to participate in a psychological study of 'prison life' for 15 dollars a day over a period of two weeks. The 10 prisoners and 11 guards who actually took part in the experiment were among those respondents judged to be the most stable (physically and mentally), the most mature, and the least inclined towards anti-social behaviour. In fact the majority of them were middle-class students.

The prisoners and guards were to live within the confines of the 'Stanford County Prison', which was situated in the basement of the psychology building at Stanford University. This mock prison was deliberately designed to be as unpleasant as possible. There were three small cells (9 ft by 6 ft), with three prisoners assigned to each. As in a real prison, the windows were barred, and in addition to guards there was a warden, a superintendent (Zimbardo), a parole board and a grievance committee. All the participants had agreed to take part in spite of having been told that those assigned to play the prisoner role could expect to be under surveillance, might be harassed, and might have some of their basic rights curtailed during imprisonment.

The happenings within the mock prison were so unpleasant and potentially so dangerous that the entire experiment had to be brought to an end after six days rather than the scheduled fourteen. Violence and rebellion broke out within less than two days of the start of the experiment. The prisoners ripped off their clothing and their identity numbers, shouted and cursed at the guards, and barricaded themselves inside the cells. The guards put down the rebellion violently using fire extinguishers, transformed the prisoners' rights into 'privileges', played the prisoners off against one another and systematically harassed them. One of the prisoners showed such severe symptoms of emotional disturbance (disorganized thinking, uncontrollable crying and screaming) after only one day that he had to be released.

On the third day a rumour spread through the 'prison' about a mass escape plot. This led the superintendent and the guards to take various repressive and preventative steps. On the fourth day, two more prisoners displayed symptoms of severe emotional disturbance and were released; a third developed a psychosomatic rash all over his body and was also released. As time passed, some of the guards seemed to derive great satisfaction from exercising power and behaving in a sadistic manner. A particularly interesting observation was that the use of force, harassment and aggression by the guards increased steadily from day to day, in spite of the fact that prisoner resistance declined and evaporated. The guards also manifested more indirect displays of power as time went by, such as rapping their sticks against their hands or against the furniture, walking with a swagger, or adopting extravagant postures. The prisoners, on the other hand, began to slouch and keep their eyes fixed on the ground.

What seems to have led to the experiment being abandoned was a comment made by Christina Maslach, Zimbardo's fiancée. She had gone to the prison to help interview the prisoners. While she was there she saw a line of blindfolded prisoners shuffling along under guard to the toilet. Miss Maslach burst into tears and exclaimed: 'It's awful what you're doing to those boys!' Naturally, Philip Zimbardo's heart melted at these words and the experiment was officially halted the next morning.

Perhaps the most vivid accounts of what it was like to take part in such a dehumanizing experience were the diary entries of those directly involved. Before the experiment one of the guards wrote in his diary that he was a pacifist and so unaggressive that he could not imagine maltreating any other living being. By the third day he appeared to be thoroughly enjoying the power to manipulate people. Before the prisoners received visitors, he warned them not to complain unless they wanted the visit to come to an abrupt end. What he really liked, he said, was having almost total control over everything that was said and done.

On the fifth day, problems arose because a new prisoner refused to eat his sausage. The guard's diary entry at this point reads: 'We throw him into the Hole ordering him to hold sausages in each hand . . . We decide to play upon prisoner solidarity and tell the new one that all the others will be deprived of visitors if he does not eat his dinner . . . I walk by and slam my stick into the Hole door . . . I am very angry at this prisoner for causing discomfort and trouble for the others. I decided to force-feed him, but he wouldn't eat. I let the food slide down his face . . . I hated myself for making him eat but I hated him more for not eating.'

As we have already noted, the guards became increasingly brutal and aggressive during the course of the experiment and ignored the warning not to use physical force. However, Zimbardo and his colleagues reported that there were differences in behaviour among the guards, and only about a third of the guards, they felt, were so consistently hostile and degrading as to be described as sadistic.

On the other hand, the prisoners became progressively more passive as the days passed, and sank into a state of depression and helplessness. Perhaps the reason for this was that they began to realize there was very little they could do to improve matters or control the environment. As the old saying goes: 'Why bang your head against a brick wall?'

Despite its premature end Zimbardo's experiment showed that brutal, ugly prison situations can develop even when upright citizens play the parts of prisoners and guards. The dehumanization which occurred in the Stanford experiment could hardly be attributed to the 'deviant personalities' of those involved. The most natural explanation was that it was the prison environment which was mainly responsible for the participants' behaviour. In Zimbardo's own words, his study revealed 'the power of social, institutional forces to make good men engage in evil deeds'.

But how similar was the mock prison to a real prison? The evidence from those with first-hand experience of real prisons is somewhat mixed. Prisoners in the maximum security wing of Rhode Island Penitentiary said that they recognized the reactions of the mock prisoners as corresponding to the confused and over-emotional reactions of many first offenders. A remark by one ex-convict throws some light on the passivity of the mock prisoners: 'The only way to really make it with the bosses [in Texas prisons] is to withdraw into yourself, both mentally and physically—literally making yourself as small as possible. It's another way they dehumanize you. They want you to make no waves in prison.'

A woman prisoner stares out of her cell window. To survive prison conditions, she will probably withdraw into herself; this will further undermine her sense of identity.

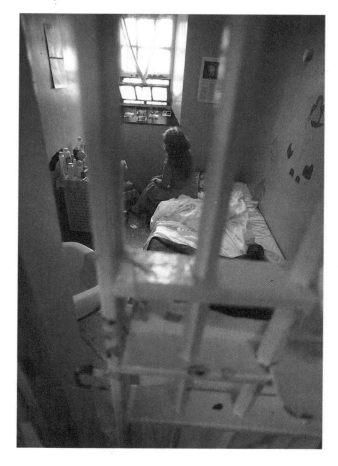

WHAT THE CRITICS SAID

The associate warden at San Quentin prison was predictably sceptical about Zimbardo's experiment when he was interviewed on television. Asked whether it was relevant to the prison system, he replied that it was worthless, biased and methodologically unsound, but he was basing his judgment on a brief news article he had read. Subsequently, Zimbardo's right to visit any of California's prisons was refused by the Superintendent of the Department of Corrections. This action suggests, at least to the cynical mind, that officialdom was frightened because Zimbardo had got it right.

The most weighty attack came from Boston psychologists Ali Banuazizi and Siamak Mohavedi, who argued that the participants in the Stanford Prison Experiment were not in a social situation that was functionally equivalent to that of a real prison; all they were asked to do was to play the roles of prisoners and guards, and since they had strong stereotypes of how guards and prisoners behave in a real prison, they simply engaged in conscious role-playing based on these stereotypes. In this connection, it is interesting to note that most of the guards, when questioned about their aggressive behaviour, argued that they had 'just played the role' of a tough guard.

Banuazizi and Mohavedi examined some of these ideas by asking people to fill in a questionnaire giving a description of the Stanford Prison Experiment followed by a series of questions. Eighty-one per cent of those questioned guessed fairly accurately what the experimenter was trying to prove; one respondent, for example, wrote: 'He believes that people are pushed about, put down, and humiliated in gaols.'

The vast majority of respondents (90 per cent) predicted that the mock guards would be oppressive, hostile and aggressive. Such a wide consensus suggests that there is a familiar stereotype concerning the behaviour of prison guards and warders. There was less agreement about the probable reactions of the mock prisoners. Approximately 30 per cent thought the prisoners would be rebellious and defiant, another 30 per cent guessed they would be passive and docile, and most of the others thought they would probably fluctuate between the two.

So, as these data indicate, the mock guards may simply have been pretending to conform to the cultural stereotype of the aggressive, unpleasant prison guard, and did not 'really' get involved in the part they were playing. However, it is less clear whether the mock prisoners' behaviour can be so readily accounted for by the stereotype argument. There are no cultural expectations concerning the typical behaviour of prisoners.

It is certainly true that the behaviour patterns exhibited by those engaged in role-playing reflect many different things, including what the role-player would like to do, what he feels is socially desirable, and what he thinks the experimenter expects him to do. In this connection, Banuazizi

and Mohavedi were correct when they criticized Zimbardo for assuming that his results could be explained fairly simply. But their own explanation of Zimbardo's results was not totally adequate either. Was the passivity, depression, helplessness and even psychological dysfunction displayed by the prisoners merely a remarkable piece of acting designed to please the experimenters? Even if severe emotional disturbance can be simulated, psychosomatic rashes presumably cannot.

The strongest evidence against the idea that Zimbardo's subjects were merely 'acting out' culturally defined roles is that extreme versions of these roles were observed mainly towards the end of the experiment. If Banuazizi and Mohavedi were correct, why was full-blown stereotypical behaviour not manifest from the beginning? Furthermore, the physical abuse and harassment shown by the guards seem to have gone quite a long way beyond what would have been expected from mere play-acting. While acting is most likely in the presence of an audience, Zimbardo actually found that harassment of prisoners was greater when individual guards were alone with solitary prisoners or out of range of the recording equipment.

A close examination of the data collected by Zimbardo suggests that there was undoubtedly some play-acting during the early stages of the study, with stereotyped expectations helping to determine the participants' behaviour. However, it is worth noting that real prison guards or warders during the early days of their employment are also likely to 'role-play'. As the experiment progressed, the participants seem to have become increasingly involved in the roles assigned to them, noticeably less self-conscious.

The aspect of the Stanford Prison Experiment which worried people most was whether it was morally acceptable to expose the participants to such degradation and hostility. Can one really justify a study in which four participants had to be released because of 'extreme depression, disorganized thinking, uncontrollable crying and fits of rage'? Was it reasonable for Zimbardo to stand by while the guards forced the prisoners to clean toilets with their bare hands, hosed them with fire extinguishers, and made them do push-ups, sometimes with a guard standing on their back?

Professor Harris Savin of the University of Pennsylvania, for instance, described the mock prison as a 'hell', and compared Zimbardo to used-car salesmen and others 'whose roles tempt them to be as obnoxious as the law allows'. He concluded as follows: 'Professors who, in pursuit of their own academic interests and professional advancement, deceive, humiliate, and otherwise mistreat their students, are subverting the atmosphere of mutual trust and intellectual honesty without which, as we are fond of telling outsiders who want to meddle in our affairs, neither education nor free inquiry can flourish.'

ZIMBARDO'S DEFENCE

In reply, Zimbardo argued that psychological research is morally justified if the gains—new knowledge, for instance—outweigh the losses[2]. He claimed that the 'losses' suffered by the participants did not persist after the end of the study. This was ascertained by means of questionnaires sent to the participants several weeks after the study, several months later, and then at yearly intervals. An attempt was made to minimize the negative effects of the study by holding day-long debriefing sessions, in which the moral conflicts posed by the study were made explicit.

Zimbardo admitted that there was a lot of suffering during the course of the experiment, but pointed out that all of the participants signed a formal 'informed consent' statement which specified that there would be an invasion of privacy, loss of some civil rights and harassment. He also pointed out that any professional psychologists who felt unhappy about the study could have lodged a complaint with the American Psychological Association Ethics Committee. In fact, only one inquiry was addressed to the Committee within two years of the study taking place, and that was from Zimbardo himself!

On the positive side, most of the participants reported that they had learned valuable things about themselves. Some of the participants volunteered to give up part of their summer holiday to work in local prisons, and most became advocates of penal reform. Another possible benefit of the study was the influence which it had on the public at large. For example, one citizens' group used the results of the study in a legal action to prevent the construction of a huge new prison in Contra Costa County, California, in favour of smaller, community-based facilities.

The moral position adopted by Zimbardo is one in which ends justify means, and in which research is evaluated by considering the benefits and costs involved. This accords with the view of most psychologists and was expressed in the following words by the American Psychological Association Committee on Ethical Standards in Psychological Research: 'The general ethical question always is whether there is a negative effect upon the dignity and welfare of the participants that the importance of the research does not warrant.' Even so there are difficulties.

First, it is all very well to justify research on the basis of likely benefits and costs, but we do not always know what the consequences are going to be until *after* the experiment has been carried out. Zimbardo claims that the high costs of his prison experiment, in terms of degradation and physical assault, surprised him. Nevertheless an earlier and smaller version of the main experiment had been carried out under Zimbardo's supervision at Stanford University, with many of the same disquieting results.

Second, one person's assessment of the bene-

Two approaches to prison organization: the bars and barriers of a closed prison, and the social and family contact allowed by an open prison. The one operates a system of punishment, the other a system of rewards.

fits and costs of a piece of research may not agree with someone else's. Many people would disagree with Zimbardo, arguing that the suffering of the participants was not justified by the kind or quality of information gained.

Immanuel Kant and others have argued that ends cannot justify means. There should be no exceptions to a moral principle, regardless of the consequences. But the rigid following of such principles can have extremely unfortunate consequences. If a madman with a gun asks you where your mother is because he wants to shoot her, would you tell him, for the sake of sticking to the principle 'Always tell the truth'? The inflexible and unrealistic nature of such a moral position has limited appeal.

IMPLICATIONS FOR PRISON REFORM

In spite of the criticisms, the Stanford Prison Experiment produced thought-provoking and striking results. What is it about the organizational structure of prisons that produces such unfortunate effects on the morale and behaviour of inmates? Zimbardo argued that one relevant factor is that prisons are designed to maximize anonymity. All prisoners are put into standard uniforms, required to have hair of a standard length, and are fed standard meals on standard plates at standard times. Of course their personal identity is under siege.

However, it was the power structure within prisons which Zimbardo identified as being the most important factor: 'Power is the most important variable in social psychology and the most neglected . . . The great discovery of American behaviourism, namely that responses that are reinforced will increase in frequency, is but a technological footnote to the primary issue of who controls the reinforcers.'

Within the prison system the guards or warders exert the power. They expect prisoners to obey all the rules, but they don't reward them for their obedience. But if prisoners disobey the rules, that *is* noticed and followed by punishment. So the best a prisoner can hope for is that the guards will behave predictably so that he knows how to behave in order to avoid punishment. When actual prisoners are asked 'What are the characteristics of a good guard?', most say they prefer guards who 'go by the book' and don't make exceptions.

The fact that prisoners are relatively unable to control their environment or obtain rewards by acting in certain ways may be of crucial importance. Laboratory research has demonstrated that such circumstances produce an apathetic state known as 'learned helplessness', which seems to have much in common with the passivity and unresponsiveness of Zimbardo's mock prisoners. Perhaps prisoners would be more contented with their lot if they were praised and rewarded for following the

prison rules rather than punished for disobeying them. Such an approach has been adopted with some success in the 'token economies' discussed in Chapter 24.

CONCLUSIONS

Philip Zimbardo set up a mock prison to investigate the failings of the prison system. He found that responsible citizens, when asked to play the part of prison guards, acted in a degrading and dehumanizing way towards other responsible citizens playing the part of prisoners. This suggested that it is the environment and power structure of prisons rather than the sadistic nature of the guards or the antisocial nature of the prisoners which lead to the horrors of prison. More specifically, prison power structures require the guards to punish the prisoners for violating the rules, and the prisoners are not allowed to control their environment to any significant extent. However, Zimbardo's work did not actually disprove alternative explanations, and there is evidence that criminals do differ in personality from the normal population (as we shall see in Chapter 24).

As well as providing new information about the prison system, the Stanford Prison Experiment raised important ethical issues. According to Zimbardo, research should be judged by the criterion of whether the benefits exceed the costs. In a study in which the costs included several days of utter misery and humiliation for some of the participants, the benefits would need to be very substantial indeed. Many people feel that Zimbardo's study was a clear case of the costs greatly exceeding the claimed benefits, and that the study should not have been carried out or should have been halted sooner.

Chapter 6
SEX, VIOLENCE AND THE MEDIA

In most Western countries there has been a marked increase in the number of violent crimes, rapes and other sex crimes in recent years. No matter how the data are analyzed and criticized, the increase is a real one, and it demands an explanation. Many people blame the media, arguing that overtly violent and pornographic material is bound to have a bad influence on the young and susceptible. Is it merely a coincidence that the amount of violence shown on television and the amount of overt and explicit sex shown in videos and pornographic magazines has also increased over the last 30 years? There does seem to be a correlation over time between the offerings of the media and higher incidence of violent crime and sexual assault, but is the one the cause of the other?

7   A large number of case histories have been published suggesting just such a relationship. Here is one very nasty example, in which a 14-year-old girl was assaulted and raped by two 15-year-old boys and one 14-year-old. The girl had been baby-sitting and returned home around 11.00 pm—the couple she had been baby-sitting for gave her a lift to the street near the flats where she lived. As she was walking towards the flats, a red sports car pulled up —it had been stolen from a nearby street that same day. In it were the three youths, none of them known to the girl. They offered her a lift but she refused.

All three followed the girl into the block of flats, where they grabbed hold of her. One of them pushed her into a dark corner and ordered her to take off her trousers, while another produced a penknife. They began fondling her but were interrupted by an irate resident who shouted at them. They then dragged the girl away from the flats and flung her down behind a tree near the river. One of them told her: 'If you don't take off all your clothes, you'll go into the river.'

The terrified girl stripped and all three boys raped her. They called to each other 'It's your turn now', and raped her again and again. They committed 'other horrifying sex acts'. One kicked the girl because she cried when ordered to perform a sex act. After several minutes three men in their thirties arrived on the scene. First they watched the boys rape the girl, then they too joined in. According to the girl, they were friends of one of the boys. At one point the boys and the men were all engaged in some form of sex activity against the girl. When the men left, the boys again had intercourse with her.

Afterwards two of the youths urinated over her. Then all three left, threatening to break her neck if she told anyone.

The girl, filthy and covered in mud, managed to gather some clothes together and went to her friend's flat, and the police were called. The woman doctor who examined her found bruises, teethmarks and scratches on the girl, but was unable to examine her properly because she was so badly swollen and also in great pain. The three youths were traced and all three made statements of confession. In all these lengthy statements there was not one single word or expression of remorse or care as to what the girl had been through.

FROM THOUGHT TO ACTION

The relevance of this horrifying story to the theme of this chapter was made clear by the prosecuting counsel, who stated: 'At the ringleader's home, a number of pornographic magazines were found, some showing explicitly the kind of beastly sex offences that had been committed against the girl.' This suggests, but does not of course prove, that these pornographic materials were, at least in part, responsible for the crime that had been committed. Even the fact that many similar cases can be quoted, in which the offence was a mirror image of an act or acts portrayed in a book, film or television programme read or seen by the defendant, does not provide such proof. However, such cases raise a genuine demand for investigation. The appearance of cause and effect cannot be ignored.

Those who argue that there is a causal relationship between media models and violent crime often use advertising as the basis for their opinions. If television, newspapers and magazines can successfully persuade thousands of people to buy product X simply by showing other people buying and enjoying product X, why should large numbers of people not follow suit when they see or read about people behaving in a violent or sexually explicit manner and apparently enjoying it? Why should advertisers pay large sums of money to have their wares touted in the media if they do not expect the publicity to increase people's motivation to buy them?

This argument has some power, but it is not logically consistent. Most of the things advertised in the media are things people want anyway, such as cars, refrigerators and holidays. They certainly

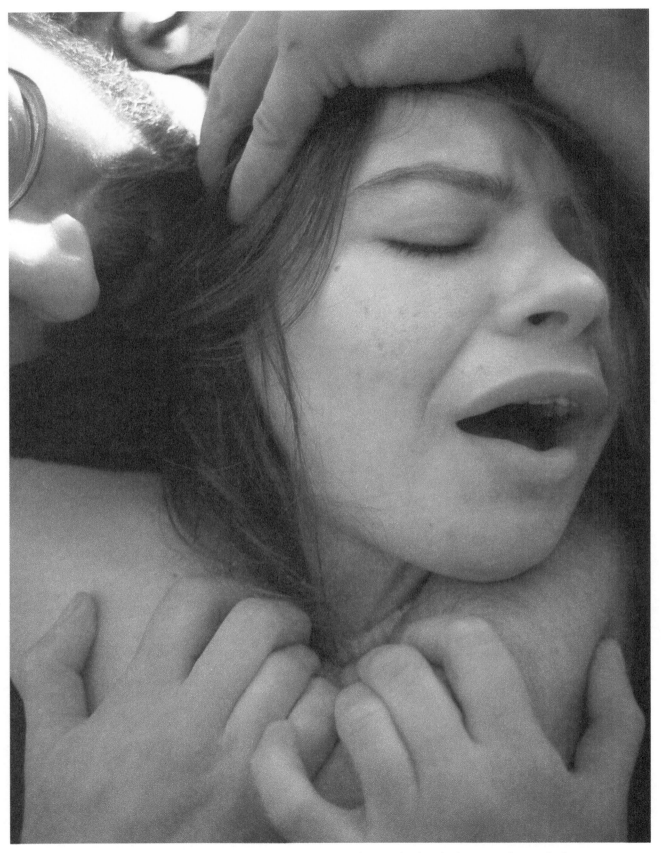

Rape is raw and ugly, and the psychological scars can last a lifetime. Saying 'no' to sexual assault does not mean 'yes'.

do not want violent or perverted forms of sex in the same way. Most advertisements tell people which company manufactures the goods or services they want, or where they can be bought. The portrayal of violence and explicit sex may wake people up to the existence of certain forms of conduct, but that is rather a different point.

Another 'causal' argument runs like this. Television presents us with a view of society and shows us how people behave in different situations. Youngsters imitate the models set before them— this is how they learn to react to situations they have never encountered before. Parents, teachers, pop stars, siblings, schoolmates, books, magazines and television all provide role models. So if violent or callous behaviour and explicit or brutal sex are freely demonstrated to youngsters, they may come to regard such behaviour as natural and acceptable. There is indeed evidence to support this argument, and it is one which is difficult to counter.

Would you let your child go past this shop? Should sex aids, rubber dolls and porno mags be on public sale?

A young boy's inner sanctum. Powerful media interests want him to consume erotica.

It is not suggested, of course, that television, videos, pornographic magazines and so on are the only or even the major source of the disturbing changes that have taken place in our society. Proving that there is cause and effect between the media and greater levels of violence in society is very difficult because so many other factors at work.

Nor is it suggested that everyone is equally influenced by the portrayal of sex and violence. What is suggested, rather, is that *some* people, admittedly a relatively small number, are sufficiently influenced by images of human callousness to turn thought into action. But let us not be hypnotized into thinking that the problem is insignificant because only a small percentage of people are affected by television, videos or pornographic magazines. In 1952 only 0.024 per cent of American citizens died in road accidents, but in a country the size of the United States that means that 37,794 people lost their lives. Small proportions can still add up to unacceptably large numbers of murders, rapes and other violent crimes.

CORRECT INTERPRETATION OF RESEARCH FINDINGS

In the last 40 years or so there have been many empirical studies—experimental laboratory studies, field studies, other studies combining laboratory and field work—which have sought to establish or disprove a connection between violent behaviour and violence in the media. Before we look at the results, however, we should be aware of the biases in such studies. In many cases strong financial interests have been involved, which is not generally a recipe for unbiased interpretation of results, and in some cases the findings of the scientists actually carrying out the work have been muzzled by sectional interests. In a Commission set up by the President of the United States to look into the effects of sex and violence in the media, the major television networks were allowed to veto the appointment to the Commission of two highly respected psychologists who were considered expert in such matters and replace them with laymen favourable to the television industry. As a result the Commission consisted mainly of amateurs as far as the evaluation of findings was concerned and by others expressly selected to represent certain interests. The conclusions of the Commission were not necessarily incorrect, but they were expressed in such a cautious and circumscribed fashion that the wrong impression was frequently given. The Commission's report on television violence, for instance, declared that television violence was harmful, but this conclusion was couched in such a convoluted manner and with so many reservations that many newspapers got the idea that the Commission had exonerated television. Thus anyone seriously interested in knowing what the findings were had to rely on the (incorrect) interpretations of newspaper reporters based on (biased) summaries written by prejudiced

amateurs incapable of understanding the voluminous and highly technical reports written by the psychologists who actually carried out the investigations!

In a recent book entitled *Sex, Violence and the Media*[1] H. J. Eysenck and D. K. Nias looked at all the original reports of the Commission and summarized their findings and conclusions, but they had the greatest difficulty in obtaining the reports from the Commission, which seemed to be quite averse to allowing anyone to read the actual experimental findings!

Another problem with research in this area is that the lay person is frequently told, by interested parties, that the data are 'conflicting', that 'nothing can be proved', and that 'more research is needed' before conclusions can be drawn and action taken. It is of course possible to criticize any individual study, but when many different studies, using different methodologies, different populations and different stimuli, arrive at similar conclusions, then those conclusions should be taken seriously. Newton's work on gravity was criticized in his lifetime and conspicuously failed to solve the three-body problem (the relationship between the movements of the sun, the moon and the earth), yet it would not have been good science to disregard his conclusions. There are no perfect scientific studies, but this does not mean that acceptable and worthwhile conclusions cannot be derived from the best.

A frequent and particularly invidious criticism of experimental work in the media violence/social violence field deserves special mention. The senior author of this book was once called as a witness before a Royal Commission (the Williams Committee) set up by the British government to look at the possible effects of sex and violence in the media. The Commission was presided over by a professor of philosophy no less, and contained many eminent people, but no scientists and certainly no psychologist. This made it quite certain that the Commission would be ignorant of the large literature on the subject, unable to understand it, and incapable of arriving at meaningful conclusions, thus ensuring solidarity with most other Royal Commissions!

When the members of the Williams Committee were told about the experimental studies that had been done, they argued that laboratory experiments (in which, for example, participants are shown films or videos depicting extreme violence or explicit sex scenes) were 'artificial' and that one could not generalize from them to behaviour in real life. They might just as well have argued that Galileo, rolling balls down inclined planes, was working in an 'artificial' environment and that his results did not apply to the real world! They made the common mistake of thinking that laboratory studies, or studies done under carefully controlled conditions, are simply inductive. This is not so.

Normally, laboratory work is done for the purpose of testing theories—a prediction is made from a theory and the prediction is then tested in

Who is he copying? The macho gesture contains a hint of menace. The macho image is under siege today—is that one of the reasons why violent behaviour is on the increase?

the laboratory. If the test bears out the prediction, then the theory is strengthened; if it does not, the theory is weakened and may have to be abandoned. It is the testing of the theory which is important. There is no attempt to generalize from the laboratory to the outside world.

Let us suppose that a particular experiment consists of showing a number of subjects videos containing typical rape scenes, and that the subjects' views on women are tested before and after the videos are shown. In such experiments it is usually found that these views change in the direction of greater callousness: after seeing scenes of rape, more subjects are inclined to believe that women enjoy being treated as sex objects and that when they say 'no' they really mean 'yes', or such beliefs are strengthened. There is a change in the direction of greater machismo, a perceptible dismantling of the accepted social view of women as individuals who have the right to accept or reject sexual advances. What kind of theory is tested by such an experiment?

THE DE-CONDITIONING EFFECT OF MEDIA VIOLENCE

Behavioural psychologists have worked out a very powerful technique for treating patients suffering from phobias and other anxiety states: desensitization. Anxiety is reduced by pairing the fear-producing situation or object, presented in a relatively mild form, with a positive stimulus (a biscuit, a piece of chocolate, etc.) while the person is relaxed. Thus, if a woman has a cat phobia, she is first taught how to relax and then, when she feels relaxed and comfortable, she is shown a picture of a kitten. The picture of the kitten provokes some fear, but not enough fear to overcome her state of relaxation or the pleasant feelings induced by eating a biscuit or a piece of chocolate; she has, to some extent, become desensitized. Gradually the strength of the fear-producing stimulus is increased (from kitten to cat, and from pictures to the real thing), but very carefully so that the anxiety provoked is always less than the positive feelings produced by the relaxation and the positive stimuli. Over and over again it has been shown that progressive densensitization can cure even the most serious phobias and anxiety disorders in a relatively short period of time. The process is one of de-conditioning or re-conditioning (see Chapter 8), in which a stimulus which once provoked fear and anxiety comes to be associated with feelings of wellbeing.

Applying de-conditioning theory to the experiment in which subjects were shown videos depicting rape, one would expect the normal socialized reactions of horror and disgust to become de-conditioned by the images on the screen if the people

Not so long ago, assaulting a policeman was a fairly rare offence. Not so today. Has respect for the rule of law been eroded by too many cop thrillers and soaps?

watching were relaxed, sitting in well-upholstered chairs and enjoying a drink or a cigarette. This is what the theory predicts and when the prediction is tested in the laboratory, it turns out to be true. We can therefore regard the theory as having been strengthened. In fact de-conditioning theory has been very strongly supported by hundreds of laboratory experiments done in various contexts, so there is no question of 'generalizing' by induction from a single laboratory experiment. De-conditioning theory has been used outside the laboratory to treat different types of neurotic disorder and with great success. So the results of laboratory experiments cannot be argued away.

WHO COMMITS RAPE?

Is it possible to predict what kind of personality would be influenced by the portrayal of rape into actually carrying out aggressive acts against women? In a book called *Sex and Personality* the senior author of this book showed that there are quite close relationships between personality and sexual attitudes, beliefs and behaviour[2]. Extroverts tend to have intercourse at a younger age than introverts, and also more frequently, with more partners and in more positions. They also indulge in longer pre-coital love play than introverts and in more varied sexual behaviour outside intercourse. On the other hand people who score high on the second major dimension of personality, neuroticism-stability, behave rather differently. Because their emotions are so changeable and because they react with fear and anxiety to even mildly stressful situations—in which category we must include social contact generally and sexual contact particularly—neurotics are more likely to worry about sex, more likely to be disgusted by certain aspects of sex, and therefore more likely to have fewer sexual partners and less frequent sexual contacts than their more stable peers. This is particularly true of unmarried people.

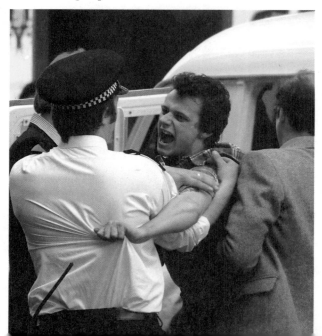

Of most interest in connection with rape is psychoticism, the third major dimension of personality. People who score high on the psychoticism scale display such traits as aggressiveness, coldness, egocentricity, impulsiveness and tough-mindedness, and behave in an anti-social and callous way. Many studies have shown that psychoticism is closely related to criminality and psychopathy (see Chapter 24). As far as sexual behaviour is concerned, high psychoticism scorers are characterized by promiscuity, curiosity, hostility and lack of satisfaction, and have few qualms about sex before marriage. One would therefore predict that people committing rape would be high psychoticism scorers, and also that people not guilty of any crime but scoring high on

psychoticism would be interested in pornography showing the use of force against women, would admit to wanting to use force against women, and would also admit to having enjoyed doing so on occasions when they did behave in such a fashion.

KEY EXPERIMENT: THE USE OF FORCE IN A SEXUAL CONTEXT

In a highly significant experiment Barnes, Malamuth and Check tested large numbers of students with respect to personality and various aspects of sexuality—sexual knowledge, attitudes, thoughts, actual behaviour. Particular attention was paid to the kind of attitudes, thoughts and behaviour associated with high psychoticism. It was found that high psychoticism scorers were less

Most of the pin-ups on this wall are erotic rather than pornographic, but the display as a whole suggests an obsessive interest in female flesh rather than in real women. Real women are not eternally promiscuous.

◄ *This advertisement, although it implies that women are for sex and men are for boardrooms, is unlikely to appeal to a potential rapist. High psychoticism scorers are more aroused by images which show the use of force.*

motivated to engage in sexual activities as an expression of love and affection; they also had more frequent thoughts associated with the use of force in sexual encounters; and they did not enjoy thoughts of more typical heterosexual activities, but did enjoy thoughts of forcing others.

Questioned as to whether they would engage in unconventional sexual behaviour if there was no chance of getting caught, high psychoticism scorers endorsed rape—forcing a woman to something sexual when she didn't want to—and also sado-masochism. When asked about their intentions towards the opposite sex, high psychoticism scorers denied intentions of having intercourse and oral-genital contact, but endorsed group sex and forcing a woman to do something against her will. As regards exposure to pornography, high psychoticism scorers reported less exposure than low psychoticism scorers except to items showing the use of force. Once again, conventional sexual activities did not, on the whole, arouse pleasurable feelings, but forced sexual activity did.

With these findings in mind, Barnes and his colleagues proceeded to test the hypothesis that high psychoticism scorers would become more sexually aroused than low psychoticism scorers by material of a violent nature[3]. Sexual arousal was measured in two ways, by self-report and by penile erection, as measured by a mercury strain gauge. The sexual material used as a stimulus consisted of various audio-taped versions of a story of about 1,000 words. There were four versions of the story, with and without violence (the woman's consent versus non-consent) and with and without the infliction of pain. The outcome was very clear-cut, and as expected. Low psychoticism scorers were more aroused by the 'no violence' and 'no pain' versions of the story, high psychoticism scorers by the violent versions. This was true both of self-reported sexual arousal and of physiologically measured arousal. So there is a clear relationship between susceptibility to violent pornographic material and strong sexual reactions to such material.

High scores on measures of psychoticism and schizophrenia have consistently been found in personality studies of convicted rapists[4,5]. Such people are usually described as hostile, irritable, unpredictable and impulsive individuals who avoid close emotional involvement, show poor judgment and poor grasp of social situations, and frequently fall foul of agents of authority. Thus the personality of the actual rapist corresponds very closely with that of the potential rapist as outlined above.

Other studies have shown that, when exposed to pornographic material involving the use of force

towards women, men with this particular kind of personality become more aggressive, domineering and forceful[6]. Their attitudes towards women move in the direction of greater callousness. Field studies and laboratory studies have, on the whole, come to a similar conclusion.

To be rigorously scientific such a conclusion ought to be tested, but since it would be barbarous to repeatedly show rape videos to high psychoticism scorers in an attempt to significantly increase the number of rapes committed, we must be content with less direct evidence.

CONCLUSIONS

In a wider context it would be worth quoting here the conclusions Eysenck and Nias came to after considering all the empirical evidence concerning violence and the offerings of the media: 'Our major conclusions are that the evidence strongly indicates that the portrayal of sex and violence in the media does affect the attitudes and behaviour of viewers; that these effects are variable, depending on the details of presentation and the personality of the viewer; and that the recommendations for action depend entirely on a person's value system. Aggressive acts new to the subject's repertoire of responses, as well as acts already well established, can be evoked by violent scenes portrayed on film, TV, or in the theatre. Pornography, too, affects many viewers, but its effects are likely to be much more variable. Variability of reaction is associated with such factors as the sex of the viewer, or his personality; general as well as environmental factors operate here. The great variability of attitudes and reactions makes it clearly impossible for recommendations to be universally acceptable; compromises are inevitable, and compromise pleases nobody. Our recommendations, which are clearly subject to debate, disagreement and argument to a degree that our factual findings are not, suggest a closer watch on the portrayal of violence in the

We live in a relentless TV culture, with many adults watching more than 30 hours of TV a week. That represents a lot of conditioning time.

media, and also certain restrictions on the portrayal of pornography, though not of erotica . . . It can no longer be said that the evidence is ambiguous or too contradictory to allow any conclusions to be drawn; the evidence is remarkably consistent and congruent . . . '

It is often argued that any kind of control over the media involves censorship and therefore the erosion of free speech and free artistic expression. Holding strong beliefs about free speech ourselves, we are not impressed with this argument. Incitement to racial violence is rightly forbidden by law. Would that such rules had been in operation in the Weimar Republic when *Der Stürmer* published its rantings against the Jews. Few people would want to argue against such rules on the basis of freedom of speech. Why should the implicit and apparently effective incitement to violence against women be treated differently? Freedom yes, license no. Incitement to violence of any kind is incompatible with the existence of a law-abiding democratic state and cannot be defended on the grounds of freedom of speech or artistic freedom.

More and better research certainly needs to be done, but we doubt if the ultimate result will be very much different from that which has emerged from the work done so far. Above all else, interested parties should not be allowed to muddy the waters by suggesting that results are contradictory, methodology inadequate, or conclusions doubtful. There is too much agreement for such criticisms and too much accord with well-substantiated theories to doubt the main conclusions. Society will reject them at a high cost.

French riot police in action. All over the world violent civil protest is met with varying degrees of official violence. But which breeds which?

Chapter 7
WHO IS MAD?

One of the great controversies among psychiatrists and clinical psychologists concerns the nature of mental illness. The dominant view is that there are important similarities between mental and physical illness, and that methods of treatment should take account of that fact. The treatment of physical illness begins with the doctor identifying the nature of the illness. Arriving at a correct diagnosis (the medical term for classification of illness) is the most crucial part of a doctor's work. Having satisfied himself that he has discovered the true nature of the physical ailment, the doctor is in a position to prescribe appropriate treatment.

Clear deviation here from footwear norms! Most societies react to unusual behaviour with suspicion and disapproval, but that does not automatically mean that such behaviour is mad.

In the same way, it is often assumed that psychiatric disorders are accompanied by symptoms which point to a particular diagnosis (schizophrenia, for example, or manic-depressive psychosis), which is then used to guide treatment. Of course, it is often a lot harder to diagnose correctly a problem when it is of a mental rather than a physical nature—even non-medically qualified people recognize blisters and broken legs when they see them. The complexity of the problem was well illustrated by one study in which three psychiatrists all interviewed the same male patients, and found they could only agree on the appropriate diagnosis in 20 per cent of the cases.

A very strong reaction against the idea that mental illness should be viewed in medical terms has developed over the past 30 years or so. Psychiatrists such as Thomas Szasz and R.D. Laing have claimed that mental illness is a myth. In

essence, they argue, anyone allegedly suffering from mental illness is simply behaving in ways which deviate from those which are expected. Society reacts to this deviant behaviour with disapproval and tends to apply a semi-permanent label of mental illness to the person concerned. And once that person has been labelled as mentally ill, society expects him to behave in accordance with the label.

The importance of labels was memorably expressed by Laing. He claimed that if someone labelled a scientist said 'All men are machines', he might receive a Nobel Prize. In contrast, if someone labelled a schizophrenic said 'I am a machine', he would promptly be locked away.

This challenge to psychiatric orthodoxy has already brought about a number of changes in psychiatric rehabilitation schemes. In California, some of the ideas of people like Szasz and Laing were used in the formulation of the Lanterman-Patris-Short Act. The effect of this act was to make it more difficult to commit patients to mental hospitals, and still more difficult to keep them there for long periods.

The bitter personal disputes between those who subscribe to the medical model of psychiatric disorders and those who believe that psychiatric diagnoses are purely in the minds of the observers has probably succeeded in creating more heat than light. An ingenious attempt to evaluate the relative merits of these two diametrically opposed positions, however, was made a few years ago by David Rosenhan of Stanford University. The repercussions of his work are still with us today.

KEY EXPERIMENT: CAN WE DETECT INSANITY?

David Rosenhan was extremely interested in the various approaches that have been adopted towards the treatment of psychiatric disorders. In particular, he wondered, is it really as simple to distinguish between normality and abnormality as is implied by the medical model? In murder trials, for example, it is not unusual for eminent psychiatrists for the defence to contradict equally eminent psychiatrists for the prosecution on the issue of the defendant's sanity. Rosenhan was also aware that what is regarded as normal in one culture may be viewed as dangerously abnormal in another. Finally he came up with a clever way of trying to determine how well we are able to distinguish between the normal and the abnormal, or between the sane and the insane. What would happen if a number of entirely sane people attempted to gain admission to a mental hospital by pretending to have one of the symptoms of insanity?[1,2] Would they be classified as insane? If they were admitted, would the staff realize that a mistake had been made?

The answers to these and other questions were obtained in a study in which eight normal people, five men and three women, attempted to gain admission to twelve different psychiatric hospitals. They consisted of a young psychology graduate, a pediatrician, a psychiatrist, three psychologists, a painter and a housewife. The twelve psychiatric hospitals were located in five different states on the East and West Coasts of America, and varied considerably, ranging from relatively new to old and shabby, and from good staff-patient ratios to severe under-staffing.

Each of the eight participants phoned the hospital asking for an appointment. Upon arrival at the admissions office, each of them complained of hearing voices (these voices were often unclear, but appeared to be saying 'empty', 'hollow', and 'thud'; they sounded unfamiliar but were of the same sex as the participant). Each gave a false name and occupation, but told the truth about significant events in his or her life.

All were judged to be insane, and all were admitted to hospital, apparently on the basis of their hallucinations. One was diagnosed as suffering from manic-depressive psychosis, the others as schizophrenic. But as soon as they had been admitted the participants stopped simulating signs of abnormality, although several experienced a brief period of nervousness and anxiety because they felt they would immediately be exposed as frauds, which would be highly embarrassing.

While they were in hospital, the participants indicated that they felt well and were no longer troubled by 'voices'. In general, they behaved in a friendly and co-operative way. The only unusual aspect of their behaviour was that they spent a fair amount of time writing down their observations about the ward they were in, its patients and the staff. To begin with, these notes were written secretly, but as it gradually became clear that no one took much notice, the note-taking was done quite openly.

The hierarchical structure of the various hospitals was such that those of greatest professional status had the least to do with their patients (and pseudo-patients). The average daily contact of the participants with psychiatrists, psychologists and doctors was 6.8 minutes. In view of the general lack of careful observation by those in authority, it is not surprising that the participants were not released very quickly. The actual length of hospitalization ranged from 7 to 52 days, with 19 days being the average.

The fact that all the participants were released within a few weeks of admission may suggest that the psychiatric staff discovered that they had been sane all the time. However, this was not the case. All the participants were discharged with a diagnosis of 'schizophrenia in remission', indicating that the deception had not been detected.

Interestingly, quite a number of the real patients became suspicious about the participants. The first three participants were placed in wards containing a total of 118 patients, 35 of whom voiced their doubts. They said things like 'You're not crazy. You're a journalist, or a professor. You're checking up on the hospital.' However, most of them were reassured by the participants' insistence that they had been sick before they came into hospital, although they felt fine once they had been admitted. Nevertheless a few bona-fide patients continued to voice the opinion that the participants were sane.

If we accept these findings at face value, they suggest that the distinction between the sane and the insane is so blurred that it is entirely possible for the sane to be mistaken for the insane, at least by psychiatrists. Rosenhan wondered whether he could show the opposite effect, namely the insane being regarded as sane. He used as his testing ground a research and teaching hospital. The staff there had heard about the experiment just described and had informed Rosenhan that they would not have proved so gullible.

We humans do nothing without reason and intent. This man may be suffering from paranoid delusions, but his actions are perfectly consistent with them.

The first thing Rosenhan did was to tell the staff of this hospital that one or more bogus patients would attempt to gain admission at some time during the following three months. Each member of staff was asked to observe all patients who presented themselves for admission or in the ward and say whether they thought they were bogus patients or genuine patients.

Judgments were obtained on a total of 193 patients admitted for psychiatric treatment. Forty-one genine patients were judged with great confidence to be pseudo-patients by at least one member of staff. Nineteen patients were suspected of being frauds by one of the psychiatrists and another member of staff. In fact, none of Rosenhan's pseudo-patients sought admittance during this time. Apparently, then, mental hospital staff do sometimes think that people committed to their care are sane.

Rosenhan's main conclusion, which is tremendously important if it is true, was as follows: 'It is clear that we cannot distinguish the sane from the insane in psychiatric hospitals'. Part of the problem may be that, under normal circumstances, doctors and psychiatrists are more inclined to call a healthy person sick than a sick person healthy. It is obviously dangerous for a doctor to fail to take appropriate action when a sick person asks for treatment. A psychiatrist who refuses to hospitalize someone who has suspicious symptoms and asks to be hospitalized may face legal action if the patient subsequently commits suicide or murder, so it is natural for him or her to err on the side of caution.

If psychiatrists become too cautious, however, they may start to apply the labels of mental illness to normal people. This could be extremely damaging for those concerned because society deeply distrusts the mentally ill. While there is more tolerance now than in the past, when the mentally ill were thrown behind bars in asylums or burned as witches, mental illness is still stigmatized.

The other main points made by Rosenhan concerned the rather degrading conditions experienced by some of his bogus patients during their stay in hospital. Rosenhan himself saw one patient being beaten for having approached an attendant and said 'I like you.' In one hospital it was customary for the morning staff to wake the patients by shouting, 'Come on, you m———f———s, out of bed!'

On several occasions, when the pseudo-patients approached staff members with courteous requests for information, nurses and attendants simply ignored the request and moved on with head averted 88 per cent of the time, compared with 71 per cent of the time when the request was addressed to a psychiatrist. Even when the pseudo-patients did receive a reply, it was often unhelpful. If the pseudo-patient said 'Pardon me, Dr X. Could you tell me when I am eligible for grounds privileges?', the doctor would often respond with something like 'Good morning, Dave. How are you

In big cities 'community care' has increased the number of seriously disturbed people living on the streets. Was institutionalisation worse?

today?' and then move away without waiting for an answer. Such treatment is hardly likely to restore the shattered self-esteem of the mentally ill.

Since Rosenhan seemed to be suggesting that most psychiatrists are wasting their time and cannot tell the difference between the normal and the abnormal, it was only to be expected that his study would be greeted with a storm of protest[3]. This was exactly what happened. The letters pages of *Science* (in which Rosenhan published his original study) began to smoulder with furious criticism.

One of the main attacks on Rosenhan's work was that it was illogical of him to argue that because the process of psychiatric diagnosis did not seem to work very well with pseudo-patients, psychiatric diagnoses are *never* of value. The weakness of this line of argument was most forcibly expressed by Seymour Kety: 'If I were to drink a quart of blood and, concealing what I had done, come to the emergency room of any hospital vomiting blood, the behaviour of the staff would be quite predictable. If they labelled and treated me as having a bleeding peptic ulcer, I doubt that I could argue convincingly that medical science does not know how to diagnose that condition.'

Another point made by several psychologists and psychiatrists concerned Rosenhan's condemnation of psychiatrists for diagnosing schizophrenia on the extremely slim evidence of a single symptom (i.e. auditory hallucinations). Of course, a further relevant factor is that the pseudo-

patients indicated voluntarily that they wanted to be admitted to a mental hospital. How many normal, sane people are desperately keen to be allowed to live a severely restricted life surrounded by extremely abnormal people? It is perhaps not unreasonable for the staff of a psychiatric hospital to suspect that something *is* seriously wrong with anyone asking to be admitted.

Rosenhan claimed that there is one well-recognized difference between physical and mental illness: people usually recover from the former, whereas the latter is supposed to be lasting. Indeed, when they were discharged from hospital his pseudo-patients were diagnosed as having schizophrenia in remission; they were *not* deemed to be entirely normal. However, it certainly does not follow from this that being discharged after less than three weeks in hospital means that the staff were remarkably alert and perceptive. It is known that schizophrenics often have short periods of remission during which they seem perfectly normal. As a result, a fairly lengthy period of observation is required before one can be certain whether or not recovery has taken place, and so 19 days as an average period before discharging 'schizophrenics' was not unreasonable.

A diagnosis of schizophrenia in remission may sound as if the psychiatrists still had serious doubts about the mental health of the pseudo-patients ('in remission' simply means 'without signs of illness'). Apparently no suggestions were made about continuing serious problems. In fact one-third of released schizophrenics require re-hospitalization within one year, and 50 per cent require it within two years. Accordingly, the diagnosis of schizophrenia in remission is prudent.

One of the things Rosenhan found particularly distressing was that the sanity of the pseudo-patients was not discovered, in spite of the fact that they behaved perfectly normally while they were in hospital. However, there are several reasons for doubting whether the pseudo-patients really did behave as they would normally. Since six of the pseudo-patients were clinically or professionally trained, it would presumably have been 'normal' for them to discuss medicine and psychology with their professional peers, which they did not. It would also have been 'normal' for them to have told the staff that they had only wanted to gain admittance to the hospital as part of an experiment, but they did not do this either.

A related and potentially more serious problem is that the pseudo-patients may unwittingly have acted in ways that conformed to their psychiatric diagnosis, and thus lengthened their stay in the hospital. This could have occurred because they knew a good deal about the purpose of the study and its probable outcome (indeed, one of the pseudo-patients was Rosenhan himself).

But perhaps the most persuasive reason for not agreeing with Rosenhan's claim that we cannot distinguish between the sane and the insane in psychiatric hospitals is that many of the real patients made precisely that distinction!

In 1975 Rosenhan replied to the growing army of his critics by suggesting that they were allowing their emotions to run away with them: 'One can have little difficulty understanding those who fight mightily, even angrily, to retain current beliefs. Those beliefs were not earned without sweat in training, research, and on the clinical firing line.'

OTHER STUDIES OF PSYCHIATRIC ASSESSMENT

Rosenhan also pointed out that there is growing evidence that psychiatric diagnoses can quite easily be distorted. In one study, the researchers played a tape-recorded discussion between a doctor and an interviewee to groups of psychiatrists and clinical psychologists. Some of those listening were given a prior suggestion by the doctor that the interviewee 'sounds neurotic but is actually quite psychotic'. The interviewee in fact gave 'healthy' responses to several of the questions relevant for a diagnosis. In the absence of the prior suggestion, everyone agreed that the interviewee was not psychotic. However, 60 per cent of the psychiatrists and 28 per cent of the clinical psychologists given the suggestion rated the interviewee as psychotic.

In some related work, Langer and Abelson videotaped an interview in which the discussion concentrated on a client's work history and on the difficulties he experienced at work. The videotape was seen by two groups of well-trained psychiatrists and psychodynamic psychologists who were told that they were observing either a job interview or a psychiatric interview. In spite of the fact that everyone saw the same videotape, those who thought they had seen a job interview rated the client as much better adjusted than did those who thought they had seen a psychiatric interview.

Once again, the message seems to be that psychiatric assessment is often biased and unreliable. One would of course expect real job applicants to be better adjusted than the average psychiatric patient, in which case information about the kind of interview (job or psychiatric) is relevant, and ought to have some influence.

Clowns allow us laugh at strange behaviour rather than feel threatened by it. As surrogate madmen, they both confirm and question our ideas of normality.

The key point here can be illustrated by imagining that you are a soldier on guard at an army camp somewhere overseas. While on duty, you hear a sound and see the vague outline of a figure. If you know that the local inhabitants are basically friendly and that the enemy is not in the immediate vicinity, you'll simply ask the other person to identify himself. On the other hand, if the local people are mostly hostile and enemy forces are known to be close, you'll probably shoot first and ask questions afterwards. In other words, you take the entire situation into account in making your decision. Similarly, it is a reasonable assumption that anyone asking to be admitted to a psychiatric hospital is far more likely to be mentally ill than average members of the public.

Rosenhan did have a valid point, however, when he pointed out that psychiatrists should be more careful about applying psychiatric labels to patients. The label not only affects the way other people regard the individuals concerned; it can also affect those individual's opinions of themselves and how they interact with others. In one experiment, male out-patients with a psychiatric history were led to believe that a confederate of the experimenter had been informed earlier of their actual psychiatric history, or that they were patients with a physical illness. Although the confederate was not in fact told anything about the patients' conditions, mental or physical, he rated patients as much more tense and anxious when they thought their psychiatric history had been revealed.

THE REALITY OF SCHIZOPHRENIA

In spite of the criticisms of Rosenhan's study,[3] it could still be argued that schizophrenia is something which exists in the mind of the observer rather than inside the patient. In other words if an individual acts counter to society's *idea* of what is normal then he is abnormal, and what one culture may regard as normal may be regarded as completely abnormal in another.

American anthropologist Jane Murphy studied various ideas about normality during a field study in which she spent a considerable time with two very different non-Western groups, the Yupik-speaking Eskimos on an island in the Bering Sea and the Egba Yorubas in Africa. The Eskimos use the word *nuthkavihak* to indicate that a person's soul or mind is out of order. *Nuthkavihak* manifests itself in various ways, including talking to oneself, screaming at people who don't exist, believing oneself to be an animal, drinking urine, making strange grimaces, and threatening people. There is an obvious closeness between the concept of *nuthkavihak* and schizophrenia, since *nuthkavihak* is never used to describe a single phenomenon, but rather a pattern of behaviour in which three or four symptoms exist together.

The Yorubas have a word, *were*, which can be translated as 'insanity'. The typical symptoms of *were* include hearing voices, laughing when there is nothing to laugh at, asking oneself questions and answering them, taking a weapon and suddenly hitting someone with it, and defecating in public and then tramping around in the faeces.

It is very striking that these two primitive groups of people, very different from each other and from Western society, should nevertheless identify a state of insanity or craziness that corresponds so well with the Western diagnosis of 'schizophrenia'. Since most other non-Western groups also have a concept akin to that of schizophrenia, one is on very flimsy ground if one defines schizophrenia primarily in terms of society's response to unusual modes of behaviour.

A major criticism of Western society is that it displays a great deal of intolerance towards the mentally ill. Are the Eskimos and Yorubas more tolerant than we are of those suffering from *nuthkavihak* and *were*? Not at all. The Eskimos sometimes place an insane person in an igloo with bars across the opening through which food can be passed. They also physically restrain insane people when they become violent, and force them to return home if they run away. In Nigeria, the Yoruba healer of the insane frequently has between 12 and 15 patients in custody at any one time. Those who have a penchant for running away are usually shackled, and various herbal concoctions are administered to them to calm them down.

Many people have argued that the complex and competitive nature of Western society plays a substantial part in causing schizophrenia. In fact, the evidence suggests otherwise. The number of people who suffer from schizophrenia is a little less than 1 in 100—this is true of the two primitive groups just considered and of several Western groups as well. The figure is much higher in America because the American standard for schizophrenia is more lenient. The United States–United Kingdom diagnostic unit found that the same patients were diagnosed as schizophrenic five times more frequently by American psychiatrists than by British.

If schizophrenia is *not* something that is merely in the minds of observers, how should it be regarded? The remarkable similarities in definition, treatment and incidence of schizophrenia across very diverse societies suggest that schizophrenia is relatively unaffected by environmental conditions. This naturally suggests that genetic factors might be important. Other evidence strongly supports this notion. Let us consider pairs of identical twins in which at least one member of the pair is schizophrenic. What is the probability that the *other* twin will also be schizophrenic? About one in two, an amazingly high probability in view of the relatively low incidence of schizophrenia in the population at large. However, it could be argued that this is really a reflection of environmental influences—it must be very disturbing to grow up in a family in which the other sibling is mentally distraught. This argument sounds plausible, but it

A local oddball entertains the occupants of a New York park bench. The context makes his antics acceptable and unthreatening, but our tolerance of odd behaviour is fairly thin.

does not explain a further finding: where one of a pair of identical twins is schizophrenic the probability of both twins being schizophrenic is also one in two *even if the twins are separated shortly after birth.*

CONCLUSIONS

Many people (not all of them schizophrenics) are in two minds about the value of Rosenhan's work. Few would deny, however, that he was successful in highlighting the dilemma facing psychiatrists. If, on the one hand, a psychiatrist fails to hospitalize and apply a psychiatric label to someone seeking admission to a psychiatric hospital, he or she runs

the risk of prosecution if that person should subsequently commit suicide or murder. On the other hand, if a psychiatrist gives a psychiatric diagnosis to someone who is not really suffering from mental illness, that person will almost certainly be stigmatized by society and probably suffer a drastic change in his or her self-image as well. There are differing views on the relative costs of turning away a schizophrenic person and admitting a sane one. Overall Rosenhan may be right that psychiatrists are too willing to risk admitting those who are sane.

The readiness of psychiatrists to diagnose schizophrenia on the basis of only *one* of the major symptoms of schizophrenia (i.e. hallucinations) certainly lends support to the view that they err on the side of professional caution. However, several psychiatrists expressed great surprise at this aspect of Rosenhan's findings, pointing out that complaints about auditory hallucinations would usually be dealt with by out-patient psychiatric care.

While Rosenhan's work is provocative and ingenious, his major conclusions must be rejected. There is overwhelming evidence that the sane *can* be distinguished from the insane with a fair degree of accuracy, except perhaps under the very unusual conditions of Rosenhan's experiment. Fur-

thermore, schizophrenia is not simply society's way of labelling and controlling those who exhibit deviant behaviour. As Seymour Kety pithily remarked: 'If schizophrenia is a myth, it is a myth with a strong genetic component'. Dramatic evidence supporting Kety's position was obtained in 1988 when the genes involved in some kinds of schizophrenia were identified.

B

LEARNING FROM ANIMALS

Most people, even if they have only a smattering of knowledge about psychology, have heard of Pavlov's experiments with dogs, and possibly of Skinner's work with rats and pigeons. Nevertheless, the general public has always been sceptical about the relevance of animal experiments to an understanding of the human psyche. Contemporary psychologists are well aware of the dangers of assuming that what is true of other animal species is necessarily true of our own. We are not some unusually complicated sort of rat or dog. Why then do researchers continue to carry out so many animal experiments? The reasons given usually fall into one of three categories.

1. In medical research it is standard practice to try out new drugs on animals before using them on human patients. While this procedure cannot guarantee that humans will not receive harmful drugs, it clearly helps to minimize the risks. Psychological methods of treating neuroses and psychoses can also be dangerous; it is merely a sensible precaution to do initial tests on animals where this is feasible.

2. Some experiments cannot be carried out with human beings on ethical grounds. For example, no psychologist would contemplate separating a mother and child for long periods of time in order to investigate the importance of the mother to the child's development. However, such experiments have been carried out with monkeys.

3. Animal experiments can also be justified if they enable us to satisfy our natural curiosity about the world around us.

The chapters in this section deal with some of the most informative and thought-provoking animal experiments ever carried out. In Chapter 8, for example, we discuss work on 'avoidance learning' in dogs. Dogs will continue to jump across a barrier to avoid an electric shock even when the shocks are discontinued. This apparently senseless behaviour resembles the sort of behaviour seen in people suffering from obsessive/compulsive neuroses. But the real value of this work with dogs was that it suggested a new method of treatment for people afflicted with such neuroses, which turned out to be considerably more effective than previous treatments.

In the late 1970s Herbert Terrace (Chapter 9) addressed himself to one of the most important and controversial questions in the whole field of animal research: Do chimpanzees have language-learning ability? The answers he found have major implications for theories of language acquisition in humans. The possibility of language acquisition by chimpanzees has been looked at by other researchers, but Terrace's work is the most thorough in the field so far, and of especial value because it compares the social, physical and emotional development of young chimpanzees with that of human children.

Another aspect of the human condition which has been gainfully studied using animal models is the problem of maternal deprivation. The consequences of a child receiving inadequate mothering are far-reaching and of great social significance. What does a mother provide that is so essential to a child's normal development? What can be done to mitigate some of the sad consequences of maternal deprivation? In Chapter 10 we discuss Harry Harlow's answers to these and other fascinating questions, based on his work with rhesus monkeys.

Chapter 8
THE GENTLE ART OF CONDITIONING

There are four very pertinent questions which psychologists are repeatedly asked. The first is: 'What is the use of psychology?' Medicine is obviously useful because it enables us to cure patients suffering from a great variety of physical disorders. Physics is obviously useful because the laws of physics govern everything we do. And biology, botany, geology, chemistry and so forth because they enable us to influence the world around us. But of what use is psychology?

The second question is a little more involved: 'Psychologists spend hours running rats through mazes, making dogs salivate to the sound of bells, and generally making animals do fairly unnatural things. Surely all this has little relevance to the behaviour of human beings? After all humans possess language, intelligence of a high order, and the benefits of culture transmitted over thousands of years. Animals don't, so what can we learn from animals that we couldn't learn much better from humans?'

The third question is this: 'Much of the work done by psychologists on dogs, rats, hamsters, pigeons and so on seems to be cruel and involves giving electric shocks and other painful treatment to innocent, defenceless animals. This should not be allowed. It may be necessary to tolerate vivisection and other cruel practices for medical purposes, if they provide the *only* means of finding better methods for treating diseases, but in psychology such practices seem to be used merely for the purpose of satisfying aimless curiosity.'

The fourth question, often asked by psychologists themselves, is this: 'Psychologists carry out experiments in laboratories and then use the results to make far-reaching deductions about the everyday lives of people at work, at play, or in their homes. But isn't the very act of conducting an experiment in a laboratory unrealistic? Isn't the artificiality of the laboratory likely to affect the behaviour of the people or animals being studied to such an extent that nothing of general value can be deduced from experiments?'

In this chapter we hope to show that there is much valuable and relevant knowledge to be gained from psychological experiments with animals. The experiments we will be discussing, which go a long way towards answering the questions posed above, all concern 'avoidance learning' and 'response prevention'. Avoidance learning means learning how to do a task in order to avoid an unpleasant stimulus, and then performing the task even when the unpleasant stimulus is absent. Response prevention means preventing the performance of a habitual action until the urge to perform it fades away. To demonstrate these concepts we have chosen a whole series of experiments done on dogs, rats and other animals rather than a single key experiment. What is important is not so much the detail of each experiment, but the general methodology and findings.

AVOIDANCE LEARNING

Imagine a large laboratory room, divided into two compartments by a barrier across the middle. The barrier is low enough for a dog to jump over quite easily, but it can be raised so that he cannot jump over it. Both compartments—let us call them A and B—have metal rods on the floor which can be electrified independently so as to give the dog a mild shock to the soles of the feet. A similar arrangement can be made for rats, using a simple box divided in two (hence the term 'shuttlebox', which psychologists often use to describe this particular arrangement).

The experiment itself is a very simple one involving training the dog to respond to a stimulus that he learns to associate with an electric shock. The stimulus might be a flickering light. We will assume that the dog is in portion A of the shuttlebox; the flickering light is put on, and 10 seconds later the floor in this portion of the box is electrified, giving the dog a mild shock; very soon he jumps across the barrier into section B, where he is safe for a while. After a few minutes the flickering light comes on again, and after 10 seconds the floor of section B is electrified; the dog jumps back into A, which is now safe. This continues for a while, the dog jumping from A to B and from B to A, until he learns to jump not when he gets a shock but when he receives the 'conditioned stimulus', i.e. the flickering light which heralds the shock. Most dogs (and rats) learn this habit pretty quickly, and will continue to jump in response to the conditioned stimulus even when it is not followed by the unpleasant sensation of an electric shock. In other words, they have become 'conditioned' to adopt an avoidance habit which is functionally useless; they jump to the signal even though there is no longer an

Dog owners, as well as psychologists, demand rather strange behaviour from their dogs. Why condition a dog to sit at table and then forbid him to take food? As a conditioning stimulus, the owner's tone of voice may be enough.

Sneaking a cigarette and trying not to look guilty about it! Bad habits are not easily undone by punishment and exhortation. The more this youngster is nagged, the more precious his smoking habit is likely to become.

electric shock to avoid. As we shall shortly see, there are important similarities between human neurosis and avoidance learning in dogs.

As in human neurosis, the avoidance habit is extremely strong, and very difficult to break. Many methods have been tried to make dogs conditioned in this way unlearn the habit of jumping when the flickering light shows, but most of them do not work at all well. One might assume that electrifying the floor in the part of the shuttlebox the dog is jumping *into* would break the habit of responding to the light. But receiving a shock when he lands does not put the dog off at all; on the contrary, he jumps all the more enthusiastically, even though he is punished with a shock every time he lands. This again is fairly typical of human neurotic behaviour, which is not usually eliminated by any form of punishment, however severe.

OBSESSIVE/COMPULSIVE NEUROSES

Before describing how this habit may be changed, let us consider a typical human neurosis which is very similar to avoidance learning, namely the obsessive/compulsive neurosis. Typically, a patient suffering from this type of neurosis shows a very strong fear of being contaminated, of coming into contact with germs, dirt or other substances. He tries to reduce this fear by cleaning and washing himself, and by avoiding all contact with suspect substances. This cleaning/washing behaviour gradually increases in frequency, until he spends an inordinate amount of time cleaning himself, washing himself, polishing door handles, chairs and tables, vacuuming the floor, and so on. In the end, cleaning behaviour becomes so compulsive that it takes up practically all the person's waking hours. He loses his job, has no social intercourse with friends or relatives, and, if he is married, probably loses his wife as well. A disorder of this kind is obviously extremely serious, and until work on 'response prevention' was done with dogs there seemed little hope of curing it. Psychiatrists tried many different methods of treating obsessive/compulsive neurosis, including psychoanalysis, electric shock treatment, psychotherapy, leucotomy (a brain operation in which parts of the pre-frontal lobes are severed from the rest of the brain—see Chapter 12). None of these treatments have proved effective, and none of them achieve results which are any better than spontaneous remission (the improvement often observed in neurotic disorders with the passage of time even when no treatment has been given). However, although spontaneous remission is quite powerful in most neurotic disorders, it is exceptionally weak in obsessional and compulsive disorders; only one patient in three recovers on his own or is much improved even after a period of five years, a poor rate of improvement compared with that for anxiety neurosis or reactive depression, where the rate of remission is something like 70 per cent after two years.

Few people who have not come into contact with obsessive/compulsive neurotics can have any idea of just how debilitating the disorder is. Here is a description of the fears and rituals which obsessed a 19-year-old boy, as narrated by his elderly father: 'When George wakes in the morning, usually at 11 am, he feels that his hands are contaminated and so he cannot touch his clothing. He won't wash in the bathroom because he feels that the carpet is contaminated and he won't go downstairs until he is dressed. Consequently, I have to dress him, having first cleaned his shoes and got out a clean shirt, underclothes, socks and trousers. He holds his hands above his head while I pull on his underpants and trousers and we both make sure, by proceeding very cautiously, that he doesn't contaminate the outside of his clothing. Any error or mishap, and he will have to have clean clothes because he must avoid at all costs passing on the contamination to others. George then goes downstairs, washes his hands in the kitchen and then spends about 20 minutes in the toilet. This is quite a palaver. He has to roll up his shirt and vest to make sure they do not touch the toilet seat and has to check that he does it properly. I then have to stand at the doorway and supervise him, my main function being to give reassurance that he has not done anything silly to contaminate his clothing. Thankfully he is now managing on some occasions to cope in the toilet without my close supervision but I still have to be on call so that I can help him if he starts to panic for any reason. Incidentally, I have to put newspapers down on the floor of the toilet and change them daily to make sure that his trousers never come into contact with any contaminating substances. If he only wants to urinate then my task is made easier. I simply have to check his trousers and boots for splashes, sometimes getting down on my hands and knees with a torch. I am for ever telling him how ridiculous I think these rituals are, especially because I never ever find anything wrong. George never flushes the toilet because he feels that his clothing could be splashed, so one of my duties is to pull the chain and to cope with the frequent blockages which occur because of George's excessive use of toilet paper. Recently he has been checking that there are no pubic hairs on the floor and he asked me to get down on my hands and knees to check the floor meticulously. Basically he has to be completely sure that there is no contamination around because if he is not sure then he will start to worry and ruminate about it later on. He has to be completely sure and therefore needs a second opinion. As soon as he has zipped up his trousers I have to march in with a pad soaked in antiseptic and give the zip a quick once-over. When he washes his hands after toileting, he meticulously scrubs each finger and methodically works his way up as far as his elbow. I used to have to watch him at every step of the way, but now he only calls me in on occasions. Sometimes he will have washed and dried his hands and then decide that he is not sure

whether he washed them properly. At this stage I usually have to supervise him so that when he is finished he is absolutely certain that the job has been done perfectly without missing a square inch of contamination.'

The story goes on and on and on like this all through the day. It takes little imagination to realize that a person so afflicted cannot have an ordinary life. George's disorder was grossly disabling. Both he and his father lived in a very special kind of purgatory.

Why do some people behave in this way? The evidence strongly suggests that they do so in order to reduce their anxiety, which would otherwise be unbearably painful. When they are prevented from cleaning themselves their anxiety mounts; sometimes they become visibly terrified. When they are allowed to wash and clean themselves, their anxiety visibly decreases.

There are obvious similarities between the case of the dog jumping in response to the flickering light (although objectively he has nothing to fear because the electricity supply has been disconnected) and the obsessive/compulsive patient cleaning himself (although objectively there is no

The pint and the daily newspaper are a common ritual—we all have rituals which are not strictly necessary but which help us to cope with anxiety, to keep things somehow under control.

danger of contamination). The dog jumps and the young man washes himself because such actions relieve fear and anxiety, even though the fear and anxiety are unnecessary.

Both in dogs and in humans neurotic disorders can go on for months or even years without any improvement, despite all attempts to cure them. Yet one method *has* been found fruitful in the case of dogs, and that is 'response prevention'[1,2,3,4].

RESPONSE PREVENTION

Essentially, response prevention works as follows. When the flickering light is put on and the dog tries to jump into the 'safe' area, the barrier is raised so high that he simply cannot jump over it. The fact of being prevented from jumping causes the dog to be 'flooded with emotion' (the term 'flooding' has become widely used to describe this method of treatment). He will yelp, howl, bark, run around the cage wildly, and may even urinate and defecate in his fear. After a while, however, his emotion clearly decreases in intensity, and after half an hour or so he is apparently reconciled to his fate, particularly as he has not received any electric shock. Repeat the treatment a few times and the dog is permanently cured; the flickering light can be put on, but he will not attempt to jump across the barrier.

Overeating is one of the commonest compulsive disorders in the West today. Food messages are everywhere, but so are messages which they say 'thin is beautiful'. The bind is an uncomfortable one which de-conditioning theory can help to solve.

Psychologically, of course, this makes sense. If we may anthropomorphize for a moment, the dog was jumping in the belief that if he didn't jump he would receive an electric shock; what the response prevention technique demonstrated to him was that he would not receive a shock for not jumping and that his fears were therefore unfounded. Previously fear made it impossible for him to 'test reality'; now that he has been forced to test reality he is able to act in a more rational fashion.

KEY EXPERIMENT: RESPONSE PREVENTION WITH HUMAN PATIENTS

Can we use the response prevention technique with human patients, and does it have the same effect? The answer is yes to both questions. Naturally experimenters have used slightly different methods of proving the point, so we will just give a fairly generalized description of the procedures used (a detailed description of these procedures is given by S. J. Rachman and R. J. Hodgson in their book *Obsession and Compulsion*)[5].

First, the psychologist explains the details of the treatment to the patient and obtains his informed consent (without the active co-operation of the patient the treatment will not be successful, and in any case the patient has the right to know what is going to be done to him, and why). The patient must also have the right to refuse if he doesn't like what the therapist is proposing.

Having agreed, the patient is brought into a room which contains little besides a table, two chairs, one for the psychologist and one for the patient, and a container filled with some dirt or other material that the patient is known to think 'contaminating'. The therapist then puts his hand into the dirt in the container, and persuades the patient to do likewise. Now comes the crucial point: the patient is urged not to go and wash his hands (as he would normally do in order to reduce his anxiety), but rather to sit still and tolerate the very strong emotions of fear, anguish and anxiety that threaten to overwhelm him. Being 'flooded' with emotion is an extremely unpleasant experience, but the emotion gradually subsides, and after half an hour or so the patient can tolerate the situation with a degree of composure that he would have thought impossible at the beginning.

This, essentially, is the kernel of the procedure now widely employed by clinical psychologists in the treatment of obsessive/compulsive disorders. Of course the process has to be repeated a number of times, but the treatment is short. Between 20 and 30 exposures are usually required.

Figure 1 shows what typically happens in cases of this kind. Thus our theoretical account of what happens during response prevention treatment is a fairly accurate mirror of the actual behaviour and subjective experience of the patient.

We must now ask two questions. First, does the treatment actually work? Second, do patients suffer relapses after being cured? The answer to the

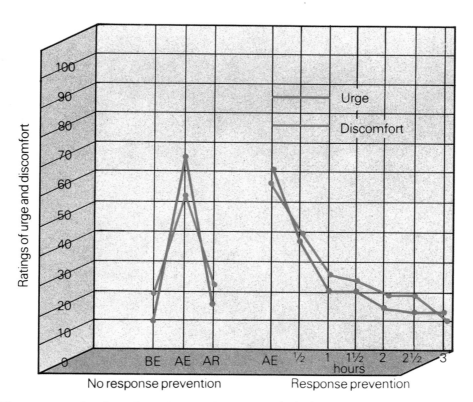

Figure 1   *These two graphs show the ratings made by an obsessive-compulsive patient of the discomfort he felt, and the urge he felt to wash and clean himself, after being exposed to 'dirt' and other 'contaminants'.*

The lines on the left show a relatively low degree of urge and discomfort before exposure (BE) but a huge increase in both after exposure (AE). AE denotes urge and discomfort after carrying out ritual cleaning and washing procedures.

The lines on the right show the effect of preventing ritual cleaning and washing responses. AE again indicates the patient's high levels of urge and discomfort after exposure to 'dirt', etc., but these levels fall to almost the same level as BE (before exposure) within 1 hour, and continue to fall for the next 2 hours.

Eventually obsessive-compulsive patients become conditioned to expect low levels of discomfort and urge when confronted with things once perceived as highly threatening. Response prevention enables them to test reality and learn that no serious consequences follow from not going through their usual ritual behaviour.

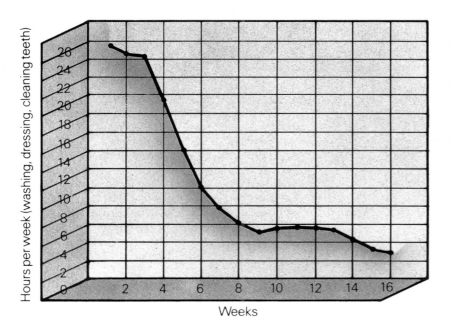

Figure 2   *This graph show the progress of one particular obsessive-compulsive patient, TN, over a period of 16 weeks during which he was given response prevention treatment. At the beginning he was spending 26 hours a week ritually brushing his teeth, combing his hair, shaving, putting on clothes, and bathing or washing himself. At the end of the period he was spending about the same amount of time most people spend on such activities – 2 hours a week.*

first question is simple. Yes, the treatment works in something like 80–90 per cent of cases, and it does so within a very short time. Usually fewer than 20 supervised exposures are necessary to produce either a complete cure or a very considerable reduction in the number of rituals carried out. Figure 2 shows a typical patient's improvement during treatment. By itself a graph like this proves nothing, but it illustrates what typically happens as a result of response intervention treatment. The treatment works, and works well. Until quite recently, obsessive/compulsive patients were received with dismay and hopelessness in most psychiatric institutions because nothing could be done for them. Now they are warmly welcomed and doctors are only too eager to try out these new methods in the almost certain hope of being able to cure them. This tremendous change has come about in just a few years, and all because of a new approach directly learned from psychologists' experiments with dogs.

But what happens once a patient is cured, or very much improved, and the treatment ceases? Freud would have called such treatment 'purely symptomatic', meaning that one may have dealt with the symptoms, but not with any underlying 'disease' or 'complex'. According to Freud, symptomatic treatment is useless; it leads inevitably to relapses or symptom substitution (i.e. the growth of new symptoms, assuming that the original symptom is successfully abolished). It is one of the tenets of psychoanalytic doctrine that symptoms are merely the outward indication of a complex underlying disorder. Unless one cures the underlying disorder, the symptoms either cannot disappear or will be replaced by others. It is this 'disease

model' of obsessive/compulsive disorders which is most fashionable among psychiatrists. Psychologists, on the other hand, believe that the disease model is inapplicable to behavioural disorders. They maintain that in the case of behavioural disorders one is simply dealing with faulty learning or conditioning patterns. So the patient needs not medical treatment but some form of re-education or re-conditioning. Instances of relapse or symptom substitution would provide crucial evidence for the disease model, but is such evidence available? What actually happens to patients after successful response intervention treatment?

The answer is simple. Although many patients have been followed up over several years, no relapses have been observed, and nothing in the way of symptom substitution—exactly the opposite of what Freud predicted. What is usually found instead is a continued improvement in the mental health and behaviour of the patient, even in areas not treated. The work record of many patients improves considerably, and so does their general happiness, their marital satisfaction and so forth. This is a very important finding, and it is paralleled by similar findings in other types of neurotic patients treated by other methods of behaviour therapy.

Why does the treatment fail in 10–20 per cent of cases? The answer seems to be that it fails for those patients who find the degree of fear and anxiety induced at the beginning of the treatment just too painful to bear. In such cases it should be possible to prescribe tranquillizers or other drugs to reduce these extreme levels of discomfort, although it should be emphasized that the disorder cannot be cured by medication, only suppressed.

There are other possible ways of dealing with patients who do not respond well to response intervention treatment, but it is still too early to say whether any of these new methods will be successful. Meanwhile let us rejoice that a disorder previously impossible to treat has now yielded to psychological investigation and innovation, and can be treated with great success in a relatively short time.

THE VALUE OF ANIMAL PSYCHOLOGY

Now, let us return to the questions asked at the beginning of this chapter. What good does psychology do? Well, in this case at least it has enabled large numbers of people suffering from distressing mental disorders to receive treatment that restores them to a healthy and happy life. That is something to be proud of. Although we chose only one example to illustrate the point, behaviour therapy has had many similar successes. Considering its triumphs and its extreme youth (the term 'behaviour therapy' was coined barely 30 years ago) many more advances can be expected. Anyone who argues that psychology is neither practical nor useful in this modern world is playing on an increasingly sticky wicket.

Agoraphobia is an overwhelming fear of being in public, open places. This woman can be helped to lose her disabling fear of crowds by response prevention therapy. Most phobias yield to this kind of treatment.

What about the value of animal experiments? Again, our jumping dogs clearly demonstrate the importance of animal work in understanding some of the mechanisms which govern human behaviour. They also suggested methods for changing and improving it. Work on response prevention in animals antedated the use of the technique on obsessive/compulsive patients. Looking back, it is doubtful whether the technique would have been considered for use with humans without previous experience with animals. Indeed, would psychologists have had the courage to use it, in the face of acute dismay and discomfort on the part of their patients, had they not known from animal experiments how successful it could be? None of this proves, of course, that human beings are simply larger, more complicated versions of rats and dogs—no psychologist would subscribe to such a view. What such a body of research demonstrates is that we share certain similarities with rats and dogs as far as our nervous system is concerned, and that it is possible to exploit these similarities. It does not follow that because there are certain mechanisms in rats and dogs, the same mechanisms are present in humans—it would be simple-minded to believe that, and animal psychologists are particularly wary of making such analogies. It is simply suggested that, where possible, similarities should be exploited and that before we try out new methods on human beings, we should try them out on animals. The methods which work with animals will not necessarily work with humans, but there are many procedures we would feel ethically compelled to reject in work with humans unless we could be sure, from experience with animals, that they stood a good chance of being successful. This is precisely the view taken by medical researchers testing new drugs, or exploring new theories in physiology and neurology. Why should psychologists be expected to adopt a different attitude?

Last, we must face the question of the cruelty involved, and the degree to which we are justified in using animals in experiments. This is not a scientific question but an ethical one and, as in most ethical problems, it is not a matter of black and white but of various shades of grey. There are rights and wrongs, advantages and disadvantages on both sides, but we believe that in cases like the one just described the relatively slight pain and discomfort suffered by the animals involved can be justified in terms of the ultimate benefit to human beings, who are themselves suffering. Others may disagree. You, the reader, must decide for yourself. In matters like this there are no convenient or categorical answers.

CONCLUSION

In summary, then, we find that an apparently trivial experiment in animal psychology had far-reaching consequences for human happiness, and for the treatment of certain neurotic disorders once considered untreatable. We also see that such experiments, particularly when their lessons are applied to humans, have important theoretical consequences; they indicate that psychoanalytic theory is, in fact, mistaken about certain disorders, and that simpler behaviouristic accounts of neurotic illness are more likely to be correct. Finally, such experiments suggest that it may be wrong to condemn animal experiments as irrelevant to human behaviour. We may yet learn a good deal from rats and dogs that will help us to understand and beneficially influence human behaviour.

Chapter 9
THE CHIMP WHO GREW UP AS A CHILD

Some of the most interesting experiments in the history of psychology have concerned chimpanzees, our nearest animal relatives. Most investigators have focused on one big question: Can chimpanzees acquire the skills of language? But there is an even larger question: Do young chimpanzees have the potential to grow up and develop in the same way as human children? An ambitious study by Herbert Terrace of Columbia University, New York, examined the socialization of a young chimpanzee and the development of his personality over a period of four years, far longer than the experimental period required for any of the other experiments described in this book.

WHY TEACH CHIMPS TO TALK?

Before discussing Terrace's work in detail, let us consider some of the background. For example, why is it important to know whether chimpanzees can be taught language? The simplest reason is that we have a natural curiosity to explore the

Introducing Nim Chimpsky, the chimp who learnt sign language. By the age of 44 months he had learnt 120 signs and could understand 200.

unknown, even when the cost is astronomically high (one has only to think of the manned landings on the moon). The idea that we might be able to communicate properly with another species, and so make contact with a point of view wholly outside our experience, is intrinsically fascinating.

A second good reason was expressed by Terrace: 'The opportunity to observe how the addition of language, as we know it, would influence the culture of a group of chimpanzees might provide a priceless glimpse of what life was like at the dawn of human civilization.'

Yet another reason for seeing whether chimpanzees can master language is that the success or otherwise of such an endeavour may help to resolve a bitter theoretical controversy about the human learning of language. The famous behaviourist B.F. Skinner claimed that humans learn language in much the same way that rats learn to press a lever for food: any kind of behaviour that is followed by reward or reinforcement will be repeated. If Skinner is right, there is no obvious reason why chimpanzees should not learn language, provided their attempts at language are suitably rewarded.

There seems to be some merit to Skinner's point of view. When a human infant makes a sound that is recognizable as a word, or as an approximation to a word, the parents usually show their approval verbally ('Good girl!') or physically (hugs and kisses), presumably reinforcing the infant's behaviour. However, when communication between a mother and her child during the first year of life is looked at closely, it turns out that the mother rewards virtually all of the baby's vocalizations, rather than just those which most closely resemble adult speech.

There have been numerous critics of Skinner's position, most of whom claim that he has proposed a grossly over-simplified account of the learning of language. The psycholinguist Noam Chomsky has argued that the sheer variety of sentences that children produce and their ability to create new sentences cannot be explained by simplistic ideas about reinforcement. Chomsky contends that the human brain is 'pre-wired' to make the various grammatical transformations that occur in any language. Others have referred to this capacity to learn language as the 'language acquisition device'. The existence of such an innate capacity would

Stages in human socialization: the 'Ya boo sucks' gesture which challenges authority (as it does in chimp language!) and bared teeth and fierce shouting (excitement in chimp language too) at a Punch and Judy show.

certainly help to explain the remarkable ability children have to produce grammatically correct sentences many years before they have had any formal training in grammar.

A HEAD FOR LANGUAGE

Some psychologists have argued that the ability to use this innate language acquisition device depends on the specialization which gradually develops in the two hemispheres of the brain. Normal children start to talk during their second year, after which their language skills improve rapidly until the age of five. Thereafter, these skills develop more slowly until puberty. The development of brain specialization closely parallels the pattern of language learning. Brain specialization is virtually complete at puberty. Until then children learn language easily, but thereafter it is difficult to learn a *second* language and the learner tends to speak it with a foreign accent. Before puberty, children readily learn to speak second languages.

Chomsky and his followers have assumed that the innate capacity to acquire language is only found in humans. Accordingly, since chimpanzees do not have the benefit of a language acquisition device, they should be all at sea when it comes to mastering language. So, on the question of whether chimpanzees can learn language, Skinner's position tends towards an affirmative answer and Chomsky's towards a negative. Who is right?

There is no doubt that the earliest attempts to impart the rudiments of language to chimpanzees produced results favouring Chomsky. They were almost unmitigated failures. Keith and Katharine Hayes spent six years trying to teach a female chimpanzee called Vicki to speak English words. At the end of that time, Vicki could only say four words: 'momma', 'poppa', 'up' and 'cup'. Her teachers had to push her lips and mouth into the correct positions at first, but she eventually learned to position her lips and mouth with her own hands to produce the sounds.

Why did this attempt fail? Undoubtedly part of the reason is that it is not at all natural for chimpanzees to make much use of their vocal chords. If they are left undisturbed, chimpanzees are usually silent. Furthermore, they are only physically able to produce approximately 12 distinct sounds compared to our 100.

CHIMP SIGN LANGUAGE

A major breakthrough occurred when Allen and Beatrice Gardner of the University of Nevada in Reno saw a silent presentation of a film made by Keith and Katharine Hayes. Even without the sound track, the Gardners were able to tell what Vicki was saying simply by watching the gestures that accompanied her sounds. This led them to wonder whether it might not be easier to use gestures than sounds, especially since chimpanzees in captivity spontaneously use a variety of begging and other gestures.

In June 1966 the Gardners began training a one-year-old female chimpanzee. They called her Washoe after the name of the county in Nevada where they lived. Washoe demonstrated the proverbial imitativeness of apes in many ways. For example, during the tenth month of the study she bathed one of her dolls in the way the Gardners usually bathed her. She filled her little bathtub with water, dunked the doll in the tub, then took it out and patted it dry with a towel.

This capacity for imitation was extremely useful when it came to teaching Washoe American Sign Language, a gesture-based language often learned by deaf people. She managed to learn four signs or words during the first seven months of teaching, nine more in the following seven months, and 21 in the next seven-month period. After three and a half years, Washoe had learned to sign a total of 132 words, and the Gardners estimated that she understood about three times as many signs as she could express. She was also able to combine words in sensible ways.

There have been some other notable studies. David Premack of the University of California invented an artificial language using plastic chips. He was so successful with his 'star' chimpanzee Sarah that she was eventually able to manipulate the chips to produce a complicated sequence such as 'Mary give apple Sarah'.

It is tempting to argue that such work demonstrates that chimpanzees can learn language. However, as the work of Terrace shows, this assumption may not be correct.

KEY EXPERIMENT: PROJECT NIM

When he first met the male chimpanzee he intended to train Herbert Terrace was a 37-year-old bachelor teaching at Columbia University. It was 2 December 1973 and the chimpanzee was just two weeks old. Terrace decided to call him Nim Chimpsky (a pun on Noam Chomsky). In contrast to the key experiments discussed in other chapters, this one lasted non-stop for nearly four years.[1]

Terrace felt that the chimpanzees in other language acquisition studies had too often been brought up in a relatively sterile and unsocial environment. Terrace was determined that Nim Chimpsky would be brought up in an environment resembling the loving and sociable atmosphere surrounding a human child. This approach had the advantage that language on Nim's part would develop as a result of social interactions, exactly as happens with human children.

Terrace was by no means convinced that chimpanzees had really acquired language in the way claimed by earlier investigators. He felt that what the chimpanzees had learned could often be dismissed as unnatural tricks. You can teach pigeons to peck at discs of different colours in a certain order to obtain food, but no one would regard that as evidence that pigeons can construct sentences. Nor would it prove anything if we superimposed the word 'please' on a white disc, 'teacher' on a red disc, 'give' on a blue disc, and 'food' on a green disc, and the pigeon 'spoke' to us by pecking in the order: 'Please teacher give food'. Terrace hoped that this sort of problem could be obviated by resisting any temptation to teach Nim language as if it were a party trick. Language learning was to be part of socialization.

The story of Terrace's experiment with Nim really divides up into two parts: Nim's general social development and, more specifically, his acquisition of language.

THE SOCIALIZATION OF NIM

Nim Chimpsky was the son of Pan and Carolyn, who were regarded as the most intelligent and stable animals in a chimpanzee colony in Oklahoma. Nim spent most of the first 18 months of his life in a large house owned by W.E.R. and Stephanie LaFarge. It was a typical New York household, consisting of Stephanie, her second husband W.E.R., three children from her previous marriage, W.E.R.'s four children from an earlier marriage, and a schoolteacher friend of the family.

During his first four months in the LaFarge house, Nim slept for 15–18 hours a day at the foot of Stephanie and W.E.R.'s bed. Just like a human

Nim, seen here with Laura Pettito, was a boisterous playmate and very demonstrative. He had an uncanny ability to see through his teachers' attempt to disguise their emotions.

infant, he had his nappies changed every few hours, was burped after feeding, tossed in the air, hugged, and held protectively by each of his caretakers.

In many ways Nim was even more childlike than a human child. His emotional reactions, for example, seemed to be much stronger than those of a human child, especially when he realized that one of his caretakers was unhappy. On one occasion when Jennie (one of the children in the household)

was crying, Nim leaped into her arms and stared intently into her eyes. He then touched her cheeks very gently and tried to wipe away her tears.

Sometimes the way in which Nim reacted to W. E. R. was strangely reminiscent of the Oedipus complex. One afternoon when Stephanie and W. E. R. were taking a nap, W. E. R. reached over to put his arm around Stephanie. In an instant, Nim stood up and bit him. (It has often been observed in chimpanzee colonies that an infant male chimpanzee will attack his father when he copulates with his mother.)

Nim's development was in certain respects more rapid than that of a human child. He could crawl by the end of his second month, and stand a month later if he had something to grasp. By the

Nim actually enjoyed washing up, and would get very cross if he was excluded from the kitchen.

time he was 20 months old, he was toilet-trained and would regularly use his potty.

His behaviour at bedtime was fairly similar to that of a human child. When he started to sleep on his own during his fifth month, he screamed or whimpered for a few minutes when put to bed. However, letting him hold on to a bottle or a pacifier was usually all that was needed to calm him down.

When Nim was almost a year old, he started using four rooms at Columbia University as both a nursery school and a day-care centre, returning to the LaFarges' at night. He was so mobile and energetic that the rooms had to be thoroughly chimp-proofed to prevent him escaping. Initially, his teachers tried using a chain-lock on the door together with a dead-bolt lock, which Nim managed to open. After that they tried spring-loaded hooks which required considerable dexterity to open. Nim still managed to escape occasionally into the main part of the psychology department. (Contrary to popular belief, it was actually quite easy to pick Nim out from among the psychologists.)

Eventually Nim's teachers and caretakers discovered that the most effective way of disciplining him was to walk away from him indicating 'you bad' or 'I not love you' in American Sign Language. His typical reaction to this was to stop what he was doing and run quickly to his caretaker, signing 'hug' or 'sorry'.

By June 1975 Nim had become so boisterous and difficult to manage that it became necessary to move him from the LaFarge house. Among other things, he had broken several valuable objects as a result of his ability to jump up onto any piece of furniture and hang from the light fittings. Fortunately, Columbia University owned a splendid 21-room mansion, Delafield, half of which they rented inexpensively to Terrace. There Nim was allocated five rooms for his exclusive use.

While he was at Delafield, Nim often behaved mischievously. On one occasion, he had heard Carol (one of his teachers) preparing a bowl of cereal for his lunch in the nearby observation room just before she left. A few minutes later his next teacher, Laura Petitto, left him on the nappy-changing table on his own while she went into the classroom to prepare for his next activity. When she went into the observation room to collect the bowl of cereal for him, it was missing. Nim was still lying on the nappy-changing table, but with an exaggerated expression of innocence. She looked severe and signed 'Where bowl?' Nim merely looked puzzled and looked around as though he was trying to help her find the bowl. It was only when Laura threatened to hit him that Nim finally took her hand and led her to the sink beside the changing table. In the bottom of it was the half-finished bowl of cereal!

He also behaved in an amusingly childish way when Susan Quinby, another of his teachers, brought her cat in. He offered a spoonful of yoghurt to the cat, and was amazed when the cat licked the spoon clean. The next time he deliberately offered the cat an empty spoon. After that, he filled the spoon up with yoghurt and fed himself.

Nim believed in joining in most of the household chores and other activities going on around him. He was particularly keen to help in the preparation of his own meals, and showed great patience and care in mixing and stirring ingredients. Another chore which he relished was doing the washing up; he had a very intense look on his face as he used a sponge to dab at the dishes. If for some reason he was excluded from kitchen activities, he would retaliate by opening drawers and cupboards and throwing out their contents, or turning on the taps or knocking over the rubbish bin.

One hundred years ago Charles Darwin suggested that a chimpanzee's expressions of emotions such as joy, anger, affection and curiosity all possess a distinctly human-like character. Well, Nim's behaviour certainly confirmed Darwin's observations, except perhaps that Nim's emotions were expressed more directly and intensely than those of a human. If he had not seen someone he liked for a long time, he would greet him or her with screeches of delight, smiling, pounding the ground with joy, hugging, kissing, and grooming.

A rather less attractive side of Nim's character was that he was very keen to establish dominance over everyone if at all possible. When a new teacher met him for the first time, he would put him or her to a severe test in order to gain the ascendancy. His unprovoked outbursts of aggression in these first meetings occurred with such speed and ferocity that new teachers often finished up scratched and bitten, and with their clothes torn.

More surprising than Nim's ability to express his own feelings was his ability to see through people's attempts to disguise their emotions. Laura, perhaps the best of Nim's teachers, summed it up when she described the important aspects of her relationship with Nim: 'It was more than just being relaxed. Nim had an uncanny ability to read one's feelings. I always felt that I had to be honest because he understood me . . . he made me feel as if I was "naked".'

LANGUAGE TRAINING

Psychologists who have attempted to teach language to the members of other species have focused primarily on chimpanzees. This is mainly because the personality of a chimpanzee resembles that of a human, which presumably makes communication easier. The importance of this became clear during Terrace's experiment, with Nim using sign language most freely with those he knew and liked best. The other major reason is that, of all the primates, the chimpanzee has a brain closest in complexity and relative weight to that of man.

Teaching American Sign Language to Nim turned out to be much more difficult than Terrace expected. (A constant shortage of funds to pay for the large number of people needed to look after

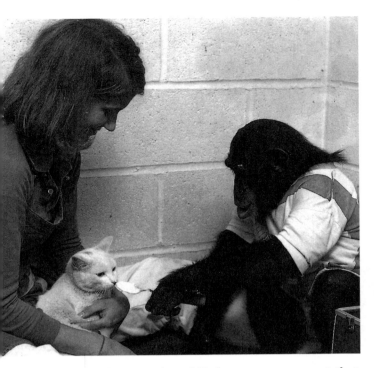 

Nim 24 hours a day, 365 days a year, meant that there was a rapid turnover in voluntary helpers to supplement the professionals. Nim was taught by 60 different teachers in only 46 months, and obviously such inconsistent relationships did not help.) This, for example, is how he learnt the sign for 'tea'. Laura, his teacher, got Nim to pay attention as she poured hot water into a cup containing a tea bag. Then she moulded his hands into the sign for 'tea', and encouraged him to take a sip. After this, Nim offered his hands to Laura so that she could form his fingers into the appropriate sign. Next Nim tried to mould Laura's hands to make the sign for 'tea'. When he had achieved this, Laura responded by giving him the cup of tea that he wanted.

After this training, Nim gradually started making the sign for 'tea' when his teacher made the sign in conversation. Finally, he would make the sign upon seeing the tea cup. Learning was still not complete, however. Just as a young child will often say 'doggie' to a wide range of animals and objects, so Nim would sometimes over-generalize, signing 'play me tea' while playing a game of chase.

In at least one respect, Nim managed to show greater linguistic versatility than his human teachers. Terrace tickled Nim when he was holding on to the branch of a tree with both hands. Nim immediately thought of an easy way to indicate that he wanted the tickling to continue: he signed both 'more' and 'tickle' with his bare feet!

One very human skill that Nim acquired as his language powers developed was the ability to lie. He had obviously noticed that his teachers were very responsive when he signed either 'dirty' (meaning that he needed to go to the toilet) or 'sleep' (meaning that he was tired). He gradually started using these signs when they were obviously inappropriate, presumably because he was bored and wanted a change.

Nim mastered his first sign ('drink') at four months, and this was quickly followed by four more signs ('up', 'sweet', 'give' and 'more'). It is interesting to note that there are several reports of deaf children learning their first sign by the age of four months. Words can be signed much earlier than they can be vocalized, probably because the muscular co-ordination required for sounds is much subtler.

In all, Nim learned to express 125 signs during his first 44 months, and he could probably understand more than 200 signs. His progress was very erratic, and depended greatly on the skills of individual teachers and the rapport they established with him. Under Laura Petitto's expert guidance Nim managed to learn five signs a month, more than twice as many as before her arrival.

In the summer of 1975, under Laura's supervision, Nim started to produce several two-sign combinations, including 'more eat', 'tickle me' and 'give apple'. By the summer of 1976 he was signing combinations of three or more signs ('me more eat', 'you tickle me' and 'me brush baby'). As time went by, he started using the words available to him more and more. Between 1 June 1975 and 13 February 1977, Nim's teachers observed him signing over 19,000 utterances consisting of two or more signs. This huge total was not achieved by mere repetition of a handful of combinations: Nim produced 5,235 distinctly different combinations. The sheer variety of his sign combinations suggests very strongly that Nim was not simply memorizing them in rote fashion. Unfortunately it was not possible to see how far Nim's learning might have gone. Because

Nim offers a spoonful of yoghurt to Susan Quinby's cat. Then an exchange of signs leads to Nim wanting to hold the cat. The cat looks distinctly uncomfortable.

of financial and other problems Terrace was forced to return Nim to the Institute for Primate Studies in Norman, Oklahoma, towards the end of 1977.

It could be argued that Nim was combining the signs which he knew in a more or less haphazard fashion. However, this was not the case. Consider a two-sign combination consisting of a transitive verb and 'me' or 'Nim'. Was Nim just as likely to sign 'tickle me' as 'me tickle', or 'tickle Nim' as 'Nim tickle'? Not at all. He signed with 'tickle' first on 107 occasions and with 'me' or 'Nim' first on 16 occasions. In other words, he chose the verb-first order 87 per cent of the time. Overall, the verb was placed first 83 per cent of the time by Nim when combining a transitive verb and 'me' or 'Nim'. Several other analyses confirmed that there was a definite structure to Nim's utterances, just as there is with human utterances.

There was another important similarity between Nim's utterances and those of children. When children are at the stage of starting to produce two-word combinations, some 80 per cent of these utterances can be interpreted as belonging to eight semantic categories. Two of these categories are object + beneficiary (e.g. 'food Nim') and action + object (e.g. 'eat grape'). When Terrace performed the same analysis on Nim's utterances, he discovered that 84 per cent of his two-sign combinations fitted these semantic categories.

The evidence discussed so far suggests that Nim developed language in much the same way as a human child. However, there were some import-ant differences. Videotapes of communications between Nim and his teachers were played in slow motion so that it was possible to see exactly when Nim began an utterance in relation to the utterance of his teacher. Although his teachers had not been fully aware of it, Nim interrupted them much more frequently than a normal child interrupts its parents. It appeared that Nim was much more interested in telling his teachers what he wanted them to do than in attending to what they were saying to him.

It has been found that less than 20 per cent of a normal child's utterances consist of imitations of its parents' utterances, and about 30 per cent of what a child says is spontaneous and not merely a response to an adult. Even after several years of language learning, 40 per cent of Nim's utterances were fairly exact imitations of what had been said to him, and only 10 per cent of his signings were spontaneous. In other words, Nim used language in a less creative and innovative way than a child.

The most important of Terrace's findings casts still greater doubt on the comparability of the language skills of Nim and of a child. When they start to speak, children with normal hearing produce utterances containing an average of 1½ words, but rapidly escalate to an average of 4 words or more per utterance (sometimes by the age of 26 months). Deaf children show the same escalation in the number of signs per utterance, but usually a little later than normal children. In striking contrast, the average length of Nim's utterances remained remarkably constant at about 1½ signs between the ages of 26 and 46 months.

Another major difference between Nim and children is that children's longer utterances usually communicate much more meaning than their shorter ones. Nim's did not, as can be seen in his longest utterance of all: 'Give orange me give eat orange me eat orange give me eat orange give me you.' A comparison of Nim's two- and three-sign combinations revealed that his three-sign combinations added practically nothing (other than

emphasis) to his two-sign combinations. His most frequent three-sign combinations included 'play me Nim', 'hug Nim hug', 'play me play', and 'eat me eat'.

If one compares learning a language to climbing a ladder, it looks as if chimpanzees are quite adept at climbing the first few rungs. After that, though, they seem to come to an almost complete stop. They may learn more words, but they do not improve their ability to combine these words into longer, more sentence-like forms. It is tempting to regard the chimpanzee's lack of a language acquisition device or something similar as the insuperable barrier to climbing further up the linguistic ladder. If so, Nim Chimpsky may have been well named, since he seems to have confirmed the views of his namesake Noam Chomsky.

CONCLUSIONS

The social and emotional development of Nim Chimpsky was remarkably similar in many ways to that of a human child. Indeed, his emotional reactions were often simply stronger and more extreme versions of human emotions. He behaved in the mishievous and boisterous way familiar to untold generations of human parents.

Nim Chimpsky was very proficient at learning signs and expressing himself in a limited way, and there is a natural inclination to regard his very real achievements as revealing a mastery of language skills. However, more careful analysis suggests that there is perhaps less here than meets the eye.

Chapter 10
LOVE AND AFFECTION

Love is not an easy field of research. Poets, philosophers and most ordinary men and women regard love as the most interesting and important of all the emotions, but psychologists have tended to give it a fairly wide berth. It is difficult to induce instant feelings of love in a laboratory, but feelings of fear are quite easy to generate if one straps electrodes to people and threaten them with electric shocks. The paucity of psychological research on the nature of love led the American psychologist Harry Harlow to the following pessimistic conclusion: 'The little we know about love does not transcend simple observations, and the little we write about it has been written better by poets and novelists.'

In our view Harlow was being over-modest about his own important discoveries concerning the nature of love. Indeed his researches on love among rhesus monkeys appear to have major implications for the development of love in human beings.

KEY EXPERIMENT: LOVE BETWEEN MOTHERS AND BABIES

Harry Harlow, at the University of Wisconsin, had spent several years looking at the ways in which monkeys learn to solve various difficult problems. During the course of this work, he noticed that many of the baby monkeys reared in the laboratory showed great attachment to the cloth pads or folded gauze nappies used to cover the floors of their cages. The infants clung to these pads and displayed violent temper tantrums when they were removed for sanitary reasons. Human infants display much the same devotion towards cuddly toys and other soft objects. Harlow began to suspect that the obvious pleasure his baby monkeys derived from clinging to cloth pads might explain a major part of the mother-baby bond. A monkey mother, after all, usually spends many hours a day clutching her baby tightly[1]. To test this idea he created two monkey 'mothers'.

One, the 'cloth mother', had a perfectly proportioned and streamlined monkey body made of wood, but she was covered with rubber and sheathed in tan cotton towelling, which made her soft to touch. A light bulb behind her radiated heat, which also made her warm. The other 'mother' was similar, but made of wire mesh and she lacked 'contact comfort'. Both 'mothers' had 'breasts'.

Infant monkeys were separated from their natural mothers shortly after birth and put in the same room as the cloth mother and the wire mother. For some of the monkeys, only the cloth mother's breast provided milk; the rest could only get their milk from the wire mother. Which substitute mother did they prefer? Overwhelmingly, the softer cloth mother which offered them contact comfort. On average they spent 18 hours a day cuddling against her compared with less than 2 hours a day against the wire mother. But the real surprise was that the results were almost exactly the same even for the group which could get milk only from the wire mother; these monkeys also spent most of the day against the cloth mother. In other words, infant monkeys do not love from hunger, rather they hunger for love.

Early critics of Harlow's work raised various objections to the validity of his experiment. Some argued that monkeys dislike wire. Some claimed that other substances might have proved more

Do little girls like to play with prams and dolls because they have a mothering instinct? Devotion to cuddly objects is instinctive, but there is a learned component to mothering.

comforting than towelling. Harlow refuted the first set of critics by pointing out that baby monkeys spend a lot of time climbing up the sides of their wire cages and exploring the wire with their mouths and hands. The preference which small monkeys have for towelling was further demonstrated by showing that they chose to spend much more time on a towelling-covered mother than on mothers covered with rayon, vinyl or rough-grade sandpaper.

Other critics wondered whether Harlow's observations had any real implications for love at the human level[2]. Harlow certainly set out to shed light on human needs for contact and affection. As he pointed out: 'The only reason for using monkeys rather than rats is that the data will generalize better to man.' Even so, monkeys are not human beings.

The most serious objection to Harlow's early work in this area was that it seemed to suggest that the only reason infant monkeys love their mothers is because of the contact comfort they provide. Harlow responded to this charge by constructing more substitute mothers. He found that a very important factor, especially during the first two weeks of a monkey's life, was the warmth of the mother. Infants really were 'turned off' by sub-

In almost every culture, young babies are given as much contact warmth and comfort as possible. A neglected baby often has a hard time becoming a sociable adult or a successful parent.

stitute mothers with icy water in their veins. They also preferred mothers that rocked backwards and forwards to mothers that remained stationary.

In later studies, Harlow set out to investigate just how strongly his monkey infants became attached to their substitute mothers. He did this by creating four 'monster mothers', all covered with towelling. One gave the infants occasional blasts of compressed air, the second shook so violently that the infants were often shaken off, the third contained a catapult that frequently flung the infants away from it, and the fourth was an 'iron maiden' which had a set of metal spikes which poked through the fabric from time to time.

Naturally enough, the baby monkeys showed signs of emotional disturbance on first experiencing the unpleasant characteristics of each 'monster mother'. But as soon as the mothers returned to normal, the infants speedily returned to them and acted as if all were forgiven. Indeed, Harlow claims that it was only the people carrying out the experiment who experienced stress!

Harlow subsequently discovered other ways in which cloth mothers appear to be a substitute for the real mother. When baby monkeys were placed in strange surroundings littered with numerous objects (boxes, cups) known to be of interest to monkeys, they used their cloth mother as a base of operations, exploring their environment a little and then returning to her for security. When the cloth mother was absent, the infants would often freeze in a crouched position. Some of them would run towards the middle of the room where the mother was usually placed, and then rush quickly from object to object, crying and screeching.

Do infant monkeys really display the same kind of love for cloth mothers as they do for their real mothers? Here is Harlow's considered answer to that question: 'Love for the real mother and love for the surrogate mother appear to be very similar . . . As far as we can observe, the infant monkey's affection for the real mother is strong, but no stronger than that of the experimental monkey for the surrogate cloth mother, and the security that the infant gains from the presence of the real mother is no greater than the security it gains from a cloth surrogate.'

One of the first things a human mother notices about her baby is that it often stares intently at her face. Harlow decided to find out how important facial characteristics were to baby monkeys. One infant was given a substitute cloth mother which

Brothers, sisters and age mates can supply some of the affection we all need to grow up into well-adjusted, purposeful adults. Adequate social behaviour cannot be learnt in isolation.

had a featureless round wooden ball for a head. The baby reacted enthusiastically to this mother substitute, which suggests that even a face that would stop a clock doesn't stop a baby loving its mother.

By the time the baby monkey, a female, had reached three months of age, the researchers had prepared a more monkey-like cloth-mother face. They proudly put it in place, but the baby took one look and screamed. She remained terrified for the next few days, then she had a brainwave: she rotated the head through 180 degrees so that she could once again look at a featureless face. When the experimenters put the head back in its proper position, the infant once again turned the head so that the face was not visible. Shortly after that she lifted the head from the body, rolled it into a corner and abandoned it. To paraphrase Harlow's interpretation of this incident, a baby is capable of loving a faceless mother, but not a two-faced one.

Harlow's work with cloth and wire monkeys became very well known and was frequently discussed during the 1960s. While Harlow welcomed the publicity, he was not entirely happy at the way things were developing. His doubts were strengthened when an eminent psychologist and a leading psychiatrist independently made the same comment to him within a single month. What they both said was: 'You know, Harry, you are going to go down in the history of psychology as the father of the cloth mother!' Not relishing that fate, Harlow began to consider other facets of love, starting with maternal deprivation and its implications.

THE EFFECTS OF MATERNAL DEPRIVATION

It may seem paradoxical, but the easiest way to study love is to look at what happens when love is missing. Prove that lack of love has serious consequences and you have proved that love is important. The vital importance of a mother's love is only too obvious in cases of 'maternal deprivation', in which a baby is separated from its mother during some or all of the early stages of its development.

The effects of maternal deprivation were studied some 40 years ago by the British psychologist John Bowlby, who was asked by the World Health Organization to prepare a report on the mental health of homeless children. This was part of a study carried out by the Social Commission of the United Nations on the special needs of children separated from their families and placed in foster homes or institutions. Bowlby concluded that maternal deprivation is liable to have unfortunate consequences, including juvenile delinquency and psychopathic behaviour.

Unfortunately for Bowlby, other workers have not been able to replicate his findings and he has been obliged to modify his views. There is now general agreement that it is not a mother that is needed so much as personal contact of a positive kind with a caretaker or peer group.

Among the primates, Harry Harlow was able to show that there are far-reaching consequences when baby monkeys are not allowed to see or interact with other monkeys for the first few months of life. When a number of monkeys isolated in this way were brought together, they reacted very aggressively. Many of them acted in a similar way to patients in a mental hospital. For example, they would freeze into bizarre postures, make apparently purposeless repetitive movements, or simply stare into space for hours on end.

Harlow discovered that another major consequence of early isolation was a virtual absence of sex life in adulthood. As part of an attempt to increase the number of his monkeys by breeding, he and his colleagues put a normal, sexually experienced male monkey into the same area as some previously isolated female monkeys. This monkey was completely unsuccessful in making any of the females pregnant. As Harlow neatly summarized it, unless a female monkey is chased when she is young, she will probably remain chaste for the rest of her life.

HELP FOR THE UNLOVED

What could be done to help monkeys reared in isolation to become more sociable? The fact that normally-reared young monkeys spend a lot of time playing with one another suggested to Harlow that placing isolated monkeys with normally-reared monkeys of the same age might be beneficial. In the event, the results were disastrous. The isolated monkeys simply froze with fear and scarcely interacted at all with the normal monkeys. They spent most of their time engaged in self-clasping, self-chewing and huddling in a corner.

Obviously, a major problem was the fear which the normal monkeys aroused in the isolates. One way of getting round the problem is to put isolates in the company of normally-reared monkeys several months younger than themselves. It appears that isolated monkeys can only learn adequate social behaviour if they are initially exposed to monkeys possessing simpler social abilities, i.e. younger monkeys. In other words, the difference between the social skills of the isolates and those they are required to mix with must not be too great.

Melinda Novak, one of Harlow's research associates, was able to demonstrate almost complete social rehabilitation in monkeys isolated for the first 12 months of life. This is a tremendous achievement. Until quite recently it was believed that the substantial social disadvantages produced by long-term isolation in infancy were irreversible.

Next page: nothing wrong with the sociability quotient ▶ of this cheeky bunch. Normal children, like normal monkeys, learn social skills by playing games.

Children who are shy with children of their own age can often be brought out of themselves if they have a slightly younger child to play with.

Novak used monkey 'therapists' who were less than one-third the age of the isolated monkeys, and was rewarded by the gradual disappearance of undesirable, maladaptive behaviour on the part of the previously isolated monkeys, combined with a slow increase in play and social contact. But almost two years of hard work were needed to complete the transformation.

These findings suggest that the love and affection that exists among monkeys (or people) of a similar age may be a more potent force for good than has been generally realized. While mother love may be the ideal, love between age-mates may be a reasonable substitute.

Many theorists from Freud onwards have argued that appropriate stimulation in early life is essential for normal development—this is the 'critical period' hypothesis. Novak's data seem to disprove this hypothesis, at least for monkeys. Optimistically, her findings suggest that human beings may also be more resilient than Freud and his successors allowed.

MATERNAL AND PATERNAL INSTINCTS

The spontaneous delight which most human mothers take in caring for their offspring has suggested to many psychologists the existence of an innate 'maternal instinct'. On the face of it this would seem to explain the months and years of selfless devotion of mothers to their children, but there are various difficulties with the notion that all women possess a maternal instinct.

In the first place, it has been fairly conclusively demonstrated that humans have much weaker instincts of all kinds than other species. More tellingly, the worryingly high incidence of 'baby bashing' and child abuse is difficult to reconcile with the concept of maternal instinct. We now know, for example, that most physically aggressive parents have themselves been neglected and abused as children, either as a result of 'bad environment', 'bad heredity', or a combination of the two.

Here too Harlow's work shed interesting light. His plan was to observe mothering behaviour in female monkeys brought up for the first few months of life in isolation. The difficulty was that these monkeys were sexually unaware, and it proved virtually impossible to turn them into mothers by simply letting nature take its course! In desperation, Harlow and his team of researchers created a device, affectionately known as the 'rape rack', in which they could be strapped down and impregnated. This had the desired effect.

What happened when these isolated females gave birth to their first baby? Typically they ignored it. Only if the infant was very persistent would they occasionally provide it with some of the contact comfort it demanded. Indeed, from the fourth month onwards, some of the first-born infants of these 'motherless mothers' were actually punished less than the babies of normal mothers and allowed more contact with the mother's nipples. When such mothers had a second baby, they tended to look after it fairly adequately.

But things did not always work out so smoothly. A few of the motherless mothers trod on their babies, or crushed their infant's face into the floor of the cage. On one or two occasions, the experimenters did not react fast enough to prevent a mother chewing off her baby's foot or fingers. The most terrible mother of all popped her baby's head into her mouth and proceeded to crunch it up like a potato crisp.

Indeed Harlow's observations seem to suggest that the notion of a universal maternal instinct may be erroneous. Many monkey mothers (and probably human mothers too) who have not been brought up in a normal loving relationship with their own mothers give every appearance of lacking a maternal instinct.

Harlow also looked at the role of the father. In all of the monkey families he studied, the father was unquestionably the dominant individual, maintaining his status without using physical force, unless one counts pseudo-slaps and nips, chasing and the occasional threatening gesture.

In humans, fathers tend to be preferred to mothers as playmates by babies as young as eight months of age, and this preference is maintained through the second year of life. Exactly the same is true of rhesus monkeys brought up in captivity. Adult male monkeys indicate their readiness to play with their own or other monkeys' offspring by making a special signal: a dazed and glazed

In human societies, all adult males hold a watching brief for youngsters, whether related to them or not. This does not seem to be true in many monkey communities.

mesmerizing stare accompanied by a casual flip of the ear. Male infants are content to play with any adult male, but female infants are more particular and prefer to play with daddy.

A recent study of free-ranging rhesus monkeys in Katmandu Valley, Nepal, revealed that wild male monkeys are less inclined than captive male monkeys to help in the care of infants. During an exhausting 1,500 hours of field observations, there were only a miserly 18 cases of pleasant interactions between an adult male and an infant. Eleven of these were brief play or grooming encounters, and only seven were more extended cases of male parental care. There were three times as many aggressive encounters, most of them involving mild slaps and swipes.

The most dramatic incident observed concerned a dominant adult male called Spock and the day-old infant of a mother who had died. At first, Spock cared for the infant in a remarkably gentle way, but he became irritated when the infant began to squirm and cry. On a number of occasions, the poor infant was held upside down or carried in the crook of Spock's arm while he ran to watch a fight. Unfortunately for the infant, Spock did not seem to realize that it needed food, and it died of starvation. The ineptitude of this large adult male was further shown by his apparent failure to grasp the fact that the baby had died. For many hours after its death he continued to groom it and carry it around with him.

Harlow found that there are important sex differences among monkeys in reactions to baby monkeys even before adulthood is reached. When

Nurturing is not something only women do. This dad seems to be managing very well!

pre-adolescent female monkeys were introduced to baby monkeys, they immediately behaved in a loving manner. By contrast, pre-adolescent males were either indifferent or mildly abusive.

Does the general inattention and indifference of the adult male monkey to his own offspring equate with the 'natural' reaction of the human father to his children? A proportion of fathers choose to devote their leisure time to traditionally male activities such as beer and football, but a higher proportion are very loving carers towards their children.

Many feminists have attacked Harlow's work because it seems to imply that human infants only thrive if they are looked after by full-time mothers. Harlow remains impervious to their accusations. In an interview with Carol Tavris in the magazine *Psychology Today*, he reacted to these attacks by saying: 'Man is the only animal capable of speaking, and woman is the only animal incapable of not speaking.'

CONCLUSIONS

Harry Harlow has spent more than 30 years investigating the importance of the phenomenon we call love in rhesus monkeys. His main strategy has been to look at the effects of removing different aspects of the normal loving environment in which baby monkeys develop. The first great success of this strategy was in identifying contact comfort as the most important contribution of the mother to the baby's wellbeing.

Harlow later found that maternal deprivation seriously affected the ability of young monkeys to mate or socialize successfully, and the same is true of humans. But he also discovered that love and attention from younger age-mates may eventually overcome the bad effects of maternal deprivation.

The love of a mother for her child is something we take for granted, but the 'maternal instinct' is not quite as innate as we assume, as Harlow very effectively demonstrated in his work with monkeys.

C

BRAINS, PERSONALITY AND EMOTION

The differences between the psychological approach and the physiological approach to human behaviour can be clarified by an analogy. Suppose a psychologist and a physiologist who have never seen a car before set out to try to understand how it functions. The psychologist focuses on the speed of the car, its road-handling, its reliability, its fuel consumption, and so on. He then uses this information to speculate on the processes and mechanisms inside it (engine, battery, gears, steering, etc.). The physiologist concentrates on the inside of the car, perhaps discovering a large black box (the battery) and paying minute attention to the lettering on the side of it. He has the difficult task of trying to decide which parts of the car do what and how they are interrelated. So the psychologist looks at things from the outside, and makes guesses about what is happening inside, while the physiologist probes inside, trying to make mechanical sense of the things he finds there.

Ideally, the approach of the psychologist and the physiologist should be complementary, and this is increasingly the case. Indeed there is a new hybrid called a 'psychophysiologist', who attempts to use physiology to clarify psychological findings, and vice versa.

In this section we consider research that has successfully integrated information from both physiological and psychological sources. Recent work on intelligence (Chapter 11) is a prime example of this multi-disciplinary approach. Ever since Alfred Binet, at the request of the French Ministry of Education, devised the first standardized test of intelligence in the early years of this century, psychologists have been interested in the marked differences that exist between human beings when it comes to intellectual ability.

As a result of their endeavours, psychologists have learned a great deal about the major factors which determine intelligence, the importance of heredity in determining intellectual potential, and so on. However, there is still a lot to learn about the workings of intelligence. Until quite recently, for instance, we knew practically nothing about the marked differences in brain activity between people of varying intelligence. This gap in our knowledge was filled by the work of Allan and Elaine Hendrickson at the Institute of Psychiatry in London in the early 1980s.

There are, of course, much more drastic and dramatic ways of exploring the workings of the brain than applying electrodes to the scalp and recording the brain's electrical activity. Parts of the brain can be severed, isolated or removed. Three main categories of psychosurgery are discussed in Chapter 12. Thousands of pre-frontal lobotomies (in which the fibres running between the frontal lobes and other parts of the brain are severed) have been performed to alleviate the misery of obsessive and melancholic patients. Sometimes they achieve their goal, but the risk of reducing the patient to a mere vegetable is extremely high. More recently, interest has switched to the use of amygdalotomy, in which part of the lower brain, the amygdala, is severed or burned out. The intention of the operation is to reduce fear and anger, but again there are many unfortunate side-effects.

But the history of psychosurgery is not entirely a catalogue of mistakes and misfortunes —there is at least one major success story. In an attempt to reduce the effects of severe epileptic attacks, surgeons developed the procedure of cutting through the corpus callosum (the bridge of tissue connecting the two halves of the brain). This had two important consequences. First, epileptic attacks became fewer and more manageable. Second, fascinating differences in the workings of the two halves of the brain were revealed.

Chapter 13 explores the roots of personality. There are two main ways of examining the biological basis of personality. The first is to examine personality similarities in identical and non-identical twins, the basic assumption being that the more similar identical twins are, as compared with non-identical twins, the greater the influence of heredity. Broadly speaking, the evidence suggests that individual differences in personality have much more to do with heredity than is generally realized.

The alternative method of investigating personality is the physiological one. There are various recording techniques (measuring brain-wave activity, galvanic skin response and heart rate, for example) which can be used to demonstrate that there are wide variations in physiological activity between one individual and another. H. J. Eysenck has used information obtained from twin research and physiological studies to propose a theory of the biological basis of personality.

If personality has a largely biological basis, it follows that attributes such as happiness are also largely influenced by biology. This contradicts the popular belief that external events and success in major areas in life produce happiness. In Chapter 14 we demonstrate that it is the kind of personality we inherit that makes us happier or more miserable than others.

In Chapter 15 we explore emotion, through the eyes of psychologists and physiologists working in tandem. Emotional states obviously depend on people and things in our immediate environment, but they usually involve distinctive physiological changes as well. The classic theory of emotion put forward by Stanley Schachter and Jerome Singer places equal emphasis on psychological and physiological causes. Their method of manipulating physiological functioning was not surgical—they achieved changes in physiological activity by means of drugs.

In sum, this section reveals the wide range of valuable overlaps between the work of psychologists and physiologists in the areas of intelligence, personality, emotion and abnormal behaviour.

Chapter 11
MEASURING INTELLIGENCE

Until recently there was fairly general agreement between experts on the concept of intelligence. Intelligence was a kind of general, all-pervasive cognitive ability which enabled you to do well at anything resembling a mental problem. This highly-prized ability was largely a genetic endowment; while the environment might influence the way in which intelligence showed itself, and might act as a handicap if very disadvantageous, it did not contribute more than perhaps 20 per cent to the total amount of variability in intelligence found in the population studied. There were also several special abilities—verbal, numerical, rote memory, perceptual—but as far as intellectual capacity was concerned these did not account for anything like as much as general intelligence. The consensus was that intelligence was of great importance educationally and socially. Your income and your job depended quite significantly on your intelligence, as did your social status. Luck, personality and family connections also played a part of course, but a less important one than innate intellectual endowment.

In recent years these views have received a lot of criticism. Many critics deny that intelligence is a meaningful concept. They do not accept that heredity determines differences in this non-existent ability, and argue instead that social class and other environmental influences are the decisive factors in educational and work success and social status.

Most of these criticisms have come from people not fully conversant with the rather technical fields of genetics, psychometry and mental test construction, and the majority of them have appeared in popular weeklies, daily papers and political tracts rather than in the scientific journals. Nevertheless, because these criticisms received such publicity, they influenced political decisions. The rejection of selection in schools and the abandonment of streaming were largely influenced by these arguments. The sad affair of Sir Cyril Burt, who fudged some of his data, gave a lot of ammunition to the critics. However, Burt's faulty data constituted a very small part of the empirical material on which the orthodox view of intelligence was based, and recent evidence has strongly supported the traditional view.

Meanwhile physiologists have come up with novel approaches to the measurement of intelligence, and these have cast new light on questions such as: Why does mental ability decline with age, why are there social and class differences in intelligence, and is intelligence more determined by nature than nurture?

Briefly, these new approaches enable us to measure intelligence by means of psychophysiological methods, i.e. by using the electroencephalograph or 'brain-wave machine'. More than that, by being based on far-reaching theories of the nature of intelligence, and its physical substructure, these new approaches give us much deeper insight into the nature of intelligence than was possible before.

IQ TESTS

In traditional ways of measuring intelligence, the candidate is set problems which as far as possible make little or no call on acquired knowledge. If such knowledge is necessary for tests, then it is important to make sure that all candidates possess it equally. The IQ test (IQ stands for Intelligence Quotient—the average person has an IQ of 100) is not meant to be a test of school knowledge, but of ability to manipulate the elements of a problem and find a solution which has not been part of any formal training. Figure 1 shows the distribution of IQs in the population at large.

Such tests have universally shown that there are marked differences between social classes, with a difference of some 30 points between middle-class and working-class groups. There are also differences between different races; American blacks score some 15 points below American whites,

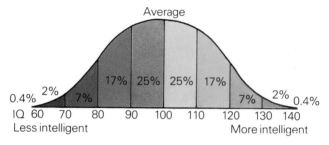

Figure 1 *This shows, in somewhat simplified form, how intelligence is shared out in the population at large. Twenty-five per cent of people have IQs between 100 and 110, and an equal percentage have IQs between 90 and 100. Only 0.4 per cent have IQs above 140 or below 60.*

Malays about the same number of points below Chinese, and middle-European gypsies below middle-European natives.

Children who do well on these tests usually do better in school and at university than children who do poorly. If children within one and the same family are studied, one finds that they differ in IQ, and that usually the brighter ones go up in the social scale and the duller ones go down. Identical twins, whether brought up together or separated early in life and brought up in different families, have very similar scores. Fraternal (non-identical) twins are much less alike. Adopted children are much more like their biological parents than their adoptive parents, although the latter may provide practically all their childhood environment.

It is sometimes said that whites are superior to other races in IQ tests because the tests are produced by white psychologists, but this is not true. In the first place, tests are not constructed at the whim of the psychologist, but must follow quite objective statistical rules. In the second place, it is found that on these tests, constructed by white psychologists, Chinese and Japanese children and adults do quite significantly better than white children and adults, in spite of lower socio-economic status and worse schooling!

These are difficult factors for egalitarians to accept. They cut across all their hopes of reaching the paradise of universal equality. Hence their criticism, and hence their hostility to anyone who dares mention the facts and defend the orthodox position. But many of these criticisms are directed at a chimaera, for the picture many people have of the mechanism of inheritance, that like begets like, is far removed from reality. If like did beget like, we might have good reason for apprehension. Reality is quite different.

HEREDITY AND INTELLIGENCE

Let us consider the well-known and well-documented phenomenon of 'regression to the mean'. This is a convenient way of saying that parents who are particularly well or poorly endowed with certain physical or mental characteristics will pass those characteristics on to their children in a less extreme form; in other words, their children will regress to the mean. Children of very tall or very bright parents will be tall or bright, but on average not quite as tall or bright as their parents. Children of very small or very dull parents will still be smaller and duller than the average, but not to the same extent as their parents.

Figure 2 shows the picture most people have of the workings is of heredity. According to this erroneous view of heredity, very dull parents have very dull children, very bright parents have very bright children, and so on. If this were so, we would have a totally static caste society, with the children of the workers forever destined to hew the coal and draw the water. But reality is quite different, as shown in Figure 3.

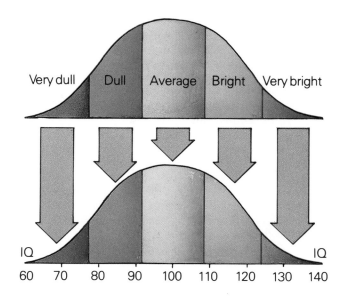

Figure 2   *This shows the quite inaccurate idea many people have of the workings of inheritance. Like does not reliably produce like – the chances of very intelligent parents producing an Einstein are only one in four! The biological principle of 'regression to the mean' ensures that all our genes are shuffled and redistributed with each generation.*

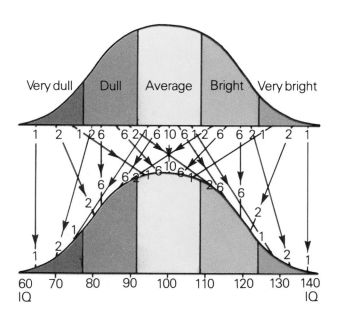

Figure 3   *This shows how 64 parents, belonging to five IQ bands (very dull, dull, average, bright, very bright) contribute intelligence to the next generation. The overall distribution of intelligence in the new generation is the same, but both the very dull and the very bright parents produce some average children, and the average parents produce some children who are duller and brighter than themselves.*

Here we see regression at work. Of the four children of the very dull parents, only one is also very dull; two are dull and one is average. Similarly, of the four children of the very bright parents, only one is very bright, two are bright and one is average. Conversely, of the four very bright children, one comes from average stock, two from bright parents and only one from very bright parents. Thus genetics ensures a constant stirring up of the gene pool, overriding class and family interests. The mixing of genes produces dissimilarities as well as similarities between parents and children. This makes any caste system biological nonsense and impossible to maintain except through political and cultural constraints. It also makes class systems difficult to maintain unless there is considerable social mobility. Significantly, the amount of social mobility in the Western world is just about what is required to keep the IQ difference between the working class and the middle class steady, for the composition of the classes changes from generation to generation, with brighter working-class children rising into the middle class and duller middle-class children sinking into the working class.

All of this makes perfectly good biological sense, and there is a tremendous amount of factual research to back it up. But clearly a vital piece of the jigsaw is still missing. We cannot inherit the way we behave, and we cannot inherit something as insubstantial as 'intelligence'. We can only inherit physical somatic, anatomical structures from which intelligence and behaviour derive, in interaction with the environment. So until we know something about the physiological mechanisms which underlie problem-solving and other types of cognitive behaviour, and can measure their functioning, we

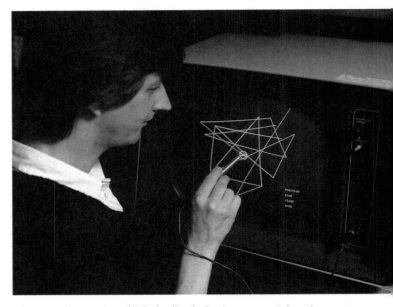

An experiment in which feedback during a spatial task is delayed in order to study the speed at which the separate halves of the brain react.

If this couple were to have four children, the odds are that one of the other three would be black and the other two somewhere between black and white. This is how inheritance works.

are relying on circumstantial rather than direct evidence, and critics can always point to possible sources of error which are difficult to eliminate completely. It is this problem on which recent research has thrown such important light.

CORRELATING PHYSIOLOGICAL DATA WITH IQ

Head size and brain size and weight have some correlation with measured IQ, but the relationship is so slight as to be of no practical importance. Electrical conductivity of the skin, which is often regarded as a sign of mental alertness and motivation, has been found to be greater in bright than in dull children, but while the relationship between skin conductivity and IQ is closer than that between brain size and IQ, it is still not close enough to be of really practical importance.

Much the same would once have been said of attempts to measure 'reaction times' as an indication of intelligence. In this type of measure the subject is confronted with a light and a press-key; when the light goes on, an electric timer is started, whereupon the subject presses the key as quickly as he can to stop the timer. The time he takes to react can be measured very accurately. At one time it was thought that the speed of conduction through the neuron pathways inside the brain might be measured by this device, and that conduction speed might be related to intelligence, but the relationship was never found to be at all close.

However, by using the same experimental idea but making certain changes, much closer correlation between reaction time and intelligence can be obtained. Figure 4 shows the type of console used in such experiments. The subject sits in front of the

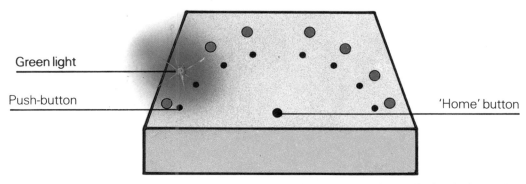

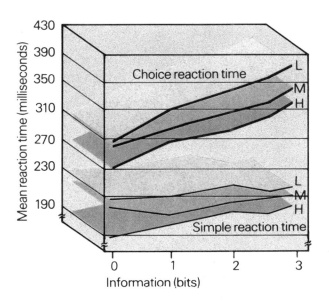

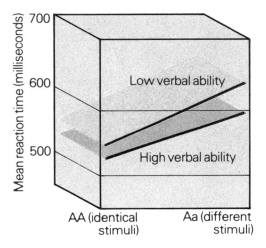

Figure 4 *This is the kind of console used in reaction time experiments. The lights can be covered so that only one, two, four or eight are exposed for subjects to react to.*

Figure 5 *This shows mean reaction times for high (H) intelligence, middle (M) intelligence and low (L) intelligence thirds of a sample of school children. Note how reaction times increase as the task gets more difficult.*

Figure 6 *This graph shows the time it took university students scoring high or low on a verbal intelligence test to recognize the physical or semantic identity of letter pairs.*

console with his index finger resting on the 'home' button. When one of the lights lights up he immediately moves his finger to press the push-button associated with that light. When only one light shows, it is 'simple reaction time' which is being investigated. When more than one light is used, it is 'choice reaction time'. Obviously, the more choices there are, the longer the reaction time. Usually we count the increase in the number of choices offered not just by the number of lights, but by 'bits' which are counted as the logarithms of the numbers, so that a choice between two lights constitutes one bit of information, between four lights two bits, and between eight lights three bits. Reaction times increase linearly with each additional bit, as Figure 5 shows. Note that the three groups tested are quite well separated, except perhaps at the simple reaction time level (zero bits of information), with the dull girls always having the longer reaction times and the bright girls the shorter reaction times.

There are other ways of using the reaction time experiment. One of them is the so-called Posner paradigm, a type of experiment in which subjects are shown stimuli which may be identical (A A) or different (Aa); the subject has to press a button to indicate as quickly as possible whether the stimuli are identical or different. Figure 6 shows the reaction times of dull students (poor scorers on a verbal test) and bright students (high scorers on a verbal test). Note that the decision 'different' takes a longer time to reach than 'identical' for both bright and dull students, but that dull students take longer for both types of stimuli, and particularly long for the more difficult task.

A third method, again different, is the so-called Sternberg paradigm, where the subject is presented with a set of digits or letters, followed immediately by a single 'probe' digit or letter to which the subject responds 'yes' or 'no', depending on whether the probe was or was not included in the set originally

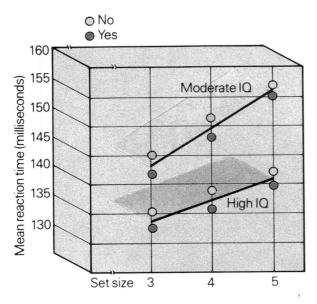

Figure 7 *This graph shows the mean reaction times of subjects of moderate or high IQ when presented with sets of digits of increasing length and asked to confirm the presence or absence of a particular digit.*

shown. The subject's reaction time or decision time in pressing the 'yes' or 'no' key is the time measured. Figure 7 shows the results of an experiment with subjects of moderate and high IQ. Note that as set size increases reaction times also increase, that 'no' answers take longer than 'yes' answers, and that bright subjects are much quicker in their reactions than dull subjects, as becomes more and more evident as the set size increases.

The obvious conclusion is that, whatever the paradigm, there is a fairly close relationship between reaction time and intelligence, and that this relationship becomes closer the more complex the task. None of the tasks set in reaction time experiments have any cultural determinants, so the results obtained can be considered almost entirely free of the environmental influences that are often said to determine success or failure in ordinary IQ tests. Here, then, we have an objective, culturally fair way of measuring intelligence.

While such tests, and other similar tests, are interesting in that they demonstrate that very simple perceptual and reaction time behaviour is highly correlated with intelligence, they do not throw much light on the theoretical nature of intelligence or on its physical basis. However, this is precisely the sort of information that can be supplied by 'evoked potentials', recorded on the electroencephalograph (EEG).

BRAIN-WAVES AND IQ

Through electrodes placed on the scalp an EEG detects the electric potentials generated by the brain and records them as a series of waves. Until a few years ago these waves did not appear to be at all

closely correlated with intelligence. Evoked potentials are series of waves that appear suddenly when the subject of the experiment has a bright light flashed into his eyes, or hears a sudden click delivered over earphones. Figure 8 shows the resulting waves for three subjects, each of whom had had an IQ test (the Otis group test) on which they scored 137, 100 and 73 respectively. This particular recording of evoked potentials was published by J. P. Ertl, the Canadian psychologist who pioneered research into the relationship between IQ and evoked potentials. Ertl measured the latency of these waves, in other words how quickly they came after the stimulus (a visual one) had been presented to his subjects, who were children. What he found was that for the brighter children the latencies were shorter. That is to say, the waves arose more quickly in the brighter children than in the duller ones. As Figure 8 shows, the waves for the dullest child are the most elongated and drawn out. This was interesting news, but not sensational. When much larger groups were tested the relationships between intelligence and latency potentials were not so close. At first, other workers found it difficult to duplicate Ertl's work, but when finally it was shown that his results did stand up to repetition, there were still disappointingly low correlations between IQ and latency potentials.

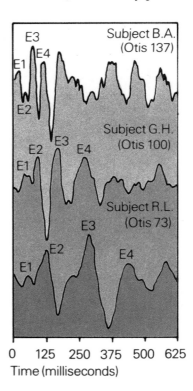

Figure 8 *These are the evoked potentials recorded from three subjects of different intelligence (as measured by the Otis test). In each case the first four waves produced by the stimulus are labelled E1, E2, E3 and E4. Note the closeness and rapidity of the first four waves in the case of B.A.*

KEY EXPERIMENT: IQ EQUALS MINIMUM PROCESSING ERROR

At this point work began at the Institute of Psychiatry in London, led by Elaine and Allan Hendrickson[1]. It was inspired by the thought that perhaps if one looked in detail at the theoretical foundations underlying the measurement of evoked potentials, and if one also improved the methods of measurement used, the observed correlations might be more significant. Elaine Hendrickson changed the stimulus from visual to auditory (partly because visual stimuli produce many artefacts in the recording of EEGs), and also began to measure the amplitudes of waves as well as their latencies. She soon found that bright people had bigger waves as well as faster ones, and by combining these two indices she achieved a much more respectable correlation—something that made one sit up and take notice. But the major step still lay ahead, the elaboration of a theoretical rationale for the whole procedure, and the working out of a proper measure based on this rationale. This was done by Allan Hendrickson.

We know that information reaching the cortex of the brain through the sense channels is encoded and then sent from one part of the brain to another via neurons connected to each other by synapses.

Electrodes being applied to various areas of the scalp to record brain activity. Large, fast brain-waves correlate with high intelligence.

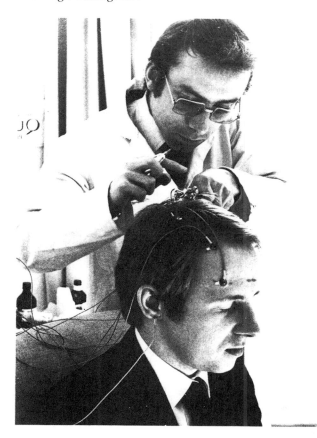

The passage of information through the cortex was the part of the process which the evoked potential was thought to tap, but there were many queries concerning the way the information was encoded, passed across the synaptic gap, and finally related through the evoked potential to IQ. Hendrickson, by virtue of his expertise in computer technology, was able to produce a theory which explains how information can be encoded in neuronic pulse trains, and he also furnished a theoretical account of the biochemical events which take place when information is passed across synapses. More important, he hypothesized that, in the processing of information, errors are likely to occur. Individuals have a consistent and characteristic mean probability of such errors occurring, and it is this mean probability which he and Elaine believed was the biological basis of differences in intelligence. It stands to reason that a person can only act quickly and appropriately on information received in so far as the incoming information is processed correctly! The Hendricksons symbolized the probability of an incoming message being correct enough to be recognized by the individual by the letter R. Individual differences in R could therefore be the biological equivalent of intelligence. The Hendricksons went on to show, by means of computer simulation, the effects on message transmission of introducing errors of varying degree, and also that the picture so obtained fitted other measures of intelligence very well.

How is all this related to evoked potentials? There is evidence, from studies of single neuron recordings, that there is some relationship between the EEG and the pulse train which transmits a given message and hence the possibility that records of the evoked potential might reveal details of the pulse train, and possible errors in transmission. Such errors should have the effect of 'smearing' the peaks and troughs, making them less distinct; transmission errors would change the shape of the wave forms. Furthermore, errors in transmission which would make recognition difficult or impossible would give a pulse train different from an error-free pulse train. This is important because several evoked potentials are usually averaged to produce the published diagrams. This averaging is necessary because of the low signal-to-noise ratio in recording, which means that wave forms only become clear when several waves are averaged. Averaging correct and incorrect pulse trains would eliminate finer details and make the resulting curve more regular.

This is indeed a feature of the three curves in Figure 8. The most intelligent subject has a curve which shows lots of squiggles and the least intelligent has a very bland, smooth curve. If it is the squiggles which represent aspects of the message being transmitted, then clearly the message is relayed much more efficiently in the cortex of subject B. A. than in that of subject R. L., with subject G. H. coming somewhere in between. Nor are these squiggle features accidental correlates of IQ in just these three subjects. Figure 9 shows the wave forms of ten bright and ten dull subjects in a study by Ertl and Schafer. Even on very cursory inspection one can see that the two sets of curves differ very profoundly in complexity, as predicted by the Hendricksons' theory, in amplitude and latency.

How can we measure this intuitively obvious characteristic of 'complexity'? As a very rough and ready measure, the Hendricksons used what they called the 'string measure'. They projected an enlarged version of the observed curves onto sheets of paper, put large numbers of pins along the contour, and then threaded a piece of string in and out of the pins; having done this, they unthreaded the string and measured its length. The result was very impressive; the correlation between string measure and IQ was as high as that between one good IQ test and another! Nothing so convincing had ever been achieved before, suggesting that perhaps theory and measurement were along the right lines. Now of course the string measure has been abandoned—the computer measures the length of the squiggles with much greater accuracy.

IMPLICATIONS OF THE EVOKED POTENTIAL TECHNIQUE

Elaine Hendrickson went on to test hundreds of children and adults using both recognized intelligence tests and the evoked potential technique, scored in the manner described above, and replications of her work have given pretty much the same results. There seems to be no doubt that we can now measure intelligence physiologically with an accuracy that compares favourably with the best IQ tests currently available. The Hendricksons achieved something truly important and novel in the measurement of intelligence. A thorough review of this and related work has been given by H. J. Eysenck and P. Barrett[2,3]. However, although there now seem to be many close links between intelligence and the physiology of the brain, we still do not fully understand the precise way in which the one produces the other.

What of the future? We can now claim to have a measure of intelligence that is free of the cultural determinants that in some degree still adhere to even the best IQ tests (i.e. the 20 per cent due to environment). We should be able to make predictions, undertake selection and give advice to people on the basis of a pure measure of their general mental ability, no matter what their education, family or life history. We should be able to investigate aspects of intelligence that have raised almost insuperable barriers to research in the past, with better hope of success. For example, the growth of intelligence in babies and young children below the age of six cannot be properly investigated by means of IQ tests. There are baby tests, but they are not really good measures of intelligence; they tend to test physical rather than mental development, and do not correlate at all well with adult intelligence. At the other end of the scale, we should be able to investigate the decline of mental powers with age. This has proved difficult in the past because previous learning interferes with the measurement of intelligence, so that tests give different results depending on whether they measure mainly 'fluid intelligence' or 'crystallized intelligence'. And finally, we should be able to say something about racial and class differences without the possibility of cultural factors interfering and causing endless argument.

There is one additional theoretical problem which it may now be possible to solve. We have mentioned the existence of special abilities in addi-

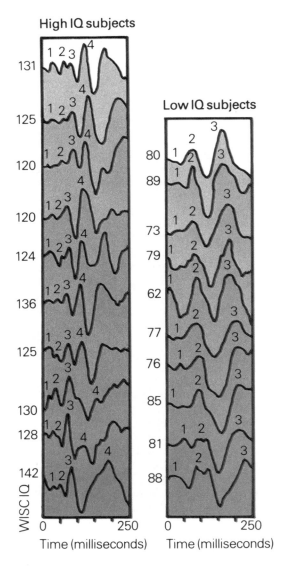

Figure 9 *These are the evoked potentials recorded from ten high IQ and ten low IQ subjects (as measured by the WISC IQ test) when presented with a visual stimulus. The first waves produced in response to the stimulus are numbered 1, 2, 3 and 4. Note how the first four waves of the high IQ group are complex and bunched together.*

tion to general intelligence. These fall into two broad categories, verbal ability, and perceptual and mechanical ability, and there appears to be a relationship between them and the two cerebral hemispheres. Verbal performance seems to be mostly controlled by the left hemisphere of the brain (certainly in right-handed people), while perceptual-mechanical ability seems to be controlled much more by the right. 'Split-brain' studies have been particularly instructive in this respect. The two halves of the brain are joined by the corpus callosum, a bundle of thickened nerve fibres. For medical reasons (to control epileptic seizures, for example), this bundle of fibres may have to be cut, leaving the two halves of the brain more or less isolated from each other. Material can be presented to one half of the brain, but not to the other, and we can study in detail how each half functions on its own (see Chapter 11).

It will be fascinating to see, in normal and split-brain people, how performance on verbal and non-verbal tests relates to the patterns of evoked potentials taken from the two hemispheres separately. In theory, we should find that among people who show discrepancy between verbal and non-verbal IQ those with a high verbal IQ should show more complex wave forms in the left half of the brain, while those with a high perceptual-mechanical IQ should show more complex wave forms in the

In this experiment both verbal and perceptual-mechanical ability, corresponding to left and right brain activity, are being monitored.

right. This is only the most obvious of the many experiments that will now be possible. We are, it seems, on the threshold of a revolution in the study of mental ability.

Chapter 12
THE DIVIDED BRAIN

The human brain has long been regarded as the repository of the mind, hence its great symbolic significance. The brain has been held responsible for many of the positive achievements of humankind, including great works of art and major scientific discoveries. But when the brain malfunctions, tragic and debilitating effects follow, including of course the bizarre patterns of behaviour found in madness and mental illness. Someone who is mentally ill is, in common parlance, 'out of his mind' or 'off his head'.

The notion that the brain is the seat of mental illness has led many people over the centuries to advocate direct action on the brain to effect a cure. Many horrifying methods of treatment have been used, one of the best known being trepanning, which appears to have been used even in the Stone Age. The patient, unanaesthetized, had a hole drilled in his skull in order to release the imagined accumulation of unwanted vapours in his head. Skulls found in Peru show evidence of healing around the hole, which means that some of these unfortunates survived the operation.

Even as far back as Roman times, there was interest in techniques that foreshadowed electroconvulsive therapy. The physician Scribonius Largus describes the application of an electric fish to a patient's head as a cure for headache, and Pliny the Elder recommends the stunning shock from such a fish as an excellent remedy for the pain of childbirth. Electroconvulsive therapy today involves administering electric shocks of between 70 and 130 volts. These induce convulsions similar to grand mal epileptic seizures. This technique was first discovered in the late 1930s, and is sometimes useful in the treatment of depression, though it is not clear why. However, it is instructive to consider the story of the new ECT machine, installed in a hospital in England, which was used with the normal success rate for over six months—until the mechanic called and found that it was faultily connected. Obviously the power of suggestion can be a key factor in producing improvement.

LOBOTOMY AND AMYGDALOTOMY
The most significant landmark in the history of brain surgery was a conference of neurologists held in London in 1935. Jacobsen and Fulton reviewed their work, in which they had significantly moderated the behaviour of two chimpanzees by surgically removing their frontal lobes. At the end of the talk, the Portuguese neurologist Antonio Egas Moniz rose to his feet and asked: 'If frontal lobe removal prevents the development of experimental neuroses in animals and eliminates frustration behaviour, why would it not be feasible to relieve anxiety states in man by surgical means?'

Moniz and his colleague Almeida Lima set to work to provide an answer to that question. They used the surgical method of prefrontal lobotomy in an attempt to modify the mental lives of obsessed and melancholic patients. What they did was to cut certain fibres running from the frontal lobes to other parts of the brain. The instrument used was a special knife called a leucotome, which they inserted through a small opening drilled in the skull. Film buffs will be reminded of Ken Kesey's *One Flew Over the Cuckoo's Nest*. In that film, it is a lobotomy operation that puts a permanent halt to Randle Patrick McMurphy's heroic struggle against Big Nurse.

The publicity which Moniz attracted for his new form of brain surgery led to a tremendous upsurge of interest in prefrontal lobotomy. In the 20 years between 1935 and 1955 approximately 70,000 lobotomies were performed in the United States and Britain. Walter Freeman, the acknowledged doyen of American lobotomists, personally performed more than 3,500 lobotomies. The fame and prestige of Moniz were such that he received a Nobel Prize in 1949.

As the years went by, however, there were increasing indications that prefrontal lobotomy was not the panacea which Moniz claimed. There were frequent reports of a variety of unfortunate side-effects, including apathy, irresponsibility, diminished intellectual powers, impaired judgment, reduced creativity, and even coma and eventual death. As the disadvantages of this form of brain surgery became more obvious the number of patients receiving lobotomies dropped, until very few were being done at all. Moniz got what some regarded as his just deserts when he was shot in the spine by one of his own lobotomized patients.

But the irony of the whole saga of prefrontal lobotomy was that it eventually came to light that one of Jacobsen and Fulton's lobotomized chimpanzees had suffered a brain abscess as a result of poor surgical technique, and that the other had not actually shown the reported good effects of lobotomy!

With the abandonment of the lobotomy operation, 'psychosurgeons' shifted their attention from the frontal lobes of the brain to the limbic system. Loosely speaking, the limbic system lies between the lower and higher parts of the brain, and part of it, the amygdala, is thought to be involved in rage and aggression.

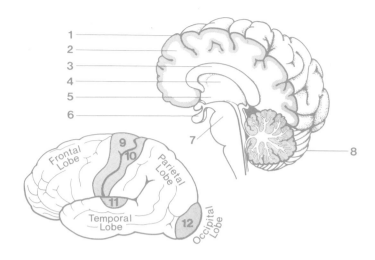

This very simplified diagram of the brain shows:
1. Cortex 2. Subcortex 3. Corpus callosum
4. Thalamus 5. Hypothalamus 6. Pituitary
7. Midbrain or brain stem, with the spinal cord
below it 8. Hindbrain or cerebellum. Projected on the
surface of the cortex are: 9. Main area controlling
body movements 10. Main area receiving messages
from the body and sense organs 11. Main area
concerned with hearing 12. Main area concerned with
seeing. The area concerned with producing speech
sounds lies in the frontal lobe, but the areas for
interpreting speech and writing lie in the parietal lobe.

Arthur Kling and his colleagues performed amygdalotomies (lesions or cutting of the amygdala) on monkeys that had been living in a free-ranging colony. The good news was that they became less aggressive and friendlier towards their human handlers. The bad news, which failed to deter some psychosurgeons, was that these animals appeared to be confused and fearful when they rejoined their old colony in the wild. They were quite incapable of coping with the complexities of social life and rapidly became social isolates.

Psychosurgeons usually get at the amygdala by directing a fine wire electrode towards the intended target through a small hole drilled in the skull and passing a strong current through the electrode, which destroys the tissue around the tip of it.

CASUALTIES OF PSYCHOSURGERY

The most notorious application of the amygdalotomy technique was in the United States, where it was used on criminals serving gaol sentences. The then Attorney General of the State of California was reported to have called publicly for amygdalotomies on all violent criminals housed in the state's prisons in order to remove 'the brain centres responsible for fear and anger'.

One case that made banner headlines involved L.S., a psychopath convicted of first-degree murder and rape, who had spent 18 years in a Michigan mental hosital. When a lawyer called Gabe Kaimowitz heard of the plan to make L. S. the first recipient of psychosurgery at the Lafayette Clinic, he told the *Detroit Free Press* of his concern and initiated court proceedings. According to L. S.'s testimony at the hearing, he had only given written consent to psychosurgery because he thought he might be released after the operation. He also claimed that he had been misled into thinking that he was agreeing only to electrode implantation and not to destructive surgery.

The three-man panel ruled that people who are involuntarily confined cannot give legally adequate consent to dangerous brain operations. They also decided that in this case psychosurgery violated the First Amendment (guaranteeing the citizen's right to free expression) in that it could have the effect of impairing memory and intellectual powers.

Another well-known case involved a 34-year-old engineer named Thomas R., who received an amygdalotomy at the hands of Vernon Mark and Frank Ervin. After surgery he was confused and delusional, and unable to work. When he was re-hospitalized because of his bizarre and dangerous behaviour, he was discovered on one occasion walking about the wards with his head covered by bags, newspapers and rags. He said he did this because he was frightened other bits of his brain might be destroyed. His mother, describing his behaviour after psychosurgery, said: 'The poor guy has been almost a vegetable . . . We know he was destroyed by that operation.'

Legal constraints on the use of psychosurgery have increased in recent years as a result of public outrage at some of its unsavoury consequences. California State Assembly Bill 4481, for example, restricting the use of electroconvulsive therapy and psychosurgery in California, was signed into law in late 1974 by the then Governor Ronald Reagan (it was later replaced by Assembly Bill 1032, operative from 1 January 1977).

It is undeniably true that the complexities of the human brain make it very difficult for surgeons to operate on it without producing a number of unpleasant and disturbing side-effects. However, there are some success stories, and this chapter is mainly concerned with one such story, based on the impressive work of Roger Sperry[1] of the California Institute of Technology and his colleagues. This work has alleviated human suffering and also produced exciting new insights into the physiological and psychological workings of the brain.

KEY EXPERIMENT: THE SPLIT-BRAIN OPERATION

The work of Roger Sperry and his associates at Caltec was done with a small number of advanced epileptics whose severe convulsions could not be controlled by medication. The first patient, for example, was a 48-year-old war veteran who had been having seizures for more than ten years, averaging two major attacks a week, each of which left him debilitated for at least a day.

The radical form of treatment decided upon for these epileptic patients was based on the fact that the human brain is a double organ, consisting of a right and a left hemisphere connected by a bridge of nerve tissue called the corpus callosum. This bridge of nerve tissue was severed surgically, the surgeons in this case being Philip Vogel and Joseph Bogen. Though this procedure is popularly referred to as the 'split-brain' operation, this is slightly inaccurate because the deeper parts of the brain remain connected.

Was such drastic surgical intervention justified? The basic idea was that cutting the corpus callosum would confine the epileptic seizures to one hemisphere, thus providing a measure of relief for the patients. There was also some evidence that possible unpleasant side-effects would be few (Ronald Myers and Roger Sperry had previously found that cutting the corpus callosum in cats and monkeys did not seriously impair their mental faculties).

After a stroke, caused by a disturbance of blood supply to a particular part of the brain, specific motor, sensory or integrating functions may be lost. This old lady is learning to walk again after partial paralysis of her right side, following damage to the left side of her brain.

Generally the effects of this operation were very beneficial. In the case of the 48-year-old war veteran not a single large-scale convulsion occurred in the several years following surgery. The second patient, a housewife and mother in her thirties, also remained free of seizures after recovering from surgery. A minority of the patients did continue to have seizures, but their convulsions were much less severe and less frequent than before, and usually confined to one side.

All the patients showed some short-term memory loss, problems of orientation and mental fatigue immediately after the operation. Some of them were unable to speak until two months after the operation. But in all cases there was gradual recovery. Within a few months none of them felt any different from the way they had felt before the operation. All in all, a substantial reduction in epileptic attacks was achieved, and at very low cost in terms of long-lasting side-effects.

Sperry's work achieved considerable publicity. Naturally the media sensationalized the difficulties the patients had in coping with their two half-brains, but considered objectively, the most remarkable result of the split-brain operation was its apparent lack of effect on ordinary behaviour. Indeed, Sperry had to devise a special test to demonstrate the drawbacks of split-brain functioning. This test was based on the fact that information presented visually to the left half of each eye is projected to the right hemisphere of the brain, whereas information presented to the right half of each eye goes to the left hemisphere. Provided the patient's direction of gaze was controlled and information was presented for a tenth of a second or less to prevent eye movements, Sperry could ensure that only one hemisphere of the brain received the information.

One of Sperry's first discoveries was that his patients had two separate visual inner worlds. If the picture of an object was presented to one hemisphere, they recognized it when it was presented again to the same hemisphere. However, if the picture was then presented in the other half of the visual field, so that it was projected to the opposite hemisphere, they responded as if they had no recollection of having seen the picture before.

More striking evidence of the existence of two quite separate visual worlds in these patients was obtained when the word 'heart' was flashed across the centre of the visual field, with 'he' to the left of centre and 'art' to the right of centre. Since language and speech are very largely left-hemisphere functions, the patients said they could see the word 'art' when it was presented to the right and projected to the left hemisphere. However, when they were asked to point with the left hand to one of two cards ('art' or 'he') to identify the word they had seen, they invariably pointed to 'he', the reason being that the right hemisphere controls the movement of the left hand and 'he' had been presented to the right hemisphere!

It has been known for a long time that language is associated to a far greater extent with the left hemisphere than with the right, although the opposite is found among some left-handed people. The original evidence for this came from studying patients who had received head injuries or suffered strokes. A gunshot wound to the left side of the head, for example, or a stroke in the left hemisphere, is much more likely to affect speech or writing ability than a similar injury to the right side.

Sperry was able to confirm this very convincingly. He found that visual material projected to the left hemisphere could be described by the patients in speech and writing in an essentially normal manner. But when the same material was presented to the right hemisphere, the patient would insist that he had not seen anything, or that there had only been a flash of light. Yet if the patient was then asked to use his left hand to point to a matching picture or object, he had no trouble in indicating the very item which he had just said he had not seen!

In an amusing variation of this experiment, a female patient was presented with a series of neutral geometrical figures. A photograph of a nude woman was then flashed to the right hemisphere. The patient said that she had not seen anything, but a sly smile spread over her face and she began to laugh. When she was asked what she was laughing at, she replied: 'I don't know . . . nothing . . . oh, that funny machine.'

We have already mentioned that the right hemisphere is not usually the one which controls speech. However, other observations made by Sperry and his co-workers indicated that the right hemisphere is able to understand both written and spoken words to some extent. If the name of an object (e.g. 'eraser') was flashed to the right hemisphere, the patient was able to select an eraser from among other objects by touch alone using the left hand (controlled by the right hemisphere).

The right hemisphere was even able to respond appropriately to a command such as 'Retrieve the fruit monkeys like best'—patients were quite capable of pulling a banana from a bag of plastic fruit with their left hand. The patients varied in terms of the linguistic powers of the right hemisphere. The most adept patient was able to spell simple words by placing plastic letters on a table with his left hand, but after he had spelled a word as directed, he could not name the word he had just spelled.

So far, we have focused mainly on the problems Sperry's patients encountered in dealing with visual information. Similar difficulties were experienced when objects were placed unseen in either the left or the right hand. Information from the left hand goes to the right hemisphere and information from the right hand to the left hemisphere. Objects placed in the right hand for identification by touch were easily described or named in speech or writing. If the same objects were placed in the left hand, the patients could only make wild guesses and often seemed unaware that anything at all was in their hand. However, if one of the objects which the patient said he did not recognize was taken from his left hand and placed among a dozen other items, he was then able to feel it out and retrieve it, again with the left hand, even after a time lapse of several minutes. The major limitation on performance here was that the patients could only retrieve the object provided that they used the same hand throughout—they could not recognize with one hand something identified only moments before with the other.

The superiority of the left hemisphere over the right across a wide range of tasks has led many people to refer to the left side of the brain as the 'major hemisphere' and to the right side as the 'minor hemisphere'. This is a profoundly mistaken view. If we move away from verbal abilities and consider other kinds of skills (e.g. spatial), the position is quite different. Tests by Sperry and Bogen at the Californian Institute of Technology showed that the right hand, which is under left hemisphere control, was unable either to arrange blocks to match a pictured design or draw a cube in three dimensions, whereas the left hand could perform both tasks quite satisfactorily.

There is interesting recent evidence that the right hemisphere may also be more intimately involved in emotional experiences. Lesions in most areas of the left hemisphere are accompanied by the feelings of loss that might be expected as the result of any serious injury, whereas damage in much of the right hemisphere sometimes leaves the patient unconcerned about his injuries and their possible consequences.

After Sperry's patients had been tested a number of times, they started using various strategies to cope with the tasks they were asked to perform. When a red or green light was flashed to the right hemisphere, the patient would at first simply guess at the colour. With practice, however, if the right hemisphere saw the red light and heard the left hemisphere guess 'green', it produced a frown and a shake of the head. This cued the left hemisphere to the fact that the answer was wrong.

Although the media have emphasized the problems that split-brain patients experience in performing relatively simple activities, Sperry found that it was sometimes a positive advantage to have two half-brains. He asked his patients to perform two different visual discrimination tasks simultaneously, with one task being presented to each hemisphere, and this they did as well as if they were performing each task on its own. In contrast, normal people find that the two tasks definitely interfere with each other if they attempt to perform them simultaneously.

TWO MINDS IN ONE?

One of the most challenging issues that arose from Sperry's pioneering research is whether he conclusively demonstrated the existence of two minds, each with its own consciousness. Sperry himself believed that he had. He announced to a distinguished Academy of Sciences: 'Everything we have seen so far indicates that the surgery has left these people with two separate minds, that is two separate spheres of consciousness. What is experienced in the right hemisphere seems to be entirely outside the realm of awareness of the left.' A very categorical statement indeed.

Experts have been in two minds, as it were, about whether or not to accept Sperry's bold assertion. Part of the difficulty revolves around what we mean by 'conscious experience'. It has been defined semi-facetiously as 'the dimension that makes you more like a dog than a computer', but various other definitions are possible.

The best attempt so far to come to grips with the question of double consciousness was undertaken by LeDoux, Wilson and Gazzaniga[2]. Since it is relatively easy to assess the nature and limits of consciousness in the 'talking' left hemisphere, but much more difficult to do the same with respect to

When we use a camera most of us use the right side of our brain to a greater extent than our left — we use both eyes, but the information they provide is mainly processed by the right hemisphere.

the mute right hemisphere, they decided to use as their subject Paul S., a boy who had greater language representation in the right hemisphere than had been observed in any other split-brain patient.

On one occasion, words were presented to one hemisphere of Paul S.'s brain and he was asked to evaluate them on a good–bad scale. Many of the words elicited quite different evaluations from the two hemispheres, with the right hemisphere rating being consistently closer to the bad end of the scale than the left hemisphere rating. Words such as 'Paul', 'mother' and 'sex' were rated very good by the left hemisphere and very bad by the right hemisphere. These differences suggest that each hemisphere may possess its own unique system for assigning subjective values to people and events.

It is especially intriguing that Paul was difficult to cope with on the day that these differences in hemisphere evaluations were obtained. It was almost as if he was literally at odds with himself. When he evaluated the same words on a second occasion he was calm and tractable. His improved mood on this occasion was mainly reflected in more positive right hemisphere evaluations, supporting the idea that the right hemisphere is more 'emotional' in some sense. On this second occasion the good–bad ratings were very similar in each half-brain.

Further evidence in favour of the notion that each hemisphere has a mind of its own was obtained when Paul was asked what job he would like. The left half-brain spelled out 'draughtsman', but the right half-brain spelled out 'automobile race'. It thus looks as if Sperry may not have been far wide of the mark in suggesting that two minds can co-exist in one body, but this may only happen when some language skills are present in each hemisphere.

Many popular writers have drawn sweeping conclusions about normal people, and even the inadequacies of human societies, on the basis of Sperry's work with a handful of severely epileptic patients. We have been told that the verbal, logical culture of the Western world is managed by the left hemispheres of its population, whereas the mystical, artistic and religious cultures of the East are based on right hemisphere domination.

This analysis has suggested to the psychologist Robert Ornstein that there ought to be a revolution in Western education, with much greater emphasis on non-verbal skills. Just as there are people who are politically left-wing and others who are right-wing, so also there are left and right hemisphere supporters. Hugh Sykes Davies, a scholar of English, attacked the 'rightist' movement to which Ornstein belongs, complaining that crucial left-hemisphere verbal skills are rapidly degenerating in our televisual society. Unfortunately most of the contributors to this controversy seem to have made the bizarre assumption that the two hemispheres of a normal man or woman are as divided as those of

If there was no exchange of information between the hemispheres of the brain, this artist would be unable to draw with his right hand something seen only with his left eye. The left side of the brain controls the right hand, but the left eye sends its messages to the right hemisphere.

Sperry's patients. The most fruitful approach would surely be to harmonize and integrate the function of the two hemispheres rather than develop one at the expense of the other.

A very important question that has almost been lost sight of by popular writers is whether or not we can safely assume that the differences between the two hemispheres in normal individuals are the same as those found by Sperry in split-brain patients. It could well be that frequent epileptic seizures, combined with all the problems of adjustment after surgery, make such patients' brains quite different from normal brains.

How can we look at the way each hemisphere performs in normal people? One useful method is to record the brain-waves evoked by some stimulus or other via small metal electrodes attached to the scalp, and to amplify these responses electronically, using special computer techniques to distinguish them from continuous brain-wave activity.

This technique measures what are known as 'evoked potentials' (see Chapter 11), and depending on where we choose to place the electrodes we can measure brain-wave activity in either the left or the right hemisphere.

In one typical experiment subjects were asked to carry out a number of verbal tasks (e.g. vocabulary test, finding synonyms) and spatial tasks (e.g. constructing a cross out of six plastic pieces, drawing a human figure). There was more pronounced brain-wave activity in the left than in the right hemisphere when a verbal task was being performed; the opposite occurred when a spatial task was being carried out. These observations fit in well with Sperry's notion that the left hemisphere is dominant for language skills and the right for spatial abilities.

There have been attempts to apply brain-wave techniques to a well-known sex-related difference, namely that women tend to be better than men at verbal tasks, while men are better at spatial tasks. Do women have better verbal skills because they have greater language representation in the right hemisphere than men, and does the organization of their right hemispheres for language interfere with the right hemisphere's attempts to handle spatial tasks? The answer to both questions seems to be yes. Women show relatively more brain-wave activity in the right hemisphere than men when engaged in verbal activities.

However, cross-cultural studies have somewhat dented the view that the right and left hemispheres have fairly specialized functions. Tsunoda Tadanobu of the Tokyo Medical-Dental College found interesting differences between the brains of Japanese people and those of other groups. He discovered that the sounds of insects, animals, rain, wind and waves activated the left hemispheres of Japanese-speaking people and the right hemispheres of everyone else! He also found that the sounds of traditional Japanese musical instruments like the *shakuhachi* produced the same pattern.

What is the reason for this unusual response to sounds? According to Tadanobu, the explanation lies in the peculiarities of the Japanese language. In Japanese, all vowel sounds and their derivatives are meaningful words. This means that many naturally occurring sounds resemble Japanese words, and so activate the language-processing systems of the left hemisphere.

All the evidence indicates that our hemispheres typically operate in an asymmetrical fashion, that is to say, many activities depend much more heavily on one hemisphere than the other. In other species symmetrical functioning of the two parts of the brain is often found. What are the advantages and disadvantages of asymmetrical brain functioning?

One advantage can be illustrated by means of a tale related by the fourteenth-century French monk Jean Buridan. An ass was faced with the dilemma of choosing between two equally appetizing and equidistant bales of hay, but it perished because it had no logical reason for moving towards one bale rather than the other. In real life, nature forestalls such tragic behaviour by equipping animals and humans with a response bias that usually leads them to select the bale on their right.

In general terms, asymmetry can be an advantage if you are trying to do two very different activities at once. If each activity can be dealt with by a different hemisphere, interference between the two activities is reduced. On the other hand, if you are attempting to cope with a single, complex task, it may be more difficult to co-ordinate behaviour if each hemisphere is doing part of the necessary processing on its own.

Marcel Kinsbourne tested some of these ideas with a very simple task that you can easily try yourself. This involves balancing a rod on either the right or the left index finger for as long as possible. If right-handed people do this while remaining silent, they can balance the rod longer on the right index finger than on the left, because the right hand is generally more skilled. However, if people are speaking while they attempt to balance the rod, then the opposite result is obtained: they can now balance the rod longer on the left index finger than on the right. It is as if speaking knocks the rod off the right index finger.

What is happening here? Speech and the right hand are both controlled by the left hemisphere, and so interfere with each other. In contrast, speech and the left hand are controlled by different hemispheres, and so only interfere with each other to a modest extent. This simple but ingenious experiment shows the potential advantages of asymmetry. If each hemisphere concentrates on a single task, two different activities can be successfully performed at the same time.

CONCLUSIONS

The history of attempts to modify human behaviour by direct action on the brain shows that it is all too easy to produce radical behavioural changes. The problem is that many unforeseen and unfortunate changes usually accompany the desired ones. This has led to increasing legal constraints on the use of various psychosurgical techniques.

However, there are some brain operations that have proved to be worthwhile under certain circumstances. The work of Sperry is especially important in this context, because it has provided major benefits in terms both of the welfare of epileptic patients and of the accumulation of knowledge about the complex workings of the brain.

Chapter 13

THE ROOTS OF PERSONALITY

Over two thousand years ago the Greek philosopher Theophrastus, then 99 years of age, wrote a book entitled *Characters*, in which he asked a question which is central to a large body of modern psychological research: 'Why is it that while all Greece lies under the same sky, and all the Greeks are educated alike, it has befallen us to have characters variously constituted?' In other words Theophrastus, like many people since, wondered why different people behave so differently, have different abilities and different personalities. He did not find an answer, but simply described various people who displayed, in exaggerated form, traits normally found in many people, such as miserliness, courage, persistence, and so on.

THE 'FOUR HUMOURS' UPDATED

The Greeks elaborated a descriptive system of personality according to which one was 'melancholic', 'choleric', 'phlegmatic' or 'sanguine'. Even today these terms are still used, in disciplines such as homeopathy for example.

Modern psychologists have found such categorization useful to some extent, but of course the majority of people are not thorough-going melancholics, cholerics, phlegmatics or sanguinics. Wilhelm Wundt, the founder of the first psychological laboratory in Leipzig, a hundred years ago, drew attention to the fact that melancholics and cholerics are alike in having strong and volatile emotions, whereas phlegmatics and sanguinics have rather stable emotions. He therefore postulated a dimension of 'emotionality', going from extreme instability to extreme stability. He also drew attention to the fact that cholerics and sanguinics are alike in being somewhat changeable in their behaviour, whereas melancholics and phlegmatics are rather unchangeable. Substituting the more modern terms 'extravert' and 'introvert' for changeable and unchangeable, we can say that Wundt foreshadowed the second major dimension of personality.

The picture painted by the ancient Greeks, and made more widely applicable by Wundt, is shown in Figure 1. It consists of two major dimensions of personality: emotionality/neuroticism as opposed to stability, and extraversion as opposed to introversion. Though each person has a position on these two axes, he or she would not necessarily fall

into one of the four quadrants. Indeed, most people centre around the point of intersection, showing personalities that are neither extremely stable nor extremely unstable, neither extremely extraverted nor extremely introverted, but 'ambivert'—half way between the two. The validity of this picture is supported by a vast body of evidence from different sources[1,2,3]. The words round the inside of the circle indicate the traits which, taken together, cause a person to be designated an introvert or an extravert, stable or unstable.

How can we measure these traits, and how can we measure 'personality'? At first sight it seems almost a contradiction in terms to speak of the 'measurement' of personality. How can we measure something so protean, complex and non-physical? In a sense this objection is sensible; we cannot measure personality as such. But we can measure different *aspects* of personality. Similarly we cannot measure the Universe, but we can

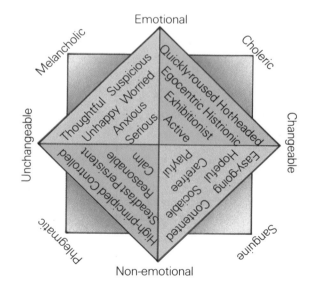

Figure 1   *The two major modern dimensions of personality suggested in the last century by Wundt, emotionality and non-emotionality and changeability-unchangeability, are in many ways a re-statement of the four main personality types recognized by the Ancient Greeks, melancholic, choleric, phlegmatic and sanguine.*

It is generally assumed that personality is constant, not something one can put on and take off at will, like make-up or a wig. Extraversion, introversion, stability, neuroticism and psychoticism are made up of many different traits or observable kinds of behaviour.

measure different aspects of it, such as stellar distances or the physical composition of the planets.

MEASURING PERSONALITY

There are in fact many different measures of personality. All have their strengths and weaknesses, but all derive from one overriding fact: personality is a concept which is derived from behaviour, and behaviour is by definition observable and measurable.

Consider a personality trait such as persistence. We call a person persistent if we have seen him exerting himself, perhaps over long periods, against pain, fatigue, boredom and other influences which would tend to make him give up. We can measure the length of time from the beginning of his exertions to the moment when he gives up, and we can measure most of the forces which he has to overcome in order to continue. Thus the concept of 'persistence' is based on observable, measurable behaviour, and much the same is true of other personality traits. Measurement is not always easy, but in principle it is usually possible to design an experiment which will be relevant to the particular trait one is looking at. In fact it is usually quite easy to design measures of personality. The difficulty lies in ensuring that they actually measure what one wants to measure.

QUESTIONNAIRES AND CASUAL OBSERVATION

The oldest and most widely used methods of personality measurement are observation and questionnaires. In fact questionnaire measurement is derived from a much older technique, namely self-observation. All that we are doing is to ask people to tell us the results of their own observations of their behaviour over the past few years. Let us assume we are interested in the trait of 'sociability'. We could observe the person, see how frequently she goes to parties, how many people she talks to at parties, how much time she spends alone by herself in her room, etc. This would be casual or uncontrolled observation; we are doing nothing here to constrain our subject, and we cannot, obviously, observe all her relevant behaviour—we cannot shadow her for 24 hours a day, and even if we could, our presence would undoubtedly modify her behaviour. So her own account of her habitual behaviour, either given verbally or given in the form of answers to a questionnaire, might be much more reliable than mere observation—after all, she is always with herself! We would of course have to trust her; if she had any good reason for deceiving us then no reliance could be placed on her answers. But for most purposes there is good agreement between outside observation and rating of a person's conduct, and self-ratings as given in response to a questionnaire or during an interview.

CONTROLLED OBSERVATION

We could refine our observation by making it controlled observation. Suppose that as part of our interest in sociability we wanted to find out exactly how sociable and unsociable people behave during discussions with strangers. Casual observation would not enable us to be very precise in our rating, chiefly because of the random nature of the strangers our various subjects would be meeting. We would not be able to tell to what extent their reactions were determined by their own personality or by the personality of the strangers. We could get over this by arranging an experimental confrontation between our subjects and a trained stooge who always behaved in a predetermined manner regardless of whom he met. For example, the stooge might be instructed to make no spontaneous remarks during the first five minutes, to become voluble during the next five minutes, and then revert to taciturnity. The confrontation could be staged in a laboratory and the conversation tape-recorded. The experimenter could also watch it through a one-way screen; he or she might even film the behaviour of the subject, to make it possible to count the number of times she smiled, blinked, looked at the stooge, etc. In this way we would get a very accurate record of exactly what took place, and could compare one subject's behaviour in this standardized situation with that of others. Controlled observation can be a very good method of personality measurement.

Risk-taking behaviour, whether it takes the form of defying gravity or asking for affection or help, is an area of personality which has been very thoroughly studied by psychologists. Extraverts tend to take more risks than introverts.

Another way of improving casual observation is to introduce a time-sampling system. Suppose that we are interested in the aggressiveness shown by children, and want to rate a group of children for this quality. We could go to the playground a number of times and observe their behaviour. But this would not be very accurate—we might pay more attention to some children than to others. The correct method would be to get a list of the names of all the children and spend exactly 60 seconds observing child one, 60 seconds observing child two, going on down the list and watching each child for an identical period. When we got to the end of the list, we would start again at the top. We would also have a list detailing precisely what behaviours we should watch out for, and a stop watch to tell us for how long each type of behaviour went on. If we continued our observations repeatedly over a period of months, we could then analyse our results and see how consistently each child behaved—in other words, is it always the same children who are aggressive, or is aggressiveness just a random type of behaviour? This type of observation would still be naturalistic, but it would be much better controlled and therefore more reliable than casual observation.

These improvements in observational technique bring us very close to an experimental technique which has been found to have many advantages for the measurement of personality, the 'miniature situation' technique. Since it is often difficult or impossible to observe people in a natural setting, and in any case the types of situation encountered by them are not usually identical, why not set up a simple situation in the laboratory, taking care that in all essentials it duplicates the sort of life situation we are interested in? This would obviate all our difficulties and enable us to take proper measurements.

Let us go back to persistence as a personality trait. It is easy to set up laboratory tasks which call for persistent behaviour; we can then measure each person's reaction to the tasks involved, and see whether statistical analysis of the data supports the notion that it is indeed persistence that we have measured. How would we set about it? We might go into a school[4] and arrange for the teachers to give their pupils a series of tests, making sure of course that the children did not realize that tests were being carried out. For instance, the teacher might take them to the gymnasium and announce a competition to see who can pull the hardest on a dynamometer (an instrument which registers strength of pull). Having found out each child's maximum pull, the teacher then announces that he wants to see how long each child can hold the dynamometer at two-thirds his maximum pull (thus ruling out differences in strength between the children). The more persistent children would, according to theory, keep going longer than the less persistent, overcoming the pain and fatigue that sets in after a very short while.

In another quite different test the teacher might give the class an intelligence test, timing each item for each child. Among the easy and the moderately difficult items there are some items too difficult for any of the children to solve. We are interested in finding out how long each child continues to grapple with these problems before giving up. This time is then a measure of his persistence.

If we devised, say, 20 persistence tests, all of this miniature situation type, and tested all the children on each test, could we show that the sum of all the scores on the 20 tests actually measured persistence?

Our first duty would of course be to demonstrate that the children who are persistent in one test are also persistent in the others. If this were not so, then the tests would not all be measuring the same trait, and it would be meaningless to add their scores together. But if all the tests do correlate together, we must next see whether perhaps this is because they all measure some other factor, such as intelligence. No, they don't; dull children do not have higher or lower persistence scores than bright children. Next we would have all our children rated for persistence by their teachers, on the assumption that teachers know their children pretty well; we would find that these correlations are positive and pretty high. Children who are rated as persistent by their teachers also perform persistently on our tests. We would then argue that persistent children probably do better in school than non-persistent ones, and indeed, when the necessary corrections are made for intelligence, we find that this too is true. Last, when we construct a questionnaire asking questions about persistence, the persistent children in the experiment are also the persistent children on the questionnaire. Taking all this together makes it pretty clear that our miniature situations do indeed measure what they are supposed to measure.

EXPERIMENTAL METHODS

Going one more step away from the commonsense approach characteristic of the techniques of observation and questionnaires, we come to experimental measures based on specific theories. These are difficult to discuss because to do so sensibly requires a detailed statement of the theories involved, which can be a lengthy and complex business, but let us take a rather oversimplified example. The theory has been advanced that introverts are more sensitive to external stimulation than extraverts. How can we test this? What follows is an example of just one experimental approach. First we measure the rate at which the subject salivates by putting some cotton wool into his mouth for 20 seconds; we weigh this before and after, and thus determine the amount of saliva which has been absorbed. After a short rest we perform the same experiment again, but this time we put four drops of lemon juice on the subject's tongue. It is known that this increases the rate of salivation for most people. Now the hypothesis states that if introverts are more sensitive, their rate should increase more than that of extraverts. So if we know our subjects' degree of extraversion or introversion from questionnaire answers, we can correlate their extraversion scores with the increase in salivary flow, and show that the correlation is in fact negative. Introverts who score low for extraversion show a greater increase in salivary flow than extraverts. That is the result we would expect, and it bears out our theory.

Experimental tests of this kind are particularly interesting and important for two reasons. The first is that they cannot be faked. In fact the subject has no idea that we are testing his personality, and even if we told him he would not know what the meaning of his scores was. And the second is that by

Herman Rorschach's inkblots. Usually the testee is shown ten different inkblots – five black, two red and black, and three multicoloured. What do you make of these?

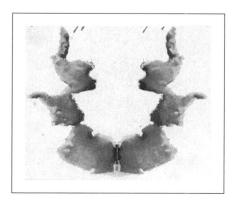

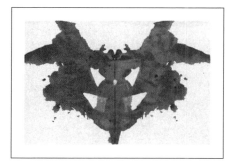

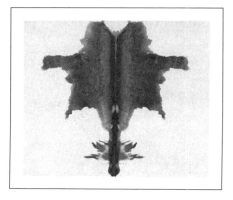

putting forward theories of this kind we hope to gain a better understanding of the mechanisms underlying our personality dimensions.

But there is also a disadvantage in using tests of this kind for practical purposes. They lack 'face validity'—in other words, they are not obviously relevant to whatever purpose they are being used for. A candidate for a job which requires introverted traits would be very surprised to find his rate of salivation being measured!

Much the same can be said of other personality tests based on physiological measures. It is well known that emotional reactions are closely connected with physiological changes; thus fear and anger are accompanied by an increase in heart rate. If we had to select candidates for a job which required them to remain very calm and stable under conditions of considerable danger, we might expose them to stress in the laboratory (threat of electric shock, say) and measure the increase in heart beat caused either by the threat or the actual administration of an electric shock. Subjects whose heart rate increased rapidly and died down again very slowly might not be the best choice for a job requiring a lot of 'cool'.

There are many such physiological indicators which can be and have been used as measures of personality, but they usually require elaborate laboratory equipment and are therefore not very useful for ordinary personality assessment. In special cases, however, and when the number of subjects involved is not too large, physiological tests can be extremely useful.

PROJECTIVE TESTS

We now come to a quite different category of tests, collectively known as 'projective devices'[5]. These are based on the hypothesis that we tend to project our ideas and fears, our ambitions and thoughts, onto material which is poorly structured. The projective expert can then study our imaginative products and argue back from these to the ideas and thoughts which gave rise to them.

The best known example of projective testing is the Rorschach ink-blot test. The subject is shown a series of ink-blots, which are symmetrical but fundamentally meaningless in shape and either coloured or black and white. He is asked to say what he thinks each ink-blot looks like. The sort of answers one usually gets are 'a couple of witches', 'a butterfly', 'two old women', and so on. There are various rules which are supposed to tell the experimenter how to argue back from these answers to the personality of the subject. Usually the experimenter tries to obtain an all-round picture of the temperamental characteristics of the subject. In this sense one might say that projective tests are the only real personality tests—all the others attempt to measure only very limited aspects of personality.

Another very widely known test is the T.A.T.

(Thematic Apperception Test). In this the subject is shown a series of drawings or pictures, the content of which is purposely vague. He then has to make up a story about each picture, and these stories are then scored and interpreted. The hypothesis in this case is that an aggressive person will write stories which contain a lot of fighting, an over-sexed person will write stories full of sexual activity, and an ambitious person will write stories in which the

A street palmist at work. Some palmists, like graphologists, accurately diagnose character with much better than chance accuracy. The same cannot be said of most projective tests. Perhaps this is because hands and handwriting are more directly expressive of essentials than words.

hero of the story succeeds in various endeavours. There are a vast number of different types of projective test, but the ink-blot test and the T. A. T. have remained the most widely used and the best known. Do they work?

After many years of great enthusiasm, the answer from literally hundreds of experimental studies is quite unequivocal: projective tests do not work very well. They do not agree with findings obtained on other tests of personality, and even identical projective information from the same person can result in quite different interpretations of his personality if scored by different experts.

One typical experiment will suffice to give the reader an idea of the sort of investigation which has been done on the claims of the experts themselves. During the war a large number of candidates for the U. S. Air Force were put through a whole battery of projective tests. These were not scored at the time but put aside until the end of the war. When the war was over an experimenter unearthed the tests of 50 candidates who had done exceptionally well in the Air Force and had come through all their trials and tribulations with flying colours. He also took out the records of 50 failures, people who had crumpled up under the stress and never got anywhere. A large number of experts in these various projective techniques were then approached and asked to sort out the old records into potential 'successes' and potential 'failures'. All of them had worked in the Air Force, knew what was involved and considered the experiment a fair one. To cut a long story short, only one of the experts gave answers outside the limits of chance, and he got his predictions significantly wrong! So much for the projective experts.

Many other similar experiments have come to similar conclusions. In one of them, 50 severe neurotics and 50 perfectly normal controls were tested with the Rorschach cards, and the results were then assessed by several experts. Not one could tell with above-chance accuracy which were the neurotic and which were the normal subjects. There is little doubt that as tests of personality these projective devices are not reliable and therefore not to be recommended.

However, such wholesale condemnation should not necessarily include the T. A. T. When the T. A. T. is used to test specific traits rather than assess all-round personality, and when pictures are specially chosen to probe one particular facet of a person's temperament (need for achievement, fear of failure, etc.) then the scores are likely to be fairly trustworthy. But apart from such specific uses, even the T. A. T. does not emerge unscathed from experimental evaluations of its usefulness.

Graphology (handwriting analysis)[6] is one method of personality assessment which correlates better with more reliable test methods. In one study 50 subjects filled in personality inventories and a graphologist attempted to predict their answers from separate samples of their handwriting. She was correct in 62 per cent of the cases, where chance or expectation would have predicted 50 per cent. On judgments of which she was particularly sure she was correct 68 per cent of the time. Subjects tended to differ in consistent ways with regard to the ease with which their handwriting could be diagnosed, and personality traits differed according to the ease with which their presence or absence could be detected in each subject's handwriting. The graphologist also succeeded in matching character sketches of the subjects, and other material, with their writing. Psychiatrists and psychologists who tried to judge personality from handwriting failed abysmally. In sum, it is possible for a skilled graphologist to diagnose personality traits from handwriting with better than chance success.

A GENETIC BASIS FOR PERSONALITY?

The very notion of 'personality' implies consistency. We assume that a person who is sociable, or talkative, or anxious shows these traits consistently over many years, rather than at odd intervals. This suggests that genetic factors may be involved in the determination of personality[7]. This is certainly what the physicians of Ancient Greece thought.

What, then, is the evidence regarding heredity? Does it influence personality? The best evidence here comes from studies of twins. Nature occasionally provides us with exciting ready-made experiments in the form of identical twins and fraternal twins, which enable us to investigate the influence of heredity along two different paths. We can examine identical twins who have been separated at birth or shortly after, and who have been brought up in quite different environments (by foster parents, in orphanages, or in some other way). Any similarities between separated identical twins can only be the effect of heredity, not environment, since they ceased to share the same environment shortly after they left the womb.

The other path allows us to make comparisons between identical twins and fraternal twins. Let us suppose that a given trait, say sociability, is due entirely to environmental causes. The only difference between identical and fraternal twins is that the former have more heredity in common, but this is irrelevant to our hypothetical trait, and consequently identical twins would be no more alike with respect to sociability than would fraternal twins. But let us now suppose that heredity does play an important part in producing differences in sociability. In that case we would expect identical twins to be much more alike than fraternal twins, simply because they share more heredity. The general rule can be stated as follows: the more similar identical twins are with respect to the trait one is studying, the greater the influence of heredity; conversely, the more similar fraternal twins are with respect to a certain trait, the greater the influence of environment.

What is the outcome of the many personality studies on twins which have been carried out in Britain and the United States, where most such work has been done? Let us take first the experi-

Part of the original manuscript of Lewis Carroll's Alice in Wonderland. *Would a skilled graphologist have divined, behind the carefully crossed Ts and even letter spacing, that the writer was a reclusive mathematics don?*

This time Alice waited quietly until it chose to speak again in a few minutes the caterpillar took the hookah out of its mouth, and got down off the mushroom, and crawled away into the grass, merely remarking as it went : "the top will make you grow taller, and the stalk will make you grow shorter."

"The top of _what_? the stalk of _what_?" thought Alice.

"Of the mushroom," said the caterpillar, just as if she had asked it aloud, and in another moment it was out of sight.

Alice remained looking thoughtfully at the mushroom for a minute, and then picked it and carefully broke it in two,

Most identical twins who are brought up together work hard to establish a separate personality for themselves, with the result that they are often more different from each other than identical twins brought up separately.

ments using identical twins brought up separately. Here the outcome is rather unexpected. It has been found that identical twins brought up apart are, if anything, slightly more alike than identical twins brought up together. Both groups, in fact, are very similar with respect to extraversion and neuroticism; knowing one twin, one can make a very good guess about the personality of the other.

But how is it possible that environment not only fails to make twins who grow up together more alike, but may actually make them somewhat less like each other than twins who grow up separately? The answer may lie precisely in the great similarity that exists between them. Often identical twins resent the fact that they are not regarded as separate individuals, and tend to magnify any small and accidental differences in behaviour simply in order to appear different. Thus one twin may take over negotiations with the outer world, while the other takes over internal management of their affairs. This parcelling out of roles is

often facilitated by the fact that identical twins interfere with each other in the womb more than fraternal twins do, because in most cases they share a common placenta. Thus one twin may deprive the other of part of its share of their joint blood supply, leading to differences in birth weight which are often correlated with intelligence, dominance, etc. Thus, contrary to expectation, identical twins share a pre-natal environment but may not share it as equally as fraternal twins. Slight differences of experience in the womb may then lead identical twins to emphasize and exaggerate these differences subsequently.

Whatever the truth about these complex matters, there is no doubt that the evidence from identical twins brought up separately demonstrates very clearly that heredity plays a very important part in producing differences in personality. The hereditary effect is particularly strong in people with more extreme scores on either extraversion–introversion or neuroticism–stability; the effect is least strong in the middle of both axes, i.e. among people who are not particularly extraverted or introverted, emotional or stable.

Experiments comparing identical and fraternal twins bear out this conclusion. Out of some 20 studies, there is not one in which the correlations for identical twins have not been larger, and usually much larger, than those for fraternal twins. This applies not only to the major personality variables, such as extraversion–introversion and neuroticism–stability, but to a large number of other measurable traits as well.

When proper personality tests are used, whether questionnaires or objective experimental procedures, the results always support the proposition that heredity plays a most important part in producing differences in personality[1]. It is not easy to give a numerical value to the propositional importance of nature and nurture. The results of tests depend in part on the actual instruments used for making the measurements. Also, the numbers of twins studied have often been too small to give very accurate results. But the minimum value for the contribution of heredity is something like 50 per cent, with the maximum being in the region of 70 per cent. Probably something like 60 per cent would be the best guess at the moment. This would apply to the heritability of major personality characteristics (i.e. extraversion–introversion, neuroticism–stability). Simpler traits, such as sociability or impulsiveness, give lower values, but still up to the 50–60 per cent mark. Thus there can be no doubt that personality has a hard core of innately determined behaviour patterns. This hard core (the 'genotype' as geneticists call it) interacts with the environment to produce the actually observed behaviour (the 'phenotype').

Modern methods of analysis applied to very large groups of twins (some in excess of 12,000 pairs) have given a great deal of information that could not be obtained from the smaller samples that were usual only a few years ago. One of the most important of these findings relates to the environmental influences which in part determine personality. These environmental influences are divided into two groups, those due to shared environments (i.e. due to the fact that children from the same family share the same home, the same parental care, and many other features of the environment) and those due to events happening to children within the same family which may cause them to differ in personality (i.e. one child having a good teacher, another one a bad one, or one contracting some kind of illness which the other escapes). The first kind of environmental influence is 'between family environmental variance' and the second 'within family environmental variance'. Modern methods of analysis enable us to estimate the influence of these two kinds of environmental variables, and the result has been rather astonishing.

Most theories of personality have given great weight to the influence of the family. One would therefore expect 'between family environmental variance' to be the crucial factor, accounting for the lion's share of the environmental contribution to personality differences. Actually all the large-scale studies done so far agree completely that there is little if any evidence for between family environmental influences. All the influences detected in these studies have been of the within family kind! In other words, the evidence seems pretty conclusive that the more orthodox types of personality theory, including the Freudian, are wrong, and that the environmental factors which contribute to personality development are not connected with the family, the type of upbringing we receive, or any of the other environmental conditions determined by the family! Five very large-scale studies, carried out in Scandinavia, England, the United States and Australia, using different methods, different twins, different inventories and different methods of analysis, all agree on this point[7].

A PHYSIOLOGICAL BASIS FOR PERSONALITY?

These findings raise some interesting problems. It is of course quite impossible to inherit conduct. We can only inherit physical structures that can be identified by the physiologist or the anatomist. Yet what we measure when we talk about personality is conduct, or behaviour. This suggests that there must be physical structures in our nervous system which give rise to behaviour of the kind which causes us to diagnose a person as extraverted or introverted, neurotic or stable. We now have some idea what structures are involved. Consider Figure 2, which is a very simple diagram of the cortex and the spinal cord. At the base of the brain is the so-called visceral brain. This co-ordinates the activities of the more primitive part of our nervous system, which governs the expression of the emotions through two sub-systems, the sympathetic and the parasympathetic nervous systems. Emotions such as fear and anger are always accompanied by physical symptoms (increased heartbeat, more rapid breathing, sweating, the cessation of digestion, dilation of the pupils, etc.) which are mediated by the sympathetic system and co-ordinated by the visceral brain. Once the occasion for the fear or anger is over the parasympathetic nervous system calms things down again (brings heart beat and breathing back to normal, re-starts digestion, and generally relaxes the organism). The visceral brain and the structures of the autonomic system are the physical base for individual differences in neuroticism and stability. In interaction with the environment, they produce the phenotypic behaviour which we measure with our questionnaires.

Extraversion–introversion, on the other hand, is closely related to the habitual arousal level of the cortex. We are all familiar with different arousal levels. We get tense and wound up, highly aroused, before an important examination, but we are relaxed and drowsy late in the evening in front of the television. The brain functions best at moderately high levels of arousal.

Introverts have higher habitual levels of

arousal than extraverts, which is why they tend to be better at learning, conditioning and remembering. The cortex also has the function of keeping the lower levels of the brain in check, which is why the behaviour of introverts is more inhibited than that of extraverts. An illustration may make things clearer. Alcohol makes people more extraverted, whereas amphetamines, which are stimulant drugs, have the opposite effect; because they increase the level of cortical arousal they make people more introverted. So do nicotine and caffeine, which is why students studying hard for an examination tend to smoke and drink coffee to keep awake and learn better. Therefore, by giving people depressant or stimulant drugs, we can alter the physical basis of their personality and thus their behaviour. The effect of such drugs can be tested,

The degree to which we seek or tolerate the company of others, in other words our sociability, depends on our habitual level of arousal. If cortical activity is high we are more likely to want to read a book than talk to friends.

by psychophysiological tests which fairly directly measure the activity of the cortex. Many such studies (EEG recordings of brain-waves, now measurable with great accuracy, recordings of heart rate, breathing rate, electrical conductivity of the skin, changes in pupil diameter, etc.) have been carried out, and in general they support the theory that extraversion–introversion is linked to levels of arousal.

Such studies are of more than academic interest. They have important practical applications and also throw light on behaviour we often find difficult to understand, such as neurosis, vandalism and criminality. Extraverts, as we have seen, have a low level of arousal, whereas introverts have a high level. In fact most people seek for intermediate levels of arousal. Too high or too low a level of arousal is unpleasant, and people try to avoid both. This suggests that extraverts will on the whole be 'sensation-seekers', that is they will seek to increase their arousal level by indulging in behaviour that brings them in contact with bright lights, loud music, sexual excitement, and so on. This sensation-seeking behaviour also accounts for the socia-

bility of the extravert; associating with other people increases his or her arousal level. Conversely, introverts avoid contact with too many people because it increases their arousal level to an unpleasant degree.

Or consider another consequence of an individual's arousal level. Neurotic symptoms and disorders are now believed to be acquired through a process of conditioning, that is through associating a painful stimulus with a neutral stimulus which, through force of circumstance, accidentally becomes linked with the painful stimulus. For example, one woman acquired a lifelong phobia for cats because her sadistic father drowned her favourite cat in front of her eyes when she was a child. But the ease of conditioning is determined to a large extent by the arousal level of the cortex. This means that introverts, having a higher arousal level, condition much more readily, and are therefore more susceptible to neurotic disorders. This association between neurosis and conditioning has been powerfully demonstrated in many studies, as we saw in Chapter 7.

Since personality has such a strong biological basis, it follows that people in general are much more different from one another than might at first be supposed. We tend to believe that most people are like ourselves, perhaps differing slightly due to events in their past. We also believe that they could quite easily be converted to our way of thinking, and change their behaviour to be more like us. But this belief is quite wrong, as we shall see in Chapter 24. The long history of our failure to rehabilitate criminals and make vandals behave like ordinary human beings is eloquent testimony to the fact that people differ profoundly from each other. Given that fact, the search for Utopia is ultimately a foolish exercise. What is heaven for one may be hell for another, and the best we can hope for is some form of compromise that does not offend or injure too many people.

This may be a very tame and unacceptable conclusion for eager idealists seeking a heaven on earth but, unfortunately or perhaps fortunately, it is an accurate statement of the facts of the case. Our differences make living together extremely difficult, whether in a family, state or international context. Understanding that people are incorrigibly different from each other is the beginning of wisdom for the budding psychologist.

Chapter 14
THE HAPPINESS FACTOR

Happiness is one of the major goals of life. Many people seek desperately for it, hence the huge (and still growing) army of those whose business it is either to reduce unhappiness or promote happiness. Social workers, psychiatrists, psychotherapists, marriage guidance counsellors and clinical psychologists all tend to the needs of the unhappy, and hundreds of popular books tell us that happiness is attainable through diet, exercise, relaxation, self-assertion, satisfying relationships, prayer, good works . . .

But is the pursuit of happiness an entirely good thing? In an interesting story by Mark Twain entitled *The Mysterious Stranger*, an angel promises to make an old man happy. This sounds very appealing to the old man and the angel keeps his promise . . . by making the old man insane. The old man spends the rest of his days in a mental institution, where he talks with imagined old friends and dispenses non-existent money and gifts. So it appears that it is possible for a happy life to be at the same time an essentially empty and meaningless one. That is not a definition that many of us would want to accept.

'Happiness' is one of those words we all feel we know the meaning of, yet find difficult to define. It clearly means a number of different things. If someone says 'Last year was a very happy year for me', he or she is not using the word 'happy' in quite the same sense as someone who says 'I felt really happy at the party last night'. In the former case, happiness is being used in the sense of long-lasting satisfaction or contentment, whereas in the latter happiness refers to an emotional high, a brief feeling of euphoria. For the purposes of this chapter, we will assume that there is some merit in both definitions. Happiness can be regarded as a combination of contentment with life and intensely positive but brief emotional experiences.

THE INGREDIENTS OF A HAPPY LIFE
The commonsense answer to the question: 'What are the ingredients of a happy life?' is that a happy life comes from having a succession of pleasant and agreeable things happen to us. So if we have a reasonable amount of money, good friends, a good family life, good health and an interesting and well paid job, we are likely to be happier than someone who is poor, jobless, friendless, has no family, and so on. The American academic Jonathan Freedman neatly caricatured this view of happiness: 'The happiest person on the North American continent is a forty-year-old Unitarian clergywoman. She lives in Canada and works full-time. She is married

for the first time, is in love with her husband and is loved equally by him, and has an active, satisfying sex life. She has a college degree (no graduate education), earns twenty-five thousand dollars a year. Both she and her husband are in good health. She is not especially religious, does not believe in ESP (extrasensory perception), has had peak experiences, has at times felt in harmony with the universe, has confidence in herself and in her guiding values; she believes that life has meaning and direction and that she has control over both the good and bad things that happen to her. She is not fat.'

There is an element of truth in the notion that our level of happiness depends on the number of pleasant things that happen to us, and on our position within society. Not surprisingly, some factors are of greater importance than others in determining our level of happiness. In several large-scale studies, age, life-cycle stage, socio-economic status, occupational status and family income are all found to influence happiness, but sex, race, education and religion were found to have hardly any influence at all.

Although it has been established that different groups within society differ in their levels of happiness, what is most striking is that the effects of socio-economic status and all of the other factors mentioned above are really rather modest. There are much larger differences *within* each group than there are *between* groups. Thus, people who are young, wealthy and of high socio-economic status are not necessarily happy, nor are the old and poor automatically unhappy. In other words, we must look elsewhere for the mainsprings of happiness.

THE 'HEDONIC TREADMILL'
Why is it that the 'good things' in life seem to have less effect on long-term happiness than is generally thought? The answer seems to be that pleasant experiences increase our level of happiness a little less each time they occur. The chocolate addict who goes to work in a chocolate factory and is allowed to eat as many chocolates as he or she wants is in a paradise on earth . . . at first. Then chocolate, and even the thought of chocolate, ceases to be pleasant. As far as the power of life's more pleasurable events to make us happy is concerned, there seems to be an inexorable law of diminishing returns operating.

Happiness depends, in part, on what has happened to us in the past. The ability of past experiences to colour present experiences was emphasized by American psychologist Harry Helson. He argued that we all have an 'adaptation level', a point of neutrality corresponding to what we expect to happen, our expectations being based on our past experiences. If what happens is the same as our expectation or adaptation level, we feel neither happy nor unhappy. If what happens is better or worse than expected, then we feel happy or unhappy.

If Harry Helson is correct in his assumption, everyone who aspires to happiness is in rather a bind. A series of pleasant experiences will produce happiness but it will also raise our expectations to a higher level. As a consequence, it becomes increasingly difficult for new experiences to be better than expected. And so, in present happiness lie the seeds of future unhappiness. This depressing view of happiness has been called the 'hedonic treadmill' —in a treadmill, you cannot make any genuine progress no matter how fast you run. Since it is most unlikely that life will consistently prove better than expected, the searcher after happiness is caught in the hedonic treadmill.

One of the commonest ways in which increasing expectations or adaptation levels reduce happiness can be seen in the lives of those millions of people who become steadily better off as the years go by. Most of them do not really feel better off, and their increasing wealth does not usually make them happier. They expect an increasingly affluent lifestyle and their escalating expectations put a damper on their happiness.

Winning a small or a large sum of money is a pleasant experience, although the euphoria does not last long. Are tombolas, lotteries and sweepstakes a way of beating the adaptation theory? We don't really expect to win, but we just might!

In spite of the predictions of adaptation level theory, most people firmly believe that more money will make them much happier. When Joyce Brothers, the American television psychologist, asked viewers whether becoming 25 per cent better off financially would make them happier, nearly all of them claimed that it would. What are the facts? In essence, the evidence supports adaptation level theory. One major study which looked at big winners of the Illinois State Lottery, many of whom had won $1 million, found that these 'lucky' people did not feel any happier after their big win than they had before. Nor, it emerged, did they expect to feel any happier two years later. A comparison between these lottery winners and other people who had received sudden windfalls also failed to uncover any positive effect of wealth on personal happiness[1]. These are striking findings. After all, American society is often regarded as being the most materialistic on earth.

Adaptation level theory makes the even more surprising prediction that individuals who suffer from severe physical disabilities will gradually reduce their expectations and so become as happy as everyone else. In other words, they will adjust to the adverse circumstances in which they find themselves. As the rather heartless Arab proverb says: 'Throw a man into the sea, and he will become a fish.'

Philip Brickman, an American psychologist at Northwestern University, Evanston, Illinois, tested these ideas with accident victims who were either quadriplegic or paraplegic (paralyzed from the neck down or the waist down). Despite the huge limitations which paralysis imposed on their lives, these people still derived as much pleasure as the able-bodied from common activities such as talking with friends or watching television. More remarkably, they expected to be as happy as other people within two years. Since their accidents were relatively recent, their current level of happiness was somewhat lower than that of other people, but there was little evidence of misery or despair.

Richard Schulz and Susan Decker, at Pittsburgh and Portland University, assessed happiness levels in quadriplegics and paraplegics who had been paralyzed for approximately 20 years and found that their satisfaction with life was only marginally lower than that of the population at large. Those who had the benefit of strong social support from relatives and friends were just as happy as other people. As part of the process of changing expectations and adaptation, many of them said that their disablement had a positive side. It had made them more patient and tolerant, and more aware that brain is more important than brawn.

One of the most remarkable endorsements of adaptation level theory comes in *One Day in the Life of Ivan Denisovich* by Russian novelist Alexander Solzhenitsyn. The book is a portrait of life in a Siberian labour camp, a topic which Solzhenitsyn was well equipped to write about, having spent eight years in a number of different Siberian labour camps. Despite the horrors of his everyday life, the hero of the book, Ivan Denisovich Shukhov, is not in the wretched state one might imagine. An inkling as to why this is so emerges when he considers the day in his life which has been described in the earlier part of the book: 'Shukhov went to sleep fully content. He'd had many strokes of luck that day: they hadn't put him in the cells; they hadn't sent the team to the settlement; he'd pinched a bowl of kasha at dinner; the team-leader had fixed the rates well; he'd built a wall and enjoyed doing it; he'd smuggled that bit of hacksaw-blade through; he'd earned something from Tsezar in the evening; he'd bought that tobacco. And he hadn't fallen ill. He'd got over it . . . A day without a dark cloud. Almost a happy day.'

Shukhov had adjusted his expectations downwards to suit the discomforts of the camp and was therefore not unhappy. His adjustment was so great that even things such as buying tobacco and not falling ill were enough to make the day a good one.

Who is happier? The little Mexican boy opposite or the owner of the Rolls Royce below? Although social and political injustice cannot be excused by saying that people adapt to circumstances, the little boy will adapt to the meagre comforts of life in a refugee camp just as the tycoon will adapt to penthouse suites and caviar.

What can we do about the hedonic treadmill? Paradoxically, one way of increasing future happiness would be to reduce the adaptation level in the present by avoiding pleasurable activities. There are numerous examples of this approach among the world's religions, which regard temporary abstinence from pleasure as a valuable experience. Consider the Christian tradition of Lent, in which the 40 weekdays between Ash Wednesday and Easter Eve are given over to fasting and penitence.

Two extroverts pull faces at one another. Their chances of happiness are greater than those of introverts, not because they have fewer negative experiences but because they have more positive ones. They behave in ways which elicit the interest, amusement and affection of others.

Another example is Ramadan, the ninth month of the Muslim lunar càlendar, during which devout Muslims fast from sunrise to sunset.

KEY EXPERIMENT: WHO IS HAPPY?
We have so far considered happiness in terms of pleasurable and unpleasurable events and their influence on expectations. Unfortunately adaptation level theory says nothing about the personality of the individual who is experiencing the pleasurable or unpleasurable events, as Paul Costa and Robert McCrae at the National Institute on Aging, Baltimore, Maryland, pointed out. The world, as Oscar Wilde might have said, consists of two kinds of people, optimists and pessimists. For the first, the glass is always half full and for the second, it is always half empty, and this must have

an influence on general levels of happiness. As the American psychologist Ed Diener once remarked: 'A person enjoys pleasures because he or she is happy, not vice versa.'

Costa and McCrae decided to focus on the subjective experience of the individual rather than external events. In psychological jargon, enjoyable emotions such as excitement, delight, enthusiasm and anticipation are known as 'positive affects'. 'Negative affects' are just the opposite—unpleasant emotions such as fear, hostility, jealousy, frustration, and so on. Costa and McCrae theorized that happy people are people who experience lots of positive affect and very little negative affect. Could it be as simple as the song says? Is happiness just a question of accentuating the positive and eliminating the negative?

To test their theory Costa and McCrae measured the amount of positive and negative affect experienced by a large number of people, and at the same time assessed them for introversion–extraversion and neuroticism–stability, the major unrelated personality dimensions put forward many years ago by the senior author of this book. The results were very striking. Extraverts reported much more positive affect than introverts, but did not differ much in terms of negative affect. In contrast, neurotic individuals reported considerably more negative affect than stable individuals, but the two groups resembled each other in reported positive affect[2]. In other words, the introversion–extraversion dimension reflected individual differences in the tendency to experience positive affect, whereas the neuroticism–stability dimension reflected individual differences in the tendency to experience negative affect.

Since extraverts are people who are both sociable and impulsive, Costa and McCrae were curious to find out which of these components of extraversion is more responsible for the high level of positive affect experienced by extraverts. They discovered that sociability, enjoying the company of others, was the component which made the major contribution to positive affect. This is not really surprising, because the majority of our most pleasurable experiences involve other people.

Happy people, therefore, are those who combine great experience of positive affect with minimal experience of negative affect, and it is the stable extravert who conforms to this pattern. Stable extraverts are indeed lucky, because their extraversion allows them to experience a lot of positive affect, and their stability or lack of neuroticism prevents them from suffering too much negative affect. The unluckiest people are neurotic introverts. On the one hand, their introversion curbs their enjoyment of life and experience of positive affect, and on the other their neuroticism makes them very vulnerable to anxiety and to negative affect.

This leaves us with stable introverts and neurotic extraverts. While both groups are intermediate in their level of happiness, they differ dramatically in their everyday emotional experiences. Stable introverts are very phlegmatic individuals who avoid all emotional extremes, rarely being down in the dumps or on top of the world. Their introversion stops them from experiencing much positive affect and their stability saves them from experiencing much negative affect. By contrast neurotic extraverts are constantly on an emotional roller-coaster, experiencing high levels of both positive and negative affect.

Costa and McCrae carried out a further study which provided even more impressive support for the notion that personality is the most important determinant of happiness. They asked whether personality measures taken at one point in time could predict happiness ten years later. Completely

Two football supporters in high spirits, despite the rain. The present moment is the only moment worth getting completely involved in.

ignoring all of the pleasurable and unpleasurable events which had happened during those ten years, they discovered that those who were assessed as stable extraverts were very much happier a decade after the assessment than those who were assessed as neurotic introverts. So if you have the luck to be a stable extravert, the future looks good!

The intriguing findings of Costa and McCrae disprove the common belief that the world is divided into emotional people who frequently experience emotional highs and lows, and unemotional people who cruise along on a smooth and rather boring plateau. Neurotic extraverts certainly tend to be rather emotional and stable introverts rather unemotional, but stable extraverts and neurotic introverts cannot be regarded simply as either emotional or unemotional. Stable extraverts experience life's emotional highs without the lows and neurotic introverts do the opposite. So, contrary to popular belief, it is possible for people to be very emotional in some ways and very unemotional in others.

Old people are not necessarily less happy than young people, despite some of the limitations imposed by aches and pains and reduced income. All of us tend to become less changeable emotionally as we get older – both the highs and the lows are less intensely felt.

DOES INTELLIGENCE LEAD TO HAPPINESS?

Intelligence is much valued by Western society because it often provides the key to job success, material prosperity and high socio-economic status. So, on the face of it, one might think that people of high intelligence would be happier, on average, than people of limited intelligence. But in spite of the advantages associated with intelligence, the overwhelming evidence is that intelligence and happiness are unrelated.

There are probably two main reasons for this. One is that people who are highly intelligent tend to have much greater aspirations and expectations than those who are not. Since happiness depends on reality exceeding expectation, high expectations

◄ Life at both ends of the age spectrum has its compensations. Relations between grandparents and grandchildren are often very happy – both parties feel free to be themselves.

are likely to prove a source of discontent. There is also the old adage 'Only cows are contented', implying that the only way to be truly happy is to be oblivious of the world's problems. To be intelligent is, by definition, to be aware of the world's problems, which again is more likely to breed discontent than happiness.

AGE AND HAPPINESS

Enjoyment of life must surely be related to age and the stage one has reached in life. Young people in the 'prime of life', usually with few responsibilities, have the time and the opportunity to change those aspects of their lives (sexual partner, job, where they live) which fail to measure up to expectation. In contrast, middle-aged and elderly people typically feel that their lives are set in a particular pattern, that the future is unlikely to present them with major new opportunities.

But what are the facts? Despite the apparently greater opportunities for happiness available to the young, there is only modest evidence to support the view that they are happier than their elders. Contentment and satisfaction both tend to rise with increasing age. What does appear to vary with age is emotional changeability. Young people experience much more positive affect and much more negative affect than older people. This greater changeability is not associated with greater happiness, however, because happiness stems from a combination of high positive affect and low negative affect.

MARRIAGE AND FAMILY INFLUENCES

The sharp increase in the divorce rate in recent years reflects a general feeling that marriage is in many ways an outmoded institution. There are certain obvious disadvantages associated with marriage, such as the substantial emotional and time demands which it imposes, and the loss of freedom, which suggest that the married state should be a recipe for unhappiness.

In fact there is very clear and strong evidence that marriage is good for you[3]. On average married people are much happier than single people. In one study it was found that a married man's chances of being very happy are about five times as great as those of widowed or separated men, and three times as great as those of divorced men. The differences were somewhat less marked for women, but they were in the same direction—women who are married experience more positive affect than women who are not, and they also experience less negative affect. Why this should be so is not altogether clear, but it probably has a lot to do with the social support which a spouse can provide. It has sometimes been argued that men are more con-

cerned than women about the restrictions and loss of freedom which marriage involves, which suggests that marriage should be more beneficial to women than men. Actually, as we have just seen, men derive rather more benefit from the marital state than women.

One of the main reasons why people get married is that marriage sanctions the begetting of children. Indeed, it could be argued that it is the presence of children in a marriage which makes married people generally happier than people who are not married. Nevertheless it has been established that having children actually tends to *reduce* marital happiness. This is true for men as well as women, and it is also true for virtually every race and religious group ever studied, but perhaps these findings should not be taken at face value. Married couples without children usually separate or divorce if the marriage is not happy, whereas unhappily married couples with children often decide to stay together 'for the sake of the children'. But this cannot be the whole story. The fact that married couples tend to become happier after their children have flown the family nest is striking confirmation that the presence of children has a definitely adverse effect on marital happiness.

Why on earth do married couples have children if their happiness is likely to be reduced for 20 years or so as a result? The most obvious answer is that there is more to life than happiness. Being responsible for the care and development of children adds meaning to life and is generally regarded as a worthwhile enterprise. Also, although having children undoubtedly produces some very deep emotional lows, it can also produce extraordinary emotional highs.

CONCLUSIONS

Happiness depends in part on the experiences we have and on our position within society. However, the number of pleasurable experiences we have has only a modest effect on our happiness. This is because we tend to have, in the long run, approximately as many pleasurable experiences as we expect, and happiness depends on reality consistently being better than we expect.

The secret of happiness lies in personality. Stable extraverts possess the 'happiness factor' —they are happy because they tend to view the world through rose-tinted spectacles. Neurotic introverts lack the happiness factor—they are unhappy because they take a gloomier view of things. So it is the way in which we react to life's events rather than the events themselves which determines whether life is heaven or hell.

Next page: It is a mistake to think that when we retire, ► when the pressure of earning a living is lifted from us, we will be happier. Unless we enjoy chewing the fat when we are young, we are unlikely to do so when we are old.

Chapter 15
CHURNING EMOTIONS

The endless fascination of emotions has kept generations of novelists and poets in gainful employment. One of the reasons for this fascination is the lack of agreement about the significance of those feelings we call 'emotions'. Consider as an example the intense emotion of love. To the poet Shelley it was 'the universal thirst for a communion not merely of the sense, but of our whole nature', but to George Bernard Shaw it was 'a gross exaggeration of the difference between one person and everybody else.'

We shall not attempt to arbitrate between them. However, we shall consider the interesting matter of exactly what it is that leads people to have emotional experiences. In other words, where do emotions come from?

KEY EXPERIMENT: INTERPRETING AROUSAL

The classic study on emotion was carried out some 30 years ago by Stanley Schachter[1] of Columbia University and Jerome Singer of Pennsylvania State University. They started by asking themselves what ingredients were vital in order for someone to experience an emotional state, and decided that there were two. One ingredient is a state of physio-

Did this taxi driver get out of bed the wrong side, or did someone do something unforgivable? Most of us would rather attribute our feelings to external events than to internal states.

logical arousal, which can include pounding of the heart, sweating, trembling hands, and a warm, flushed face. The second ingredient is the way in which the person interprets this state of arousal; he must explain the arousal in emotional terms in order to feel in an emotional state. If he accounts for the arousal in non-emotional terms, he will not experience emotion.

Normally, of course, arousal is interpreted as an emotional experience. A man who becomes aroused at the sight of an attractive woman normally attributes his arousal to feelings of sexual attraction. However, according to Schachter and Singer, it is entirely possible for us to feel aroused or 'stirred up' without experiencing any emotion at all. Some work done by a medical doctor named Maranon in the 1920s suggests the reason why. He injected 210 of his patients with adrenalin (epinephrine), a drug whose effects mimic almost perfectly a naturally occurring state of arousal. When he asked his aroused patients to say how they felt, 71 per cent simply reported their physical symptoms, attaching no emotional overtones to them whatsoever. But the remaining 29 per cent did respond in an apparently emotional fashion. The really interesting thing here was that the great majority of patients described their feelings in a way that Maranon described as 'cold' or 'as if' emotions.

Why did most of Maranon's patients fail to experience any true emotion in spite of their aroused state? Presumably because there was a clear and unequivocal reason for it, namely the drug they had been given. Because they could neatly account for their high level of arousal in non-emotional terms, they felt no emotional state.

Schachter and Singer argued that much the same state of physiological arousal was associated with all kinds of emotional experience: 'Precisely the same state of physiological arousal could be labelled "joy" or "fury" or "jealousy" or any of a great diversity of emotional labels depending on the cognitive aspects of the situation.' That is, the great variety of emotions we experience are the result of changes in the way we interpret our aroused state.

If it is true that there is very great flexibility in the way in which we apply emotional labels to aroused states, then we are likely to make mistakes, in other words apply them incorrectly, from time to time. For example, many women experience an increase in irritability and tension just before their periods. Often they attribute this to external causes, to other people being awkward or irritating, rather than to their monthly cycle.

The 'Romeo and Juliet effect' is another example of misattribution of emotions. The more parental interference young people in love are confronted with, the greater the amount of romantic love they tend to experience. It may be that the attitudes of the parents create a state of unpleasant arousal which is then re-labelled romantic attrac-tion. Or, to put it another way, adrenalin makes the heart grow fonder.

Schachter and Singer carried out quite a complicated experiment to investigate some of these ideas. Their basic prediction was fairly simple and straightforward: for genuine emotion to be experienced, there must be a state of arousal, and it must be interpreted in emotional terms. If either ingredient is lacking, no emotion will be experienced.

They decided to test their prediction by varying both the amount of arousal that was experienced, and the way in which the arousal was interpreted. All the participants were told that the experiment was designed to find out how the vitamin compound Suproxin affects vision. Although they were told that they had been injected with this vitamin compound, they actually received either adrenalin (which increases physiological arousal) or a saline solution placebo (which has no effect on arousal).

The various groups of participants were told different stories about the side-effects of the drug. Those receiving adrenalin were either correctly informed about the effects of the drug, misinformed ('Your feet will feel numb, you will have an itching sensation over parts of your body, and you may get a slight headache'), or kept in ignorance, being told merely that the injection was mild and harmless and would have no side-effects. Those given the placebo were also told that the drug would have no side-effects.

After they had received the injection, all the participants were told that the vision tests would begin in 20 minutes, so as to allow time for the Suproxin to get into the bloodstream. During that time, each individual was placed in a situation designed to produce either euphoria or anger.

In the euphoria situation, the participant and a confederate of the experimenter waited together. The confederate doodled on a notepad, threw crumpled pieces of paper at the waste-paper basket in a mock 'basketball game', made and flew a paper plane, made a catapult out of a rubber band and used it to shoot bits of paper at a tower of manila folders, and played with a hula hoop. The general idea was that the participant would respond to the boisterous enthusiasm of the confederate by becoming happy or euphoric (it has since been pointed out that other emotions might be aroused by such behaviour, including curiosity, disgust and extreme annoyance!).

In the anger condition, the participant and the confederate spent the 20 minutes filling in question-naires which became increasingly personal and insulting, finishing up with the question: 'With how many men (other than your father) has your mother had extra-marital relationships?' The confederate became progressively more annoyed and agitated, and eventually tore up his question-naire, screwed up the pieces and flung them on the floor, saying, 'I'm not wasting any more time on this. I'm getting my books and leaving.'

How much emotion should the various groups have shown in both these conditions? According to Schachter and Singer, those given adrenalin and told about its arousing effects should not have experienced much emotion; they would interpret the arousal they felt as stemming from the drug rather than from their reaction to the behaviour of the confederate ('I feel this way because I have just received an injection of adrenalin').

Those given the innocuous placebo should also have experienced relatively little emotion: they would not be in an aroused state because they had not received an arousing drug. In contrast, those given adrenalin and misinformed about its effects should be highly aroused, and would be unlikely to interpret their arousal as due to the drug; they would presumably tend to attribute their aroused state (anger or euphoria) to the behaviour of the confederate. A similar prediction followed for those given adrenalin and told it would have no side-effects; they should be aroused and would account for their arousal in emotional terms.

In view of the fact that Schachter and Singer's experiment constitutes one of the most celebrated investigations of emotion, the striking thing about their findings was that some of them did not accord too well with their predictions. The basic problem was that those who had been given the placebo, and were therefore supposed to be relatively unaroused and unemotional, actually experienced quite a lot of emotion. A further experiment designed to probe this particular problem will be considered in a moment. However, there was reasonable evidence that states of high arousal are labelled in different ways in different circumstances. Of the people injected with adrenalin, it was only those who were told precisely what they would feel, and why, who remained relatively unmoved by the anger- and euphoria-provoking situations, presumably because they believed that the drug rather than the situation was producing the arousal.

It is possible that those given the placebo rather than adrenalin did, in fact, become aroused as a result of being exposed to the confederate, in which case, of course, the assumption that they were relatively unaroused was false. Schachter and Singer argued that the way to prevent people becoming aroused was to give them a drug that actually *reduces* arousal rather than a placebo. The drug they chose for this purpose was the depressant chlorpromazine. Everyone was told that they would receive Suproxin, a highly concentrated vitamin C derivative with no side-effects, but they were actually injected either with chlorpromazine, the placebo or the arousing drug adrenalin. They then watched a 15-minute excerpt from a Jack Carson film called *The Good Humour Man* involving a slapstick chase scene.

Since everyone was expected to attribute any feelings of arousal to the same source, namely the film, the prediction was that the amount of emotion experienced would depend mainly on the amount of arousal caused by the injections given. Thus, the adrenalin-injected people should have been most aroused and most amused, and the chlorpromazine-injected people least aroused and amused.

Reactions to the film were assessed by asking the participants how enjoyable and funny they had found the film and by observing the number of smiles, grins, laughs and belly laughs during the showing of the film. Exactly as predicted, those injected with adrenalin found the film funniest and showed most signs of overt amusement, and those injected with chlorpromazine were the least amused by the film. The placebo-injected participants tended to react to the film with quiet amusement, whereas several of the adrenalin-injected participants reacted with belly laughs. Interestingly, some of those injected with adrenalin were aware of a discrepancy between their actual behaviour and their impressions of the film. For example, one participant said: 'I just couldn't understand why I was laughing during the movie. Usually, I hate Jack Carson and this kind of nonsense.'

MORE QUESTIONS

In the 30 years or so since this seminal work, much has been said both for and against Schachter and Singer's viewpoint. Some of the most critical points were made by Gary Marshall and Philip Zimbardo[2] of Stanford University, who did a follow-up study in 1979. They noted that, despite the obvious importance of the Schachter and Singer study and the unclear nature of some of their results, no one had attempted to replicate it in the intervening 20 years. In their study, Marshall and Zimbardo used only the euphoria situation, because the Stanford University Medical School Human Subjects Committee argued that it was unethical to induce anger in unsuspecting people.

In essence, Marshall and Zimbardo found that the injection of adrenalin failed to make the participants more happy or euphoric than those receiving the placebo. They were disappointed by these results, and tried larger doses of adrenalin. People injected with these larger doses and then exposed to the euphoric confederate actually reported that they were unhappier than the other groups, which is precisely the opposite of what Schachter and Singer would have predicted.

Why didn't the high level of arousal produced by adrenalin make the participants more receptive to a pleasant state of emotion? It may be that unexplained arousal is normally regarded as

Everyone in this crowd is exposed to the same stimulus – a football game – but levels of excitement vary, depending on identification with the players. Adrenalin alone, it seems, it not enough for us to feel real excitement.

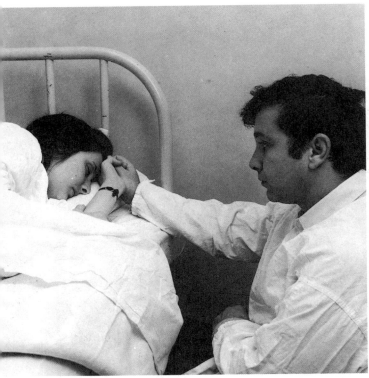

In real life, feelings often lie too deep for words. Few of our feelings are as simple as 'fear', 'joy', 'anger', and so on, nor is a lack of emotion on the surface any guide to what is going on underneath. This man, at his wife's bedside, is probably struggling with a mixture of emotions – love, sympathy, worry, perhaps guilt and anger too.

unpleasant. After all, substantial levels of physiological arousal are far more often associated with negative emotional experiences than with positive ones, the universal exception being sexual excitement.

Even when the adrenalin-injected participants behaved in a mildly euphoric way, it was still something of a pretence. As one participant said: 'It's like being at a party when everyone is clearly having a good time and you have a headache or feel depressed for some unknown reason. You don't want to rain on their parade. You might even laugh and try to join in, but you don't really feel happy.'

Schachter and Singer hypothesized that all emotional states involve the same churned-up physiological state. Other psychologists, however, have wondered whether things are really that simple. For example, Daniel Funkenstein found some support for the idea that anxiety is associated with the production of adrenalin within the body, with noradrenalin (norepinephrine) release being associated with anger or aggression. Some fairly fanciful support for this notion comes in the finding that predatory species of animals such as lions and tigers produce more noradrenalin than non-predatory species such as deer and sheep. But how does this relate to human emotional states?

Lennart Levi tested Funkenstein's idea in a study in which he asked people to watch four films designed to elicit different emotional reactions: *Paths of Glory* (an early Stanley Kubrick film about a First World War episode in which several French enlisted men were accused of cowardice, court-martialled and shot, in order to cover up the bungling of an incompetent general); *Charley's Aunt* (a comedy in which the main male character capers about in woman's clothing to avoid the consequences of some supposed breach of family propriety); *Mask of Satan* (a horror film in which there are several gruesome killings); and a neutral film of nature scenes.

Those watching the films experienced anger while watching *Paths of Glory*, amusement during *Charley's Aunt*, and fear during *Mask of Satan*—different emotional reactions in each case. It was found that adrenalin flow increased to a similar extent during all three of these films, but not during the neutral film. This of course agrees with Schachter and Singer's notion that all emotional experiences have a common underlying physiological basis. (Unfortunately for Funkenstein's own theory, noradrenalin flow did not significantly increase during *Paths of Glory*, but it did increase during *Mask of Satan*.)

A final important way of assessing the value of Schachter and Singer's contribution to the study of emotion is to consider the emotional life of paraplegics and quadriplegics, whose spinal cord injuries are so severe that they have little or no direct experience of physiological arousal. If Schachter and Singer's theory is right, they should lead relatively unemotional lives, and this does indeed seem to be the case. Although they sometimes behave in an apparently emotional way, they tend not to feel very emotional: 'Sometimes I act angry when I see some injustice. I yell and cuss and raise hell . . . but it just doesn't have the heat to it that it used to. It's a mental kind of anger'.

EXCITEMENT MAKES THE HEART GROW FONDER

On the face of it, romantic love is an odd topic to try to study within the walls of the psychology laboratory. However, some bold researchers have done just that. The usual idea has been that romantic love, or at least sexual attraction, can be produced in the laboratory, provided those taking part in the experiment are aroused and the situation enables them to interpret their state in sexual terms.

Stuart Valins took this argument one step further. He wondered whether it was really necessary for people to be physiologically aroused; perhaps if they mistakenly believed themselves to be aroused, that would prove sufficient for them to experience pleasant feelings of a sexual nature.

Valins asked a number of young men to look at slides of semi-nude women taken from the pages of *Playboy* magazine. While they were performing this arduous task, they listened to what they were told was an amplified version of their heartbeat. In fact the heartbeat was completely faked; it remained steady for some of the slides, but speeded up or slowed down for others at random. The semi-nudes associated with the apparent increase in heart rate were rated as the most attractive and appealing, followed by those associated with the decreased heart rate, and then those for whom the heart rate had remained steady. When the men were looking at a slide that apparently caused their heartbeat to speed up, they tended to look at the slide more closely, obviously in an attempt to justify their fast heartbeat by magnifying the girl's positive characteristics.

Valins apparently demonstrated that sexual attraction can be enhanced by an imaginary increase or change in arousal. However, it has subsequently been found that fake changes in heart rate when watching female nudes trigger off genuine changes in heart rate, so that actual changes in arousal may be necessary to increase sexual attraction. It has also been found that men watching slides of male nudes were not affected emotionally by fake heart rate increases. They merely found the whole experiment distasteful and offensive.

Does physical excitement make the heart grow fonder? These youngsters will probably think of each other as closer buddies for having experienced the excitement of the helter-skelter together.

Joanne Cantor showed excerpts from an erotic film called *Naked Under Leather* to young men either immediately after or five minutes after they had performed vigorous physical exercise (bicycle pedalling). She found that those who viewed the film five minutes after exercise, rather than immediately afterwards, were more sexually aroused by it. Immediately after exercise, people are physically aroused but attribute arousal to the after-effects of exercise. A few minutes later, however, people are still aroused but do not realize that they are. In Cantor's experiment this residual arousal combined with the arousal produced by watching the film led to an augmented erotic response to the film. Thus, if you take up jogging, you may find yourself giving your partner the glad eye after your daily run!

This research showed that arousal produced by one aspect of the environment (in this case exercise) can sometimes be attributed to a completely different aspect of the environment (in this case an erotic film). The notion that sexual attraction can be increased by arousal from an irrelevant source has a long history. In classical times, a Roman expert on love recommended that would-be lovers should take their ladies to gladiatorial contests, presumably on the principle that the ladies would misattribute the arousal and excitement generated by the events in the arena to their male companions and fall in love with them.

Many authorities have even suggested that the arousal produced by unpleasant emotions such as fear, anger and frustration can often fuel the flames of desire. In the words of Sigmund Freud: 'Some obstacle is necessary to swell the tide of libido (sexual energy) to its height.' The same thought was expressed less bluntly by the Greek writer Vassilikos: 'Once upon a time there was a little fish who was a bird from the waist up and who was madly in love with a little bird who was a fish from the waist up. So the Fish-Bird kept saying to the Bird-Fish: "Oh, why were we created so that we can never live together? You in the wind and I in the wave. What a pity for both of us." And the Bird-Fish would answer: "No, what luck for both of us. This way we'll always be in love because we'll always be separated".'

Donald Dutton and Arthur Aron of the University of British Columbia wondered whether the emotion of fear could be used to enhance sexual responsiveness. Men on their own were approached either by an attractive female interviewer or by a male interviewer. The interview took place either on a sturdy bridge overlooking a 10-ft drop, or on a 5-ft wide, 450-ft long suspension bridge which tilted, swayed and wobbled rather alarmingly, creating the impression that one might easily fall 230 ft to the rocks and shallow rapids below. It was assumed, with some justification, that the suspension bridge would create more fear than the other bridge. The interviewer asked each man to invent a story based on a picture, and found the greatest number of sexually toned responses

The girl who is the focus of attention in this picture clearly feels embarrassed at having her chest written on! In this case it is more likely that interpretation of the situation triggered arousal than vice versa.

when the interviewer was female and the interview took place on the fear-provoking suspension bridge. The female interviewer also gave each participant her phone number and the men on the suspension bridge showed more sexual interest in her than the men on the sturdy bridge, because more of them telephoned her afterwards.

Dutton and Aron may have succeeded in showing that arousal associated with fear can be misperceived as sexual attraction, but it seems a little far-fetched to suggest that the men on the swaying bridge really interpreted their sweaty palms and trembling legs as due to the irresistible charms of the female interviewer. It is more likely that she helped to reduce their fear by distracting them from their dangerous situation, and that this is why they responded to her so positively. Alternatively, she may have been perceived as more daring or thrill-seeking in the more fear-inducing situation, and the male participants assumed or hoped that this would also be true of her sexual behaviour.

CLINICAL IMPLICATIONS

Most, if not all, forms of mental illness involve a considerable amount of emotional disturbance. If there is any validity to the theoretical approach to emotion pioneered by Schachter and Singer, then it ought to have some implications for clinical treatment. Some work has already been carried out, and some intriguing results have been obtained.

Imagine that you are faced with the problem of treating people suffering from chronic insomnia, who report taking almost an hour to get to sleep every night. You have in your possession some sugar pill placebos, which are entirely innocuous. Should you tell the insomniacs that these pills will increase their level of arousal or that they will decrease arousal and help to relax them? One's initial reaction would be to tell the insomniacs that the 'drug' will relax them.

However, let us assume that the insomniac's problem is that he tends to go to bed in a state of arousal, and that he associates that arousal with emotionally-toned thoughts. If he then takes a 'drug' that allegedly reduces arousal but is actually a placebo, he is likely to start thinking: 'If I feel as I do now, when a drug is operating to lower my arousal, then I must be very aroused indeed.' In contrast, if he takes a placebo which he believes to be capable of producing arousal symptoms, he may very well attribute most of his arousal to the drug and only a small proportion of his arousal to his worries and problems.

Paradoxically, then, insomniacs might worry more and take longer to get to sleep when given a 'relaxing' drug than when given an 'arousing' drug, and this is what researchers found. Insomniacs given the 'arousing' placebo got to sleep at least 20 per cent faster than previously, whereas those taking the 'relaxing' placebo took over 40 per cent longer than usual to get to sleep.

Why were the results exactly the opposite of those usually achieved with placebos? Part of the answer may be that insomniacs are all too familiar with their own symptoms and therefore know that their overall state of arousal at bedtime is neither much greater nor much less than usual. If they believe that the 'drug' lowers or raises arousal level, as the case may be, they can only suppose that the amount of emotion-generated arousal must be more, or less, than usual in order to achieve the same result.

The same technique has been applied to pain tolerance. People who were led to believe that their experience of pain was due to a placebo (because they were told it would cause heart pounding, increased rate of breathing, and hand tremors) were able on average to tolerate 1,450 microamperes of electric shock, whereas those who had no reason to attribute pain to the placebo could tolerate only 350 microamperes. The former group also reported less experience of pain. Strange though it may sound, a visit to the dentist might be less unpleasant if the dentist gave you a 'drug' which you thought would cause sweating, hand clenching and a feeling of blind panic! You would blame the 'drug', not his treatment.

Rather than allowing people to become aroused and then trying to persuade them to give a non-emotional label to their arousal, it might be easier to prevent the arousal occurring in the first place. Richard Lazarus of the University of California adopted the latter approach. The stimuli he used were anxiety-provoking films. In one film, adolescent boys had their penises deeply cut in a Stone Age ritual. In another, a board is caught in a circular saw and rammed with tremendous force through the body of a worker, who dies writhing on the floor.

Most people responded to these films with considerable arousal and anxiety. However, if they are asked to consider the Stone Age ritual from the perspective of an anthropologist watching strange customs, and to remember that the people shown in the factory accident are actors, there is a marked reduction in arousal and anxiety. Similarly, one

Ironically, if we are told that something will hurt, we experience less pain if we think the pain is due to something other than the thing actually causing the pain.

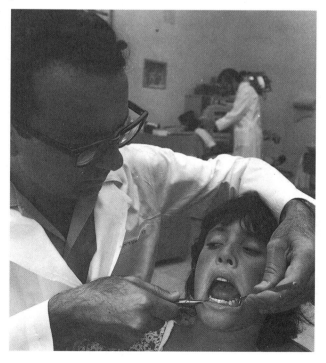

might be frightened by strange noises in the night, until one discovers that the neighbour's cat is the culprit. Whenever possible, it seems, we try to cope with unpleasant situations by giving them a non-emotional interpretation.

CONCLUSIONS

In broad terms, Schachter and Singer were correct in assuming that the most important ingredients in producing an emotional experience are a state of physiological arousal and an emotional interpretation of the reasons why the arousal has occurred. They were also right in saying that a similar state of physiological arousal seems to be involved in several quite different subjective states.

The theory implies that people frequently misperceive the cause of their stirred-up physical state, and this may help in the treatment of some clinical patients. The theory also suggests explanations for some of the puzzling aspects of romantic love, particularly the way in which unpleasant emotions such as fear and anger can amplify romantic ardour.

However, it would be fair to say that Schachter and Singer adopted an over-simplified view, a view which requires certain modifications and extensions. They focused on the notion that a state of arousal triggers off an interpretation of that state. But it is equally true to say, as Lazarus does, that the way in which a situation is interpreted affects the level of arousal.

D

PERCEPTION AND PROBLEM-SOLVING

Psychologists attempting to understand how people process information and cope with situations often resort to the use of analogies. Some of Sigmund Freud's theories, for example, imply that human 'drives', including the sexual drive, operate on a simple hydraulic principle. Using the analogy of a water tank, if one lowers the water level, the pressure on the sides of the tank is reduced; similarly by indulging in sexual activity (or some other energy-releasing activity) the strength of the sexual forces (or other pent-up forces of the Id) can be reduced to a tolerable level.

Another favourite analogy in recent years has been between the human brain and the data-processing system of computers. Computers can store information for long periods of time, a capacity which mirrors long-term memory. Computers sometimes hold information only briefly while they perform various operations on it, a capacity which is similar to our short-term memory. Computers also have executive programmes which direct the sequencing of processing operations, and it has been argued that in human beings conscious attention serves the same function.

The approach we propose to adopt is rather different. Our basic assumption is that the best way of trying to understand our flexible information-processing system is to consider some of the major situations in which the system seems unable to cope with the demands placed on it.

Under normal circumstances, we are quite proficient at attending to important information in our environment while ignoring the trivial and the non-essential. This is not always the case, however. If a very important event occurs suddenly and unexpectedly, we do not always manage to notice vital details about it. Such failures of observation are especially unfortunate when they occur while a crime is being committed. Chapter 16 is about eyewitness testimony, and deals with the difficulty witnesses have in reconstructing the details of crimes. The inaccuracies of eyewitness reports have been well documented in the media; here we consider why these errors occur, and what can be done to prevent them.

As overworked housewives and harassed business executives are well aware, it is often impossible to do two or more things at once. In Chapter 17, we show that this is because our powers of attention are limited. But there are ways in which we can overcome the narrowness of our attention, several of which are discussed in Chapter 18.

One of the most obvious weaknesses of our information-processing system is our inability to remember some of the things we want to remember. Students taking examinations, housewives shopping in supermarkets and college professors trying to track down elusive references have all wished that they had been blessed with a better memory system. The whole question of forgetting (and what to do about it) is dealt with in Chapter 18. It may come as a relief to know that being blessed with perfect and total recall is no blessing at all!

Most people like to behave in ways that are consistent with their attitudes and beliefs. However, there is often strong conflict between what people do and what they think—for example smokers continue smoking although they know that smoking can give them lung cancer. Such conflicts can be upsetting and difficult to resolve, producing what American psychologist Leon Festinger calls 'cognitive dissonance'. He has shown very clearly that people in a state of cognitive dissonance often experience bizarre and unpredictable attitude changes. His work in this field is discussed in Chapter 19.

The message implicit in all the chapters in this Section is that although we are generally successful at coping with our environment, we are fallible and in some circumstances find it extremely difficult to make sense of our world. However, gaining an understanding of our cognitive limitations is the first step towards overcoming them.

Chapter 16
EYEWITNESS TESTIMONY

One of the earliest attempts to step outside the narrow confines of the laboratory in the pursuit of psychological knowledge was made shortly before the turn of the century by a leading German psychologist called Hugo Munsterberg. He was interested in the relevance of psychology to the presentation of evidence in court and it was his work which first revealed that eyewitness testimony is often very unreliable. Munsterberg was worried that innocent people might be being imprisoned solely on the basis of what one or more witnesses said they remembered, but might have remembered wrong.

Several cases of apparently mistaken identity were considered by the recent British television series *Rough Justice*. In some of these cases it was possible to demonstrate beyond a shadow of a doubt that innocent individuals had been put behind bars because of inaccurate eyewitness testimony.

Somewhat surprisingly in view of the valuable work that has been done, the fruits of psychologists' endeavours to unravel the complexities of eyewitness testimony and its reliability have had very little impact on the admissibility of evidence. We believe that psychologists have a valuable contribution to make. Nevertheless, the 1976 Devlin Report on Evidence of Identification in Criminal Cases, which considered whether studies in psychology threw any light on such problems, said: 'It has been represented to us that a gap exists between academic research into the powers of the human mind and the practical requirements of courts of law and the stage seems not yet to have been reached at which the conclusions of psychological research are sufficiently widely accepted or tailored to the needs of the judicial process to become the basis for procedural change.' Even today the legal system continues to endorse the sentiments expressed in the Devlin Report.

THE ACTIVE MEMORY
Let us consider the nature of the processes of perception and memory which are the basis for eyewitness testimony. It is commonly thought that perception and memory are copying processes, in other words that the human brain handles the wealth of sensory information reaching it from the external world in a similar way to tape-recorders and cine cameras, which provide semi-permanent records of sounds and visual events. So failure on the part of a witness to remember what happened can be put down to a lack of effort or to unwilling-

ness. It is probably not an exaggeration to say that that is the view of many, if not most, of those in the legal profession.

However, most psychologists feel that it is very misleading to regard perception and memory as being straightforward copies of the world outside. They prefer to regard perception as an active and constructive process, depending not only on information arriving from the external world but also on personal attitudes, beliefs and motives.

The most obvious implication of this theory is that there will often be systematic, though unconscious, distortions in perception. At an informal level, the notion that people see what they want to see rather than what actually happens can be confirmed any Saturday afternoon at a football game. The award of a penalty to one team is seen as fair and reasonable by that team's supporters, but as outrageous by the other team's supporters. The referee is either seen as an excellent judge of the game or as someone of dubious parentage in urgent need of a white stick!

KEY EXPERIMENT: DISTORTING THE EVIDENCE
Elizabeth Loftus and John Palmer [1] of the University of Washington wondered whether the memory of eyewitnesses might be similarly susceptible to distortion by information encountered after an accident or crime. To explore whether this was in fact the case, they carried out two experiments. In the first, participants were shown seven different films, each showing a traffic accident, and were then asked to answer a series of questions about each accident. Those who were asked the question 'About how fast were the cars going when they smashed into each other?' consistently gave higher estimates of their speed than those asked to answer the same question, only with the word 'smashed' replaced by 'collided', 'bumped', 'contacted' or 'hit'. Indeed, the average estimated speed was almost 10 mph higher when 'smashed' was used than when 'contacted' was used. The *actual* speed at which the cars were travelling was almost irrelevant to estimates of speed. The average estimate was 38 mph when the cars collided at 40 mph, and 38 mph when they collided at 20 mph!

These findings clearly suggest that our memory for events is relatively fragile and fairly susceptible to distortion. Even stronger evidence was obtained in the second experiment, in which participants watched a short film of a multiple car accident. In this film, the first car made a right hand

This street scene is full of memorable events.
Memorize as many of them as you can in 60 seconds,
then turn to page 162.

turn to enter the main stream of traffic, causing cars in the oncoming lane to stop suddenly with the result that five cars were involved in bumper-to-bumper collisions. At the end of the film the participants answered a series of questions about the accident. One of the questions was either 'About how fast were the cars going when they smashed into each other?' or 'About how fast were the cars going when they hit each other?' As in the previous experiment, the average estimate of speed was greater for those interrogated with 'smashed' than for those questioned with 'hit'.

One week later, all the participants returned and answered a series of questions about the same accident, but without viewing the film again. One of the questions asked was 'Did you see any broken glass?' Of those who had answered the question about cars 'smashing' into each other the week before, 32 per cent said they had seen broken glass; only 14 per cent of those who had answered the question about cars merely 'hitting' each other said they saw broken glass. Since there was, in fact, no broken glass in the accident, it appears that fairly subtle wording of questions can lead eyewitnesses to 'remember' details that did not actually occur.

INFORMATION OVERLAY

How did Loftus and Palmer account for their findings? Basically, they argued, two kinds of information go into our memory when we witness a complex event like an accident or a crime. The first is information obtained from perception of the original event, and the second is external information

supplied subsequently. As time passes, information from these two sources is integrated in such a way that it is not possible to say from which source any specific detail is recalled. All we have is one homogeneous 'memory'.

Of course, those involved in the legal process are aware of some of the difficulties inherent in the way in which questions to eyewitnesses are worded. Questions which either by their form or their content suggest to the witness what answer is desired, or 'lead' him to that desired answer, are called 'leading questions' in the courtroom. Most countries have rules designed to exclude such questions. In the United States, for example, these are enshrined in the Supreme Court Reporter of 1973.

But in spite of such precautions, there is still the obvious danger that a witness's fragile memories of an event will be systematically distorted either by conversations with other witnesses or by police interrogation long before the start of court proceedings. Apparently trivial changes in the wording of questions can exert considerable influence. Take, for example, another memory experiment conducted by Elizabeth Loftus and Guido Zanni. This time the film showed a minor collision between a man backing out of a narrow space in a supermarket car park and a woman pedestrian carrying a large bag of groceries. The observers were then asked questions about items that were not in the film. Those who were asked questions which included the definite article ('Did you see the bottle?') were more than three times as likely to say they saw the item as observers asked the same questions with the indefinite article ('Did you see a bottle?').

Wet streets, a speeding car, dazzling headlights . . .
Unless our attention is especially alerted, we retain a
general impression of events, but few useful details.

TRANSFERRING ONE MEMORY TO ANOTHER

In further research, Elizabeth Loftus studied what is known as 'unconscious transference'. This occurs when a person seen committing one act is confused with a person seen committing another act. In one real-life case, a ticket clerk at a railway station was robbed at gun-point. He subsequently identified a sailor in a line-up as the criminal, but the sailor had a watertight alibi. It turned out later that the sailor had bought tickets from the man on three separate occasions prior to the robbery. In other words, the ticket clerk mistakenly assumed that the familiarity of the sailor's face related back to the robbery, when in fact it related back to the three ticket-purchasing occasions.

In one particular experiment on unconscious transference, Loftus presented participants with a tape-recorded narrative about six college students, each student being introduced by a slide at the appropriate point in the story. The narrative went like this: 'Steve Kent picked up a heavy paperweight and threw it at Fisher, hitting him on the back of the head; one of the onlookers was Robert Dirks.' Dirks was shown wearing a small brown hat. Approximately one hour later, the participants in the experiment were either asked 'After the guy with the hat threw the paperweight at Fisher, did he run away?' or the same question with the words 'with the hat' omitted.

Three days later, the participants tried to pick out the culprit from among the slides of the six students. Fifty-eight per cent of those who had been asked the leading question (implying that the person with the hat committed the deed) chose the real culprit (Steve Kent); 24 per cent chose the man with the hat. Eighty per cent of those who had been asked the straightforward question made a correct identification, and only 6 per cent chose the man with the hat. The implication of this experiment is alarming: suggestive questions can quite easily induce a witness to accuse an innocent person of something he or she didn't do.

AT THE SCENE OF THE CRIME

The fact that perception of a complex event such as a crime can be affected by the past knowledge and experience of witnesses, as well as their attitudes, needs, beliefs and expectations, was clearly demonstrated in the 1920s by Gordon Allport of Harvard University. All he did was to ask a number of people to take a brief look at a drawing of several people on an underground train. The drawing included a black man and a white man standing close to each other. In spite of the fact that it was the white man who was holding the cut-throat razor, almost 50 per cent of Allport's observers said they saw the black man holding the razor. At the time the razor was regarded by many white Americans as a stereotyped symbol of black violence. Presumably it was this common prejudice which caused the distorted recollection of the event.

In most violent incidents, people are more concerned with fight or flight than with noting the particulars of their attackers. Fear tends to scramble our recall of events.

The clear message from the Allport study was that people tend to see what they expect to see. This has now been demonstrated many times. Two prominent American researchers, Jerome S. Bruner and Leo Postman of Harvard University, showed observers a display of playing cards for a few seconds, and then asked them to report the number of aces of spades they thought they had seen. Most people said they saw three aces of spades. In fact, there were five, but two of them were coloured red. Once again, past experience distorted the process of perception.

Apart from the biasing effects of past knowledge and prejudice, are there any other reasons for assuming that eyewitnesses often misperceive events? At first glance, it would appear not. After all, people with amazingly good memories for visual information often turn up in laboratory studies. In one American study, it was found that observers were able to recognize 90 per cent of a huge set of 2,500 photographs of unfamiliar paintings, scenes and events presented for a few seconds each. Even when 10,000 photographs were presented, there was still correct identification 86 per cent of the time.

But in contrast to these laboratory studies, recollection of staged events in which actors pretend to steal purses, attack each other and so on, is sometimes extremely poor. Why is there such a large difference in the two sets of findings? The answer is that the circumstances are entirely different. Observers in a laboratory know what to look for, they know where the visual information will be presented, and they know when it will be presented. Eyewitnesses to a crime are taken by surprise, are exposed to a complicated series of events, and are often quite naturally more concerned about their own safety than about memorizing the number-plate of the robbers' getaway vehicle.

A point that is often overlooked is that people tend to pay more attention to those aspects of an event or another person which they find interest-

None of the witnesses of this multiple crash was able to give a full picture of what happened. Many hours of careful questioning were necessary before the sequence of events could be pieced together.

ing. In everyday life, women always notice if another woman is wearing clothes which do not match or if she is wearing false eyelashes, whereas men notice that Mr Smith along the road has bought himself a new car or a lawn-mower. Peter Powers of the University of Washington investigated this phenomenon. Observers watched slides showing a man and a woman walking through a car park and spotting two people apparently fighting each other. The man rushes in to stop the fight while the woman goes off to telephone for help. Female observers were more accurate than male observers in recalling the description and actions of the female main character, whereas male observers were more accurate in recalling information about the main male character and about a nearby car.

The effect of fear on memory has been researched by examining eyewitness reports noted down by policemen within minutes of their arrival on the scene. The typical report conveys a general impression of the assailant, but lacks specific features such as colour of hair or eyes. In general terms, less complete descriptions are obtained in connection with the more fear-provoking crimes (rape, assault) than with other crimes (robbery). Irrespective of the type of crime, uninjured victims give more complete descriptions of their assailant(s) than injured victims.

It is often said that the members of a different race 'all look the same', and there is partial support for this assertion. White witnesses show much greater accuracy in identifying white faces than black faces. However, black witnesses show equal accuracy whether identifying black faces or white faces. It is also true, of course, that some races are

easy to remember because they are distinctive. Indeed, it is the unusual features of a face that we remember best.

It is plausible to assume that witnesses will pay less attention to trivial crimes than to those which are more serious. In one experiment witnesses saw an object being stolen; some believed it was worth about £1, others that it was worth aout £25. Fifty-six per cent of the witnesses who believed the object was worth £25 picked out the correct person from a six-person photo spread, compared with only 19 per cent of those who believed the object to be relatively cheap. However, witnesses who saw an expensive item being stolen showed worse recall of the various physical characteristics of the thief than people who thought they were witnessing the theft of the cheap item. When eyewitnesses believe that a serious crime is being committed, they pay attention to just one crucial visual aspect of the scene (i.e, the facial features of the criminal). Thus, an attempt to devalue all the testimony of a witness during cross-examination by demonstrating the fallibility of some of his recollections may be unfair.

MUGSHOTS AND LINE-UPS

The crucial test of eyewitness testimony is when the witness is confronted with the suspect, either 'live' in an identity parade or among a set of photographs or mugshots. It is important that the other people included in the line-up or set of photos should be broadly similar in appearance to the suspect. If it is generally agreed that the person who committed a crime was very tall and white, there is little point in having a line-up comprising a huge white man and several short black men.

There are some real-life examples of such bias. Consider the case of the militant black activist Angela Davis in the 1960s. A set of nine photographs used to check identification included three pictures of the defendant taken at an outdoor rally, two police mugshots of other women with their names displayed, a picture of a 55-year-old woman, and so on. Any witness could immediately rule out most of the nine pictures as ridiculous choices. The chances of selecting one of the pictures of Angela Davis was therefore at least 75 per cent!

Robert Buckhout has claimed that one kind of bias in the use of mugshots is the implicit assumption that the witness ought to be able to pick out the suspect. In other words there is social pressure to 'co-operate' with the police. Buckhout staged an assault on the California State University campus in which a distraught student 'attacked' a professor in front of 141 witnesses. Another person of the same age as the distraught student was present as a bystander. After the incident, the witnesses were asked to pick out the assailant from a set of six photographs; the unbiased photo spread used equivalent photos of all the suspects, whereas the biased photo spread had the assailant's photo at an angle to the others and with a different expression. The instructions to the witnesses were either unbiased ('Do you recognize any of the people in these photos?') or biased ('The culprit is among this set of photos').

Identification performance was affected by both kinds of bias. More witnesses picked out the culprit under biased than under unbiased conditions, and they were also more confident that they had selected the right person. The combination of biased photo spread and biased instructions led to over 60 per cent of the witnesses selecting the perpetrator. Only 40 per cent were correct in their identification under unbiased conditions.

It is obviously worrying that the way in which suspect identification is carried out can produce such large effects on the apparent accuracy with which eyewitnesses remember events. It is also worrying that 25 per cent of all the witnesses (including the attacked professor) mistakenly identified the innocent bystander whose picture was also included in the photo spread (Suspect No. 2) as the attacker.

In further research, Buckhout very clearly showed that witnesses are usually prepared to identify *someone*, perhaps because they feel they would be wasting everyone's time unless they did. Fifty-two students witnessed a live purse-snatching incident in a classroom and were then exposed to two different identity parades with five people in each. One line-up included the purse-snatcher and the other line-up included someone who looked like the purse-snatcher. Eighty per cent of the witnesses picked out a suspect, even though most of them were mistaken. Fourteen witnesses correctly identified the culprit in one line-up, but half of them rather spoiled things by going on to identify the person who merely resembled the culprit in the other line-up. Seven more witnesses only picked the look-alike, 18 selected an innocent person who didn't even look like the culprit, and three went so far as to pick out two innocent people, neither of whom resembled the culprit.

One of the difficulties with mugshot identification is that we tend to remember some kinds of information better than others. For example, all of us know what it is like to recognize someone but not be able to 'place' him or her. This typically happens when we normally see someone in just one setting, and then see him or her in a different setting. The TV star buying groceries or the company chairman prowling the red-light district of town provide examples of this phenomenon. In one experiment, students were presented with 25 photos of faces in one room, and with 25 more two hours later in another room radically different from the first. In a subsequent test, the faces were correctly recognized 96 per cent of the time, but most observers could not remember at better than chance level in which room they had seen the faces. This inability to remember the circumstances in which a face has been seen can be especially troublesome if the eyewitnesses to a crime have encountered any of the suspects in other circumstances.[2]

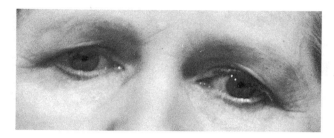

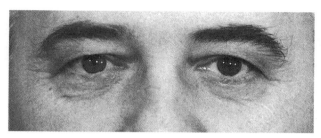

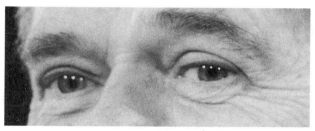

Have you seen these eyes before? Would you recognize their owners (see p. 161) if you saw them in your local supermarket? The chances of recognizing a wanted man or woman, only fleetingly seen at the scene of the cirme, in unsuspicious circumstances are fairly small.

The accuracy of mugshot identification is also affected if suspects look the way they looked at the time of the crime, In one British study, 91 per cent of faces were correctly recognized when there was no alteration between initial viewing and the identification test. However, correct recognitions dropped to 82 per cent when the pose and facial expression were changed, with a drastic decline to only 45 per cent correct when the faces were disguised by adding or removing beards or glasses or changing the hair style. Those criminals who invest in false beards and dark glasses obviously have an intuitive appreciation of some of the principles of psychology.

The police often use an identity parade in addition to mugshots to try to secure an identification. Very confusing things can happen when this is done. In one study, a staged crime was followed by the witnesses being shown a number of mugshots and then a 'live' line-up of suspects. The key finding was that anyone seen in a mugshot was more likely to be picked out at the line-up as the guilty party! The 'criminals' were selected by 65 per cent of the witnesses when seen in mugshots, but by only 51 per cent when seen only at the identity parade. Innocent people previously seen in mug-

TERRORIST ALERT

DO YOU RECOGNIZE THEM?

Saturday 10th October there was an explosion in Ebury Bridge Road which killed two people.

WERE YOU IN THIS AREA BETWEEN 5 a.m. AND 1 p.m.?

Portraits of police suspects seldom look anything like the real culprits. This is because our ability to describe a face, or fit together the different elements of a face, is much poorer than our ability to simply recognize a face.

EYEWITNESS TESTIMONY: FRAGILE BUT INDISPENSABLE

Many psychologists who have investigated eyewitness testimony and discovered its fallibility have said how dangerous it is for the courts to place much reliance on the recollections of witnesses. However, if we were to discount all eyewitness testimony, it would be impossible for an innocent defendant to prove an alibi.

Psychologists also tend to think—without having provided much evidence—that judges and jurors believe witnesses to be more reliable than they actually are. But in fact there are grounds for supposing that eyewitnesses are less fallible than psychologists believe them to be. In a number of ways, staged crimes differ importantly from real-life crimes. Participants in experiments nearly always know that the 'crime' was staged by the time they are given an identification test, and so may be relatively unconcerned about pointing the finger of suspicion at an innocent person. In real life, criminals often have distinctive characteristics, but in experimental studies researchers often go to great lengths to ensure that the 'criminal' has no outstanding features. Finally, while the police usually focus their attention on those witnesses who indicate that they might be able to make a positive identification, researchers nearly always ask *all* the eyewitnesses to attempt identification. All of these differences may mean that real-life witnesses are not quite so prone to make mistakes as has sometimes been thought.

While there is probably no way of making eyewitnesses pay more attention to important details at the time of criminal events, it may be possible to improve their ability to recall vital information by means of hypnosis. On one occasion the California Police Department used hypnosis on the 55-year-old driver of a school bus with 26 children on board which was hijacked. Interviewed by the police shortly after the crime, he remembered very little about the vans the three criminals had used to transport the children from the bus to an underground hideout. However, under hypnosis he managed to provide a vital clue in the form of the last five letters and digits of the licence-plate of one of the abduction vans.

Hypnosis has been used fairly extensively by the Israeli police. In one year they made 17 arrests on evidence obtained under hypnosis. It is not yet entirely clear why hypnosis should be so successful. However, under normal conditions we always devote some attention (known as 'spare processing capacity') to monitoring the environment for possible sources of important information. In contrast, under hypnosis people stop monitoring the environment, leaving their attention entirely free to concentrate on the task in hand (e.g. recollecting a criminal event).

The main focus of attempts to improve the value of eyewitness testimony ought to be to prevent recollections of the details of a crime being

shots were unjustly picked out 20 per cent of the time at the line-up, compared to 8 per cent of the time when not previously seen in mugshots. Obviously, a false identification rate of 20 per cent is far greater than ought to be allowed by any reasonable system of criminal justice.

A final potential problem is that of unintentional (or even intentional) bias caused by the actions of the police officer organizing the identity parade or mugshot identification procedure. If the policeman knows which person is the prime suspect, then he may communicate this knowledge by subtle changes in facial expression when the witness is looking at that person. This kind of bias has even been found to influence the behaviour of rats. Students who are told they have been given clever rats find their rats running mazes more rapidly than students who are told they have been given dull rats, even though the rats are allocated on an entirely random basis. It may well be that people are even more sensitive than rats to the cues provided by a human experimenter.

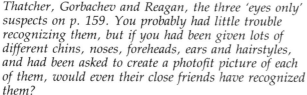

Thatcher, Gorbachev and Reagan, the three 'eyes only' suspects on p. 159. You probably had little trouble recognizing them, but if you had been given lots of different chins, noses, foreheads, ears and hairstyles, and had been asked to create a photofit picture of each of them, would even their close friends have recognized them?

systematically contaminated by subsequent occurrences. Police questioning should be entirely neutral, and should not suggest, directly or indirectly, that certain events actually occurred. When attempts are made at identification, whether by mugshots or by identity parade, the person directing proceedings should have no knowledge at all of the case; this will help to eliminate any bias. Witnesses should be told emphatically that they are only expected to identify someone provided they are confident that they have picked the right person; failure to identify anyone is entirely acceptable. Finally, either a videotape of the line-up or a set of the mugshots used should be made available to the defence lawyers so that checks for bias can be carried out.

CONCLUSIONS

The main reason for psychological investigation of eyewitness testimony is to clarify the conditions under which such testimony can be relied on. While many psychologists are inclined to discount the

value of witnesses' recollections altogether, they may have overstated the case. Eyewitness testimony *can* provide extremely useful information, but it is vital to recognize the fragile nature of the memory of a criminal event. Simple questioning of a witness, unless handled with extreme care, can produce profound distortions of memory and thus render his or her testimony almost valueless. Similarly, identification procedures must be conducted in an entirely unbiased way if further distortions of memory are not to occur. If the judicial system would listen to psychologists, and if all reasonable attempts were made to prevent distortions of memory, then eyewitness testimony could become a much more reliable source of evidence in court.

Without turning back to the cartoon on page 156, can you say what is different about this version of events? Give up? *Turn to page 256*

Chapter 17
DOING TWO THINGS AT ONCE

Everyday experience tells us that we are often surprisingly good at doing two things at once. For example, most people can hold a conversation while driving a car, or whistle a tune while they are working. On the other hand, there are some simple things which we find rather difficult to do simultaneously, such as tapping our head while rubbing our stomach. Unless one really concentrates, there is a tendency to start either rubbing the head or tapping the stomach, or both. And try asking a friend to multiply 24 by 17 while you are walking along together. Unless he is a mathematical wizard, he will probably have to stop walking so that he can devote all his attention to doing the mental arithmetic.

There are large differences between people in the extent to which they can pursue several activities at once. As a result of long practice, an individual can become a one-man band or a simultaneous translator, listening to a communication in one language while at the same time translating the meaning and speaking it out loud in another language. In general terms, we would expect highly intelligent people to be most proficient at doing two things at once. This was presumably what Lyndon B. Johnson, the former American President, had in mind when he said of Gerald Ford that he couldn't fart and chew gum at the same time. This comment has often been toned down in the re-telling with 'walk' replacing 'fart', but in either case it is an unflattering reflection on Ford's intelligence.

One the first systematic attempts to evaluate man's powers of attention was made nearly 40 years ago by an English researcher called Colin Cherry. His pioneering work has served as the basis of much subsequent interest and research.

KEY EXPERIMENT: THE 'COCKTAIL PARTY PROBLEM'

In the early 1950s, Colin Cherry was working in an American laboratory at the Massachusetts Institute of Technology. Despite the fact that he was engaged in psychological research, he was working in an electronics research laboratory, and his exciting discoveries were later published in a physics journal, thus exemplifying the multi-disciplinary nature of contemporary psychology.

Cherry was very interested in what he referred to as the 'cocktail party problem'. Cocktail parties can pose a number of problems, but the one that concerned Cherry was how people manage to follow just one conversation when there are several others going on within earshot[1].

One obvious possibility is that we make use of the fact that each conversation concentrates on a different topic, and we simply 'tune in' to one topic. Of course, at an actual cocktail party the various conversations come from different directions, and people's voices tend to be distinctive, so there are other possible reasons for this ability to attend selectively to what one person is saying. Cherry eliminated these other factors by playing his subjects a tape-recording of two different messages on the same tape spoken by the same person.

His subjects reported that it was extremely difficult to follow just one message while ignoring the other, and shut their eyes some of the time to help themselves concentrate. While they always worked out what the message was in the end, some of the phrases had to be played up to 20 times. In other words, focusing on meaning is *not* the way in which people at a cocktail party cope with the information overload to which they are exposed.

If they do not use meaning to tune into the right conversation, what do they use? Cherry argued that the direction from which the sought-for conversation was coming was probably vitally important. He tested this notion by equipping his listeners with headphones and feeding one spoken message into their left ear and a different message into their right. Although the two messages were spoken in the same voice, they experienced no difficulty in listening to either message at will while simply tuning out the other one. Thus the fact that the different speakers at a cocktail party are in different spatial locations may be of great importance in solving the cocktail party problem.

With a different message coming in at each ear, listeners were then instructed to repeat back one of the messages while they were listening (this is known as 'shadowing' the message). Their shadowing was slightly delayed behind the message, and they spoke in a very monotonous voice, although they were not aware of this.

Cherry's most important findings were obtained with this shadowing technique. He discovered, for example, that listeners showed an amazing degree of ignorance about the message that was not shadowed. When this message was in German, and they were asked about the language spoken on the unshadowed ear, they simply said that they had no idea what it was but assumed it was English. When the unshadowed message consisted of reversed speech, a few listeners reported that there was 'something queer about it,' but most claimed that it was normal English speech. Even when the unshadowed message was in English, the listeners could not recall *any* of the words or phrases in it immediately afterwards. However, when there was a change from a male to a female voice on the unshadowed message, or a pure tone was played, these changes were obvious enough to be detected.

In later work, it was found that listeners shadowing one message showed absolutely no retention of English words presented 35 times in a different message played at the same time. This was true even if the listeners were told to try to remember as much as possible of the unshadowed message.

What will the bartender remember next morning? The glamorous woman or the glittering conversation of her companion? He is very aware of her, but listening most attentively to him.

DIVIDED ATTENTION

Cherry's findings were widely regarded as demonstrating that we can really only attend to one thing at a time, since extremely little of the information played to the unshadowed ear appeared to leave any impression. However, it would not be true to say that the ear receiving the unshadowed message hears nothing. This was shown rather ingeniously by Zelniker, using what is known as 'delayed auditory feedback', in which one hears what one is saying with a delay of a fraction of a second. Many tape recorders allow you to examine the effects of delayed auditory feedback for yourself. Simply set the machine to record and speak into a microphone while wearing headphones. What usually happens is that speech is disrupted and you start to stutter.

As the listeners repeated the message heard in one ear, Zelniker tape-recorded their voices and played them back, with a short delay, to the other ear. If that ear were doing nothing, then there should have been no disruption of the shadowing. However, his listeners showed a certain amount of stuttering, enough to suggest that some attention was being paid to the unshadowed message.

Most psychologists argued that Cherry's findings could best be accounted for by assuming that human beings have only limited attentional capacity, and that the shadowing task is so demanding that it uses up virtually all of this capacity. While this certainly explains why so little of the unshadowed message is registered, things are actually more complicated than this simple theory might suggest.

An important additional factor which must be considered can be demonstrated quite straightforwardly. Try to form an auditory image (e.g. the sound of a train or a musical instrument) and then a visual image (e.g. a person's face, a favourite picture). The chances are that you found it useful to close your eyes while forming the visual image, but quite unnecessary to do so while forming the auditory image. Why is it easy to keep looking at our immediate surroundings while imagining a sound, but difficult to combine seeing with visual imagery? The answer seems to be that the more dissimilar two activities are, the easier it is to attend to them both at the same time, because it is more likely that different parts of the brain are involved.

Perhaps what Cherry really demonstrated is that we cannot attend to two extremely similar activities at the same time. What happens if shadowing an auditorily presented message is combined with the very different activity of looking at a series of pictures? Cherry tried this, and found that his subjects could remember some 90 per cent of the pictures afterwards. In other words, it is possible to attend to two activities at once, even when one of them is the complicated task of shadowing a message. Several of the participants in this experiment were surprised how easy it was to combine the two activities, although at first they felt a strong desire to look away or close their eyes while shadowing in order not to be distracted by the series of pictures.

It seems to be just as difficult to attend to two visual scenes at once as to two auditory messages. Paul Kolers of the University of Toronto devised and wore a headgear fitted with a half-silvered mirror which brought both the view ahead of him and the view behind him into his field of vision together. He reported that it was quite easy to concentrate on the front or the rear view—the other view simply disappeared. You can achieve the same effect by looking at a window from a lighted room at dusk. If the intensities of illumination are adjusted appropriately, you can choose whether to watch the outdoor scene or the reflection of the room, but you will find it is virtually impossible to look at both at once.

Ulric Neisser and Robert Becklen had a more systematic look at this phenomenon. They used two videotapes, and either presented one videotape superimposed on the other to both eyes of their subjects, or presented one videotape to each eye. In either case, it was extremely easy to follow one videotape or the other. It was easier when a different videotape was presented to each eye—the

unwanted videotape just disappeared. When both videotapes were presented to both eyes, the viewers were always aware that 'something else was going on'. When the viewers tried to follow both videotapes at the same time, however, they discovered it was virtually impossible. However, they did find it a little easier to cope when the videotapes were presented to both eyes.

PRACTICING DOING TWO THINGS AT ONCE

From the evidence discussed so far, it would seem improbable that someone could read a text and understand it while at the same time understanding words copied under dictation (if you doubt the difficulty, just try it). But Ulric Neisser and his co-workers Elizabeth Spelke and William Hirst decided to train two students, John and Diane, to perform those two activities together.

When John and Diane first attempted to read short stories by American, English and translated European writers while taking dictation, their reading speed dropped dramatically and the quality of their handwriting during dictation was much worse than normal. However, after some 30 hours of practice, they were able to combine reading and taking dictation very efficiently. At this stage, they seemed to be taking down the words in an unthinking way, for they often copied a list of related words (e.g. 'trolley, skates, truck, horse, airplane, tractor, car') without realizing that they belonged to the same category.

With several more hours of training, John and Diane learned to spot sets of related words in the dictation list and could even write down the categories to which the words belonged rather than the words themselves—all the while reading a text as rapidly and with as great a degree of comprehension as if they were reading it on its own.

The main message of this study is that the ability to attend to two activities at once can be improved dramatically as a result of extended practice. Altogether, John and Diane had over 80 hours of training each before reaching their final level of performance. This is borne out by the familiar example of car drivers who talk while driving, a feat that can safely be performed only by those with considerable experience!

Practice also has a profound effect on the task of shadowing one of two messages presented together, as in Colin Cherry's experiment. Beginners only manage to detect 4 per cent of the key items presented on the unshadowed message. But Neville Moray, who spent hundreds if not thousands of hours taking part in shadowing experiments, was able to detect no less than 83 per cent of them.

Extended practice also plays a major role in two recent striking demonstrations of the ability to perform two activities together. Highly skilled pianists were able to play unfamiliar music at sight while shadowing passages read aloud from a book, with

It takes years of daily practice to perform a feat like this. Although one would hate to ask it of him, this circus performer could probably recite nursery rhymes and continue juggling. Balance and coordination are handled by the cerebellum, speech by the cortex.

both the piano playing and the shadowing being done as well as they would normally be done on their own. In the second study, a skilled typist was able to type at about 100 words a minute while shadowing an auditorily presented passage or reciting nursery rhymes continuously.

The reason why practice of one activity (such as typing or piano playing) allows us to combine that activity readily with another activity is that less attention is required to perform a well-learned skill. Indeed, experienced typists are often not consciously aware of the order of the letters on the keyboard; it is as if the fingers 'know what to do' with only minimal guidance.

SPARE ATTENTION AND JOB PERFORMANCE

Suppose you were to go for a 10-mile run with an Olympic long-distance runner, and that he was kind enough to slow down to your pace so that you both took exactly the same amount of time to complete the distance. Would that mean that you were equally good runners? Obviously not, because you would be red in the face, sweating profusely and lying moaning on the ground afterwards, while he would be relatively unaffected by the run. In other words, although you would both have run at the same speed, you would have had to use more of your available resources than he would. If you were to attempt a repeat performance with both of you wearing very heavy army boots, the champion runner would be slowed down, but you might not be able to run at all.

It follows that it may be very misleading to assume that two people who do a task equally well have achieved that level of performance at equal 'cost' to themselves[2]. In the case of activities that require attention, some people may need to use much more of their attentional capacity than others to perform them adequately.

Ivor Brown of the Applied Psychology Research Unit in Cambridge, England, applied these ideas to a very practical problem. A large number of men were taking a course of instruction in bus driving with a view to passing the test for public service vehicles. The problem was that several of them failed this test, thus wasting their own and the bus company's time and money. It was not possible to use driving performance during training as a basis for weeding out potential failures, because there were no obvious differences in performance between those who subsequently failed or passed the test for public service vehicles.

Brown's ingenious solution to the problem was

to read out a set of eight digits every few seconds while the men were driving. Each set of digits was the same as the immediately preceding set except for one digit, and the task was to spot the digit that had changed. Those trainees who later passed the crucial test did this digit task almost twice as well as those who failed. In other words, the unsuccessful trainees had to put much more effort and attention into driving than the successful ones, and so they were unable to cope with additional demands made on them.

The same basic notion was applied to a comparison of two aircraft instrument display systems. The issue was whether it was preferable to have a conventional instrument panel or a pictorial display generated on a cathode-ray tube. It was difficult to decide because pilots doing flight simulations performed equally well with either display system. However, when they were also asked to read out digits appearing on a separate display, performance using the pictorial display remained high whereas errors increased with the conventional display. It being less attentionally demanding to read the pictorial display, this was the system that was chosen.

Another interesting example of using a second task to assess the attentional demands of the first occurred during test simulation of the X.15 rocket aircraft. The pilot handled all the various phases of the simulated flight satisfactorily, but it was argued that a more automated system would be less tiring. This was tested by requiring the pilot to turn off a periodically appearing light as well as performing the flight simulation. Performance on this extra task indicated that the more automated system demanded less of the pilot's attention, especially during the highly critical release from the parent aircraft,

Experienced keyboard operators have no difficulty shadowing messages relayed over headphones; it is as if their fingers are on automatic pilot.

Give a wide berth to this phone user! Even if the mouthpiece and pick-up are not held in the hand, radiophone conversations quite dramatically reduce concentration while driving. Passengers in the front seat do not seem to have such a dangerous effect!

Cleared for take-off, a commercial airline pilot makes a final instrument check. Instrument displays in aircraft today are designed to demand minimum attentional capacity at critical times.

after engine burn-out, and at the time of re-entry into the atmosphere. Findings such as these led to a number of improvements in the design of the X.15.

Attending to two activities at once may cause problems that have not yet been fully appreciated. One example is the increased number of radio-phones fitted to road vehicles, or the citizen's band radio transmitters which are common in the United States. Ivor Brown wondered whether a driver's judgment might be adversely affected by using a phone at the same time. In simulated driving tests he arranged a series of gaps that were either just large enough to allow a car through or were just too small, and found that drivers who were on the phone were much more willing to try to drive through gaps which were smaller than their cars. Indeed, 47 per cent of the time they attempted to get through a gap that was 3 inches less than the width of their cars!

It is obviously a good idea to give a wide berth to any driver you see talking on his radiophone. It seems rather strange that, in the United Kingdom at least, a driver is permitted to use a telephone but risks prosecution if he performs the much less attentionally demanding task of shaving with an electric razor.

At a more commonplace level, is it advisable even to listen to a car radio while driving? Most road users feel that listening to a car radio has a beneficial effect on driving in that it wards off monotony and

drowsiness. However, it has been found that brak-ing and gear-changing are occasionally delayed when there is something particularly interesting on the radio.

The reason why these two activities can nor-mally be performed together is that driving and listening involve different senses (vision and hear-ing). However, if you listen to a football game on your car radio, and try to follow the play by forming visual images, you may quickly find yourself in the ditch.

ANXIETY AND ATTENTION

We all know that anxiety often disrupts perform-ance, especially under stressful conditions. This was convincingly shown by Mitchell Berkun of the United States Army Leadership Human Research Unit. New army recruits were taken up in a plane, and led to believe that it was about to make a crash landing. The plane lurched, one of the engines stopped, and the recruits could see fire engines and ambulances down on the airfield. The pilot announced that the landing gear would not func-tion properly, and that they would have to ditch in the sea. Not surprisingly, his terror-stricken pass-engers showed very little ability to follow the details of the emergency procedures. Their memory pro-ved only half as good as that of recruits who were not exposed to the stress.

Berkun's work was done some 30 years ago, and no present-day ethics committee would let anyone get away with an experiment like that.

Pedestrians plugged into personal stereos tune out in a very real sense. If they look a little out of touch, they probably are.

The work of an air traffic controller is extremely stressful, but this does not lead to poor performance. If anything, short periods of stress heighten performance because more attentional resources are brought to bear on the task in hand.

However, everyday anxiety is typically less intense, and we can study its effects on attention and performance. Since people suffering from anxiety usually become self-conscious and start concentrating on their worries, the obvious prediction is that anxiety should impair performance. The actual effects are both more interesting and more complex than that.

Gershon Weltman of the University of California locked student volunteers into an altitude chamber, and led them to believe that the chamber had descended through water to a depth of 60 feet—with a little ingenuity (extraneous hissing noises, an artificially manipulated pressure gauge) it was not too difficult to be convincing. This produced a certain amount of anxiety induced by the claustrophobic feeling of being confined in a small space, fears of the dreaded 'bends', and apprehensions about the life-support system failing. During the time they were apparently 60 ft down, the volunteers were given the task of detecting small gaps in rings. In addition, their subsidiary task was to detect a light source when it came on.

Weltman found that anxiety had no effect at all on the accuracy with which the main task was done. This was unexpected. The probable answer is that, while anxiety has a natural tendency to worsen performance, the volunteers compensated for this by using more of their attentional capacity than they normally would when not anxious. Dr Samuel Johnson may have had something similar in mind in 1777 when he observed: 'Depend on it, Sir, when a man knows he is to be hanged in a fortnight, it concentrates his mind wonderfully.'

Since these anxious people were only maintaining reasonable performance on the main task by employing most of their resources, they should have been at a disadvantage on the subsidiary task of detecting the light. This proved to be the case; the subsidiary task was only done half as well under the anxiety-inducing conditions.

What can be done to prevent anxiety having undesirable effects on attention and disrupting performance? There is intriguing evidence that the body can learn to develop certain coping mechanisms. Novice parachutists are most reluctant to jump and most 'stirred up' physiologically just before they jump. This means that they are highly anxious during the crucial phases of the parachute jump. Experienced parachutists are somewhat anxious on the morning of the jump and on landing, but remain relatively calm at the moment of jumping. As a result of practice, people can apparently either inhibit anxiety or displace it before and after the main part of a task in order to prevent anxiety from disrupting performance.

CONCLUSIONS

There is no simple answer to the question of whether we can attend to two things at once. If two activities are dissimilar and they have been extensively practiced, then it is often surprisingly easy to combine them effectively. If they are similar and have not been practiced, then it is usually impossible to attend properly to both at the same time.

It is not always easy to tell how much attention a person is devoting to a task. However, we can obtain some idea by giving him a second task to do at the same time; the worse the second task is done, the more of his available attention and resources must have been applied to the first task. This approach has been used with some success to answer a number of practical problems and to shed light on the effects of anxiety on performance.

Chapter 18
REMEMBERING AND FORGETTING

No one can deny the importance of memory. Without it everything would seem as novel and surprising to us as it does to a newborn infant[1]. When asked about their memory, most people admit to having a fairly poor one. There is an interesting contrast here with what happens when you ask people about their intelligence or sense of humour—only a very small percentage of people will admit to below-average intelligence or a poor sense of humour!

Is it true that human memory is fairly inefficient? This is a difficult question to answer. Memory can certainly perform some impressive feats that we tend to take for granted. For example, if someone asked you whether 'sextant' was a word in the English language, it would take you less than a second to decide it was, and you would decide just as quickly that 'mantiness' wasn't.

But forgetting wedding anniversaries, birthdays, people's names, book and film titles, addresses, telephone numbers and the punchlines of jokes is a common failing. This is usually what we mean when we say we have a poor memory.

Since the workings of memory are immensely complicated, it should come as no surprise to discover that forgetting can occur in several different ways. This chapter is devoted to a consideration of some of the reasons why our memories fail us.

KEY EXPERIMENT: MEMORY CUES
Endel Tulving, an Estonian-born psychologist now working in Canada, has perhaps shed more light on forgetting than anyone else[2, 3]. He has pointed out that at any one moment we only think about or remember one event, which means that memory must work in an extremely selective way. How is this single event selected? The French philosopher Henri Bergson supplied an answer with which Tulving agrees: 'We trail behind us, unawares, the whole of our past, but our memory pours into the present only the odd recollection or that which in some way completes our present situation.'

Tulving takes this to mean that remembering an event depends on two things, both of which are essential: a memory trace containing information

about that event, and something in the immediate situation that reminds us of the event (he calls this a 'retrieval cue'). Tulving has sometimes likened the way in which these two things combine to form a memory or recollection to the way in which sperm and egg combine at the moment of conception.

Thus, there may be two major reasons for forgetting: either the memory trace has deteriorated or decayed, or there is no suitable retrieval cue to trigger off the memory. It seems natural to argue

Where did you leave your car? A moment of inattention as you lock the door and walk away, and you may be parted from your car for some time . . . until a little clue jogs your memory.

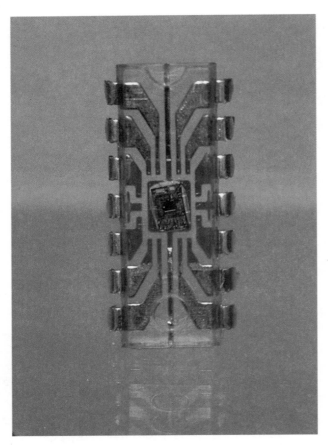

The human memory is often imagined as a complex piece of circuitry not unlike an integrated chip, but the analogy is misleading. With a computer, what goes in is what comes, out, but the brain is a living organism, constantly evolving and constantly reshuffling memory traces in the light of experience.

that we forget things because the memory trace in the brain has faded. However, this is often not the case. For example, most people find that their recollections of childhood become fainter as the years go by. Is this due to fading memory traces? But when they return to the streets and fields they played in as children, or visit their old school, they are often amazed at the number of childhood experiences which come flooding back. The fact that the appropriate environment can trigger off these memories proves that many of the memory traces laid down in childhood are not wiped out. They are there waiting to be activated by the appropriate cue.

Endel Tulving and his colleague at the University of Toronto, Joseph Psotka, were interested in finding out whether forgetting is due to a fading of memory traces or to a lack of appropriate triggers or retrieval cues. They asked the participants in their study to learn lists of 24 words, four words in each of six categories. A sample list was as follows: hut, cottage, tent, hotel; cliff, river, hill, volcano; captain, corporal, sergeant, colonel; ant, wasp, beetle,

mosquito; zinc, copper, aluminium, bronze; drill, saw, chisel, nail. The words were presented by means of a closed-circuit television system.

Some groups of participants were presented with one list, some with two lists, and others with three, four, five or six lists. Immediately after each list had been presented, the participants wrote down as many words as possible from that list. All of the groups did equally well on this test.

After they had learned the appropriate number of lists, the participants were asked to write down as many words as they could remember from all of the lists which they had received. Tulving and Psotka were especially interested to see how well the different groups managed to recall the first list. They expected that those who had learned several lists after the first list would be somewhat confused by all the words they had seen, and therefore forget more of them, a phenomenon known as 'retroactive interference'[3]. Furthermore, the time interval between learning the first list and recall was greater for those who had learned several lists, and this might also lead to a greater tendency to forget.

This is indeed what happened. The more lists people learned after the first list, the more forgetting they showed for the words in that list. Indeed, recall fell from about 70 per cent when only one list was learned to under 30 per cent when five other lists had been learned. Does this mean that the memory traces for the words in the first list faded more for those learning many lists than for those learning only one or two?

Tulving and Psotka tried to show that this was not the case. The experiment continued with the participants spending ten minutes completing as much as possible of an intelligence test, and then they tried again to recall all the words; this produced very similar results to the previous recall. Finally, the participants were supplied with the names of all the categories of words they had learned (for the sample list these were types of building, earth formations, military titles, insects, metals and carpenter's tools) and were asked to use these to aid their recall of all the words.

This cued recall produced a dramatic change in the number of words remembered from the first list. On average, about 40 per cent more words were recalled than before, demonstrating that much of the previous forgetting was not due to decay of memory traces. Indeed, the retrieval cues were so powerful that they allowed the participants to recall virtually as many words as they had originally learned. In other words, the forgetting of the originally learned words was practically eliminated by the retrieval cues. The use of cues also greatly reduced the differences in recall between participants which had been so pronounced before.

Order is important when it comes to remembering, even if it is not apple-pie order! We remember where things are – even eyelets, nails and inner soles – when we put them into a category of some kind.

Apparently, retroactive interference is much more a question of a lack of appropriate retrieval cues than of trace decay.

MNEMONIC AIDS

A great deal of everyday forgetting occurs because the environment does not supply the appropriate memory prompts. If you have to remember to perform an unusual action like buying a book for a friend or flowers for someone in hospital, you are quite likely to forget to do it. What can be done to avoid such embarrassing omissions? Anecdotal evidence suggests that the humble knotted handkerchief will often do the trick. This is because it acts as a retrieval cue.

There are various other experiments, in addition to those conducted by Tulving and Psotka, which have shown that forgetting can be reversed when more powerful or appropriate retrieval cues are used. It is therefore tempting to argue that everything we have ever learned is still stored in the brain, although much of it is inaccessible of course. This was exactly the conclusion which American neurosurgeon Wilder Penfield came to as a result of his work with epileptics. Penfield performed over 1,000 craniotomies involving unilateral removal of a portion of the temporal lobe and adjacent areas in an attempt to relieve focal epilepsy. The patients were conscious during the operation, and in 520 cases Penfield used mild electrical stimulation to explore one or other of the temporal lobes.

About eight per cent of patients reported 'flashbacks' during stimulation, in which they became suddenly aware of experiences from the past. Penfield's most interesting discovery was that electrical stimulation of the temporal lobes sometimes produced detailed re-enactments of a single experience that had been unavailable to normal recall for many years. Many of the patients spontaneously remarked on the very vivid nature of these memories. These findings suggest that much more information about events and experiences is stored than we are able to recall under normal circumstances. However, Penfield interpreted his data in far more dramatic fashion, claiming that he had shown that storage of information was permanent.

There are some weaknesses in Penfield's data. It appears that several of the recollections produced by electrical stimulation could quite easily have been recalled without it. For example, patient J. T. could hear his two cousins Bessie and Ann laughing when he was electrically stimulated. A greater problem is that the small percentage of epileptic patients reporting these vivid recollections may merely have been very suggestible. Also, unfortunately, Penfield had no way of testing the accuracy of these memories.

A practical way of using some of Tulving's ideas to reduce forgetting is to carry your own retrieval cues around with you. A popular way of doing this owes its origins to a tragic accident in Greece 2,500 years ago. The bard Simonides was chanting a lyric poem at a banquet when he was called away by a messenger. During his absence, the roof of the banqueting hall fell in, crushing and mangling the guests so that their bodies were unrecognizable. Simonides remembered the places at which they had been sitting, and so was able to point out the dead to their grieving relatives.

This led Simonides to propose a memory technique in which he stressed the importance of orderly arrangement as an aid to memory, and in which he showed how this could be achieved by linking images of places and of facts or objects. This developed into the 'method of loci' technique, which involves starting with something very familiar, such as an individual's favourite walk. Several places along the walk are then associated, by the use of imagery, with facts which that person wants to remember. When recall is required, the person simply uses the places on the walk as self-generated retrieval cues that allow him to 'read off' the needed facts in the correct order.

A similar technique was proposed in the 1930s by Dale Carnegie, author of *How to Win Friends and Influence People*. The first task is to learn a rhyme scheme for remembering 20 items. Carnegie suggested the following: one-run, two-zoo, three-tree, four-door, five-beehive, six-sick, seven-heaven, eight-gate, nine-wine, ten-den, eleven-a football eleven, twelve-shelve, thirteen-hurting, fourteen-courting, fifteen-lifting, sixteen-licking, seventeen-leavening, eighteen-waiting, nineteen-pining and twenty-horn of plenty.

The next step is to learn images which correspond to the critical words (e.g, 'run' might suggest a sprint race and 'zoo' a caged lion). Finally, a series of up to 20 objects or ideas are visualized in bizarre association with the critical words. Forgetting is quite rare with this system, the main reason being that the individual has equipped himself with powerful retrieval cues.

SOME APPLICATIONS OF TULVING'S IDEAS

The general approach propounded by Tulving has been applied with some success to the clinical problem of understanding memory deficiencies in patients with severe amnesia, many of whom are chronic alcoholics who have developed Korsakoff's psychosis. On most memory tasks their performance is so much lower than that of normal adults that it is tempting to conclude that there must be either some sort of inability to learn or a substantial decay of memory traces.

Elizabeth Warrington and Larry Weiskrantz of the National Hospital in London compared the memory of amnesics with that of normal people. In one experiment, in which recall of a list of words was asked for, normals recalled three and a half times as many words as amnesics. A similar result was obtained in a second experiment. However, when fragments of the words or their initial letters were available as retrieval cues, there was no difference in recall between normal people and amnesics. So, perhaps surprisingly, at least part of the amnesic's tendency to forget is due simply to unusual difficulty in gaining access to stored information.

Other evidence indicates that amnesic patients are able to name only about one-sixth as many photographs of famous faces taken from different time periods as normal people. However, if they are supplied with one or two letters of the surnames as cues, their performance resembles that of non-amnesics who are not given cues. The optimistic implication of recent work on the amnesic syndrome is that the chronic levels of forgetting typically shown by amnesic patients can be partially reversed.

STATE-DEPENDENT MEMORY

A question which greatly occupied Tulving and others is that of deciding which retrieval cues are most useful in reducing forgetting. In general terms, the answer seems to be that effective retrieval cues are those which help to re-create the original event or experience, or the context in which the event occurred. This appears to extend to a person's internal state too. What is experienced in an alcoholic haze is best remembered in an alcoholic haze. The term 'state-dependent memory' has been coined to refer to the finding that memory is at its best if learning and recall both occur when the individual is in the same internal state.

This phenomenon was amusingly illustrated in the film *City Lights*, in which Charlie Chaplin saves a drunk millionaire from attempted suicide and is befriended in return. When the millionaire sees Charlie again he is sober and does not recognize him. However, when the millionaire becomes drunk again, he catches sight of Charlie, treats him like a long-lost friend and takes him home with him. The next morning, when the millionaire is sober again, he forgets that Charlie is his invited guest and gets his butler to throw him out.

In a laboratory setting, Herbert Weingartner persuaded several people to drink about $4\frac{1}{2}$ oz of vodka mixed with 6 oz of fruit juice. As expected, alcoholic intoxication made learning a lot slower than normal. But those who attempted recall four hours later in an intoxicated state remembered more than those who were by then sober, presumably because alcoholic euphoria helped in the re-creation of the learning experience. If you find yourself trying desperately hard to remember something important that you were told while drunk, then the phenomenon of state-dependent memory provides the ideal excuse for some more drinking.

Those who smoke marihuana commonly report that they cannot remember events experienced while intoxicated by the drug until they take the drug again. Here too investigation has shown that information learned in a drugged state is better remembered under drugged conditions.

State-dependent memory has not only been demonstrated with extreme states created by drink or drugs. Gordon Bower of Stanford University used hypnosis to make people happy or sad, asking them to imagine a scene in which they had been delightfully happy or grievously sad. They then learned lists of words while happy or sad, and later recalled the words in one of those two emotional states. In one of the experiments, 78 per cent of the words were remembered when the mood during learning and recall was the same, compared with only 47 per cent when the mood was different. The practical application of this finding is that you may be able to reduce forgetting if you can re-create the emotional state you were in when the crucial event occurred, if you can remember what the emotional state was of course!

MEMORY MONITORING

Given the fallible nature of our memory system, is there any simple way in which it can be made to function more efficiently? One obvious answer would be some kind of memory monitoring system that could tell us how likely it was that the information we were trying to remember was actually stored in the memory. Obviously, we would not waste time and effort trying to remember information not in the memory store. Conversely, it would be useful to know that sought-for information can probably be found somewhere in the memory if we try hard enough.

It may seem paradoxical that we can know that information has been stored even though we cannot locate it, but evidence suggests that we are in fact able to do just this. We do in fact have a memory monitoring system. The most dramatic example of it is the tip-of-the-tongue state, in which you know that a memory is on the verge of coming back to you. However, the system is not only in evidence in the tip-of-the-tongue state; it operates in a much more general and ubiquitous way.

An interesting attempt to assess the accuracy with which we monitor our memory store was made by J.T. Hart of Stanford University. He asked people general knowledge questions such as 'Which planet is the largest in our solar system?' If they could not remember the correct answer, they were asked to indicate on a 6-point scale the extent to which they felt they knew the answer, even though they could not remember it at that moment. The accuracy of this feeling of knowing was assessed by giving them four possible answers for each question, and asking them to guess which was correct. For the sample question, the four answers were: (a) Pluto; (b) Venus; (c) Earth; and (d) Jupiter.

Next page: Strobe lights, pounding music, a few drinks . . . You may have difficulty remembering what happened until you are in the same setting again. ▶

When someone felt very strongly that he knew the correct answer to a question he turned out to be right 75 per cent of the time. But he was right only 30 per cent of the time if he was sure he did not know the answer. Thirty per cent is, of course, very close to the chance figure of 25 per cent. Clearly, then, we can monitor our own memory system and do so with considerable accuracy.

The most intense and even emotional form of feeling that you know something but can't recall it is the tip-of-the-tongue state. The greatest problem for psychologists studying this state is to work out a way of producing the tip-of-the-tongue state to order. Roger Brown and David McNeill of Harvard University came up with the ingenious idea of reading out the definitions of rare words and asking people to think of the word being defined. They were told: 'If you are unable to think of the word but feel sure that you know it and that it is on the verge of coming back to you, then you are probably in a tip-of-the-tongue state.' This technique was successful in producing the tip-of-the-tongue state.

However, does the tip-of-the-tongue state indicate that we really are close to recalling what we are searching for? Brown and McNeill claimed that it does. The initial letter of the missing word was guessed correctly 57 per cent of the time when someone was experiencing the tip-of-the-tongue state. The number of syllables in the missing word could also be approximated. If the word actually had one syllable, the average guess was $1\frac{1}{2}$ syllables, and when it had five syllables the average guess was $3\frac{1}{2}$ syllables. Furthermore, there was some ability to think of words that rhymed with the missing word, and these words usually had the stress on the same syllable as the missing word.

If Tulving and Psotka are right, nothing is lost from memory provided the right key can be found to unlock it. We even seem to know, before we turn the key, whether our memory contains what we are looking for. Nevertheless, anxiety seems to interfere with the process of storage and retrieval!

Among other things, Brown and McNeill have provided us with a plausible answer to the paradox of how we can feel sure that we know something in spite of being unable to retrieve it from our memory. Their work tells us that the simple idea that we either recall a word in its entirety or not at all is wrong. It is entirely possible to recall some of the information about a word (such as its initial letter), and it is this partial retrieval of information that allows us to be so confident that we know what we are looking for. This is similar to the *modus operandi* of Sherlock Holmes, supremely confident that he was on the track of his quarry on the basis of a single hair or a broken twig.

In practical terms, you will find you remember more if you pay close attention to any fragments of information produced by your memory system. If the letter 'D' occurs to you when you are trying to remember someone's name, don't assume that the information is wrong. Write the letter down, and focus on it in an attempt to produce more fragments of information. Finally, take the memory monitoring system's advice—when it fails to indicate any feeling of knowing the required information, give up trying.

HOW ANXIETY AFFECTS MEMORY

As a result of his extensive clinical experience, Sigmund Freud claimed that most forgetting was due to repression. By repression he meant forgetting motivated by the desire to prevent anxiety-toned ideas and episodes intruding into our consciousness. Of course, clinical impressions are much less reliable as a source of information than the results of properly designed experiments, and so several experiments have been carried out to study repression.

Fortunately, there is little likelihood of psychologists being allowed to induce in a laboratory setting the life-crippling traumas alleged to produce clinically observed repression, and so it has proved impossible to test the Freudian theory of repression in a satisfactory way. Nevertheless, there are plenty of informal indications that anxiety makes us forget things. Students are prone to explain poor examination results by saying that anxiety caused them to forget a lot of the information they had painstakingly learned.

In the early 1970s Irwin Sarason tried to decide whether there was any validity to such claims, or whether examinees merely try to rationalize or explain away poor results by blaming them on anxiety. After he had handed back some examination essays to his students, and discussed with them how easy it was to forget relevant material and become confused during the tense exam situation, he asked them: 'Do you really think you would have performed any better under more relaxed circumstances?' Nearly all the students said yes.

As a result, Sarason started giving the students two tests instead of one. The arrangement was that if a student got a higher mark on the second test than the first, that would be the mark entered in the book. If the score on the second test was lower, there would be no penalty. He found that performance was indeed superior under the less anxiety-producing conditions of the second test. He also discovered that students who rated high scores on a test of anxiety showed four times as much improvement from the first to the second test as students who rated low.

Why does anxiety have this effect? The evidence does not really support Freud's theory of repression. Rather it looks as if anxiety involves a 'stirred up' state of physiological arousal together with worry about oneself and one's level of performance ('I'm stupid', 'I can't do this'). Worry appears to be the culprit. If you are thinking about your own problems, you obviously cannot focus properly on the task in hand.

PERFECT MEMORY AND PHOTOGRAPHIC MEMORY

Most of us who have fallible memories must have wished at one time or another that we were blessed with a 'photographic memory'. This sort of memory (or 'eidetic imagery' as it is usually called by psychologists) is a lot rarer than is generally supposed, probably occurring in fewer than 1 per cent of Western adults, although there are reports that it is more prevalent in children and primitive groups. The reason for this difference may be that the majority of adults in Western societies rely more heavily on language than on visual imagery.

The most striking demonstrations of eidetic imagery were reported some 20 years ago by Charles Stromeyer of Bell Telephone Laboratories, working with a young and intelligent teacher at Harvard called Elizabeth. A skilled artist, Elizabeth could readily project an exact image of a picture or scene onto her canvas.

In Stromeyer's experiments, the usual procedure was that two computer-generated stereograms were presented, each consisting of a 10,000-dot display. If you look at these patterns without the aid of a stereoscope they appear completely meaningless. However, when viewed through a stereoscope, which presents one pattern to the right eye and the other pattern to the left eye, you see a three-dimensional figure.

In one early experiment, Elizabeth viewed one 10,000-dot pattern for one minute through her right eye. After a short rest of 10 seconds, she looked at the other pattern with her left eye. When Stromeyer asked her to superimpose the remembered image of the first pattern on the visible pattern, she unhesitatingly reported that she saw the letter 'T' coming towards her. Amazingly, she had stored a detailed image of the arrangement of 20,000 dots!

In a later experiment using the same technique, Elizabeth was able to retain an exact image of a 10,000 dot-pattern for 24 hours. On another occasion, she formed images of four 10,000 dot-patterns

presented to her right eye. The next day, she viewed a single pattern with her left eye, and recalled in turn each of the four eidetic images viewed by the right eye the day before. When these images were superimposed on the left-eye pattern, each created a different figure seen in depth.

It would be misleading to say that Elizabeth possessed a photographic memory. For one thing, her eidetic images were dynamic and fluctuating and, just like more commonplace images, they could be altered and manipulated voluntarily. They were not formed in the same rapid way that a camera takes a photograph. Instead, Elizabeth sometimes took several minutes to form an eidetic image of a complex pattern, moving her eyes around the various parts of the pattern. She claimed that eidetic imagery had been less useful to her than one might imagine. She had found it of some use when taking school and university examinations, but it was less helpful in her graduate work.

The most convincing evidence that phenomenal memory powers can be a mixed blessing was obtained by the Russian neurologist A.R. Luria in the mid-1920s. One day a man he referred to as S. appeared at his laboratory. S. was a newspaper reporter and had been sent to Luria by his editor, who had noted his apparently remarkable memory capacity. Although most people occasionally combine experiences in different sense modalities (e.g. high-pitched sounds can be 'seen' as bright colours), this tendency was very pronounced with S. He once commented to a colleague of Luria's: 'What a crumbly yellow voice you have.'

S.'s powers of imagery were so strong that, after only three minutes of study, he could reproduce a table of 50 numbers by calling out the numbers vertically, horizontally or diagonally at great speed. He claimed to be able to see the table so that he merely had to 'read it off'. On one occasion, he recalled a series of words accurately 16 years after learning them.

These powers of imagery produced a variety of disadvantages for S. His compulsive tendency to turn everything into visual imagery often made it very difficult for him to think effectively at an abstract level. His imagery tended to be laden with vivid but irrelevant details, leading him to remark when trying to understand what someone was saying to him: 'Each word calls up images; they collide with one another, and the result is chaos. I can't make anything out of this. And then there's your voice . . . another blur . . . then everything's muddled,' In other words, the trouble with superb but uncontrollable imaging powers is that you cannot see the wood for the trees.

Next page: Although Freud's theory of repression is difficult to test, hysterical amnesia or 'fugue' does occur, usually following an emotional crisis. A person may, for example, be so severely affected by the death of a loved one that he or she 'forgets' the painful events leading up to it. ▶

CONCLUSIONS

The main reason why we forget is that our environment does not always provide the appropriate cues to trigger off recollection of the missing information. It is often helpful, when trying to remember something, to be in the same internal state you were in when it entered your memory system. A state of anxiety can lead to increased forgetting. However, decay or fading of memory traces almost certainly plays a part as well.

In spite of the fallibility of human memory, we are lucky enough to have a memory monitoring system that gives us a reasonably accurate idea of whether we shall be able to remember forgotten information if we keep trying. Finally, it is not at all clear that an infallible memory system is really desirable; there is the danger that one's mind would be cluttered up with a vast quantity of indigestible information.

Chapter 19
RESOLVING INNER CONFLICT

It is a matter of everyday observation that people often become worried after making decisions in case they have made the wrong decision. Anyone who has bought a secondhand car will know the feeling—we all know, in our heart of hearts, that we only get what we pay for. So from the outset our common sense is at odds with our expectations. One way of resolving this conflict is to seek reassurance from friends and colleagues: 'Not bad is she, considering she's done 80,000 miles!' People are astonishingly forbearing in such situations. Rather than give a hurtful but honest opinion—'You've got a heap which won't last five minutes'—they give the only socially acceptable answer: 'Yes, you've got a good bargain there'. In other words they play along with our need to feel comfortable about our actions and decisions.

Our constant need to justify our decisions, to produce consistency between our opinions and our behaviour, inspired one of Aesop's best-known fables, the one about the fox and the grapes. An extremely hungry fox spies some luscious grapes several feet above him. His best efforts to jump up and pluck them are in vain, producing inconsistency between his energetic attempts to reach his goal and his failure to attain it. He then manages to reduce this inconsistency by convincing himself that the goal is not worth the effort anyway—he decides that the grapes are probably sour anyway. Of course, this rationalization would have been less appropriate had he spent the whole afternoon struggling to reach the grapes, since if the grapes were sour it would have made little sense to keep jumping up at them. But if he *had* tried all afternoon, unsuccessfully, our fox might have convinced himself that the exercise was good for him, enabling him to make nimbler escapes from farmers when they saw him making off with their chickens.

One of the most topical examples of major conflict between belief and behaviour is that of the cigarette smoker who is well aware that smoking can cause cancer and other kinds of illness but nevertheless continues smoking. How do people handle this sort of conflict? Two obvious ways of reducing it would be to alter one's behaviour (i.e. stop smoking) or else refuse to believe that smoking is dangerous. The causal link between cigarette smoking and cancer first impinged on the public consciousness in America in 1964 after a report issued by the United States Surgeon General.

Shortly afterwards a survey was done to investigate its effects on smokers. Only 9 per cent of the smokers interviewed had even attempted to give up smoking. Forty-one per cent of heavy smokers (compared with only 11 per cent of non-smokers) refused to accept the link between cigarette smoking and cancer. So it appears that people will attempt to reduce disturbing conflicts in any way that is open to them.

KEY EXPERIMENT: LYING UNDER PRESSURE

Leon Festinger and James Carlsmith of Stanford University were extremely interested in the ways in which people coped with conflicts of the kind described above[1]. In particular, they wondered how people's opinions would be affected by the unpleasant realization that they had been deliberately dishonest to someone.

Belief and behaviour are often at odds where junk food is concerned. Although we know that naked calories, saturated fats and additives ultimately cause ill health, we eat them just the same. Furred up arteries are not going to happen to us!

In their experiment, every subject was asked to perform two mind-numbing and utterly pointless tasks, each lasting for 30 minutes. The first task involved putting 12 spools on a tray, emptying the tray, refilling it with spools, and so on. The subjects were given a board containing 48 square pegs for the second task, and were asked to turn each peg a quarter turn clockwise, then another quarter turn, and so on.

After this hour of unrelieved tedium, the experimenter explained that he was interested in the effects of prior expectations on the performance of the tasks. Some subjects had been led to believe that the experiment was very enjoyable, a lot of fun, very interesting, intriguing and exciting, the experimenter continued—he had given the job of misinforming the subjects to a student who had been hired specifically for the purpose. Unfortunately, the experimenter went on in a somewhat confused and embarrassed manner, this student was no longer available. Would one of the participants be prepared to fill in for the missing student? In some cases he or she was offered $1, in others $20, for agreeing to perform this dishonest service and for agreeing to be available in future if a similar emergency occurred.

Nearly all the subjects agreed to do as the experimenter suggested, and were then introduced to the next subject, who was a girl. When the subject-stooge began talking in glowing terms about the experiment, the girl said she was surprised because a friend of hers had done the experiment a week earlier and had told her that it was boring and that she ought to try to get out of it. Most of the subjects dealt with this problem by trying to reassure the girl, saying something like 'Oh no, it's really very interesting. I'm sure you'll enjoy it.'

Finally, the experimenter took each subject to an 'interviewer', who said that it was his job to evaluate the experiment, and others, so that it could be improved in future. Among other questions, the interviewer asked each subject to rate how interesting and enjoyable the tasks were.

How do you think the subject's opinion of this boring experiment was affected by the amount of money offered as an inducement to be dishonest and claim that the experiment was very enjoyable? It would be natural to assume that people's attitudes towards the experiment would be made more positive by the large sum ($20) than by the small sum ($1), simply because it is more pleasant and rewarding to receive a large amount of money than a small amount. But in fact the results were quite the opposite. Paradoxically, those subjects who were offered only $1 rated the experiment as much *more* enjoyable and interesting than those offered $20! The telling of a lie (pretending the experiment was much more interesting than it actually was) produced a state of conflict, since most people regard themselves as basically honest. Those offered $20 could justify their behaviour by the large amount of money given to them: 'Anyone

would tell a lie if it was worth their while.' But those offered only $1 could not square their conscience with their dishonesty quite so easily. The solution to their conflict was to convince themselves that they had not really been very dishonest because the experiment had been genuinely interesting. In other words, the *less* money they were offered, the *greater* the conflict produced.

As sometimes happens in social psychology, the subjects were thoroughly deceived about several aspects of the experiment. The missing student who had been hired to tell subjects that the experiment was very interesting did not exist, the female subject was actually a confederate of the experimenter, the interviewer was employed by the experimenter and, worst of all, the subjects were asked at the end of the experiment to give back the $1 or $20!

COGNITIVE DISSONANCE

However, whatever the rights and wrongs of this experiment, Festinger's findings enabled him to propose that the first crucial step in persuading people to change their opinions is to produce a state of 'cognitive dissonance'. This is an unpleasant state which exists whenever an individual simultaneously holds two ideas or opinions that are inconsistent with each other. For example, in the Festinger and Carlsmith experiment, the participants may have said to themselves, in almost the same breath, 'I have just been dishonest' and 'I am a basically honest person'. Since basically honest people do not go round telling lies, it is the conjunction of these two thoughts which produces cognitive dissonance.

Festinger then went on to argue that, since the occurrence of dissonance is relatively unpleasant, individuals are motivated to reduce it by whatever means they can. One way to do this is by adding extenuating ideas or thoughts. Thus, those offered $20 for lying could think about the large sum of money involved and persuade themselves that, under those particular circumstances, lying was justified. Alternatively, dissonance can be reduced by changing one or both of the dissonant ideas or beliefs so that they fit together better. Those offered only $1 for lying could not readily justify their behaviour in terms of money, and so were unlikely to change their minds about being basically honest. Thus, the only way in which they could easily reduce their dissonance was by changing the thought 'I have just been dishonest'. This they did by convincing themselves that the experiment had been quite interesting, in which case they had not told much of a lie.

Festinger also proposed that the amount of dissonance created would be highest when the dissonant ideas are of great importance to the individual. One of the reasons for the amount of opinion change observed by Festinger and Carlsmith is probably that most individuals' self-concept includes the belief that they are basically

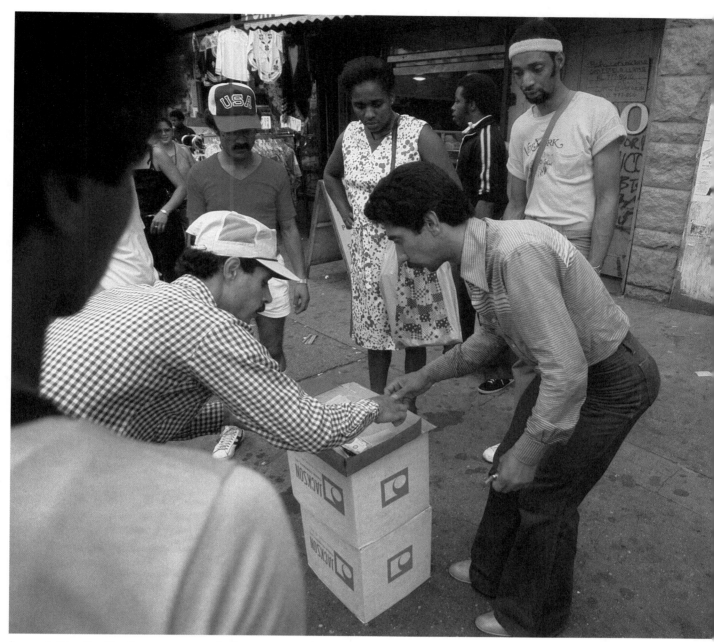

honest. Finally, Festinger proposed, the amount of dissonance experienced depends on the number of ideas that are consonant or dissonant with an action or decision.

Festinger's theory of cognitive dissonance obviously provides a plausible explanation of the results he and Carlsmith obtained. However, psychologists are sceptical by nature, especially when confronted with counter-intuitive findings, and one point that bothered many of them was the amount of money offered to the participants. Some suggested that those offered $20 probably didn't change their opinion of the experiment just because of the money—after all $20 doesn't buy very much. Others suggested that some of the participants were so disconcerted by the sum of $20 that their judgment was grossly distorted.

Now you see it, now you don't! We all know we are going to be duped by confidence tricks, yet we keep watching. By calling them 'tricks' we feel better about being deceived; by labelling the con man a trickster we can continue to believe that we are intelligent.

Neither criticism, however, turned out to have much validity. Arthur Cohen persuaded Yale students to write essays favouring the repressive actions of the New Haven Police Department in quelling a student riot by offering them $1 or 50 cents. Those offered the smaller sum came to believe in the truth of what they had written to a greater extent than those offered the larger sum.

Are people always most likely to change their opinions, when asked to do something unpleasant, for a small rather than a large bribe? Festinger's

Will he come or won't he? Waiting for someone, especially a new boyfriend, can be a very dissonant experience. If he doesn't come, will she try to minimize her disappointment by saying 'I knew he wouldn't come anyway'?

basic idea that people will justify their own actions in any way they can suggests that there might be exceptions to this tendency. For example, if participants can be persuaded to tell lies about the enjoyableness of an experiment, the thought 'I was compelled to tell lies' might provide just the justification they need for their dishonesty. Again the result would be reduction of dissonance. Under such circumstances, Festinger found, there was an exact reversal of the usual picture. Those who had been given $1 said they found the experiment more enjoyable and rewarding than those who had been given 50 cents, or half that amount.

Dissonance can also be reduced if the confederate who is told that the experiment is very interesting refuses to be convinced ('Well, you're entitled to your opinion, but I've never enjoyed an experiment and I don't think this one will be much fun'). When that happens, the participant can justify his dishonesty ('Since it had no effect, it didn't really matter that I lied'), and his feelings about the experiment are unaffected by the size of the reward.

THE MECHANISM OF SELF-JUSTIFICATION

All of the available evidence suggests the following basic rule of thumb for working out what will happen when people act in a way inconsistent with their own opinions: if behaviour can quite easily be justified for some external reason (payment, lack of choice, no bad consequences), then opinions change very little; if behaviour cannot be justified, there will be an opinion shift to bring opinions and behaviour into line.

Festinger's ideas have been related to an enormous variety of situations. For example, Philip Zimbardo (already mentioned in Chapter 4) wondered how highly disliked foods, fried grasshoppers for example, could be transformed into a prized delicacy. He argued that if people were asked to eat fried grasshoppers by someone who acted in a pleasant and friendly way, they might just do so and justify their behaviour by arguing 'I did it because he's a nice guy'. On the other hand, if the person doing the persuading was snobbish, tactless, bossy, cold and hostile, they could not use the 'nice guy' justification for tackling their plate of grasshoppers, and so dissonance would be created. Then the easiest way to reduce dissonance would be to convince themselves that they quite liked grasshoppers. Zimbardo actually put these ideas to

the test and found that approximately half his participants agreed to eat at least one fried grasshopper, but that it was only those who were persuaded to eat by an unpleasant person who consistently came to like the thought of eating grasshoppers (e.g. 'They taste like shrimp'). The non-eaters actually went the other way, expressing increased repugnance for grasshoppers.

There is one important part of Festinger's approach that has received less attention than it deserves, and that is the notion that dissonance is experienced as a state of discomfort and tension. In one study most of the students who had agreed to write essays in favour of compulsory military service experienced dissonance, and changed their opinions in the direction of the attitudes they were

In these four pictures, the woman is trying to make the man change his mind. She tries reason, cajolery and making fun of him. He feels cornered and tries to buy time.

asked to express. They did this to reduce the feelings of tension produced by dissonance. What if other students were given an innocuous drug before essay-writing, but were told it would produce feelings of tension? Would they be able to attribute any tension they felt to the temporary effects of the drug, and therefore not experience any need to change their opinions? This is exactly what happened. It was found that the usual dissonance effect of opinion change did not occur after an allegedly tension-inducing drug had been given.

Are there any real bargains here? If we buy a not-quite-genuine antique, we tend to blame the seller rather than our own gullibility.

SOCIAL IMPLICATIONS

We have seen that opinions change much more when there is insufficient justification for our actions than when there are good reasons for behaving in a certain way. It has been argued that most of the history of medicine can be explained in terms of cognitive dissonance!

Most forms of medical treatment used to be thoroughly unpleasant, ranging from putting cholera patients into scalding hot water to bleeding patients with leeches. If medical treatment is disagreeable, time-consuming or embarrassing, then there is potential dissonance between the two thoughts 'I have consented to a repulsive method of treatment' and 'I am still as ill as before'. The dissonance can be eliminated and the treatment justified only if the patient can convince himself that he is actually getting better. When people say 'It tastes so awful it must be doing me good' they are being more perspicacious than they realize. (Of course, many illnesses do not permit this kind of self-delusion.)

A similar kind of analysis can be applied to the cost of medical treatment. As doctors discovered a long time ago, raising the price of a treatment can considerably augment its healing powers. The patient says to himself: 'I'm paying a lot of money so I must be getting the best possible treatment, therefore I must be getting better'.

Dissonance theory has also been applied to the important issue of moulding children's behaviour to fit the moral values of the society they live in. It is relatively easy to stop a child behaving inappropriately if you threaten him with punishment. However, if the socialization process is successful, the child must also learn to behave properly in the absence of direct pressures or sanctions, and this is a much more difficult task.

Applying the dissonance theory, it is better to

If this death-defying leap was your initiation into adulthood – as it is in the Solomon Islands – you would regard adulthood as a very serious business indeed.

stop a child performing an antisocial act by means of a mild rather than a strong threat of punishment. If the child stops doing something he wants to do, i.e. throwing stones, because of a strong threat of punishment, then his justification is 'I was *forced* to stop but I still want to go on throwing stones'. If he stops throwing stones in response to a mild threat, however, he is likely to justify himself by saying 'I didn't really want to throw stones anyway'.

The realization that strong pressure can be counter-productive has dawned on generations of parents. All too often, the more pressure parents put on teenagers not to associate with disreputable members of the opposite sex, the more enamoured of them they are likely to become ('If I want to keep on seeing him in spite of my parents' disapproval, he must be important to me').

Support for the notion that mild threats can be much more effective than strong threats was obtained by Elliot Aronson and James Carlsmith. They told four-year-old children not to play with a preferred toy, such as a battery-powered fire engine, using a mild threat ('If you play with it, I'll be annoyed') or a severe threat ('I'll be very angry. I'll take all the toys away and go home and never come back again . . . You're behaving like a baby'). While both threats effectively stopped the children playing with the toy while the adult was out of the room, mild threat led to decreased liking for the forbidden toy but severe threat didn't.

The cognitive dissonance principle has also been applied to the question of whether individuals think more highly of a club or organization that goes in for an embarrassing or rigorous initiation than one that has only mild inititition procedures. Since most people do not like being embarrassed, one might think that an organization that provides unpleasant experiences would be disliked. According to dissonance theory, however, the two ideas 'I have agreed to join this organization' and 'I have allowed myself to be embarrassed for the sake of membership' cause dissonance, and this can only be reduced by exaggerating the positive aspects of belonging to the organization.

Elliot Aronson and Judson Mills at Stanford University tested these ideas by requiring female college students to undergo an initiation in order to become members of a group discussing the psychology of sex. The mild initiation involved reading aloud non-obscene words related to sex (prostitute, virgin, petting), whereas the severe initiation involved reading aloud obscene words (cock, fuck, screw) and then reading aloud two vivid descriptions of sexual activity from contemporary novels. After this initiation, they listened to a very boring and banal group discussion of secondary sex behaviour in the lower animals. The girls who underwent the severe initiation condition evaluated the tedious discussion much more favourably than those who underwent the mild one.

Nevertheless, other explanations have been offered for the above findings. Perhaps girls who underwent the severe initiation became sexually aroused rather than embarrassed, and this produced pleasure and increased the attractiveness of the discussion group. However, incidental observations indicated that the girls did become embarrassed (hesitating, blushing, looking at the floor). Another possibility is that these girls felt relief from sexual anxiety when they found the group discussion innocuous instead of embarrassing, and this increased their positive evaluation of it.

However, explanations in terms of sexual arousal or sexual anxiety are not applicable to a later study, in which those who underwent a series of severe electric shocks in order to gain admission to a dull discussion group rated the group more favourably than those who only experienced mild shocks.

THE RELIGIOUS DIMENSION
The effects of cognitive dissonance have also been observed in various religious sects. In an investigation by Festinger and his co-workers, a number of psychologists managed to infiltrate a sect called the Lake City group. A woman belonging to the group received written messages from a number of 'guardians' who lived in outer space, and these extraterrestrial beings informed her that on a given date, just before dawn, a cataclysmic flood would cover most of the North American continent. The activities of the group received considerable publicity when one of its members was asked to resign from his job as physician at a student health centre because of his beliefs.

In the face of much taunting and sarcasm from non-believers, the members of the sect attempted to keep a low profile while they prepared themselves for evacuation before the flood. Four days before the flood was due, they were told, a flying saucer would land in the back garden of one of their houses, at four in the afternoon, to pick them up. Although they waited hopefully with coats in hand, the saucer did not arrive. They were then informed that the flying saucer would come at midnight, and they waited in vain for many hours on a cold, snowy night. Eventually, after several more false alarms and the non-appearance of the flood, there was a message from God to say that He had saved the world and stopped the flood for the sake of this one small group and the light and strength they had spread throughout the world.

How did these people cope with the conflict produced by the failure of their predictions? While abandonment of their beliefs might have been possible if their commitment to the cause had been lukewarm, many members of the sect had given up their jobs and discarded precious possessions in readiness for evacuation from this planet. The only way in which they could reduce dissonance was to convert as many other people as possible in order to provide themselves with more social support. This they did enthusiastically, replacing their earlier secrecy with an avid desire for publicity.

Nuns and fast food joints? The dissonance created by our stereotyped ideas of nuns and fast food is unsettling. So we say to ourselves: 'So what? Nuns must eat, after all.'

However, different reactions were found among the members of the Church of the True Word, a group which accepted the message of the Bible in a literal sense. From the Book of Revelations they calculated that one third of the earth's population was about to be obliterated by nuclear warfare, and they expected to play a divinely inspired role in healing and converting the survivors. Over one hundred members of the group prepared for this emergency by moving to a remote area of the southwestern United States, where they set to work building bomb shelters.

Upon receipt of a prophetic message, 'The Egyptians are coming', 103 of the devout spent 42 days underground awaiting a nuclear attack that never came. When they re-emerged into the sunlight, they reduced dissonance by claiming that God had used them to warn a non-vigilant world, and had tested their faith. They all decided that they had passed the test and were thus especially worthy in the sight of God. However, they did not busily try to convert others as the Lake City group had done. Probably the difference between the behaviour of the two groups was due to the fact that the True Word group was larger and more cohesive than the Lake City group, and therefore had more social support in its hour of discomfiture. The True Worders were fairly benevolently treated by the surrounding community, which helped to defuse dissonance and conflict.

DOUBTS ABOUT DISSONANCE

So far all the examples of dissonance we have discussed have been relatively straightforward —there is little doubt that strong conflicts are produced by inconsistent ideas. However, it is not always so easy to be sure whether or not dissonance is created. Suppose you have told all your friends that a particular contemporary artist is your favourite painter, and it then transpires he is a chronic alcoholic. This may well not cause dissonance, because you can always argue that artists are a law unto themselves. On the other hand, you would probably experience some dissonance if you discovered that a very prominent and well-respected member of the church had been an alcoholic for many years and consistently ill-treated his wife.

What determines whether dissonance is felt? Generally speaking, dissonance is only likely to occur when an expectation is violated. We have a definite expectation that churchmen will avoid the perils of drink, but tolerate considerable permissiveness where artists are concerned.

Another difficulty which rather undermines the dissonance approach is that we all have different opinions about ourselves. Lying, as in the

Fervent beliefs of all kinds tend to thrive in the teeth of sarcasm and unbelief. To reduce dissonance, believers may find it necessary to regard non-believers as misguided, sinners, agents of darkness, and so on.

Festinger and Carlsmith studies, only produces dissonance if the liar regards himself as basically honest. If the liar regards himself as a callous psychopath he may actually relish the thought of deceiving others and experience no guilt or dissonance at all.

The implication is that dissonance theorists must pay more attention to the individual's self-image. For example, successful performance of a task would not usually be thought likely to produce dissonance. However, people who expect to fail have been found to become rather anxious when they actually succeed in something.

Finally, it would be potentially disastrous if we always did our utmost to reduce dissonance—that would be like weaving a permanent cocoon around ourselves. We would continually be justifying our own actions, never admitting that we make mistakes, to the point where we would be unable to profit from our mistakes[2].

CONCLUSIONS

The dissonance theory suggests that we are rationalizing creatures rather than rational ones. We attempt to justify our behaviour and appear rational both to ourselves and to others. This need for self-justification is a powerful one, and can be seen in the field of medicine, in the acquisition of moral values, in the behaviour of religious sects and in countless other aspects of life.

Because we are so eager to justify ourselves, we sometimes behave in strange and apparently unpredictable ways. However, largely as a result of the pioneer work of Leon Festinger and his colleagues, psychologists are beginning to understand how people deal with inner conflict.

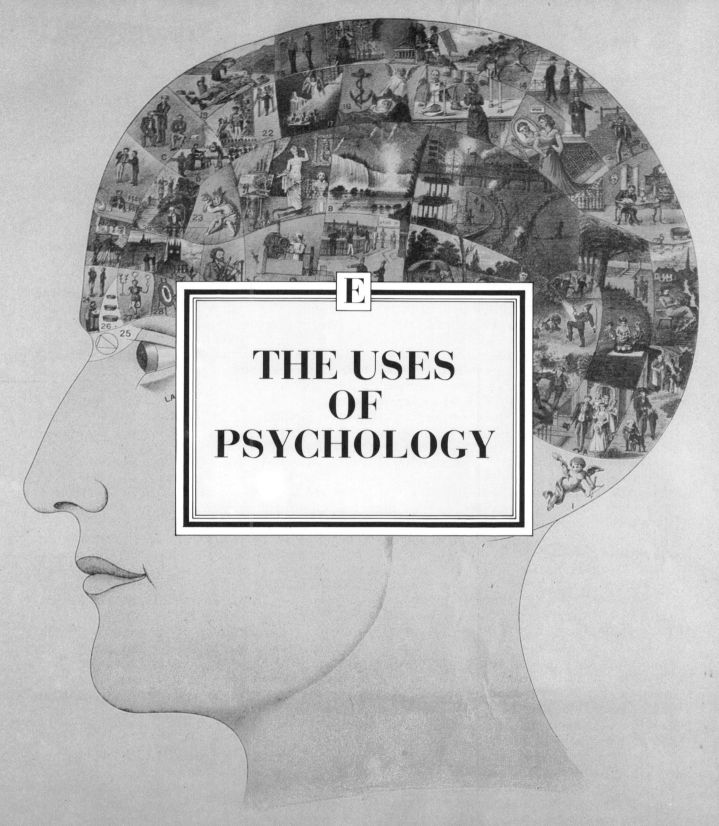

THE USES OF PSYCHOLOGY

A NEW SYMBOLICAL HEAD AND PHRENOLOGICAL CHART

WITH THE NAME AND DEFINITION OF EACH ORGAN,

by R. B. D. Wells, Phrenologist, West Bank, Scarbro'

1.—AMATIVENESS. Love between the sexes. *Excess*—Sensuality. *Deficiency*—Coldheartedness.

A.—CONJUGALITY. Desire to marry. *Excess*—Envy towards love rivals. *Def.*—Inconstancy.

2.—PARENTAL LOVE. Love of children, parents, and pets. *Excess*—Pampers and spoils children.

3.—FRIENDSHIP. Social feeling, love of society. *Excess*—Inordinate attachment to friends.

4.—INHABITIVENESS. Love of home, patriotism. *Excess*—Home sickness. *Def.*—Neglect of home.

5.—CONTINUITY. Concentration of thought, application. *Excess*—Prolixity. *Def.*—Love of variety.

courage, defence. *Excess*—Quarrelsomeness and love of conflict.

7.—DESTRUCTIVENESS. Propelling force, energy. *Excess*—Tendency to destroy, cruelty, malice, revenge.

8.—ALIMENTIVENESS. Relish for food. *Excess*—Gluttony, drunkenness. *Def.*—Little desire for food.

9.—ACQUISITIVENESS. Desire to earn money, trade, economise and accumulate. *Excess*—Avarice, selfishness.

10.—SECRETIVENESS. Policy, reserve, self-control. *Excess*—Evasion, cunning. *Def.*—Frankness, bluntness.

11.—CAUTIOUSNESS. Anxiety, guardedness, hesitancy. *Excess*—Indecision, fear. *Def.*—Indiscretion.

12.—APPROBATIVENESS. Desire for popularity, love of approbation

rity, dignity. *Excess*—Egotism. *Def.*—Servility.

14.—FIRMNESS. Stability, tenacity of will, decision. *Excess*—Obstinacy. *Def.*—Fickleness.

15.—CONSCIENTIOUSNESS. Circumspection, integrity, justice. *Excess*—Undue self-condemnation. *Def.*—Inconsistency.

16.—HOPE. Speculation, cheerfulness, hope in a future state. *Excess*—Castle building.

17.—SPIRITUALITY. Impressibility, trust, faith. *Excess*—Superstition. *Def.*—Scepticism.

18.—VENERATION.—Deference, worship, antiquity. *Excess*—Idolatry, bigotry.

19.—BENEVOLENCE. Sympathy, liberality, kindness. *Excess*—Prodigality in giv-

21.—IDEALITY. Refinement, love of the perfect, poetical sentiment. *Excess*—Fastidiousness. *Def.*—Lack of taste and refinement.

B.—SUBLIMITY. Love of the grand, sublime, and terrific. *Excess*—Bombast. *Def.*—Cannot appreciate the sublime.

22.—IMITATION. Power to copy, to draw, imitate, and mimic. *Excess*—Buffoonery. *Def.*—Eccentricity.

23.—MIRTHFULNESS. Wit, humour, sense of the comic. *Excess*—Ill-timed ridicule. *Def.*—Cannot appreciate mirth.

24.—INDIVIDUALITY. Power of observation and desire to be an eye witness. *Excess*—Curiosity, and impudent observation.

25.—FORM. Memory of shape, configuration, and faces. *Def.*—Inability to remember

27.—WEIGHT. Sense of gravity, ability to balance, ride, climb, shoot, &c. *Excess*—Too risky in climbing. *Def.*—Liability to stumble.

28.—COLOUR. Ability to match and compare colours, and evince taste in their arrangement. *Def.*—Colour blind.

29.—ORDER. Neatness, system, method. *Excess*—Too particular and precise. *Def.*—Slovenliness.

30.—CALCULATION. Mental computation, ability to estimate. *Def.*—Inability to reckon.

31.—LOCALITY. Memory of places, desire to travel. *Excess*—Constant roving desire. *Def.*—Forgets places.

32.—EVENTUALITY. Memory of facts, historical records and events. *Def.*—For-

34.—TUNE. Love of music, modulation of harmony. *Def.*—Inability

35.—LANGUAGE. Memory of what and ability to communicate and ideas. *Excess*—Loquacity

36.—CAUSALITY. Philosophical and planning capacity. *Excess* theoretical. *Def.*—Lack of con sciveness.

37.—COMPARISON. Criticism, analysis, ability to compare and illustrate. *Def.*—Inability to apply knowledge.

C.—HUMAN NATURE. Intuitive insight into character, sagacity, penetration.

D.—AGREEABLENESS. Youthfulness, suavity. *Excess*—Abruptness, importent.

Psychologists are often attacked for living in ivory towers, for studying trivial problems which have no relevance to broader social issues. There is an element of truth in the charge, especially with respect to the activities of some American psychologists, whose motto seems to be 'Publish or perish'. However, it would be a big mistake to imagine that psychological research is broadly irrelevant. An increasing number of professional psychologists are making significant contributions to society in the occupational, clinical and educational fields.

Common sense suggests that psychology ought to be of immense benefit to society at large. After all, it deals with the understanding and prediction of human behaviour, and the whole functioning of society ultimately depends on the ways in which people behave and interact.

Bringing up children is difficult at the best of times, but parents today have to cope with a lot of conflicting 'expert' advice as well. Should they choose the permissive approach or the more 'old-fashioned' disciplinary approach? The merits of both are discussed in Chapter 20, but important new research indicates that both these extreme positions are wrong. There is, it seems, a saner middle way.

It is ironical that education—to which psychological principles and findings are especially relevant—has benefited little from psychological insights. The main reason for this is that major changes in educational practice are typically made by people who are influenced more by ideology than by the available evidence. As we point out in Chapter 21, it is particularly unfortunate that most educationalists have the mistaken view that all children are likely to react in the same way to any given instructional method. In fact, some children learn better when taught by one method rather than another. Clearly, a satisfactory educational system would be one which fully catered for individual differences.

In Chapter 22 we discuss some of the exciting possibilities of 'biofeedback'. Biofeedback is a psychologically-based method of treating certain physical disorders and it has attracted enormous publicity in recent years. The basic idea is that problems which have a clearly defined physiological basis can be cured if the physiological abnormalities are rectified. Patients can help to treat themselves if they are provided with information about their success (or otherwise) in altering their physiological state. Biofeedback can help towards a cure, or at least control, of a host of problems, including hypertension, migraine, a peripheral circulatory ailment known as Raynaud's disease, and certain sexual disorders.

The two biggest killers in contemporary Western society are cancer and heart disease. Because of this, vast sums of money have been spent on medical research, but with relatively modest success. A more optimistic note is struck in Chapter 23, in which we discuss exciting new psychological approaches to preventing cancer and heart disease.

The incidence of crime, especially violent crime, has increased in virtually all Western countries. Is there anything we can do about it? It is argued in Chapter 24 that the first step is to understand the factors which lead some people to become criminals and others to remain relatively virtuous. There is some evidence that a long period of punishment-based conditioning can lead to the development of a 'conscience'. The permissiveness of contemporary society may therefore be an indirect contributory factor to increased rates of crime in that it reduces the number of such conditioning experiences. There are encouraging signs that psychological methods of treatment may prove effective in reforming some, if not all, criminals. Various conditioning techniques have been used to induce both juvenile delinquents and adult offenders to adopt more socially desirable attitudes.

As we shall see in Chapter 25, psychology also has important applications to political and social thought, from Communism to Fascism. Over the centuries, many people have distinguished between 'left-wing' and 'right-wing' attitudes; now psycholgists have identified a radical-conservative dimension which corresponds to this distinction. However, some radicals (i.e. left-wingers) are tough-minded and others tender-minded, and the same goes for conservatives. This has led to the introduction of a tough-minded/tender-minded dimension within broad ideological categories.

Why do different people have different social and political attitudes? Common sense suggests that such attitudes are determined environmentally by family, friends, and other social contacts. However, there is exciting new evidence that heredity plays a substantial role.

In sum, psychology is of ever-increasing significance to society. There are very few areas of life in which it has no contribution to make.

Chapter 20
HOW NOT TO BRING UP CHILDREN

Most parents worry how best to bring up their children. In their anxiety, some of them turn to psychologists or psychiatrists, or even psychoanalysts. This may not be a wise move. Professionals and so-called experts have a poor track record in advising worried parents. J. B. Watson, the father of the behaviourist movement, was the first of the best-sellers on bringing up children. His influential *Psychological Care of the Infant and Child* sold more than 100,000 copies within a few months of publication. Bertrand Russell, a man not easily duped, became a strong supporter of Watson's beliefs. But professional psychologists were decidedly critical. Some felt that the book damaged his status as a serious scientist. Watson's message was a simple one: children should be brought up on a scientific rather than an emotional or traditional basis. He advocated that one should not molly-coddle one's offspring, show them too much affection, or even kiss and cuddle them, for to do so encourages a dependent mentality; feeding should be on schedule, not on demand. Watson tried this regime on his two sons. One committed suicide, and the other, to Watson's intense annoyance, became a psychoanalyst. In the end, Watson regretted writing his book, not he said 'because of its sketchy form but because I did not know enough to write the book I wanted to write.'

After the tough, anti-loving, non-permissive Watson the pendulum swung back, as pendulums do, and the psychoanalytic Dr Spock with his extremely permissive, feeding-on-demand not on schedule, hugging and kissing prescription, appeared on the scene. His *Baby and Child Care* was outsold only by the Bible. Mothers everywhere gratefully relapsed into a more emotional relationship with their children, something Watson had warned explicitly against. But both the permissive and scientific child-rearing models were based on too narrow a view. Spock finally acknowledged that his recommendations had been wrong. Bringing up children his way failed to bring the results he had hoped for.

Both Watson and Spock, in their different ways, illustrate the evil of giving advice, supposedly scientific in nature, on the basis of preconceived opinions instead of firmly established scientific theories grounded in fact. The truth is that psychologists simply do not know enough about the upbringing of children to assume the role of omniscient advisers.

Watson relied on the narrow basis of a fundamentalist behaviourism, Spock on the narrow and insubstantial basis of the Freudian credo. Neither of their systems is supported by sufficient facts to bear the weight of the superstructure they and other writers erected on top of them. We know very little about the bringing up of children, but we do know enough by now to realize that Watson and Spock both gave advice that was wrong for most children—the one being too tough, authoritarian and unemotional, and the other too soft, permissive and lovey-dovey. Most mothers would have

Perhaps the best advice that psychology has to offer when it comes to bringing up children is that parents should suit the method to the child, not vice versa.

brought their children up more successfully if they had never read either. Beware of psychologists bearing advice—this is one gift horse into whose mouth it would pay parents to look most carefully!

Can we then offer nothing to parents who ask our advice? In fact, we can . . . a little. Interesting and important studies have been carried out in recent years which do suggest a few guidelines. The first—and most obvious, since few mothers need reminding of it—is that children are all different and that there is no one way of bringing them up. Each child should be treated as an individual. The second is that heredity is very important, both for intelligence and personality. Parents are not presented at birth, as Watson maintained, with a shapeless mass of putty which they can mould into any shape they like.

THE DIFFICULTIES OF CHILD RESEARCH

A lot of money and energy has gone into child research, so why is it that we still know so little? There are two interlinked reasons. The first is that research in this field is very difficult. It is usually thought unethical to expose children to regimes which might provide us with control data. The second difficulty is that psychologists have preconceived ideas which they are often unwilling to expose to experimental proof in case they are proved wrong. Psychologists (and psychiatrists and psychoanalysts) are only human and subject to all the usual human foibles—they can be just as wrong-headed, obstinate, aggressive and downright perverse as anyone else, and child-rearing is a topic which seems to bring out the worst in them.

Here is a typical example. Imagine a psychologist (or perhaps a sociologist, psychiatrist or psychoanalyst) who wishes to investigate the hypothesis that beating children as a punishment does not improve their behaviour, but makes them behave worse. Imagine him setting up an experiment in which he studies an experimental group of children whose parents do not beat them at all, or who at most only beat them occasionally, and then compares them with another group, a control group, of children whose parents beat them often and mercilessly. He then investigates the adult careers of these two groups of children and finds that those who were beaten tend to grow up into aggressive, hostile, often vicious adults (the correlation is not very high in the studies that have been done, but the trend is unmistakable). Then he will claim that he has proved his point, that beating children is bad. But is this really true?

Obviously he may be right. The data do not contradict such an hypothesis, but neither do they confirm it. There are alternative hypotheses which explain the facts equally well, without implicating parental punishment. For example, it is possible that the genetic constitution of the parents, which causes them to behave in this brutal fashion towards their children, is inherited in part by the children and causes them too to behave in a brutal fashion when they grow up, regardless of the punishment they have suffered. In fact, without punishment they might have been even more aggressive and brutal! There is much evidence for the importance of heredity in aggressive and hostile behaviour, so this alternative hypothesis is a genuine possibility.

A third possibility would be that some children are by nature so badly behaved, and so uncontrollable, that they can only be held in check by severe beatings; but as they grow up, their original behaviour, no longer curbed by physical correction, manifests itself again in vicious and unruly conduct. There is also a lot of evidence to show that the behaviour of parents is often provoked by the behaviour of their children. In other words, parents react to what their children do, rather than the other way round. Thus we have another explanation for the original findings of our hypothetical psychologist.

This example neatly illustrates a fundamental fallacy in much modern sociological and psychological research into upbringing, namely the fallacy of interpreting observed correlations as causes and effects. The unruly behaviour of the children as they grow up *is* correlated with brutal treatment handed out by parents, so researchers assume that the former is the result of the latter, but they have not proved it. In Copenhagen there has been a continuous decline in the number of babies born over the past thirty years; similarly there has been a decline in the number of storks nesting in the city. But this does not prove that the storks bring the babies! This 'sociological fallacy', as it has been called, because it is a fallacy sociologists are particularly prone to wander into, vitiates a large number of research studies in this field and makes it very difficult to come to any logical conclusions about real causes and effects.

There are two ways of side-stepping this difficulty. One is to do a genetic study which weeds out genetic from environmental effects. Thus we might study identical and fraternal twins, their spouses and their children to obtain information on different genetic relationships and different environmental relationships which lend themselves to proper statistical analysis. The drawback of such studies is that they require large numbers of twins, and are also difficult and expensive. With few exceptions, psychologists have avoided experiments of this kind and concentrated instead on observing the effects of given forms of treatment on randomly selected experimental and control groups of children.

A good example of this second kind of approach to child research was a study done by Mary Gribbin[1]. She was interested in the effects of 'permissive' and 'old-fashioned' upbringing on pre-school children.

KEY EXPERIMENT: PRE-SCHOOL PLAYGROUPS

In her experiment, Mary Gribbin looked at differences in play patterns between children attending two different pre-school groups, one the formal, old-fashioned sort, and the other run on new, permissive lines. Both groups consisted of boys and girls between two and four years of age. What particularly interested Gribbin was 'agonistic behaviour', or patterns of aggressive play among the children. Both groups had a similar social background, so any differences between them were unlikely to be due to socio-economic or other social factors. As Gribbin said: '. . . differences between the groups' overall behaviour must be largely a result of the different play environments.'

In the 'new style' group, children were forbidden to bring any guns or violent toys to play with, a prohibition presumably based on the hypothesis that playing with guns leads to antisocial and violent behaviour. In the 'old style' group, children were allowed to bring any toys they wanted, and more often than not they chose guns, tanks and similar weapons.

The second difference was that in the new style group there was a lavish supply of climbing frames, creative toys and an outdoor play area. There was also little direct supervision of play. In the old style group, however, which was restricted to an indoor hall with less equipment, the behaviour of the children was more closely supervised. Supervision included strict rules of acceptable behaviour, and transgressors were confined to a 'sin bin' for serious misdemeanours (such as biting another child). Anti-social behaviour in the new style group was looked upon by the supervisor as a sign that the naughty child needed love and understanding, which he or she duly received, often at the expense of the victim who was virtually ignored while the social problems of the aggressor were dealt with.

Thus the two groups provide a clear contrast between the permissive and the restrictive organization of society at large. We shall see later whether the lessons learnt from this small-scale experiment can indeed be extended to society as a whole. Readers are invited to guess what the effects of these two styles of treatment were on the children involved before they read the next paragraph.

Gribbin defined 'agonistic interaction' (aggressive play) in terms of a variety of behaviours, ranging from mild abuse, accompanied by verbal and non-verbal threats, at one end, to actual physical violence at the other. Boys in the old-fashioned group showed 5 instances of aggression, but in the progressive group there were 89 instances! Girls showed no instances of aggression at all in the old-fashioned group, but 42 in the progressive group. For the two sexes combined, the totals were 5 instances of agonistic behaviour in the old-fashioned and 131 in the progressive group. The five incidents in the old-fashioned play group were all simple verbal personal abuse. In the pro-gressive play group something like 65 per cent of incidents led to blows being exchanged, often with scratching and biting. Thus there was a tremendous difference between the two groups, with the 'no guns' permissive group showing vastly more agonistic behaviour than the old-fashioned group.

Gribbin commented: 'Are the children who have no violent toys, lots of sympathetic understanding, few restrictions on play within the group and a slightly more "affluent" society in terms of available toys, more able to cope with social interactions and co-operative behaviour? Far from it.' As she went on to point out, one of the most interesting features of her study was that the children in the 'no guns' group were busily engaged in making guns, tanks and swords out of harmless Lego kits. 'The forbidden fruit clearly tastes sweeter, especially when the results encouraged an adult response along the lines of "Now, Nigel, that isn't a gun you're making, is it?" ' In the old style group, by contrast, even the violent toys were generally treated by the children simply as comforting reminders of home, and seldom used for any 'violent' or even mock-violent purposes.

There were many other differences between the two groups. The children in the old style group played in bigger units (three or four individuals) than those in the new style group, where children played mostly in pairs. Inevitably this meant that there were more mixed groups of boys and girls playing together in the old style than in the permissive group. These and many other differences were discussed by Mary Gribbin in her account of the experiment[2], but the most important difference she left to the end: 'We also formed the distinct impression (admittedly a subjective interpretation, but still one based on hours of watching at each group) that the children in the old-fashioned group were just plain happier than those in the progressive group.' This bears out the observation frequently made by psychologists that children actually prefer a structured environment, and feel lost and unhappy when such structure is not provided by adults or older children. Chaos, even if labelled permissive, does not make for happiness.

This experiment strongly indicates the importance of the environment for the behaviour of children. The different treatments given the two groups overrode even the most basic biological difference of all, namely that between the sexes. In both groups boys were more aggressive than girls, but this sex difference fades into insignificance compared with the much greater difference between old-fashioned and progressive types of behaviour.

This is hardly the result that would have been predicted by the advocates of progressive teaching, who in the last 80 years or so have turned our pre-school groups, kindergartens and primary schools into permissive places of no work and all play, from which all socializing and restraining influences have been banned. The motives no doubt were

This is the kind of behaviour which 'progressive' education – minimal supervision, no violent toys, lots of outlets for creativity – has sought to eliminate. Ironically, the progressive approach may have contributed to the greater levels of aggression in society today.

good, but the effects were not. The hoped-for improvement in the happiness and mental health of our children did not happen. Progressive methods have not helped them to grow into well-adjusted, socialized human beings. Gribbin's experiment is

Research suggests that rather than delete guns and tanks and other 'undesirable' elements from juvenile consciousness, parents and teachers should concentrate on providing a social environment with incentives, clear rules about give and take, and opportunities to take responsibility.

not the only one to demonstrate the adverse effects of permissiveness, but it does show how complex social interactions can be studied experimentally.

ACADEMIC ACHIEVEMENT

Let us turn to another, larger study undertaken to investigate the influence of secondary schools on the accomplishments and behaviour of children. Here too there has been much poorly informed discussion in which the permissive climate of opinion and the erroneous views of 'experts' have played havoc with our educational system. Some of

the background of this troubling story is worth retelling.

In 1966 James Coleman published a very influential report in the United States entitled *The Equality of Educational Opportunity*. He conducted a large-scale survey of the achievements of some 645,000 students in 4,000 secondary and elementary schools. He believed that the results showed that educational attainment was largely independent of the schooling a child receives, and this conclusion was supported by Christopher Jencks in *Inequality: A Reassessment of the Effect of Family and Schooling in America* in 1972. Jencks concluded his complex statistical analysis by stating that 'equalizing the quality of high schools would reduce cognitive inequality by 1 per cent or less', and that 'additional school expenditures are unlikely to increase achievement, and redistributing resources will not reduce inequality.'

In the United Kingdom, the Plowden Report of 1967, which was in many ways comparable with the Coleman study, concluded that home influences far outweighed those of school. Altogether there was widespread pessimism about the extent to which schools could exert any influence on children's development. This view was well expressed by Basil Bernstein when he said: 'Education cannot compensate for society' (meaning that where education has failed, revolution must take its place).

These conclusions, so contrary to common sense, were largely based on statistical and theoretical fallacies (experts in education are generally as fallible as experts in child upbringing). For example, Coleman compared two factors which supposedly promote achievement at school, the environment provided by parents and the environment provided by the school. But such a comparison is meaningless because it takes no account of genetic differences in intelligence between children. Whatever precise figure we use to index the contribution of genetics, no serious researcher has come up with a figure below 50 per cent, and the majority would rate it much higher than that; 70–75 per cent is probably the most accurate estimate available at the moment.

By leaving out this extremely important factor, Coleman in fact confounded it with the environmental influences exerted by family background, socio-economic status, and so on, thus increasing the hypothetical importance of these factors out of all proportion. If his analyses are repeated with the proper introduction of genetic factors into the equations, the picture alters completely, and schools can be shown to be very important indeed in producing differences in achievement. How so many 'experts' could overlook Coleman's error and acquiesce in his conclusions is a mystery.

SCHOOLS DO MATTER

In 1979 Michael Rutter and his colleagues at the University of London wrote a book entitled *Fifteen Thousand Hours*[2], analysing a small group of secondary schools and their effects on children. Compared with the studies mentioned above, the scope of Rutter's study was very small, but that in no way detracts from its value—quite the contrary. Large-scale studies are usually conducted at too great a distance from the actual details of children's behaviour and activity. Close contact is a powerful corrective, and Rutter's book is far better factually than any of the large-scale exercises. Here we only have room to discuss Rutter's conclusions, but interested readers should read his book for themselves—not a difficult task because the book is short, full of properly researched facts, and written in clear, incisive English (Rutter eschews the atrocious jargon that normally afflicts educationists).

He found that secondary schools in Inner London differed markedly in the behaviours and attainments shown by their pupils. This was evident from the children's behaviour during school hours (as observed by researchers, teachers and the pupils themselves), from the regularity of their attendance, from the proportion who stayed on beyond school-leaving age, from their success rate in public examinations and from their delinquency rate.

His second finding was that although schools differed in the proportion of behaviourally difficult or low-achieving children they admitted, these differences did not wholly account for the variations between schools and their pupils' later behaviour and attainment. Children were more likely to show good behaviour and good scholastic attainment if they attended some schools than if they attended others. The implication here is that experiences at school *do* influence a child's progress. It was also found that variations between schools in terms of post-school success or failure were reasonably persistent over periods of at least four or five years.

Rutter's third conclusion was that individual schools performed fairly consistently on all the various measures of 'outcome'; that is to say, schools which did better than average in terms of their children's behaviour in school also tended to do better than average in terms of examination success, post-school success, and so on.

The fourth, and particularly important, finding was that these differences in outcome between schools were not due to such physical factors as the size of the school, the age of the buildings or the amount of space available. Differences in administrative status or organization were also irrelevant.

The fifth conclusion was this: 'The differences between schools and outcome *were* systematically related to their characteristics as social institutions. Factors as varied as the degree of academic emphasis, teacher actions in lessons, the availability of incentives and rewards, good conditions for pupils, and the extent to which children were able to take responsibility were all significantly associated with outcome differences between schools. All of these factors were open to modification by the staff.'

The sixth conclusion was that outcomes were also influenced by factors outside teachers' immediate control, such as academic balance in pupil intake. Examination success tended to be better in schools with a substantial nucleus of children of at least average intellectual ability, and delinquency rates were higher in those with a heavy preponderance of the least able. The intake factor was most marked with respect to delinquency and least marked with respect to observed behaviour in the classroom and elsewhere about the school.

Lastly, Rutter observed, 'The association between the *combined* measure of overall school process and each of the measures of outcome was much stronger than any of the associations with individual process variables. This suggests that the *cumulative* effect of these various social factors was considerably greater than the effect of any individual factors on their own. The implication is that the individual actions or measures may combine to create a particular *ethos*, or set of values, attitudes and behaviours which will become characteristic of the school as a whole.' In conclusion he wrote: '. . . to an appreciable extent children's behaviour and attitudes are shaped and influenced by their experiences at school and, in particular, by the qualities of the school as a social institution.'

These conclusions, we believe, follow pretty directly from the facts recorded in the book, and are of considerable importance to teachers, administrators and politicians, and particularly to parents. They may seem obvious to most people with some experience in the field, but as Rutter and his colleagues commented: 'One of the common responses of practitioners to any piece of research is that it seems to be a tremendous amount of hard work just to demonstrate what we knew already on the basis of experience or common sense . . . After all, it is scarcely surprising that children benefit from attending schools which set good standards, where the teachers provide good models of behaviour, where they are praised and given responsibility, where the general conditions are good, and where the lessons are well-conducted.' Perhaps so, but as they go on to say: 'It might have been equally obvious if we had found that the most important factors were attending a small school in modern, purpose-built premises on one site, with a particularly favourable teacher-child ratio, a year-based system of pastoral care, continuity of individual teachers, and firm discipline in which unacceptable behaviours were severely punished. In fact *none* of these items were significantly associated with good outcomes, however measured.' This point is well taken, and certainly justifies the length of time and hard work spent amassing, recording and analysing the data. The book is an example of how such research should be done, and puts to shame the much more ambitious efforts of Coleman, Plowden and the like.

NEW REALISM

May one hope that those in authority will pay some attention to the results, sack teachers who set a bad model, and promote those who influence children in a positive way? The last 30 years have seen an ideological preoccupation with unrealistic theories, poorly done research, invalid conclusions, bad statistics, and a firm desire to depart from reality in favour of utopian ideals of very limited appeal to parents anxious for the future of their children. Mercifully this period seems to be drawing to a close, and reality is again moving into conjunction

Schools matter, whatever the home environment. There is a correlation between good bahaviour and good scholastic achievement. Children are influenced not only by the quality of the teaching they receive but by the quality of their school as a social institution. The behaviour and attitudes of these two groups of children reflect the schools they go to.

with the educational process.

Some readers may feel that we are advocating a return to Victorian rules of discipline and classroom organization. This is not so. As Rutter and his colleagues pointed out: '. . . firm discipline in which unacceptable behaviours were severely punished' was not associated with particularly favourable outcomes. Imposing too harsh a discipline and too severe punishments is just as misguided as being too permissive. As usual, wisdom lies in moderation. Both extremes have their advocates, of course, but the evidence solidly opposes them. Setting a good example, maintaining good discipline with the minimum of punishment, and trying to achieve an ethos which leads to the children being socialized almost unconsciously seems to be the best way of achieving goals which most parents and teachers would agree on.

To conclude, recent empirical studies do offer helpful advice to parents on how to bring up children. The answer seems to be to avoid the extremes of Watsonian and Spockian ideology, and to create an ethos at home which reinforces co-operative and socialized behaviour. Anti-social and agonistic behaviour should be discouraged rather than absolutely vetoed. The task for parents and teachers alike is not an easy one, but the evidence shows that we can produce children who are reasonably happy and well-adjusted, provided we reject irrational prejudices, harmful ideology and the advice of 'experts' who fail to back their preaching with sound research.

Chapter 21
TAPPING EDUCATIONAL POTENTIAL

We have already seen (in Chapter 13) that human beings are very different from one another, and that these differences are much more profound than most people realize. Furthermore, they are based on firm genetic predispositions which, while they can be modified by environmental influences, nevertheless strongly determine a person's behaviour and conduct. So it seems very likely that certain methods of teaching might prove useful and helpful for extraverts, say, but exactly the opposite for introverts[1]. Thus if we compare a new method of teaching with an old-established method and find that the new method is neither better nor worse than the old, this may indeed mean that there are no differences between the two methods. But it may also mean, and this is much more likely, that the new method is *better for some people* and *worse for others*. The new method only appears neither better nor worse than the old because the two effects, one positive and one negative, appear to cancel each other out.

Take the relationship between personality and academic achievement. It has often been found that extraverted children do better than introverted ones in primary school, and in the early years of secondary school. But in the later years of secondary school, and at university, introverts do considerably better than extraverts. This seems to be largely due to the fact that the relatively free and easy methods of teaching adopted in most primary schools suit extraverted children, who thrive on informality and like to flit from topic to topic fairly quickly. Introverts prefer the formal teaching atmosphere of the later secondary school. They like to get their teeth into a topic and persevere with it, and generally do better at secondary and tertiary levels where the emphasis is on specialism.

In other words, one simply cannot say that one method is 'better' than another. All we can say is that one method suits the extravert, another suits the introvert. Perhaps introverted children would do better at primary school if a more formal system were adopted. Similarly extraverts might do better in the later years of secondary school and at university if courses were less specialized and allowed their interest to range wider.

PASSIVE VERSUS ACTIVE LEARNING
One of the traditional great divides in teaching theory is that between the 'discovery' method and the direct instruction method. The essence of the discovery method is that the pupil is told the law or principle underlying a phenomenon but has to discover it for himself by experiment (he is of course given the wherewithal to conduct experiments). This is very different from the usual 'reception' type of teaching, in which the pupil is presented with facts and simply has to learn them. Reception learning has been criticized because it tends to make the pupil a passive recipient of wisdom. Discovery learning has been praised because it enables the pupil to find out for himself. On the other hand, critics have pointed out that most school children are too young and immature to discover complex laws for themselves, and that they may actually prefer to do their work and their experiments in the context of knowledge transmitted to them by the teacher. Who is right?

KEY EXPERIMENT: PERSONALITY AND LEARNING ABILITY
Comparisons carried out to study the relative superiority of discovery learning over reception learning or vice versa have usually failed. Professor G. O. Leith[2] examined the possibility 'that the greater readiness of extraverts to become bored by routines but likely to respond to stimulus variation, and of introverts to be disturbed by changes of set but able to maintain attentiveness to a highly-prompted task, would result in a method × personality interaction.'

Leith arranged for teaching materials for a course in genetics to be carefully prepared to give equal amounts of discovery learning and instruction learning in randomly chosen groups of students. 'The materials were so chosen as to cover a range of personal discovery, tolerance for uncertainty and error-making as well as of differences which may be described as plunging into the deep end or stepping into the shallow end of the pool.' Two hundred students took part in the experiment, and were tested one week after the course and again five weeks later. They were also tested for introversion/extraversion.

The major finding was a highly significant interaction between personality and method. On both testing occasions introverts and extraverts learned equally well *on average*. In other words there was no overall superiority of one method over the other. But extraverts learned much better with the

Introverts do well at subjects which involve a high degree of concentration and application. They enjoy being meticulous and accurate in their work.

discovery method than introverts, while introverts learned much better with the direct teaching method.

At the final count, introverts had a mean score of 17 using the discovery learning method, but a mean score of 26 using the traditional reception learning method. Extraverts had a score of 24 using the reception learning method and a score of 30 using the discovery learning method. Leith's experiment illustrates very clearly the danger of comparing different methods of teaching without also measuring personality and looking for the different reactions of different personality types to the methods of teaching being investigated.

PAIRED LEARNING

Another interesting area of education in which personality interaction is particularly marked is that of 'paired learning', in which learners work in pairs. In one such study, pairing was arranged on the basis of ability and also of neuroticism-stability. Thus, pairs matched or mismatched for ability were also matched or mismatched for neuroticism-stability, giving a total of ten pair categories. The improvements in learning ability were very dif-

ferent indeed, and depended not on the ability of the pupils involved but on their personality. Neurotic-stable pairs showed something like a 100 per cent superiority over the neurotic-neurotic and stable-stable pairs, regardless of the differences or similarities between ability. So if we want to raise the academic achievement of our children, we should put high-neuroticism scorers together with low-neuroticism scorers!

Quite a different picture emerged when extraversion-introversion and ability were made the basis of pairing. In this situation similar ability pairs performed better than different ability pairs, whether the pair consisted of two extraverts, two introverts or an introvert and an extravert. In short, high-neuroticism scorers of all abilities could benefit most from being paired with children of stable character whose abilities are similar. As we saw in Chapter 17, anxiety is an inhibitor of all kinds of performance, so putting high-anxiety pupils with low-anxiety pupils would be one way of combating the effects of anxiety on learning.

SUPPORTIVE AND EXPLORATORY TEACHING STYLES

Another way of combating the effects of anxiety on academic performance was suggested by an experiment done by Trown and Leith[3], in which nearly

500 boys and girls took part. The experiment was designed to contrast the effects of 'supportive' and 'explorative' strategies in mathematics teaching in four junior schools (the average age of the children involved was 10½). As Trown and Leith reported: 'In the case of the supportive strategy, the sequence employed over each of the twelve sections of learning material was that of teacher-provided statements of organizing principle, followed by related pupil activity with mathematical models, and subsequent restatements of principle by the teacher. Such statements were both spoken and written on the blackboard.

'The same activities, with models, were used in the exploratory strategy, but this time at the beginning of each section of the learning sequence. Each statement of principle by the teacher was now delayed until pupils had been given the opportunity to perceive the relationship themselves and had been encouraged to attempt an appropriate generalization.'

Differences in neuroticism (anxiety level) produced clear differences in performance in the learner-centred exploratory situation; some children profited from it, others were handicapped by it. Mean scores in the test for remembering what they had learned were almost twice as high for low-anxiety as for high-anxiety children. However, when they learned in the supportive situation, there were no differences between low- and high-anxiety children. Again, overall differences

between the two teaching strategies were minimal when the personalities of the children were ignored.

The lesson is clear: had the experimenters failed to take the children's personalities into account, they would have come to the quite erroneous conclusion that both strategies were identical in their effects. Both extraversion and neuroticism play a part in a child's reaction to these different methods of teaching. No method is good or bad in itself—its usefulness or otherwise depends very much on the personality of the child it is applied to. The stable extravert child flourishes in discovery and exploratory situations, whereas his introverted peer, particularly when he is anxious, is heavily penalized. The anxious introvert does much better with supportive strategies and reception learning.

MATCHING TEACHING METHODS TO PERSONALITY

Leith summarized the conclusions he believed could be drawn from his many studies as follows: 'The evidence . . . does not lead to definitive con-

Learning in pairs is a strategy often used in the classroom. For the best results a stable child should be paired with an anxious child; this increases the learning ability of both, whether their academic ability is the same or different. Few teachers are aware of this fact.

In many infant schools individual progress is closely monitored and teaching methods are fairly flexible; the needs of older pupils are seldom catered for in the same way.

clusions which can be applied immediately with confidence in classrooms. It can be claimed, however, that the repeated findings of interactions between personality (as measured by neuroticism and extraversion scales) and instructional methods (defined in terms of both global differences and experimentally manipulable variations) require that educationalists pay serious attention to the need for adapting learning situations to learners.'

An examination of the interaction between personality and teaching methods shows that extraverts are not intrinsically poorer students. They have simply been disadvantaged by methods more suitable for teaching introverts. In an age of educational innocence, this may have been tolerable, but today it begins to look more like discrimination. Much more research should and must be undertaken.

If future research supports the findings of Leith and others, what should be done? Certainly it would be wrong to stream on the basis of personality and/or ability. The type of teaching system which treats class units as relatively homogeneous blocks of children is administratively convenient rather than educationally enlightened. A teaching system which fully recognized personality differences is more likely to be based on the methods

used in many infant schools; in other words it would provide a variety of approaches and tailor those approaches to individual children by closely monitoring their progress. Investigations into cooperative learning were a step towards finding ways of giving individual instruction in destreamed, comprehensive-type classes. Co-operative learning would provide not only learner-centred activities, but also continuous feedback, progress checks, and the means to make the most of the social environment of school.

TEACHER TRAINING

Above all, prospective teachers (and practicing ones, too!) need to be taught the facts of personality structure, and the interaction between personality and teaching strategies and systems. At the moment the kind of psychology taught to teachers is almost entirely useless as far as dealing with children in classrooms is concerned. It consists of irrelevant Freudian shibboleths and similar snippets of misinformation which may make teachers think they understand the psychology of the teaching situation but which are unhelpful in practice. Given some knowledge of the behaviour patterns of extraverted and introverted, stable and unstable children, and provided with questionnaires to test their pupils in order to spot extremes, teachers should be able to work out the best methods of motivating and instructing children of different ability and personality. To go on pretending that all children are alike is unrealistic, and most teachers

◀ Previous page: Most classroom situations favour extraverts – extraverts in this primary school class will be the first to put up their hands, for instance. But as long as academic achievement is equated with passing written exams, introverts will be the higher achievers.

know it. But at the moment little help is given to them in their professional training, although enough is already known to make better teaching possible, and detailed instructions on how best to apply existing knowledge are readily available. Lecturers in teacher training colleges have no excuse for avoiding what should be a central task in the preparation of teachers for their job. It is time that the facts became more widely known and were applied to the better and more successful instruction of our children.

What has been said here in relation to education is equally true in relation to all other aspects of psychology—experimental psychology, social psychology, clinical psychology, industrial psychology, and so on. In all these fields practitioners and experimentalists alike refuse to face the fact that individuals differ greatly in their reaction to any kind of experimental or social situation, and that a person's reaction is powerfully determined by his personality. Just as the physicist does not expect mercury to behave like gold, or aluminium like iron, so it is completely irrational to expect an introvert to behave like an extravert, whether in the laboratory or in social situations. Similarly, an emotionally unstable person reacts quite differently from an emotionally stable person and recognition of this fact is an absolute necessity in psychology generally and in its application.

So far we have dealt only with academic, abstract learning, but of course the task of the teacher goes far beyond mere scholastic attainment. There is a tradition, particularly in English schools, of 'character building', which insists that children should not only possess a knowledge of the three Rs but should also be educated to become well-integrated, honest members of society. We have already cited experiments (Chapter 8) to show that this can be accomplished through a process of conditioning, and that the great innate differences in conditionability produce great differences in socialized or anti-social behaviour. But there are other ways in which personality subtly interacts with education.

EXAM NERVES AND SCHOOL PHOBIA

Most people have heard of examination anxiety, and most of us have, in some degree, experienced how debilitating it can be. We feel too nervous to give of our best in the examination room. Examination anxiety is widespread. So is school phobia, a fear of going to school that is so strong that the child absolutely refuses to go, plays truant, and may become a very real problem to his parents, his teachers and himself.

Examination anxiety and school phobia tend to occur mainly in children who have a high degree of emotionality or neuroticism, i.e. who are innately predisposed to feel very fearful in situations they perceive as threatening. Fortunately these minor neuroses are fairly easy to dispel, by a method of therapy called 'desensitization'. In desensitization, the patient is trained in methods of physical relaxation, relaxation being as incompatible with anxiety as tenseness is with euphoria.

During the actual treatment session, the person is first completely relaxed and then asked to imagine the scene which normally causes him intense anxiety (getting up in the morning and getting ready to go to school, for example). This produces some anxiety, but not enough to overwhelm the anti-anxiety properties of the relaxation. Consequently the person learns to tolerate a small degree of anxiety. He becomes conditioned to respond with 'non-anxiety' to a previously threatening situation.

Gradually the therapist builds up to situations which normally evoke more and more anxiety, always being careful not to overstep the mark where relaxation is a sufficient countervailing force against the anxiety provoked. The patient is led through a number of imaginary scenes of an increasingly threatening nature (getting up in the morning, getting ready for school, actually walking out of the house, down the street and boarding the bus, seeing the school in the distance, seeing other schoolchildren approaching the school building, walking into it . . .). When all this can be done in imagination without producing undue anxiety, the therapist asks the person, again in a condition of complete relaxation, to go through all these stages in real life, accompanying him all the time. Gradually the person becomes 'desensitized' and manages to go to school, make a trip to the supermarket, pick up a spider, step into an elevator . . . The success rate of desensitization treatment is almost 100 per cent, and the treatment does not take long.

Examination anxiety can be treated in this way, again with practically 100 per cent success. The student is taught to relax, and then imagines himself in examination situations, progressing from low-anxiety situations to actual examination conditions.

Desensitization is now very widely used to treat children who suffer from school phobia and exam funk. Teachers are not usually trained in these methods, but there would be no difficulty in training them. Exam nerves and school phobia are such frequent problems that it would be well worth while introducing treatment methods into teacher-training courses.

Even more worth while would be prophylaxis—preventing the problems in the first place. To do this it would be necessary to identify those children most likely to suffer from examination anxiety or school phobia. This is relatively

Sweet comforts to ease the pain of swotting for exams! Exam phobia can actually interfere with swotting strategies.

easy—questionnaires of neuroticism and introversion could be given, and children scoring high on both would be singled out as the most likely to succumb to exam nerves or school phobia. The teacher (or therapist) could then 'inoculate' such children by the desensitization method just described *before* they showed signs of phobia or anxiety. In American schools special school psychologists are employed to do this kind of work, and it might be a good thing if British schools were to follow suit. Unfortunately, there is never much money for prophylactic schemes. Governments tend to wait until things have gone wrong and then spend money putting them right, even though it would have cost much less to prevent the problem in the first place.

CONCLUSIONS

Both at school and university level students with high neuroticism-instability-emotionality scores tend to do less well than their more stable peers. A great deal can be done to help them to make the most of their talents. But high academic achievement is not all that counts. It would be just as valuable to learn how to manage the overly strong and unstable emotions which interfere with learning and application. School teachers and university staff should be familiar with these facts, should have some insight into personality dynamics, particularly where neuroticism and extraversion are concerned, and should be able to help directly or refer their pupils to a psychologist capable of dealing with their problems. It is unnecessary cruelty to allow emotionally unstable people to suffer breakdown, failure and anxiety when the remedy is available, and usually works. A society is judged by the efforts it makes to look after the deprived, the unfortunate and the unlucky. Our society could certainly do better than it has done in the past.

Chapter 22

BIOFEEDBACK: MIND OVER MATTER

If you were asked to walk with a simulated limp, putting more weight on one leg than the other, you might think it bizarre but you would have no doubts about your ability to do it. On the other hand, if you were asked to make more blood flow through one of your ears than through the other, you would think it even more bizarre, and probably consider it physically impossible.

We have voluntary control over many activities, such as walking, thinking and speaking, but the workings of our internal organs (heart, liver, stomach, kidneys, and so on) are outside our conscious control—physiologists refer to these internal organs as the 'viscera'. And there are good reasons why we do not need to exert voluntary control over them. It would be most tiresome, for example, if we had to stop doing everything else after a meal in order to supervise the digestive processes of the stomach. But while it is clearly very convenient that our internal organs should look after themselves, there are times when the ability to control them would be extremely useful. The man with a hangover or the seasick traveller would dearly love to be able to discipline his protesting innards.

The notion that bodily activities can be divided up into voluntary and involuntary has a long history. Two thousand years ago, Plato drew a distinction between the superior rational soul inhabiting the head and the inferior souls inhabiting the body. More recently it has been argued that voluntary behaviour is possible only for skeletal responses produced by the central nervous system, whereas involuntary behaviour characterizes the visceral and emotional responses of the more primitive autonomic nervous system.

This simple distinction held sway for a very long time among philosophers, psychologists and physiologists. However, there are several intriguing examples of voluntary control over apparently 'involuntary' responses which suggest that this view may be over-simplified. The famous memory man S., briefly mentioned in Chapter 15, who had an exceptional capacity to imagine vividly, was able to control his heart rate and temperature. Merely by visualizing himself as asleep or vigorously active, S. was able to alter his heart rate abruptly over a range of nearly 40 beats per minute (70 beats per minute is average when at rest). Even more dramatically, S. could raise the skin temperature of his right hand by imagining that it was on a hot stove, while at the same time lowering the temperature of his left hand by imagining that it was holding an ice cube.

Illusionist and escapologist Harry Houdini also had exceptional control over 'involuntary' responses. In spite of the careful scrutiny to which he was exposed—whenever he performed one of his famous escapes, his clothes and body were searched beforehand by sceptical spectators—he escaped from his chains, padlocks and handcuffs every time. The method he used was to hold a key suspended in his throat and then regurgitate it when he was unobserved. Since the natural unlearned reaction to having an object stuck in one's throat is to gag, it is not surprising that no one thought of Houdini's throat as a possible hiding place for keys. Houdini's real trick was that he had learned to control his gag reflex. This he had achieved by practising for hour after hour with a small piece of potato tied to a length of string.

Amazing claims have been made about the powers of Indian yogis, including the ability to make the heart stop beating. It is difficult to evaluate most of these claims, and undoubtedly some yogis have been motivated by the desire to part the gullible from their money. However, a serious attempt to study yogis scientifically was made by Dr Bal K. Anand of the Department of Physiology at the All-India Institute of Medical Sciences in New Delhi. He tested over 400 yogis under carefully controlled laboratory conditions. Though most of them proved disappointing, a handful demonstrated unusual abilities. One was able to reduce his heartbeat to half the normal rate by blocking the action of the so-called cardiac pacemaker, and another could make his forehead break out in perspiration without moving a muscle. Two more yogis were able to slow down their metabolism until they were functioning at less than half their normal waking metabolic rate—approximately *five times* as great a drop in metabolic rate as occurs in very deep sleep!

The first thorough attempt to see whether the internal organs or viscera can learn in the same way that rats learn to press a lever for food was made by the distinguished American psychologist Neal Miller in the 1960s. His painstaking research helped to initiate today's scientific interest in 'biofeedback'.

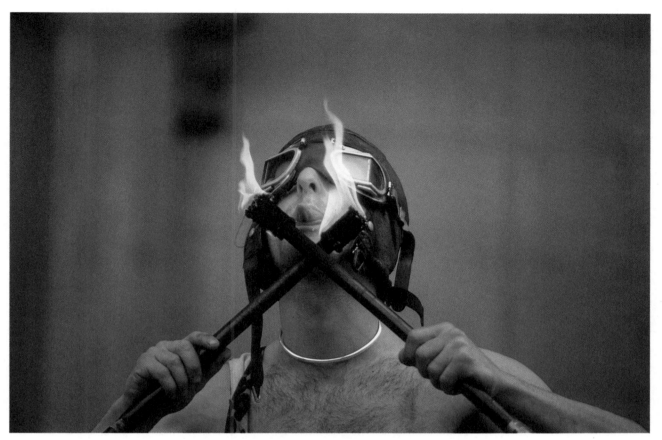

Warning: this experiment should not be performed at home unless you have learnt to control your swallowing reflex!

KEY EXPERIMENT: CAN THE INTERNAL ORGANS LEARN?

As Neal Miller stared intently at his own reflection in the bathroom mirror of his weekend house in Guilford, Connecticut, he saw a stocky, energetic man, bald except for a white fringe behind the ears, with a firm jaw, broad nose and deep-set green eyes. However, the focus of his gaze was his ears, because he was trying to teach himself to wiggle his right ear without moving his left. He believed that all learning requires the appropriate use of reward or reinforcement. Accordingly, he was looking carefully for the faintest indication that he was beginning to master the trick of wiggling one ear on its own so that he could reward this elusive wiggle with a burst of self-congratulation.

He tried various techniques, including imagining that the left side of his face was cold or numb, so that the ear on that side would be unable to wiggle; they all failed. He finally discovered that standing in front of the mirror and approaching the task little by little was the best strategy. He explained his technique in the following way to Gerald Jonas of the *New Yorker*: 'I'd start by trying to produce the most minute independent movement with my right ear. Then I'd try to increase it a little bit each day. If my left ear started to move at any time, I'd drop

back until I was sure that only the right one was moving. Then I'd start increasing the movement again, little by little. Eventually . . .' At this point in his conversation with Jonas, Miller paused and seemed to be concentrating deeply. His right ear began to twitch while the left ear remained motionless. After a while, he relaxed and broke into a wide grin, indicating that success is its own reward.

This story illustrates the way in which people can learn to do strange and unusual things if they are suitably rewarded, and if they receive direct information or feedback about the success or otherwise of their efforts. Could heart rate voluntarily be lowered or raised if constant information about the speed of functioning of the heart were available? Miller felt this ought to be possible, and argued that it could occur in two very different ways: directly through actual visceral learning, and indirectly through voluntary control of skeletal (voluntary) activities such as exercise or breathing (e.g. if you take long slow deep breaths your heart rate will tend to slow down).

Miller regarded the alteration of heart rate by indirect, non-visceral means as 'cheating', and pointed out that an impressive demonstration of genuine learning by the internal organs required the elimination of the possibility that skeletal (voluntary) activities were responsible. The technique he chose was to use injections of curare, a drug which causes virtually complete paralysis of the skeletal muscles, including those involved in

breathing, but which permits the internal organs to function fairly normally.

Curare was originally obtained by South American Indians from the roots, stems and bark of jungle plants, and they used it to envenom the darts they used in hunting, the poison causing death from respiratory failure within minutes. Later on curare was used as an anaesthetic during surgery. Since the patients remained completely immobile, it was generally assumed that they felt nothing during the operation. Their screams after the effects of the curare wore off were at one time dismissed as hallucinations. Then it was discovered that they suffered excruciating agony with every cut of the surgeon's knife.

The basic contention of Miller and his col-

Meditation is a very ancient method of altering both physical and mental states. Breath control is central to many forms of meditation – through the breath, the body's involuntary mechanisms can be influenced. They are less easily influenced merely by thinking about them.

leagues at New York's Rockefeller University was that if the visceral responses of curarized animals could be manipulated by reward or reinforcement, this would show conclusively that the internal organs are capable of learning. Since there are obvious dangers in using a powerful drug like curare on humans, and because it might have been difficult to find people prepared to submit themselves to temporary paralysis, Miller decided to use rats in most of his experiments. Since curarized rats cannot breathe unaided, their breathing had to be maintained by artificial means.

Miller decided that the major reason why the internal organs do not normally seem to show much learning is that we are not normally aware of their activities. In order to facilitate the learning of heart rate changes in the rats, Miller arranged a complicated system to provide the rats with information about their heart rates. Each rat was initially given an operation in which electrodes were sewn under its skin in such a way that they could be attached to an electrocardiograph, a machine which records and monitors heart rate. The apparatus was set up so that a small spontaneous increase in heart rate (usually a 2 per cent rise) was followed by a reward. As time went by, the rat had to increase its heart rate by larger and larger amounts in order to obtain a reward.

How on earth do you reward a rat that is totally paralyzed? Miller got round this tricky problem by briefly stimulating that part of the rat's brain which acts as a kind of 'reward centre'. He found that by rewarding progressively greater increases in heart rate with brain stimulation he could increase the curarized rat's heart rate by 80 beats a minute in just $1\frac{1}{2}$ hours of training! Thus it looked as if the internal organs *could* learn by the reward method in spite of the then widespread belief that such a thing was impossible[1, 2].

Could rats learn to alter the functioning of other internal organs? Miller found that curarized rats could learn to increase or decrease intestinal contractions, vary the amount of blood in the stomach wall, and even control the rate of urine formation!

Miller was still not satisfied that he had shown visceral learning to be the same as the learning of skeletal responses such as pressing levers for food. For instance, 'normal' learning is usually remembered reasonably well. To prove the point that visceral learning is also remembered Miller tested rats who had spent $1\frac{1}{2}$ hours learning to increase or decrease their heart rates three months earlier and found that they did indeed remember how to control heart rate.

Finally, Miller argued that 'normal' learning of any physical skill shows a progressive improvement in the precision with which movements are made. Does visceral learning show the same precision? Apparently so, because curarized rats were able to make more blood flow through one ear than the other when rewarded for doing so!

Why on earth has nature endowed us with the capacity for visceral learning if it is so little used that most people believe that we do not even possess it? As Miller himself pointed out, it would be very strange if evolution had created a mechanism that had 'no normal function other than that of providing my students with subject matter for publications.'

The answer to that puzzle may be related to the fact that most aspects of our internal environment need to be kept fairly stable all the time; this is known as 'homeostasis'. Innate control systems usually suffice to maintain homeostasis, but visceral learning may be available as a supplementary mechanism if the internal environment is seriously threatened.

An ironical footnote to Miller's work is that back in the 1930s he and his mentor Clark Hull had vigorously promulgated the notion that all forms of learning, whether of the skeletal or the visceral variety, depended on reward or reinforcement. With hindsight, Miller was amazed that none of Hull's research associates had seriously investigated visceral learning all those years ago: 'With so many other people insisting that it couldn't be done, even the smallest positive result would have been a terrific coup for the theory . . . I may have dodged this particular application of Hull's theory because I felt that it might be refuted . . . and I was unconsciously reluctant to face this possible outcome.' But perhaps the greater irony is that, in spite of his well-merited reputation as a meticulous experimenter, it has proved rather difficult to replicate Miller's findings. Researchers at other institutions have had some success, but Miller himself, in collaboration with Barry Dworkin, has not.

Whatever the ultimate scientific value of Miller's research, there is no question at all about the huge influence of his work. In particular, the entire development of biofeedback as a medical tool in the treatment of various human problems might never have occurred without Miller's seminal work.

MEDICAL USE OF BIOFEEDBACK

At the level of ideas, Miller's work has apparently shown that the difference between human reason and human emotions may be less extreme than previously believed, since both can be controlled in the same way. At the more practical level, the notion that we can control our internal organs opened up new vistas for the treatment of a wide range of complaints, ranging from migraine headaches to heart irregularities. Of course, Miller did most of his work with rats, but since people are more intelligent than rats they ought to be able to train their internal organs at least as well.

Some support for this general position was obtained by Lee Birk of Harvard Medical School, who volunteered to be injected with curare. After the injection, he could not lift his head from the chair, nor was he able to lift any extremity, open his eyes, swallow or utter intelligible sounds. Even in this state, he continued to show evidence of remembering a visceral response learned previously while not curarized.

The media have devoted a lot of attention to 'biofeedback'. The term simply refers to a technique in which biophysiological instruments provide the patient with information about changes in bodily functioning of which he is usually unaware. The patient's 'reward' is to observe his increasing control over the workings of a part of his own body, and the apparatus is set so as to gradually 'shape' the visceral response in the desired direction.

CASE HISTORIES

One of the most spectacular success stories for the biofeedback approach was reported by Peter Lang and Barbara Melamed of the University of Wisconsin. They treated a nine-month-old boy, A.T. His birth weight was 9 lb 4 oz, and at six months his weight had gone up to 17 lb. However, he suddenly started regurgitating and vomiting most of his food within 10 minutes of each feed, so that at nine months of age his weight had fallen to less than 12 lb. He was in an advanced state of dehydration and malnutrition, and was being fed through a stomach pump. He was not expected to live.

Psychoanalysts have argued that such symptoms in children are due to a disruption of the mother-infant relationship in which the mother's inability to fulfil an adult psychosexual role prevents her from providing warm and loving care for her child. The infant reacts by seeking its own gratification from within by regurgitating its food and retaining it in the mouth. Unfortunately for this idea, the prescribed remedy of very warm and intensive nursing had no effect whatsoever on the vomiting.

Lang and Melamed measured the muscle potentials along A.T.'s œsophagus, and discovered that the first wave of reverse peristalsis just preceded regurgitation. They arranged things so that the infant received unpleasant electric shocks which started whenever the œsophagus started to back up and continued until the vomiting had stopped. After only a few meals, the infant stopped vomiting. One month after discharge from the hospital his weight had more than doubled to 21 lb. He had become a healthy toddler.

Biofeedback has also been applied to the treatment of male sexual problems. In spite of the claim by the well-known sexologists Masters and Johnson that 'erections develop just as involuntarily, and with just as little effort, as breathing', penile tumescence *can* be trained and controlled. In one early study, Raymond Rosen found that penile tumescence could be greatly increased when there was information about the rate of progress and when financial incentives were offered. However, he remained sceptical of the alleged ability of some experienced yogis to withhold the ejaculation of sperm during orgasm.

Rosen applied his biofeedback technique to the treatment of Mr W., a 45-year-old school janitor who had been married for 22 years. Mr W. was arrested in a supermarket car park for exposing himself while dressed as a woman. Rosen's first step was to videotape a 30-minute sequence in which Mr W. masturbated to orgasm in his usual female attire. For the treatment sessions, Mr W.

was fitted with a mercury-in-rubber gauge, which measures even momentary changes in penile blood flow. At first when Mr W. viewed the videotape of himself he showed consistent and protracted erections on the gauge. In order to prevent this happening, an amplified recording of Mr W.'s alarm clock was played whenever his penile tumescence exceeded a particular level, and the volume of the recording was regulated according to the degree of erection. Mr W. was told to try to prevent the recording (and himself) coming on, and by the twelfth session there was total suppression of the penile response to the videotape.

On the more positive side, Mr W. manifested great penile tumescence to a typical heterosexually-oriented stag film, and this reaction was encouraged. Rosen's dry comment was 'Mr W. is a relatively inhibited, naïve lover whose sexual repertoire is currently being expanded'. At home all was well for a time. Sexual relations with his wife improved, and Mrs W. started to have orgasms. She also agreed with some reluctance to wear more erotic articles of clothing during sexual contact. Unfortunately, Mr W. resumed his transvestite activities, and was arrested and imprisoned for again exposing himself while dressed as a woman. Thus the success of his biofeedback treatment was only temporary.

Is it possible that biofeedback produces sexual arousal simply because the individual 'thinks dirty'? In one study, the vaginal blood flow of two sexually experienced unmarried women in their twenties was examined while they thought of the most erotic fantasies possible, based either on their own experiences or on activities they imagined to be erotic. Interestingly, only the more sexually experienced of the two women showed an increase in vaginal blood flow while fantasizing. In contrast, both women showed a substantial increase in vaginal blood flow when fantasy was combined with biofeedback which indicated whether the flow was increasing or decreasing. So in this case biofeedback had an effect over and above that of sexually-oriented thinking.

VOLUNTARY CONTROL OF BLOOD PRESSURE

One of the most important applications of biofeedback has been in the treatment of hypertension (high blood pressure). There has been a dramatic increase in degenerative disorders such as coronary heart disease and hypertension in the complex and fast-moving societies of the Western world. Estimates of the prevalence of hypertension vary from 10 per cent to as high as 30 per cent of the total adult population, depending on the definition of what constitutes high blood pressure. More than 90 per cent of all cases are of unknown cause, and so fall into the category of 'primary' or 'essential' hypertension. Hypertensive individuals are at greater risk than others of succumbing to such

Erotic fantasies usually increase the pleasure and intensity of sexual activity, so in a sense biofeedback is superfluous. But it has been found that awareness of changes in genital blood flow can be used to increase or decrease arousal.

disorders as myocardial infarction, congestive heart failure, stroke and damage to the kidneys, eyes and other organs.

Hypertension is normally treated by various drugs, including tranquillizers. However, many drugs have undesirable side-effects, and biofeedback might be a preferable method of treatment. Treatment of essential hypertension has most often used the 'constant cuff' method, which permits continuous, beat-by-beat feedback of blood pressure. A crystal microphone is mounted inside a standard pressure of cuff and placed over the brachial artery on the inner surface of the elbow. The cuff is inflated and set at a constant pressure close to the patient's average systolic or diastolic blood pressure. Biofeedback in the form of a light and/or sound signal is given if the patient manages to achieve a slight reduction in blood pressure.

Biofeedback training with hypertensive patients has often been successful in achieving reductions of 10–15 per cent in systolic blood press-

ure, and slightly less in diastolic blood pressure. This sounds quite impressive, but it turns out that if one simply asks hypertensive patients to attempt to reduce their blood pressure, without telling them how to do it and without using the elaborate equipment of biofeedback, one can obtain blood pressure reductions nearly as great as those achieved by means of biofeedback! It may be that biofeedback works simply because the patient is being attended to, and feels that something is being done.

The most serious doubt about the efficacy of biofeedback in reducing blood pressure is that its beneficial effects have typically only been demonstrated in the laboratory. No one has any clear idea of whether the reductions in blood pressure can be maintained under the more stressful conditions of everyday life. 'At present we have no convincing evidence that essential hypertensives can achieve clinically relevant and persistent blood pressure reductions through feedback training.'[3]

OTHER APPLICATIONS OF BIOFEEDBACK

It is known that people suffering from migraine tend to have cold extremities, and it has been argued that if blood flow to the peripheral regions were increased, this would decrease the blood flow to the head, and so ease the migraine headache.

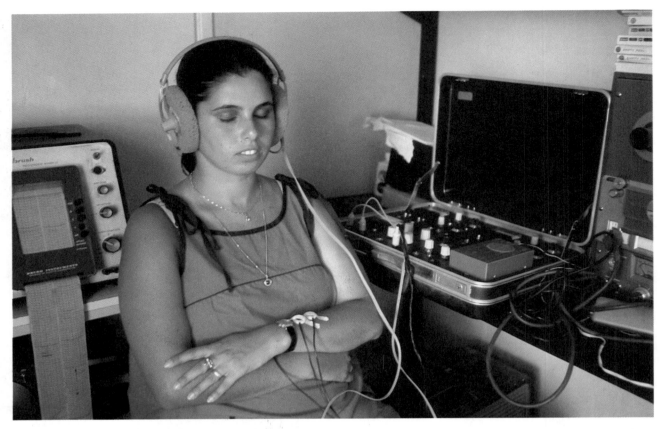

In this experiment the subject is trying to control her heart rate by listening to her pulse. The electrodes on her wrist pick up the rhythm of her pulse and relay it over the headphones.

When biofeedback has been used to increase finger temperature, there has usually been a modest reduction in the incidence of migraine headaches, but it is not clear whether this is caused by increased blood flow to the periphery or not.

A further application of biofeedback is to a peripheral circulatory ailment known as Raynaud's disease. This disease is sometimes treated by means of surgery to the sympathetic nervous system, but the effects are permanent and irreversible, and not always desirable. Biofeedback has been able to produce an increase of about 9°F in hand temperature, and shows some promise as a method of treating circulatory ailments.

A more psychological application of biofeedback has been to use it to increase alpha wave activity in the brain in order to create the 'alpha experience', a state of consciousness usually described as being pleasant, relaxed and serene, characterized by a loss of body and time awareness, and an absence or reduction of thought. The pleasantness of the alpha experience is apparently so great that many people have shown an extraordinary enthusiasm for spending large sums of money on the necessary biofeedback equipment. But the evidence indicates convincingly that these people are wasting their money. The feeling (whether justified or not) that one can control one's brain waves, combined with the power of suggestion, produces the alpha experience. If people are fooled into believing that alpha is increasing even when it is not, they report the usual strong alpha experience!

So far biofeedback has turned out not to be the medical cure-all promised by best-selling authors. But why is it that rats have a greater capacity for visceral learning than humans? One of Miller's findings offers a clue. He discovered that curarized rats showed much better visceral learning than undrugged rats, and speculated that curare helped to eliminate the various sources of distraction that interfere with learning. In other words, human patients may also need to be paralyzed in order for biofeedback to work properly!

CONCLUSIONS

In spite of a prevalent belief that the internal organs are incapable of learning, there is now strong evidence that they can learn and, moreover, acquire very specific kinds of skills. This suggests that a re-thinking of the old division of mind and body, or reason and emotion, may be called for.

These exciting new discoveries have helped to generate interest in treatment by means of biofeedback. However, the medical use of biofeedback, while much trumpeted, has proved rather disappointing so far.

Biofeedback techniques have also been applied to the treatment of migraine headaches. These headaches typically involve increased blood flow to the head, resulting in painful distention and pulsation of the cranial arteries. There are several substances available, such as benzedrine, caffeine and ephedrine, which cure migraine by producing vasoconstriction. However, these drugs can have unfortunate side-effects.

Massage achieves its effects because it stimulates the involuntary nerve fibres which control the diameter of blood vessels.

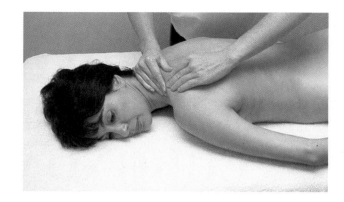

Chapter 23
PSYCHOLOGY VERSUS CANCER AND CORONOARY HEART DISEASE

Some 4,000 years ago an Indian sage declared: 'There are two classes of disease—bodily and mental. Each arises from the other. Neither can exist without the other. Mental disorders arise from physical ones, and likewise physical disorders arise from mental ones.' This flatly contradicts the notion, propounded by the seventeenth-century French philosopher René Descartes, that body and mind are entirely different substances which cannot influence each other. Nevertheless, as we shall see, the Indian sage was right and Descartes was wrong.

The debate between duality and unity has been going on for many, many years. Most practitioners of orthodox medicine aim to treat disease symptoms or disease organisms, but others, going back to Hippocrates, declare that it is their aim to treat the person rather than the disease. They consider that factors such as stress, personality, social support, housing, nutrition and many other variables play a part in the development of disease. This suggests, of course, that prophylaxis (prevention) and treatment should be just as concerned with manipulating these factors as with killing the bacteria, viruses and other organisms which attack us when our immunity is low.

There is, for instance, a long tradition linking cancer with personality. The theory dates back some 2,000 years, and many observant physicians have contributed to its evolution. Cancer-prone individuals, and people actually suffering from cancer, seem to be over-cooperative, appeasing and compliant towards authority figures, unassertive, over-patient, and inclined to bottle up negative emotions—especially anger—rather than express them and risk conflict. Recent work[1,2] has confirmed that there is indeed a link between cancer and personality, and that people with the kind of personality traits outlined above, once they develop cancer, succumb more rapidly than sufferers who are less compliant, more assertive, more complaining and willing to express their anger.

In recent years there has been a growing belief that personality and coronary heart disease (CHD)[3,4,5] are also linked in some way. This concept was pioneered by two American physicians, R. H. Rosenman and M. Friedman, who proposed that 'Type A' behaviour[6] was a reasonable predictor of stress-related heart disease. The typical Type A person was seen as almost totally work-oriented, aggressive, driven, highly competitive and impatient; he had a sense of urgency in everything he did, and explosive speech patterns which reflected his physical tension. A Type B person was quite the opposite—peaceful, normal, healthy. There was also the cancer-prone type, subsequently labelled Type C, who differed in many ways from Type A. So we are apparently dealing with three different personality types as far as susceptibility to disease is concerned: the healthy Type B, the cancer-prone Type C, and the CHD-prone Type A.

There is a large literature on the relationships between these types and the diseases to which they succumb, and on the whole it is kinder to Type C than Type A. However, prognostic studies, interviews and questionnaires have proved rather inconclusive in predicting coronary heart disease from Type A behaviour—some studies have been positive, others negative—and it is now accepted that the net was cast too wide. Only some Type A traits—hostility, aggression and anger—seem to be relevant to CHD.

Nevertheless three studies carried out over the last 20 years by Dr Grossarth-Maticek, a Yugoslav psychologist who now lives in Heidelberg, West Germany, have shown that there is a strong relationship between disease and personality type[7].

KEY EXPERIMENT: HOW STRESS AND PERSONALITY INTERACT
All the people who took part in these studies were assigned to one of four personality types on the basis of a questionnaire which, among other things, ascertained whether they were under any kind of

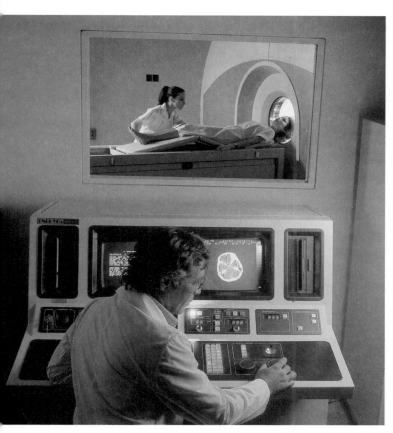

A patient enters a scanner for a check-up. When it comes to cancer and heart disease, prevention makes more sense than cure. By the time symptoms appear, the damage has been done.

'interpersonal stress'—bereavement, family rows, etc.—and how they reacted to stress. The questionnaire was administered by an interviewer who explained any questions which were not clearly understood and asked for specific examples of relevant conduct.

The personality categories to which Grossarth-Maticek's subjects were assigned were Type I (cancer-prone), Type II (CHD-prone), Type III (psychopathic personality, but otherwise reasonably healthy) or Type IV (healthy). Type I corresponds with Type C, Type II with Type A (minus those aspects of Type A thought to be irrelevant to CHD) and Type IV with Type B.

In the first study, a small town in Yugoslavia was selected and the oldest person in every household was contacted and asked to take part; a number of highly stressed individuals who were not the oldest in the household were also asked to participate. In the second study, carried out in Heidelberg, a random sample of people within preselected age and sex norms was approached. In the third study, also done in Heidelberg, the participants were severely stressed individuals, either family members or friends nominated by the participants in the second study.

Ten years went by. Then Grossarth-Maticek and his colleagues re-contacted everyone who was still alive and ascertained their state of health. For those who had died, the cause of death was noted. Figures 1, 2 and 3 on pages 222 and 223 show the results of the three studies.

A higher proportion of people in the Yugoslav group died than in the Heidelberg normal group, which was only to be expected since the incidence of cancer and coronary heart disease increases with age. However, the Heidelberg stressed group, though not older than the Heidelberg normal group, showed a much higher incidence of death from cancer and coronary heart disease, suggesting that severe stress of the interpersonal kind can indeed be a killer. Differences in smoking and other variables were not responsible for the difference.

In all three groups Type I individuals were more likely to die of cancer than coronary heart disease and Type II individuals of coronary heart disease rather than cancer. By comparison, very few Type III and Type IV individuals succumbed to either disease, although given time they may have died of one or the other. Even the 'healthiest' personality cannot postpone death indefinitely.

In short, these three studies demonstrate fairly conclusively that the connection between personality and disease is real and that stress *does* contribute to death from cancer and coronary heart disease.

BEHAVIOUR THERAPY: PREVENTION OR POSTPONEMENT?

Two very important questions follow from the studies just described. If stress, and the way we react to stress, can influence whether or not we develop cancer or coronary heart disease, it is possible, through some form of psychological treatment, to alter our behaviour in such a way that we escape them? Also, if a person is already suffering from cancer or coronary heart disease, can psychological treatment prolong his or her life? There is now evidence that the answer to both of these questions is yes.

Both cancer-prone and CHD-prone individuals seem to have difficulty coping with stress. Instead of finding ways of defusing or avoiding stress and generally behaving as if they and not external events are in control, they develop feelings of hopelessness and helplessness, retreat into themselves, become depressed or display other abnormal emotional reactions, or indulge in angry, hostile behaviour of a socially unacceptable kind. However, it is possible to teach them proper coping strategies which enable them to escape from the corner into which they have penned themselves. They can be shown how to take control of their lives, how to get over depression, how to express anger and hostility in socially acceptable ways, and generally behave in a more reasonable and self-rewarding manner.

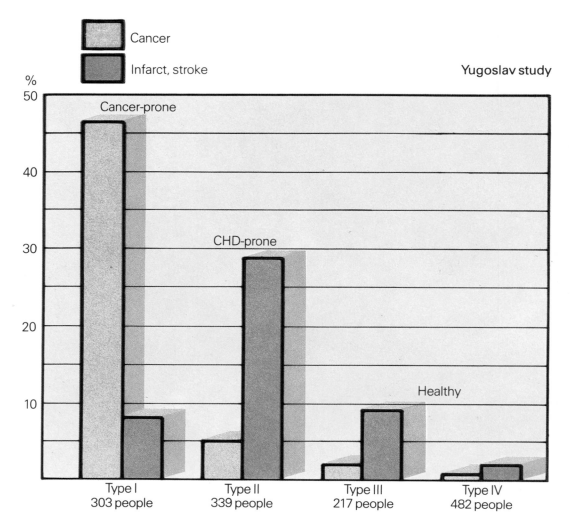

Figure 1 *In the first of Grossarth–Maticek's studies, 1,341 people – the oldest people in every other household in a small town in Yugoslavia – were contacted, assigned to one of four personality groups on the basis of a detailed questionnaire, and followed up ten years later. As this diagram shows, personality type is a good predictor of susceptibility to cancer and heart disease. Nearly half of those assigned to Type I developed cancer and nearly three in ten of those assigned to Type II developed cardiovascular problems, leading to infarct (death of heart muscle due to a blocked coronary artery) or stroke (brain damage due to disrupted blood supply to the brain).*

Grossarth-Maticek worked out a method of behaviour therapy designed to do precisely this, using techniques which included suggestion and hypnosis. The goal of such therapy is to make the disease-prone person realize the unrewarding nature of his or her usual responses to stress and replace them with healthier responses.

Figure 4 shows the results of a study which tested the effectiveness of behavioural techniques in reducing susceptibility to cancer and coronary heart disease. In this study 100 cancer-prone and 92 CHD-prone individuals were approached and divided into a control group and a therapy group (50 in both cancer-prone groups and 46 in both CHD-prone groups). Those in the therapy groups were then given 25–30 hours of individual treatment. Thirteen years later 36 of the cancer group and 38 of the CHD had died—of cancer, CHD and other causes—but the survivors from the therapy groups outnumbered the survivors from the control groups by more than two to one.

Behaviour therapy clearly has considerable potential for preventing, or at least delaying, the development of cancer in cancer-prone individuals and CHD in CHD-prone individuals, so the theory that certain behaviour patterns increase the risk of disease is clearly correct. Changing neurotic and unsuccessful behaviour patterns can lead to a longer, healthier life, not to mention a happier one. It would therefore pay anyone assessed as being cancer- or CHD-prone on the basis of personality diagnosis to undergo a short course of prophylactic therapy.

In another study small groups of up to 20 cancer-prone and CHD-prone individuals were

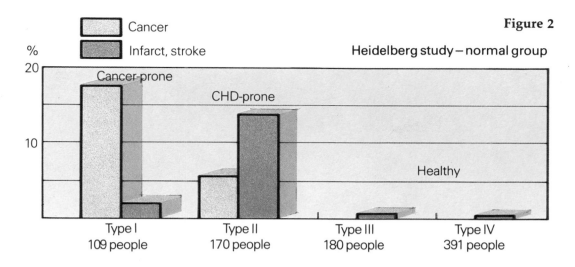

Figure 2

Heidelberg study – normal group

Cancer

Infarct, stroke

Cancer-prone

CHD-prone

Healthy

Type I
109 people

Type II
170 people

Type III
180 people

Type IV
391 people

Figures 2 and 3 *In two further studies done in Heidelberg, Grossarth–Maticek followed up 'normal' and 'stressed' individuals after ten years to see what effects stress has on disease-prone and healthy groups of people. As can be seen from the graphs above, the results were fairly dramatic. Stress, it seems, can just about double one's chances of developing cancer or CHD if one has a disease-prone personality*

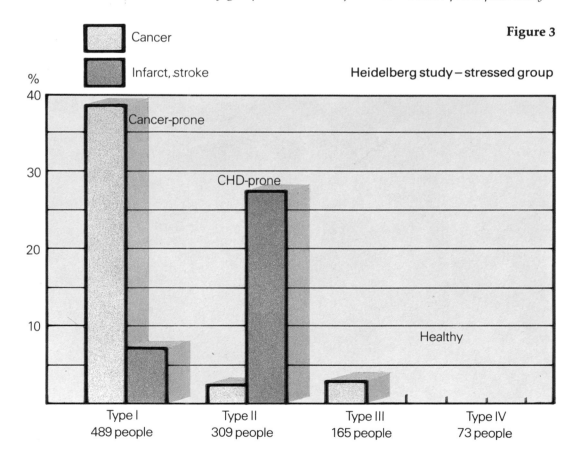

Figure 3

Heidelberg study – stressed group

Cancer

Infarct, stroke

Cancer-prone

CHD-prone

Healthy

Type I
489 people

Type II
309 people

Type III
165 people

Type IV
73 people

treated by means of group therapy, typically for six hours in all, spread over two or more separate days. They were then followed up over a period of eight years. In the therapy groups 48 people died, but in the matched control groups 180 died. So group therapy can also be an effective prophylactic.

Yet another study was done with 1,200 people, 600 of whom constituted the therapy group, 500 the control group and 100 a 'placebo' group—the latter received a form of treatment not anticipated to have any effect beyond that of making them feel that they were receiving some form of treatment. In this case

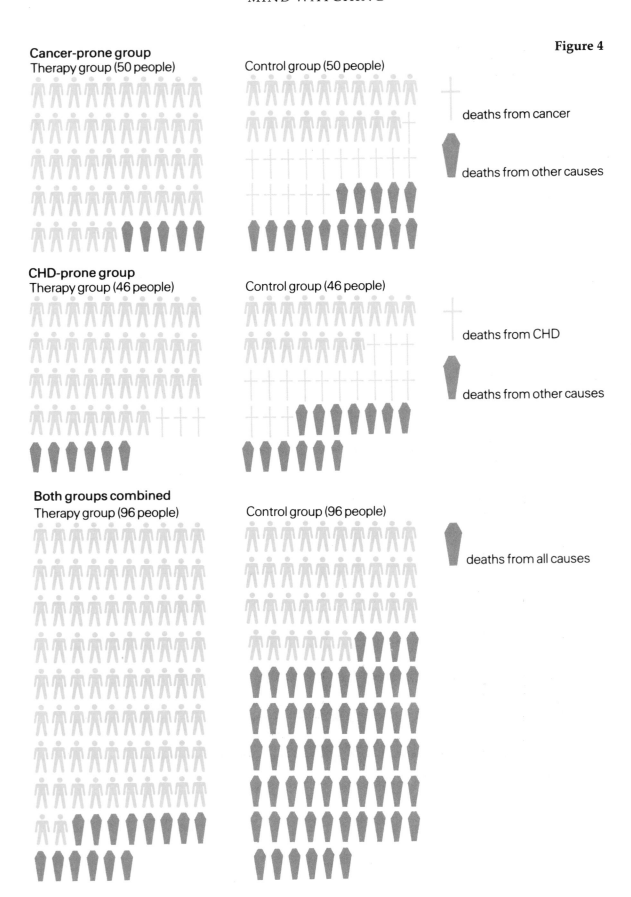

Figure 4

Figure 5

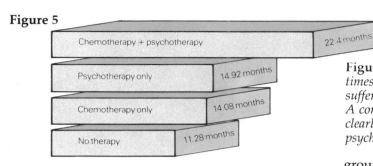

Chemotherapy + psychotherapy   22.4 months

Psychotherapy only   14.92 months

Chemotherapy only   14.08 months

No therapy   11.28 months

Figure 5   *Shown here are the mean survival times, in months, of four groups of 25 women suffering from terminal breast cancer. A combination of drug treatment and psychotherapy is clearly much more effective than chemotherapy or psychotherapy on its own.*

the bona fide prophylactic treatment consisted of one hour's individual treatment and the therapist giving each patient a page of instructions about the meaning of coping behaviour, autonomy (being in control of one's life rather than at the mercy of events), etc. By now it will come as no surprise to the reader to learn that far fewer people in the therapy group died of cancer or CHD. The control group and the placebo group showed much the same record of death.

A LONGER LEASE OF LIFE

If behaviour therapy can delay or prevent the development of cancer and CHD, what effect does it have on the survival rates of people already suffering from them? The table opposite shows 24 pairs of cancer patients, matched for type of cancer, in which one person received therapy and the other did not—the decision as to which person received therapy was made by tossing a coin. Those who received therapy survived two years longer on average than those who did not. Only four control patients of the 24 outlived their therapy 'twins'.

Figure 5 shows the results of a study of 100 women terminally ill with breast cancer. Half of the women selected were receiving chemotherapy because they had elected to do so, but the other half had refused chemotherapy; half of those selected also received psychotherapy but the other half did not. This meant that 25 women were receiving both therapies, 25 neither, 25 chemotherapy only and 25 psychotherapy only. Mean survival time was greatest for the chemotherapy + psychotherapy group and lowest for the no therapy group. The chemotherapy only and psychotherapy only

Figure 4   *Given appropriate psychological treatment, both cancer-prone and CHD-prone individuals have an excellent chance of living longer. The diagrams opposite show the results of behaviour therapy on two groups of people, one at risk of cancer and the other of coronary heart disease, 13 years after therapy. None of the therapy groups died of cancer in that time. In both the cancer and CHD groups there were deaths from other causes, but only a half or a third as many in the therapy groups as in the control groups. Taking both the cancer and the CHD groups together, only 14 individuals in the therapy groups died within 13 years as opposed to 60 individuals in the control groups.*

groups survived only two or three months longer than the no therapy group. Clearly psychotherapy is at least as effective as chemotherapy in prolonging life, and equally clearly both therapies together have a synergistic effect; in other words they are a great deal more effective together than separately.

The results of these and other studies strongly suggest that psychological treatment can have a

Survival of cancer patients receiving behavioural therapy

Type of cancer	Number of patient pairs	Survival time in years	
		Therapy group	Control group
Scrotal	1	5.8	3.2 +
Stomach	1	4.8	1.8 +
	2	2.4	2.3 +
Bronchiolar	1	1.7	2.4 −
	2	5.6	1.5 +
	3	4.2	1.6 +
	4	3.2	1.1 +
	5	1.7	1.7 =
	6	4.5	1.2 +
	7	5.2	1.0 +
Uterine	1	6.8	4.2 +
	2	4.5	4.8 −
	3	7.2	3.5 +
	4	8.2	3.1 +
Cervical	1	5.5	4.2 +
	2	6.1	4.0 +
	3	3.2	3.3 −
	4	4.5	4.1 +
	5	2.8	3.6 −
Colon and rectum	1	9.5	4.2 +
	2	7.5	2.1 +
	3	6.3	4.9 +
	4	4.8	4.3 +
	5	5.7	4.1 +
	24	av. 5.07	av. 3.09

strong prophylactic effect and also a life-prolonging effect in cases of terminal illness. Is there a possibility that behaviour therapy might actually *cure* cancer?

In a small study recently carried out in Holland the participants were eight terminal cancer patients who had recovered without treatment. Such cases are rare, but they do exist, and the diagnosis of cancer is fact not fiction. What is of interest is that all eight people showed very strongly the healthy personality type (Type IV) described by Grossarth-Maticek. It would certainly be worthwhile to try to reverse the progress of cancer in certain types of people by behaviour therapy. Success is unlikely, but the experiment ought to be made.

THE IMMUNE SYSTEM: WHERE MIND AND MATTER MEET

Why does stress, or the body's reaction to stress, negatively influence a physical disease like cancer?[8] The answer is probably that stress weakens the immune system. We produce or develop cancerous cells every day, but if we are healthy these are killed off by the immune system before they can do any harm. The greater incidence of cancer in people over 60 is probably due to the fact that the immune system, together with most other body systems, becomes less efficient with age. What is not so commonly known is that the immune system is greatly influenced by peptides (sub-units of proteins used, among other things, for making antibodies) and hormones. Cortisol, for example, is a hormone naturally produced by the adrenal glands in response to stress. Depression, which is a form of stress, is associated with high levels of cortisol, and one of the effects of large quantities of cortisol is suppression of immune responses (in fact cortisol is used to prevent rejection after transplant operations). Persistently high levels of cortisol weaken the immune system. In one study of old people in a home and suffering a good deal of stress, it was shown that behaviour therapy involving the teaching of coping behaviour not only increased life expectancy but also led to a significant decrease in blood cortisol levels. A control group did not show these positive changes.

Indeed the effects on the immune system of quite slight environmental stimuli are immediate and easily measurable. In one study subjects were shown a humorous video or a control video, and there were significant increases in immune response to the funny film compared with the control film (immune response was measured before and after the film by taking a blood sample and measuring the value of the antibody Immunoglobulin A). Perhaps the Marx Brothers would have a more beneficial effect on cancer control than many more expensive and a lot less funny forms of medical intervention!

In another study, this time with students, it was shown that there is an intimate relationship between mood and levels of Immunoglobulin A,

immune system responses being lower on 'down' days and higher on 'up' days.

Once again the evidence seems to point to the possibility of defeating cancer through some form of behaviour therapy. If the mind can be manipulated, surely the immune system will follow, up to a point.

THE NEED FOR NEW APPROACHES

Despite the prophylactic and even curative possibilities opened up by the findings of studies of the kind mentioned above, very little in the way of funding has gone into psychological approaches to cancer and other life-threatening diseases, and for a very simple reason. Orthodox medicine is still wedded to the idea of treating symptoms rather than individual people, and there is a generally frosty attitude to involving personality, stress reactions and other psychosocial variables in the disease and treatment process. These are not concepts familiar to most doctors—they are not taught in medical school and do not form part of medical orthodoxy. They are therefore regarded with suspicion or downright prejudice, and starved of research funds. This is extremely sad, because there is now a considerable body of evidence that these novel ways of looking at prophylaxis and treatment may be of considerable help. Meanwhile many thousands of sufferers are voting with their feet and seeking help from 'alternative' and 'complementary' therapies. Many thousands of people are also dying unnecessarily, whose lives might have been saved if there was greater readiness to support research into these novel areas.

People who subject themselves to apparently high levels of stress to earn a living – driving a taxi or working on the Stock Exchange, for example – do not automatically weaken their immune system. The amount of stress they feel depends on their personality.

The perfect antidote to stress? Feeling contented and at one with nature can translate directly into a more efficient immune response.

We simply have to give up the notion of body as opposed to mind and accept the notion of a body–mind–soul entity, just as physicists have had to give up the notion of time and space as separate entities and now deal with a space–time continuum.

If these new ideas are along the right lines, and the evidence suggests that they are, then the National Health Service in the United Kingdom and many healthcare and health insurance organizations in other countries would do well to consider paying doctors to keep their patients healthy and ceasing to pay them when their patients fall ill—this was the system the old Chinese emperors adopted towards their court physicians. This emphasis on prophylaxis and health rather than treating fully-fledged disease has a powerful appeal. If we could avoid cancer and CHD by suitable psychological treatment, or at least postpone their onset by 15 years or more, then we would not only add immeasurably to the sum of human happiness but also lessen the financial burden on the state and the individual. The cost of preventive treatment is extremely small compared with the cost of treating cancer and CHD patients in hospital. Considering the growing cost of state and private health care all over the civilized world, it would pay governments to set up schemes to diagnose cancer- and CHD-prone personality types and offer prophylactic psychological treatment. But given the opposition of the medical profession and the general inertia of the bureaucracies involved, this is almost certainly one of those ideas whose time has not yet come.

Health services all over the world are geared to providing last-ditch, high-tech, high-cost forms of treatment for established diseases rather than preventing diseases in the first place.

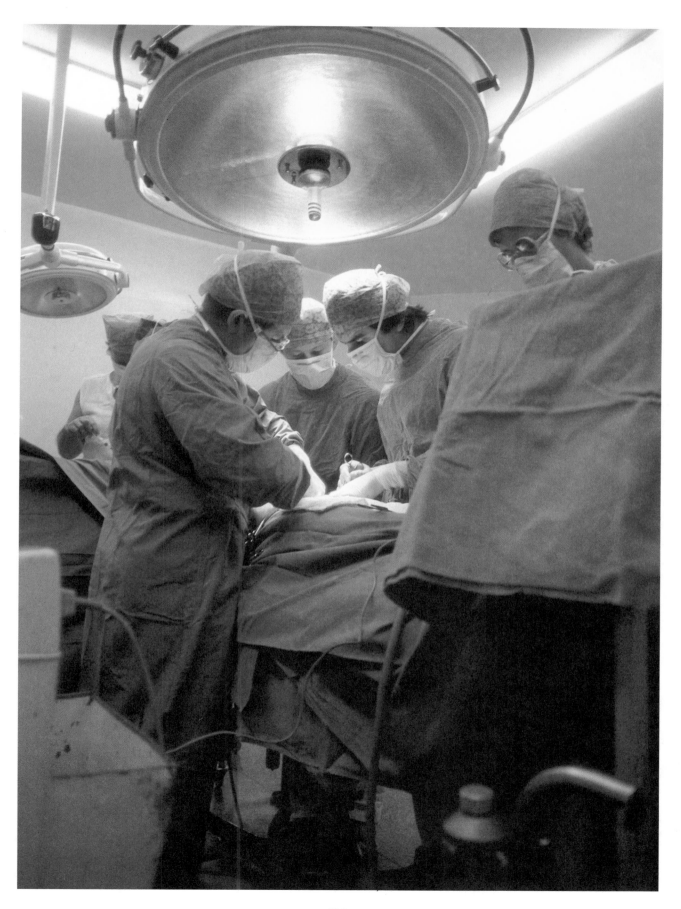

Chapter 24
CRIME AND PUNISHMENT

Ever since 1859, when Charles Darwin published his theory of evolution and established that human beings are descended from lowlier species, all students of the human sciences have had to take the animal ancestry of *Homo sapiens* into account, none more so than the well-known American neurophysiologist P. D. McLean. The human brain is clearly divided into three parts—when the brain is dissected, they can be seen with the naked eye —each of which evolved at a different time in our long human and pre-human history. McLean calls the human brain the 'triune' or three-part brain[1].

At the bottom is the brain stem and the lower part of the brain, what McLean calls the 'reptile brain'. It is the most ancient part of the brain from the point of view of evolution, and descends to us from our reptile ancestors. Superimposed upon this, and enveloping it, is the paleocortex, or limbic system, a brain structure which developed later and which governs the expression of emotion. Superimposed upon both of these structures, and enveloping them again, is the neocortex, the grey matter that above all else distinguishes us from our animal relatives. It is the neocortex which enables us to reason logically, use language and break the bounds of biological evolution. We inherit more than genes; we inherit culture too. Of course there is communication between these three parts of the brain, nevertheless they all have their separate functions and no attempt to account for human nature can be successful unless it allows for these differences.

The growth of the neocortex has made possible the interlinked functions of reasoning and language, but because they derive from a 'separate', later structure, reasoning and language have little power over the limbic system of the paleocortex and the emotions which it governs. However, the limbic system also has a language, but it is the language of Pavlovian conditioning. Most people will be familiar with Pavlov's famous experiment, in which he conditioned dogs to salivate to the sound of a bell by pairing the bell with food on a number of occasions; after a certain number of pairings the dogs salivated to the sound of the bell, even though no food was forthcoming. The importance of Pavlov's experiment is often forgotten. It was important because it showed that emotions and physical reactions can be conditioned in the same way (see Chapter 8). This is what makes conditioning theory relevant to the manipulation of human behaviour, in particular to the treatment of criminal behaviour. In fact it is not too sweeping a generalization to say that an adequate theory of criminality, like an adequate theory of neurosis, is crucially dependent on Pavlov's conditioning experiments. But let us briefly mention two alternative theories first, neither of which, in our considered opinion, really accounts for criminal behaviour.

THE SOCIOLOGICAL AND THE PSYCHOANALYTIC APPROACH

Sociological theory links criminality with such factors as poverty, inequality of wealth, capitalism, poor housing, and so on. During the past 40 years or so all these factors have been growing weaker in the major European countries and in the United States. In that time there has been a decline in the total wealth owned by the top 10 per cent of the population. In Europe and the United States there is greater equality, better housing and a higher standard of living. So, on the sociological hypothesis, crime should have decreased. In fact the evidence is conclusive that it has increased, in some cases many-fold. This seems to disprove the notion that it is economic deprivation which causes crime. True theories should predict consequences accurately.

Psychoanalytic theory regards criminal behaviour as a sub-species of neurotic behaviour caused by infantile complexes and curable by psychoanalytic treatment. We will merely mention two studies which contradict this hypothesis. The first was the Cambridge–Somerville study in which large numbers of potentially criminal youths in Boston, Massachusetts, were divided at random into two groups. The experimental group received a great deal of psychoanalytic guidance, interpretation and treatment, but the control group received no such treatment. The hope was that the psychoanalytic treatment would act as a preventive. But after the groups had been followed up over a period of 30 years, the outcome proved to be the opposite of what the theory predicted. Such differences as were found favoured the control group; the group that had received psychoanalytic treatment committed, if anything, more crimes than the control group.

Along similar lines, Grendon Underwood Prison in Britain was created to give prisoners psychotherapeutic treatment along psychoanalytic lines. Recidivism at Grendon was compared with that of a typical old-fashioned prison (Oxford). As Figure 1 shows, recidivism was exactly equal for the psychoanalysed group and the unpsychoanalysed

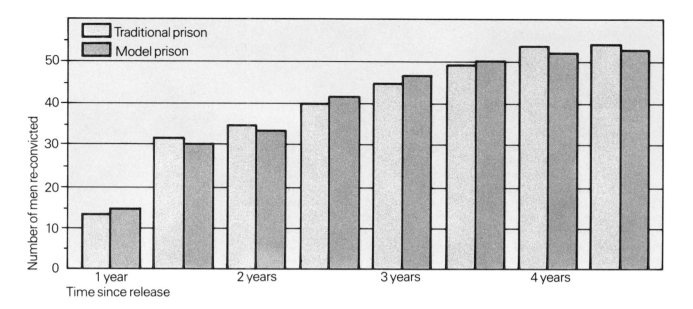

Figure 1   *Two groups of prisoners, one in a traditional prison and one in a prison where psychoanalytic therapy was given, showed no difference in re-conviction rates in the four years following their release.*

group. And there is a lot more evidence to show that the psychoanalytic interpretation of criminality does not conform to the facts, and that psychoanalytic treatment is irrelevant in reducing criminal conduct.

IS CRIME BAD OR INADEQUATE CONDITIONING?

The conditioning theory of criminality, however, accords much better with the facts. For the sake of brevity we have stated the theory much more dogmatically than we would have liked, and readers are referred to H. J. Eysenck's book *Crime and Personality*[2] for a more detailed statement. The first point to be made is that moral conduct is not the result of rational decisions, and is not influenced very much by rational considerations. Very few of those who commit crimes are caught and punished —that is a widely known fact. Anyone who organizes his life along purely rational lines might choose a life of crime as more likely to advance him materially than a life full of virtue. So the real question is: Why do relatively few people commit crimes when the rewards are so immediate and obvious, and the probability of punishment so remote?

The answer, we suggest, lies in the concept of 'conscience', conceived not as a religious mechanism implanted by God but rather as a conditioned response implanted by a long period of 'Pavlovian' conditioning. Consider the events that take place when a young child grows up. He naturally misbehaves, is selfish and anti-social and dishonest. Whenever he behaves in such a fashion, he is punished by his parents, his teachers, his peers or whoever else happens to be around. Such punishment, whatever it is—a box on the ear, standing in the corner, going to bed without supper—is painful and disagreeable. We thus have a regular chain of events. First comes the *conditioned stimulus*, the sound of the bell in the Pavlovian experiment, but in the case of the child his or her intention to commit an anti-social act and the actual carrying out of that act. The *unconditioned stimulus*, corresponding to the appearance of food in the Pavlovian experiment, is the punishment meted out by parents, teachers or peers. The *unconditioned response*, corresponding to the salivation of Pavlov's dogs, is the pain, anxiety and fear which the punishment causes in the child. According to Pavlovian principles, the conditioned stimulus should become associated, after a number of reinforcing episodes, with the unconditioned response, so that after a time anti-social intent or behaviour should become connected with the anxiety typically resulting from punishment. This anxiety, coupled with the intention of carrying out some anti-social activity, is what we commonly call 'conscience', and it effectively prevents most people from indulging in anti-social and criminal activities, even though these might be undetectable and very much to their advantage.

To many people this account may seem to endow conditioning with a far greater force than seems credible, and they may reject the theory on these grounds. However, there is experimental evidence to suggest that conditioned responses are extremely powerful in producing socialized behaviour. We have, for example, the work of R. L. Solomon and his colleagues[3, 4], which was carried out both with very young children and with puppies. Here we will merely recount briefly their work with puppies, but their results with young children were equally impressive.

KEY EXPERIMENT: THE DEVELOPMENT OF 'CONSCIENCE'

This, essentially, is what Solomon did. The puppies, starved for one whole day, are brought into a room which contains the experimenter sitting on a chair, a plate full of boiled horsemeat (which the puppies like very much) to the right of the chair, and a plate full of commercial dog food (which the puppies don't like very much) to the left of the chair. The experimenter holds a folded newspaper in his right hand and whenever the puppies try to eat the horsemeat, the eating of which he has arbitrarily decided is an anti-social activity that must be discouraged, he slaps the puppy over the rump with the folded newspaper. Note that this 'punishment' is mild and does not really hurt the puppies or cause them any degree of pain; it simply signifies the displeasure of the experimenter. After a few attempts to eat the boiled horsemeat the puppies start eating the commercial dog food, in a rather disgruntled fashion. That concludes the experiment for the day, and it is repeated the day after, and the day after that, until the end of the week.

The next stage of the experiment begins at the start of the following week. This time the experimenter is absent when the puppies, again foodless for the previous 24 hours, are brought into the room; instead he surveys the scene through a one-way glass screen. The boiled horsemeat is there for them to eat if they want to, and there also is a very small portion of commercial dog food. What will the puppies do now that they are free of the presence of the experimenter, and apparently free to disregard the 'socializing' influences set up by him? Will the puppies' conditioned 'consciences' make them act counter to their desires and instincts? For most of the puppies this was indeed the case; they circled the boiled horsemeat and looked at it yearningly, but ate the commercial dog food and left the horsemeat untouched. A few succumbed to temptation, but the great majority did not. After half an hour the puppies were taken back to their kennel, starved for another 24 hours, then brought out again, and the same procedure was repeated. This time a few more decided to eat the boiled horsemeat, but the majority still resisted the temptation. To cut a long story short, it seemed that many of the puppies would rather have died of starvation than act counter to the conditioned 'conscience' implanted in them by the experimenter (of course the experimenter did not allow this to happen, and the puppies were fed long before they starved). But note that the very mild 'punishment', the unconditioned stimulus, set up a sufficiently strong conditioned response for many of the puppies to prefer death to the simple act of doing what their newly acquired 'conscience' forbade. Much the same result was obtained with young children, so we cannot comfortably dismiss the experiment as only applicable to animals.

FROM PUPPIES TO PEOPLE

This of course is only one illustration of the 'conscience' theory. There is an enormous mass of experimental material to indicate that this theory is, if not 100 per cent correct, then at least along the right lines. It suggests two things. One is that the reason we have seen such a tremendous increase in crime since World War II may simply be that over the past 40 years the general climate of 'permissiveness' has reduced the number of 'conditioning' experiences children receive at the hands of parents and teachers. In other words the amount of social conditioning has decreased. This would automatically reduce the strength of the child's 'conscience' and make him much more likely than his pre-war counterparts to indulge in anti-social or criminal activities. Again there is much observational material to support this hypothesis. There seems to be no doubt that schools where greater 'permissiveness' is practised have a higher delinquency and criminal record among their pupils than schools where the atmosphere is more formal, 'old-fashioned' and less laissez-faire[5]. We do not have time here to go into all the experiments and studies which support this view.

The second point about the 'conscience' theory is that it can be related to the treatment of criminals, whether children, juveniles or adults. It suggests ways in which their anti-social and criminal conduct might be changed, so that they become socialized human beings with a proper 'conscience'. What is needed is not psychoanalytic treatment of non-existant complexes and neuroses, nor verbal appeals to reason and the 'better nature' of the wrong-doers. What is needed is simply a supply of what has been lacking in their upbringing, namely a suitable number of occasions for conditioning to take place.

TOKEN ECONOMIES

There are many ways in which re-conditioning can be achieved, and one of them is the 'token economy'. This concept was originally introduced by an English penologist whose work was done over a century ago, Maconochie of Norfolk Island. Norfolk Island was a penal colony off the coast of Australia, to which all of Britain's worst offenders were sent. When Maconochie arrived there he discovered that the treatment of the prisoners was inhumane, cruel and bestial. Norfolk Island, far from having any reforming influence, produced a high degree of recidivism.

Maconochie introduced a system of points which prisoners could earn by working hard, by not fighting, and by generally behaving in a socialized manner; punishment was the withdrawal of points. Very soon the effect of this regime was very noticeable. Prisoners began behaving much better than when they had been brutally punished. Equally noticeable were its effects of recidivism. From the universal testimony even of his critics, it appears that Maconochie succeeded in inculcating in his

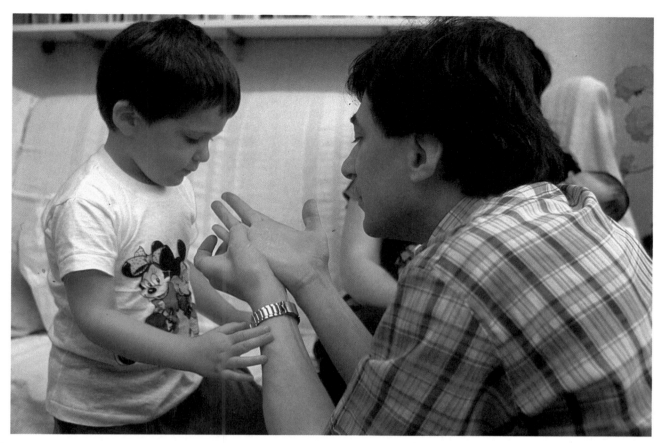

Explaining the rules of behaviour is a responsibility abdicated by too many parents today. A 'conscience' is not something we are born with – it is instilled into us by a consistent system of 'reward' and 'punishment'.

prisoners concepts of socialized behaviour which lasted well beyond their stay in prison. Unfortunately his efforts at revolutionizing the prison system were constantly attacked and ultimately thwarted by the British Home Office, which finally relieved him of his post.

In more recent years token economies of this kind have been tried out by American psychologists with many different groups, mainly juvenile delinquents. Research into outcomes is of course difficult, and many more years of follow-up will be required before we know the full extent of the success or otherwise of these trials. Nevertheless, it can already be said that token economies, properly implemented, can reduce the recidivism rate of young offenders by something like 50 per cent over a period of three years after they are released from custody. This is of course nothing like complete success, but if the whole prison population could be reduced by half the saving in money alone would repay the cost of the enterprise thousands of times over[5, 6, 7, 8].

Recent research has tended to move away from treating criminals in institutions like Borstals or prisons, for the very simple reason that in institu-

tions peer groups are a strong countervalent against re-conditioning procedures. In such settings all attempts at re-conditioning tend to reinforce and even strengthen the criminal inclinations of the inmates. There seems to be no doubt that the process of 'de-institutionalization' has much to be said for it. It is also much cheaper. In some of the experiments done in the United States it has been found that new psychological methods of treatment, administered outside institutions, not only cost as little as one third of the cost of traditional treatment, but are much more successful in preventing recidivism as well. Despite this, most European countries have shown little interest in these developments.

We do not wish to exaggerate the success already achieved. What has been done so far may not work with all types of prisoners. What has worked in America may not work in Britain or Germany. What we would like to suggest, however, is that small-scale research trials should now be made with suitable offenders, particularly juveniles, to test these methods and see to what extent the successes of our American colleagues can be copied elsewhere.

IS THERE A CRIMINAL PERSONALITY?

The picture of criminality we have painted so far lacks certain important features. The first of these is related to the problem of personality. It has often been suggested that criminals are characterized by particular personality profiles, and there is now solid evidence to support this view.

Secondly, different people have different predispositions to form conditioned responses quickly and strongly. Pavlov observed this in his dogs. Some dogs formed the association between bell and salivation after only five exposures to the bell–food connection, whereas others took 100, or even 200 or 300 exposures before forming the conditioned response.

Theory suggests, and many experiments demonstrate, that introverted humans form conditioned responses much more readily that extraverts do (see Chapter 8). People who are sociable, impulsive, happy-go-lucky and generally outgoing in their behaviour find it rather more difficult to form conditioned responses.

Figure 2 shows the results of an experiment done with human subjects, illustrating the marked difference between extraverts and introverts. The experiment used the eyeblink reflex, i.e. closure of the eyelid when a puff of air is directed against the cornea. Subjects wear goggles which are penetrated by a nozzle connected through a rubber hose to an external air supply; a stream of air can then be directed against the cornea of the eye. The conditioned stimulus is a tone relayed over earphones, and the experiment consists of measuring the closure of the eyelid in response to the tone. At first there is no reaction but as the tone is repeatedly followed by a puff of air, the subject gradually

becomes conditioned to respond to the tone with closure of the eyelid (this closure is not a voluntary reaction; voluntary reactions are much slower than conditioned ones, and can therefore be clearly differentiated from them).

It turns out that introverts are markedly quicker at learning to blink that extraverts. In other words they are 'conditioned' more easily. So we would expect extraverts to be more difficult to condition in other respects, and consequently, other things being equal, to be more likely to indulge in anti-social behaviour. There are many studies which have shown that this is so, the subjects of these studies including schoolchildren, adolescents and adults.

Another personality trait shared by criminals

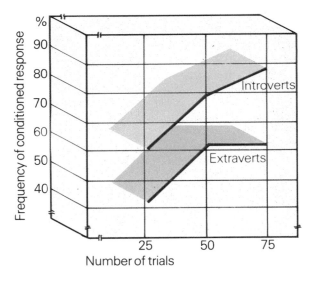

Figure 2 *This graph shows the greater conditionability of introverts. The conditioned stimulus, a tone relayed over earphones, was associated with a puff of air directed at the cornea, stimulating the eyeblink reflex. After 50 trials the frequency with which extraverts blinked in response to the stimulus stayed the same, but with the introverts it continued to increase.*

and by people who indulge in anti-social behaviour is strong emotionality, i.e. over-responsiveness of the limbic system (based in the paleocortex) which controls the expression of emotions. There are other personality traits also associated with criminality, but it is not necessary to go into detail here in order to make the point that anti-social behaviour is strongly associated with certain personality types.

This association is found not only in Western European countries and in the United States but also in Communist countries like Hungary and Czechoslovakia, and in Third World countries like India. In other words, the association is not culturally determined, as some Marxist thinkers would like to believe, but is universally valid.

THE GENETIC COMPONENT OF CRIMINALITY

It is now well established that the personality dimensions in question here are strongly rooted in the genetic constitution of the individual, with genetic factors accounting for something like three-quarters of the total amount of variability encountered, and environmental factors accounting for something like one quarter. This suggests

Easy money at the slot machines. Theft is also easy money, and all we have between us and breaking the law is childhood conditioning that says 'that's yours and that's mine' and 'nothing is for free'. Extraverts are less susceptible to conditioning than introverts.

strongly that criminality, like intelligence, has a genetic component, and indeed the evidence fully supports this view.

One line of evidence comes from studies of identical and fraternal twins. In investigations of this kind the psychologist goes into a prison to look at the records of all the inmates in order to find out which of them are twins. He then looks for the other twin, to find out whether he is an identical or fraternal twin, and whether he too is 'concordant' for criminality (whether he too has broken the law). As identical twins share 100 per cent heredity, as against an average of only 50 per cent for fraternal twins, one would expect identical twins to show greater concordance than fraternal twins if heredity is at the root of criminal behaviour. There have now been a dozen or so studies of this sort, carried out in many different countries. And the universal finding is that identical twins show concordance about four times as frequently as fraternal twins. So the brother of a criminal twin is four times as likely to be a criminal himself if he is identical rather than fraternal.

The other line of evidence comes from studies of adopted children. Children adopted early in life receive their genetic baggage from their true parents and their environment from their adoptive parents. Which of the two is stronger in determining criminal or non-criminal behaviour as they grow up? Again, judging by several studies done in different countries, it seems that the genetic component is much the more important. Adopted children tend to behave very much as their true parents did, rather than as their adoptive parents being them up to behave. Here too environment can be shown to be less important than heredity, although both are important and both play a part in causing anti-social behaviour. We have stressed the genetic aspects here because in the past 50 years there has been a tendency to stress environment to the exclusion of genes.

We can now see why would-be reformers have found it so difficult to change criminal behaviour, to manipulate motivation and conduct, and to persuade offenders to become law-abiding citizens. There is a strong genetic factor, working through a rather primitive part of the brain (the paleocortex), which speaks a language quite different from, and

It has been estimated that alcohol plays a part in at least 60 per cent of violent crimes. Alcohol affects every part of the brain, but especially the cortex, which keeps aggressive and anti-social impulses in check.

alien to, the language of reason appreciated by the neocortex. This is why the rational approach—appealing to reason and a sense of social responsibility—has so often failed, just as better housing and better social conditions have failed, just as psychoanalytic appeals to the subconscious have failed. If we want to succeed we will have to learn to speak the language of the paleocortex, and discover how to apply the laws of conditioning to the problems posed by criminality.

RE-CONDITIONING VERSUS PUNISHMENT

This is a daunting task, but a beginning has been made, and success, even if limited, has already been achieved. The point we want to make here has often been misunderstood. People tend to jump to the conclusion that the theory of conditioning we have described justifies savage correction. It doesn't. A great deal is known about the effects of punishment, and what stands out above all else is that severe punishment increases the emotional responsiveness which is already part of the criminal's innate character, and may make things worse rather than better[9]. Remember that in Solomon's experiment with puppies the punishment—a light slap with a folded newspaper—was very mild, so mild as hardly to constitute a punishment. It is only when relatively mild punishments or rewards are administered under closely controlled conditions that the desired results are obtained. The conditioning theory gives no justification for particularly harsh treatment of criminals, although it does not justify mollycoddling either.

Another of Solomon's findings from the puppy experiment may be of interest, and indeed of practical importance. Conditioning the puppies to develop a strong 'conscience' was far more successful if the experimenter was also the person who, before the experiment, had fed them and looked after them. In other words, a previous personal bond between man and animal made the conditioning process much more effective. This suggests that the effective inculcation of a 'conscience' in human beings must be the task of the parents rather than anyone else, and that any punishment handed out must be handed out against a general background of love and affection if it is to have the desired result.

From the point of view of preventing delinquency and crime it is vitally important that this message is brought home to parents generally. In this permissive era many parents evade their duty to transmit the social message of their culture to their children. It is only by re-educating parents to accept and perform this duty that we can prevent our civilization from deteriorating even further.

In advising parents, teachers and others in authority about the need to establish a 'conscience' in children by a process of conditioning, it is important to bear in mind one final finding of Solomon's.

He found that the *timing* of the slap with the folded newspaper was extremely important. If the slap occurred as the puppy approached the boiled horsemeat and before it started eating, it had the effect of a deterrent. The puppies learned not to approach the meat and eat it, which is of course what the 'conscience' training was supposed to accomplish. However, if the slap came later, after they had begun to eat, the result was dramatically different. Left to themselves, the puppies approached and ate the meat, but thereafter showed strong evidence of guilt (by avoiding the experimenter, slinking into corners and generally behaving as if they were aware of having done something naughty). It therefore seems that untimely or wrongly applied conditioning can lead to guilt feelings rather than avoidance of anti-social behaviour, and this of course is not the desired result. There is little point in making people feel guilty once the anti-social act has been performed. The aim must be to prevent performance of the act in the first place.

DEALING WITH 'TOUGH NUTS'

There is one further personality trait which is extremely important in relation to anti-social behaviour and criminality. This trait relates to psychotic and psychopathic behaviour, and consists essentially of egocentric, hostile, aggressive and selfish types of conduct, associated with a lack of empathy and care for others' rights and privileges, placing personal satisfaction and gratification before all else. This trait, which might be called 'tough-mindedness' or 'thinking tough', has also been found to be strongly heritable. As one might expect it is related to masculinity—males show it far more frequently, and to a much stronger degree, than females. This accords well with the fact that most crimes are committed by males, that males show much more aggression than females and are also much more impersonal in their social relations. Tough behaviour is probably causally related to testosterone secretion (the amount of male hormone characteristic of a person). When present to an extreme degree, tough-mindedness leads to psychopathic behaviour and even to psychotic (mainly schizophrenic) disorders.

Tough-mindedness is particularly related to crimes which have a vicious and aggressive element. Crimes against the person—muggings, sexual crimes and grievous bodily harm—are the criminal acts most often associated with this personality trait. And it is crimes of violence which are particularly destructive to society, and they are increasing more than any other sort of crime, particularly in the Western world. Here again it seems likely that permissiveness has been the crucial factor, with parents and others failing to restrain children from acting tough.

Tough-mindedness is also important from the therapeutic point of view because it has been shown many times that tough-minded individuals

There is, it seems, a large genetic component to acting tough. Getting behind a real gun at an army open day does not, of itself, breed toughness, but a tough environment plus tough genes can result in psychopathic behaviour.

are much less receptive to psychotherapy, behaviour therapy, or indeed any method of treatment. It might almost be said that the degree to which a person's behaviour can be altered by any kind of social interference is determined largely by his degree of tough-mindedness; the more tough-minded he is, the more difficult it is to alter his behaviour. The only known way of affecting the tough-minded person is by way of token economies (strict conditioning programmes) or by administering phenothiazines or other anti-psychotic drugs which temporarily reduce his tough-mindedness and make him amenable to treatment. Unfortunately phenothiazines have a feminizing effect—male patients who take them over any period of time may start to grow breasts, etc.

Whether society is justified in using drugs for the purpose of reducing a prisoner's tough-mindedness to make him more amenable to a course of conditioning or psychotherapy is an ethical point which we cannot discuss here. It must be left to experts in the fields of ethics and political science. In this instance we are merely concerned with setting down the facts rather than making recommendations.

One last point. It would be a gross oversimplification to say that criminals form a homogeneous group, or that any generalization ever applies to all criminals. In our work we have found that a whole range of crimes can be committed by persons of different personality structure. As we have already said, prisoners high on tough-mindedness are much more likely to have committed crimes of violence. But murder within the family, the most common kind of murder in the Western world outside America, is usually associated with introversion. Potential murderers tend to be rather mild, introverted people who allow resentment and hatred to grow until an explosion occurs which leads to murder. Confidence tricksters, on the other hand, are extremely extraverted, but low on neuroticism and tough-mindedness. This again makes sense, because a confidence trickster relies on making a good impression, and abnormal behaviours

Wanted for murder. Murder within families is more often committed by mild-mannered introverts than by tough-minded psychopaths. Outside the family the picture tends to be different.

such as those associated with neuroticism and tough-mindedness would not impress his victims favourably.

CONCLUSIONS

Treatment must always depend on the personality of the criminal, which means that none of the methods discussed here would be suitable for all criminals. The broad outlines are fairly clear, but much detailed work still needs to be done to discover the best methods for different personalities.

In addition to personality, age and sex may form important sub-groups for deciding on the best treatment.

However, all the evidence so far suggests that while the traditional methods are almost completely ineffective, modern psychology holds out a promise that effective methods can be worked out for manipulating attitudes and behaviours in a direction favourable to the survival of society. The rehabilitation of criminals is not a visionary or impossible task, but one well within our means.

Chapter 25

POLITICS, PERSONALITY AND PREJUDICE

To most people today the word 'ideology' (not coined incidentally until 1817) has strong overtones of struggle, terror and violence, and with good reason. Political violence has found 20th century defenders in leaders like Hitler, Mussolini and Stalin, and in philosophers like Sorel, Fanon and Sartre. As the British socioloigst M. Cranston has pointed out: 'It is characteristic of ideology both to exalt action and to regard action in terms of a military analogy. Some observers have pointed out that one has only to consider the prose style of the founders of most ideologies to be struck by the military and war-like language that they habitually use, including words like struggle, resist, march, victory, and overcome; the literature of ideology is replete with martial expressions. In such a view, commitment to an ideology becomes a form of enlistment so that to become the adherent of an ideology is to become a combatant or partisan'.

Is there not a suggestion here that perhaps personality traits play a powerful part in defining the ideologue, the person who believes in an ideology, adheres to it, and becomes identified with it? Such a person, according to Cranston's suggestion, would be aggressive, violent, physically active and 'committed'. At this point this can be no more than a suggestion, but we shall see later that there is empirical evidence to support such a view.

A narrow definition of ideology would confine it to fairly recent political systems such as Communism and Fascism, but there is a case for following J. Plamenatz, the American sociologist, in defining it as 'a set of closely related beliefs or ideas, or even attitudes, characteristic of a group or community'. This definition would allow us to regard as ideologies the religious and nationalistic beliefs, ideas and attitudes characteristic of groups and communities in eras of history preceding ours. It also has the advantage that the attitudes, beliefs and ideas which constitute particular ideologies can be presented for approval or rejection to groups of people in the form of tests. In other words, ideologies can be studied systematically by psychological methods. Ideologies have played and are playing such an important part in the politics of the modern world that it is the duty of psychologists to examine them carefully.

CONSERVATIVES AND RADICALS

Psychologists have from the earliest days of attitude-measurement proposed a dimension around which attitudes can be structured, namely that of radical-conservative or progressive-reactionary, or left-right . . . there are many names for this dimension, but they all amount to much the same thing. Furthermore this dimension embodies a theory which stretches back over the centuries, and which is almost universally accepted by politicians as well as by the man or woman in the street.

Following the custom of the French Revolution, when moderates and conservatives sat on the right and the Jacobins and other militants sat on the left of the Assembly, political parties favouring the working classes, such as the Labour Party and the Communist Party in Great Britain or the Social Democratic Party in West Germany, have been called 'left wing', and the political parties favouring the middle classes, such as the Conservative Party in Great Britain and the Christian Democratic Party in West Germany, have been called 'right wing'. Even in the USA, supposedly less class-ridden than European countries, there is a tendency for Democrats to be relatively 'left' and Republicans relatively 'right'.

Investigation of this radical-conservative dimension has formed a large part of psycho-political research, but there have been many difficulties to overcome. In the first place, there are many different kinds of 'conservative'. One may be conservative when it comes to socialist proposals for the nationalization of industry, but radical in one's aesthetic preferences in music or painting—many millionaires, by definition 'conservative', like modern painting. Different scales have been constructed for the measurement of 'conservatism', but they correlate poorly. In the second place, parties of the extreme left (like the Communists) or the extreme right (like the Fascists) create difficulties. Is it really true to say that Communists are more left than orthodox Labour Party members? The Labour Party is opposed to the death penalty, but respect for individual human life has never been characteristic of Communism. Is it really true to say that Fascists are more right than Italian or German Conservatives? Mussolini appealed powerfully to the Italian working classes and Hitler included the word socialist in the name of his party (National-sozialistische Deutsche Arbeiterpartei).

E. Schils, the well-known American sociologist, has argued that modern world history has repeatedly demonstrated the inadequacy of the notion that ideologies fit into a simple left-right continuum ranging from Liberalism to Conservatism[1]. As he points out, Italian and German Fascism were not consistently right-wing in nature, nor has

Environmental concerns, once synonymous with 'fringe' or liberal views, are moving centre stage throughout the industrial world. Left, right and centre parties espouse anti-pollution programmes with varying degrees of commitment.

Soviet Communism been consistently left-wing. Fascism introduced such policies as government control of private enterprise. In the name of Communism Stalin conducted purges, reintroduced patriotism as official policy and repressed national and religious minorities. Welfare legislation has often been used to sugar the pill of political repression. Hostility to private property has co-existed with racial and ethnic prejudice. Shils expressed all this clearly when he wrote of the similarity between Fascism and Communism: 'Their common hostility towards civil liberties and political democracy; their common antipathy for parliamentary institutions, individualism, private enterprise; their image of the political world as a struggle between morally irreconcilable forces; their belief that all their opponents are secretly leagued against them, and their own predilection for secrecy; their conviction that all forms of power are in a hostile world best concentrated in a few hands; and their own aspirations for concentrated and total power—all these show that the two extremes have much in common.'

F. A. Hayek, Nobel laureate economist, tried to combine this notion of the similarity between Fascism and Communism with the opposition between right wing and left wing.[2] As he pointed out: 'The picture generally given of the relative position of the three parties (Conservative, Liberal, Labour) does more to obscure than to elucidate their true relations. They are usually represented as different positions on a line, with the Socialists on the left, the Conservatives on the right and the Liberals somewhere in the middle. Nothing could be more misleading. If we want a diagram, it would be more appropriate to arrange them in a triangle with the Conservatives occupying one corner, with the Socialists pulling towards the second and the Liberals towards the third.' We can see, then, that there are empirical problems involved in making models of attitude relationships. We must tread very carefully if we are to reach a proper understanding of modern ideologies.

AUTHORITARIANS AND DEMOCRATS
The first psychologist to suggest explicitly that there might exist a dimension in the field of social attitudes other than the right-left or conservative-radical one was the pre-war German writer and experimentalist E. R. Jaensch of the University of Marburg[3]. He is perhaps best known for his work on eidetic imagery (the ability to imagine absolutely clear and life-like images—see Chapter 18), but for our purposes it is his book *Der Gegentypus* which is the most relevant. As Jaensch makes clear, the *Gegentypus* (lit. 'against type') person is opposed lock, stock and barrel, to the philosophy underlying Hitlerian national socialism; he is characterized as liberal or even extreme liberal in his attitudes. As we shall see, the *Gegentypus* is the opposite, in many ways, of the *authoritarian personality* of Adorno and others[1].

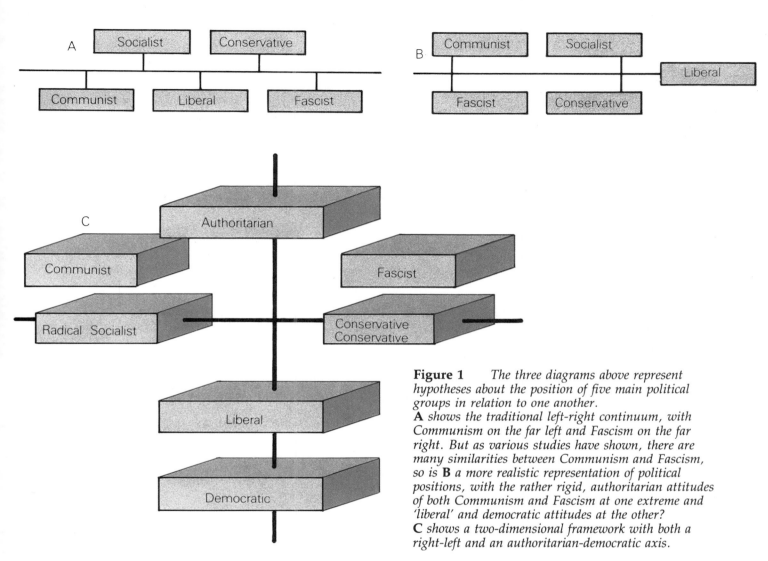

Figure 1 *The three diagrams above represent hypotheses about the position of five main political groups in relation to one another.*
A shows the traditional left-right continuum, with Communism on the far left and Fascism on the far right. But as various studies have shown, there are many similarities between Communism and Fascism, so is B a more realistic representation of political positions, with the rather rigid, authoritarian attitudes of both Communism and Fascism at one extreme and 'liberal' and democratic attitudes at the other? C shows a two-dimensional framework with both a right-left and an authoritarian-democratic axis.

Jaensch was an avowed follower of Hitler long before the Nazi movement came to power. T. W. Adorno, E. Frenkel-Brunswick and the other authors of *The Authoritarian Personality* (1950)[4], however, were victims of Hitler's persecution and strongly anti-Fascist. Our understandable revulsion at Hitler's appalling crimes makes it almost impossible for us not to side with the Adorno and oppose Jaensch. But in the interests of truth we must resist partiality. At worst we can learn from our enemies; at best we must realize that Jaensch, however misguided, was on to something very important.

In the writings of Jaensch the attitudes held by the *Gegentypus* person are intimately linked with the description of personality. It is this relationship which constitutes the original part of Jaensch's book, and we will return to it later. For the moment let us note that the *Gegentypus* has attitudes which are somewhat radical, though his main characteristics might be typified as 'extreme liberal'. In many ways the *Gegentypus* is the exact opposite of the authoritarian personality, which is tilted towards

the conservative side, but which is conservative in a very specific, authoritarian manner. The precise meaning and position of these two theoretical concepts can best be understood by looking at Figure 1.

Diagram A shows the traditional single dimension from Communism on the left to Fascism on the right, and B shows the hypothetical contrast between Liberals on the one hand and Communist-Fascist ideologies on the other. In our theory these two single dimensions are combined in a two-dimensional framework, diagram C. Note that the radical-conservative dimension is supplemented by another dimension ranging from authoritarian at one end to democratic at the other.

We would also suggest that authoritarianism is characterized by a type of personality structure which may be called 'tough-minded', while the democratic attitude is characterized by a personality structure which may be called 'tender-minded'. Again this is a concept we shall return to later.

The authoritarian personality and the *Gegentypus* do not lie along either of the two dimensions proposed in diagram C. As shown in Figure 2 the

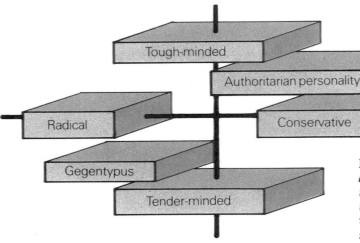

Figure 2 *In a two-dimensional model of political and social attitudes the authoritarian personality and the Gegentypus lie at opposite extremes. Unopposed, the extreme liberalism favoured by the Gegentypus would lead to the dissolution and destruction of society.*

authoritarian is tough-minded, but tilted towards the conservative side, whereas the *Gegentypus* is tender-minded but tilted towards the radical side. Many critics have pointed out this tilt, which is not really in accordance with the data and which arose primarily from the political biases and preferences of the authors of the books dealing respectively with the authoritarian personality and the *Gegentypus*. What we shall be concerned with in this chapter is the tough-minded versus tender-minded axis, or the T axis rather than the radical-conservative or R axis.

A hypothesis such as that developed here naturally requires empirical proof, and this can only be given by a correlational analysis of endorsements or rejections of attitude statements relevant to these dimensions made by large samples of the population. Many such studies have been reported. Data from the original studies which inspired H. J. Eysenck's *The Psychology of Politics*[5] show that tough-minded conservatives display attitudes one would now tend to regard as Fascist, while tough-minded radicals adhere to beliefs commonly identified as Communist. Tender-minded attitudes are identified with Liberalism. This is merely an interpretation of the data. However, many empirical studies have demonstrated that members of the Communist and Fascist Parties, as well as members of the Socialist (Labour), Liberal and Conservative Parties, hold attitudes which assign them to the particular parts of the two-dimensional framework proposed in Figure 1, diagram C. Descriptively, therefore, the two-dimensional system of attitude measurement we propose offers a reasonably accurate picture of the position of the two major modern ideologies, and their relationship to the more ordinary social attitudes and beliefs held by members of the traditional parties.

KEY EXPERIMENT: FASCISTS AND COMMUNISTS

The crucial experiment which investigated these various relationships, as well as the connection between ideology and personality which will be

discussed later, was carried out by the Canadian psychologist Thelma Coulter. She administered many attitude and personality questionnaires and tests to members of the Communist and Fascist parties, not to student members but to working-class members of long standing (with a sprinkling of middle-class members, also of long standing). This point is important because students are apt to join extreme parties and leave them after a very short while; therefore they cannot be considered as 'committed'[6].

Coulter had many difficulties in getting her subjects, all of them male, to take part in the experiment. Ideologues tend to be very suspicious, even paranoid, and regard anyone who is not with them as against them. In the interests of research, therefore, she was forced to join both parties at the same time, a very daring and indeed dangerous procedure. Fortunately she was never found out, and went to meetings, canvassed, sold newspapers for both parties and joined them in other activities without the one ever getting to know of her affiliation with the other. With her as a party member, both Communists and Fascists were more willing to take part in the testing, and her thesis records what must be one of the most adventurous as well as one of the most interesting social psychological investigations ever carried out.

The differences and similarities between the two groups were striking, and the personalities of members of both parties were remarkably similar, as we shall see. The study was done in the 1950s, when there was still a Fascist party in Britain; nowadays no such party officially exists, although the National Front has taken over many of its policies. It would be interesting to repeat the study with a new generation of Fascists and Communists, perhaps using American, German and other national samples as well as British.

What were the main personality traits of Coulter's Fascists and Communists? She noted strong hostility and aggressiveness, very much as Cranston's description at the beginning of this chapter would have led one to expect. Another marked similarity which differentiated both ideological groups from a normal control group was the rigidity of their attitudes; Fascists and Communists were much more rigid in their mental processes than the controls. They were also much more emphatic in their attitudes—whatever they believed in they felt very strongly about, and interpreted criticism or denial as hostility. They were intolerant of ambiguity, i.e. they could not tolerate doubt or uncertainty, and demanded immediate decision and action. Dogmatism and dominance were other traits which emerged, the former more associated with the Fascists, the latter more with the Communists. Altogether, there were marked similarities between the two ideological groups compared with the controls, but also a few differences. The Communists, for example, displayed less direct aggression than the Fascists. On the whole, though, the similarities far outweighed the dissimilarities.

PERSONALITY POLITICS

Jaensch originally postulated a close relationship between personality and the social attitudes characteristic of the *Gegentypus*: 'In our long-continued investigations of the fundamental differences of human beings, we have again and again come upon a type which in our circle we called "the type of dissolution and destruction" . . . This type, in its most clear-cut and definite form, is characterized by extreme liberalism. For this type, there are no ties, and this general failure to relate, to be tied, is firmly grounded in biological reality . . . In our work, we have tried to construct a bridge between empirical and experimental psychology on the one side, and cultural psychology and philosophy on the other . . . Extreme liberalism is not only a political, but a much more all-embracing, biological-psychological fact, which is primarily, and in extreme form entirely, found in the dissolution type . . . Psychophysics has show by experiment that liberalism has a biological basis, and thus goes far beyond a simple political doctrine'.

Adorno and his colleagues also attempted to link personality with the concept of authoritarianism, making much use of psychoanalytic concepts in the process. With them, as with Jaensch, the rigour of the experimental studies was rather weak, and many criticisms have been made of their work. Let us merely note that both the concept of gegentypism and the authoritarianism have been linked very closely with personality by their authors, and that a genetic basis has been implied, at least by Jaensch, for this connection. Is there any evidence for a genetic determination of R (radicalism-conservatism) and T (tough- and tender-mindedness)?

The majority of writers on social attitudes have not even considered the possibility that attitudes are anything but the product of environmental influences. To date the only empirical study concerned with evaluating the possibility of genetic determination of attitudes is one reported by Eaves and Eysenck[7]. This study used the Eysenck questionnaire for the measurement of R and T, and also measured an additional variable called 'emphasis', which is simply the sum of the degrees of extremity shown in the endorsement of the various items (items are judged on a five-point scale from Agree Very Strongly through Agree, Doubtful and Disagree to Disagree Very Strongly; the emphasis score adds together the number of very strong agreements and disagreements, disregarding the direction of the endorsement).

This questionnaire was administered to a total of 708 twins, 451 of whom were identical and 257 fraternal. The results were analysed using the very powerful biometrical genetical methods of analysis pioneered by the Birmingham School of K. Mather and J. L. Jinks. These methods have enabled us to construct a model of genetic action which not only gives us the heritability of the trait involved, but also information about other aspects of genetic architecture.

Only the briefest summary of these results can be given here. First, for the R factor (radicalism-conservatism) heritability was 65 per cent; for the T component (tough-minded/tender minded) heritability was 54 per cent. For emphasis, heritability was 37 per cent. These values are much higher than one would have expected on *a priori* grounds, and certainly disprove the widely held notion that attitudes are determined by environmental factors alone. Such a belief in the potency of the environment never had any empirical support in any case—it was purely a manifestation of the *Zeitgeist*.

In the Eaves and Eysenck study mentioned above personality inventories were also obtained. It

Demonstrators against Cruise missiles. In Russia and the West, the 'keep nuclear weapons' philosophy is predominantly a conservative one, appealing to the tough-minded sector of society.

was known from previous work done by both researchers that personality factors show strong genetic determination, and the same effect was observed again in this study. The personality traits investigated were E (extraversion-introversion), N (neuroticism-stability) and P (tough-mindedness). Extraversion-introversion refers to the opposition of sociable, impulsive, physically active traits with non-sociable, non-active, non-impulsive behaviour patterns. Tough-mindedness is a personality dimension which is characterized by cold indifference, hostility, aggressiveness, disregard for social conventions, non-conformity and a certain degree of paranoia. Neuroticism is characterized by emotional over-reactivity and the persistence of emotional reactions long after the occasion for them has passed.

Eaves and Eysenck hypothesized that extraversion would be correlated with tough-mindedness, and also that tough-mindedness would be even more powerfully correlated with authoritarianism. Statistical analysis of the results of the twin studies confirmed both hypotheses. The study confirmed the correlation between E and T, showing that it has a genetic, rather than an environmental basis. There was also a significant genetic correlation between P and emphasis, which suggests that individuals who achieve high P scores share the strong conviction of being right, which is characteristic of some psychotic behaviour. There was an even more significant tendency for high P scores to be associated with authoritarianism, very much as expected. Eaves and Eysenck went on to conduct several further studies involving familial relationships and adopted children, and these strongly supported the major conclusions derived from the original work described above.

To summarize, then, there seems no doubt that there are relationships between personality and authoritarianism, that these relationships have a genetic basis, and that consequently it is impossible to discuss ideologies simply in terms of rational beliefs[8]. Endorsement of these belief systems is determined very largely by genetic and hence philosophically irrelevant factors.

The relationship between the emphasis score and P on the one hand, and authoritarianism on the other, is of particular interest. The general bellicosity of ideologies noted at the beginning of this chapter, and the 'commitment' involved, are shown in the emphatic endorsement given to statements by tough-minded subjects, and by the generally aggressive nature of the high P scorers.

WHY THE MIDDLE WAY SELDOM TRIUMPHS

All of this seems to leave open the most fundamental question of all: Why do ideologies arise in the first place? We can suggest what sort of person is likely to fall prey to ideologies, we can predict the sort of ideologies which are consistent with right-wing or left-wing political ideals, and we can show how the dynamism of certain ideologies fits the personality features of the people who adopt them. But the question of origin requires an answer which must go beyond psychology, although it inevitably must include certain psychological principles.

In outline, what we would suggest is this. Right-wing and left-wing political ideas, capitalism and socialism, contain within themselves contradictions which inevitably lead to conflict, change and dissolution. The contradictions of capitalism have been pointed out by many writers, including of course Marx; unless restrained by government action and trade union pressure, capitalism leads to monopoly and the enrichment of the few at the expense of the many. The contradictions of socialism have been pointed out by F. A. Hayek, K. Popper[9] and many others. The egalitarian principle underlying socialism is in conflict with biological reality and can only be enforced by dictatorship. In other words, full-blooded capitalism and full-blooded socialism can only be maintained by repression and denial of human rights. Ideologies are, by definition, coercive. Capitalism, however democratic in intent, requires fascist-type dictatorship to preserve its privileges. Socialism, however democratic in intent, requires communist-type dictatorship to enforce its policies.

Neither the enforcement of social ideals nor the maintenance of privilege is, of course, successful. Fascism only preserves the empty shell of capitalism, shorn of all real power, and Communism only preserves the empty shell of socialism, shorn of all its ideals. In practice both right-wing and left-wing ideals need to be restrained by government action, otherwise they end in impasse. But government action finally congeals into government control, dictatorship and loss of freedom. The only valid alternative is to compromise, to give up right-wing and left-wing ideals in favour of a middle-of-the-road position which reconciles both capitalist and socialist doctrines, which allows for both a private sector and a state-run sector of industry.

Why is this compromise so often disregarded in favour of extreme and militant ideological postures? The answer may lie largely in the 'principle of certainty' enunciated by the British psychologist R. H. Thouless on the basis of his work on religious beliefs. He defined the certainty principle as follows: 'When, in a group of persons, there are influences acting both in the direction of acceptance and of rejection of a belief, the result is not to make the majority adopt a lower degree of conviction, but to make some hold the belief with a high degree of conviction, while others reject it also with a high degree of conviction'. This observation applies closely to political beliefs too.

One of the authors of this book did a study in which he tabulated the distribution of 22,208 votes, on a 7-point attitude scale, on a variety of social and political questions where there were clearly 'influences acting both in the direction of acceptance and of rejection' of the beliefs in ques-

Without repression and brutality, there can be no martyrs. Extreme regimes make more extreme the views they find difficult to tolerate.

'principle of certainty' which makes it difficult for many people to hold their beliefs with a low degree of conviction, although a low degree of conviction would certainly be appropriate to our lack of knowledge of the consequences of social actions.

Repression, of course, begets rebellion, as inevitably as action begets reaction in Newtonian physics. Thus one ideology begets its opposite ideology. The political process further exacerbates the tensions created by the 'principle of certainty'. The conviction that he is ultimately right drives the ideologue farther and farther away from the possibility of compromise, and leads him finally to genocide, to the murder of whole classes or races and to other obsenities which recent history chronicles only too well.

The principles outlined briefly here are, of course, likely to have wider applications. We need only substitute Catholic and Protestant or Christian and Muslim, for capitalist and socialist and we immediately see the same picture, with minor changes to fit the religious content. There are inner contradictions in religious systems just as there are in political systems, and the 'principle of certainty' operates with equal force for any set of beliefs one chooses to name.

In conclusion, we contend that it is impossible to study modern or ancient ideologies properly without paying close attention to psychological principles, and in particular to the relationships between ideology and personality. As yet our scientific implements have only scratched the surface of this absorbing and complex set of problems. Nevertheless, the results are significant enough, and coherent enough, to suggest that in due course we will understand the springs of ideology far better than we do at present.

DISSOLVING PREJUDICE

But is understanding enough? Can psychology not help us to *do* something about the pressing problems produced by modern ideologies, problems such as prejudice? Consider the following experiment, recently carried out by R. Grossarth-Maticek, H. J. Eysenck and H. Vetter in Germany[10]. In this study a random sample of 6,796 men aged between 45 and 55 were interviewed about their prejudices, which were classified as anti-democratic, anti-Semitic, anti-Arab, anti-Slav, anti-Christian, anti-race, anti-American or anti-Communist. Out of this large group 530 individuals were selected who expressed extreme prejudice. These individuals were then paired off according to their prejudices—anti-Semitic with anti-Semitic, anti-Arab with anti-Arab, and so on—and one of each pair was assigned to treatment, the other to a control group. Harking back to Chapter 23, which investigated susceptibility to cancer and coronary heart disease, these were all people who had a 'disease-prone' personality. Those in the treatment group were offered, and accepted, the group behaviour treatment outlined in Chapter 23. However, to guard

tion. The result showed a distinct tendency for extreme values (+3 and −3) to be more frequent than intermediate values. It was also found that when the different groups which took part in the study were compared, there was a marked tendency for the more extreme groups to be more certain of their opinions, which leads one to speculate that in any society which contains haves and have-nots (in effect all but the most small and primitive societies), conservative and radical attitudes would be found among the inhabitants partly as a reflection of their social status and partly as a reflection of their personality. These attitudes would be held with varying degrees of conviction, again depending on the personality of the holder. P+ personalities would have a high degree of conviction, P− personalities low conviction.

Given a particular form of social organization, whether capitalist or socialist, the internal contradictions of that organization would bring about its eventual breakdown unless those who were strongly convinced of its essential rightness ensured its survival by physical force and the suppression of civil rights. Ideologies would arise as a natural consequence of two factors, the internal contradictions of existing political systems and the

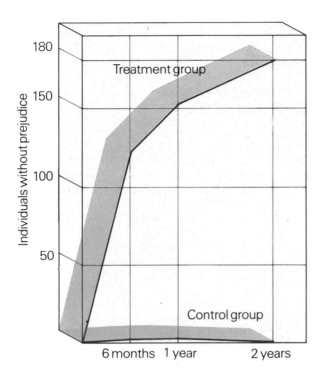

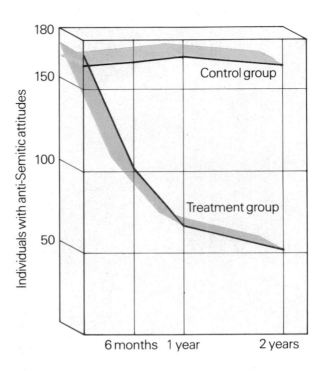

Figure 3   *This graph shows the dramatic effects of behavioural therapy in dissolving prejudice. In the two-year period covered by this study 180 of the 265 individuals who received therapy abandoned their prejudices. In the control group, there was no change in level of prejudice.*

Figure 4   *This graph show much the same story as Figure 3. Within two years of receiving therapy two out of three individuals with strong anti-Semitic opinions had abandoned them. The control group, which did not receive therapy, continued to be prejudiced against Jews.*

against the possibility of the effects of the treatment being attributed to direct suggestion, the treatment made no reference to social attitudes, prejudice, or anything outside the field of health.

The hypothesis behind this experiment was that prejudice is a form of aggression, and that since aggression is the result of frustration, a reduction of frustration ought to lead to a reduction in aggression and prejudice. This is known as the frustration-aggression hypothesis. Individuals who are prone to cancer and coronary heart disease display considerable stress and failure to cope with stress, both of which are intimately coupled with frustration. In this experiment, therefore, the hypothesis was that reduction in stress and improvement in coping behaviour would lead to a diminution of frustration, aggression and prejudice.

Members of the two groups were re-tested after six months, one year and two years, and Figure 3 shows the results. At the beginning of the experiment, none of the participants was without prejudice—indeed that had been the condition of acceptance for the experiment. The control group showed practically no change in attitudes over the two years, but over the same period there was a dramatic increase in the numbers of treated individuals who swung from extreme prejudice to no prejudice. It goes without saying that such a

swing is highly significant statistically. Psychological treatment would seem to be a powerful tool in dissolving prejudice.

Figure 4 shows the effect of treatment on a particular prejudice, that of anti-Semitism. Anti-Semitic attitudes remained at pretty much the same level in the control group, but two-thirds of those who received treatment showed no discernable prejudice at the end of the two-year period.

It is difficult to generalize from these results, and it is equally difficult to know how they could be used in practice, but they do seem to suggest that reducing frustration in a population would also reduce prejudice and that this would be a more fruitful approach than attacking specific prejudices head-on. Directly attacking prejudices makes people very defensive and often extreme in defence of their views. It also leads to resentment and, if anything, a greater entrenchment of attitudes. Tackling the more deep-seated reasons for prejudice may therefore be more practical and succesful. Clearly this is an area of human behaviour which deserves further investigation. Prejudice, particularly racial prejudice, is one of the most evil human emotions conceivable—we are all familiar with the results it had in Hitler's Germany. Anything that psychology can do to combat it should be welcomed.

Epilogue

In this book we have discussed some of the most fascinating and important discoveries ever made by psychologists. But we have not covered even a tenth of all the major areas of research in which psychologists are active. It would take many weighty volumes to do that. Psychology is concerned with human behaviour and is therefore relevant to almost any activity involving human beings.

Let us review quickly a few of the areas we have had to omit. Take architecture. Most people feel that buildings should be designed to be pleasing to look at and comfortable to live in. Psychologists have a valuable contribution to make at this man-building interface.

Overpopulation, one of the major nightmares of recent years, is another important field for the psychologist. In 20 or 30 years from now the world's population will have grown explosively, causing starvation and social strife on a gigantic scale, unless of course successful birth control programmes can be implemented and implemented now. While it is tempting to leave the problem to politicians to deal with, it is not they but psychologists who will directly supervise such programmes or advise on effective advertising campaigns.

Another important area in which psychology is of universal value is ergonomics, the interaction of people and machines. If you think about it, the entire organization of our work environment is increasingly influenced by occupational and industrial psychologists. The problems posed by decaying industries, poor worker morale, low productivity and technological change all basically call for answers at the psychological rather than the political level.

Psychology pervades many facets of our daily lives. Some people find this vaguely sinister, suspecting that the insidious horrors of George Orwell's *Nineteen Eighty-Four* lurk just around the corner. The authors of this book totally reject such a pessimistic view. Apart from anything else, it is quite unfounded. As we have been at pains to show, the richer understanding of human nature which psychology provides is already revolutionizing major aspects of society (our education and penal systems, the treatment of mental illness) in ways which are wholly beneficial.

What of psychology tomorrow? It is of course foolhardy to attempt to predict the future. However, we are prepared to risk making the following three forecasts (call them informed guesses if you prefer) as to the ways in which psychology will develop in the future.

First, psychology will be perceived as being more and more relevant to social problems, and to an increasing number of them, than is the case today. For example, most orthodox medical practitioners have little knowledge of, or interest in, psychology. They simply treat the physical symptoms of the patients who visit their surgeries. Yet many of their patients are more in need of psychological attention than of pills and potions. The 'placebo effect' (patients recovering rapidly even when given dummy drugs) strongly suggests that physical illness and recovery can be aided (as well as caused) by psychological processes. Hopefully there will be a more fruitful marriage of psychological and medical knowledge in the future.

Second, some of the experiments in modern psychology which have hit the headlines have done so because of the ethical issues they pose. If we look into the future, it seems highly probable that research psychologists will be under increasing pressure to justify their work in moral terms. Our only wish is that a proper balance be struck between the concern of the psychologist to carry out relevant and useful research, and the duty of administrators, politicians and the general public to protect the rights and dignity of those who take part in this research. It would be a tragedy if a witch hunt were started against psychologists, leading to a total shackling of their research endeavours.

Third, major advances in any science often occur as a direct consequence of important technological breakthroughs. The radio-telescope dramatically widened the scope of astronomy. In similar fashion Allan and Elaine Hendrickson's exciting new discoveries about intelligence would not have come about had new ways of measuring brain-waves not been devised.

If the future is anything like the past, then the crucial research of the 1990s will depend on further technological developments. We cannot know just what these developments will be, but we confidently predict that there will come a time when our present attempts to unravel the mysteries of the human mind will seem like the uncertain steps of an infant learning to walk.

Bibliography

Chapter 1
[1] Darley, J. M. & Latané, B. 'Bystander Intervention in Emergencies: Diffusion of Responsibility', *Journal of Personality and Social Psychology*, 8, 377–383 (1968)

[2] Latané, B. & Darley, J. M. *The Unresponsive Bystander: Why doesn't he help?* London, Appleton-Century-Crofts (1970)

Chapter 2
[1] Efran, M. G. 'The effect of physical appearance on the judgment of guilt, interpersonal attraction, and severity of recommended punishment in a simulated jury task', *Journal of Research in Personality*, 8, 45–54 (1974)

[2] Berscheid, E. & Walster, E. 'Physical attractiveness', *Advances in Experimental Social Psychology*, Vol. 7. London, Academic Press (1974)

Chapter 3
[1] Argyle, M. & Dean, J. 'Eye-contact, distance, and affiliation', *Sociometry*, 28, 289–304 (1965)

[2] Patterson, M. L. 'An arousal model of interpersonal intimacy', *Psychological Review*, 83, 235–245 (1976)

Chapter 4
[1] Milgram, S. 'Behavioural study of obedience', *Journal of Abnormal and Social Psychology*, 67, 371–378 (1963)

[2] Milgram, S. *Obedience to Authority*. London, Harper & Row (1974)

Chapter 5
[1] Zimbardo, P. G. 'On the ethics of intervention in human psychological research: with special reference to the Stanford prison experiment', *Cognition*, 2, 243–256 (1973)

[2] Zimbardo, P. G. 'Transforming experimental research into advocacy for change'. In Deutsch M. and Hornstein H. A. (Eds.). *Applying Social Psychology: Implications for Research, Practice and Training*. London, Halstead (1975)

Chapter 6
[1] Eysenck, H. J. & Nias, D. K. B. *Sex, Violence and the Media*. London, Maurice Temple Smith (1978) and New York, Harper & Row (1979)

[2] Barnes, G. E., Malamuth, N. M. & Check, J. V. 'Personality and sexuality', *Personality and Individual Differences*, 5, 159–172 (1984)

[3] Barnes, G. E., Malamuth, N. M. & Check, J. V. 'Psychoticism and sexual arousal to rape depictions', *Personality and Individual Differences*, 5, 273–279 (1989)

[4] Armentrout, J. A. & Haner, A. L. 'MMPIs of rapists, rapists of children and non-rapist sex offenders', *Journal of Clinical Psychology*, 34, 330–332 (1978)

[5] Groth, S. N. & Birnbaum, H. J. *Men who Rape: The Psychology of the Offender*. New York, Plenum Press (1979)

[6] Malamuth, N. M. & Donnerstein, E. (Eds.). *Pornography and Sexual Aggression*. New York, Academic Press (1983)

Chapter 7
[1] Rosenhan, D. L. 'On being sane in insane places', *Science*, 179, 250–258 (1973)

[2] Rosenhan, D. L. 'The contextual nature of psychiatric diagnosis', *Journal of Abnormal Psychology*, 84, 462–474 (1975)

[3] Spitzer, R. L. 'On pseudoscience in science, logic in remission, and psychiatric diagnosis: a critique of Rosenhan's "On being sane in insane places" ', *Journal of Abnormal Psychology*, 84, 442–452 (1975)

Chapter 8
[1] Baum, M. 'Rapid extinction of an avoidance response following a period of response prevention in the avoidance apparatus', *Psychological Reports*, 18, 59–64 (1966)

[2] Carlson, N. J. & Black, A. H. 'Traumatic avoidance learning: Note on the effect of response prevention during extinction', *Psychological Reports*, 5, 409–412 (1959)

[3] Page, H. A. & Hall, G. F. 'Experimental extinction as a function of the prevention of a response', *Journal of Comparative & Physiological Psychology*, 46, 33–34 (1953)

[4] Polin, A. T. 'The effects of flooding and physical suppression as extinction techniques on an anxiety motivated avoidance locomotor response', *Journal of Psychology*, 47, 235–245 (1959)

[5] Rachman, S. & Hodgson, R. *Obsessions and Compulsions*. New York, Appleton-Century-Crofts (1980)

Chapter 9
[1] Terrace, H. S. *Nim*. New York, Alfred Knopf (1979)

Chapter 10
[1] Harlow, H. F. 'The nature of love', *American Psychologist*, 13, 673–685 (1958)

[2] Harlow, H. G. & Mears, C. *The Human Model: Primate Perspectives*. Washington, D.C., Winston (1979)

Chapter 11
[1] Hendrickson, D. E. & Hendrickson, A. E. 'The biological basis of intelligence'. In Eysenck, H. J. (Ed.). *A Model for Intelligence*. New York, Springer-Verlag (1982)

[2] Eysenck, H. J. & Barrett, P. 'Psychophysiology and the measurement of intelligence'. In: Reynolds, C. R. and Wilson, V. L. (Eds.). *Methodological and Statistical Advances in the Study of Individual Differences*. New York, Plenum Press (1985)

[3] Barrett, P. T. & Eysenck, H. J. 'Brain electrical potentials and intelligence'. In Gale, A. and Eysenck, M. W. (Eds.). *Handbook of Individual Differences: Biological Perspectives*. Chichester, Wiley (in press)

Chapter 12
[1] Sperry, R. W. 'Hemisphere deconnection and unity in conscious awareness', *American Psychologist*, 23, 723–733 (1968)

[2] Gazzaniga, M. S. & LeDoux, J. E. *The Integrated Mind*. New York, Plenum Press (1977)

Chapter 13
[1] Eaves, L. & Eysenck, H. J. 'The nature of extraversion: A genetical analysis', *Journal of Personality and Social Psychology*, 32, 102–111 (1975)

[2] Eysenck, H. J. (Ed.). *A Model for Personality*. New York, Springer (1980)

[3] Fulker, D. W. 'The genetic and environmental architecture of psychoticism, extraversion and neuroticism'. In Eysenck H. J. (Ed.). *A Model for Personality*. New York, Springer (1980)

[4] MacArthur, R. S. 'An experimental investigation of persistence and its measurement at the Secondary School level'. London, Ph.D. thesis (1951)

[5] Zubin, J., Eron, L. D. & Schumer, F. *An Experimental Approach to Projective Techniques*. New York, Wiley (1965)

[6] Eysenck, H. J. 'Graphological analysis and psychiatry: an experimental study', *British Journal of Psychology*, 35, 70–81 (1945)

[7] Eaves, L., Eysenck, H. J. & Martin, N. G. *Genes, Culture and Personality: An Empirical Approach*. New York, Academic Press (1988)

Chapter 14
[1] Eysenck, M. W. *Happiness: Facts and Myths*. London, Erlbaum (in press)

[2] Costa, P. T. & McCrae, R. R. 'Influence of extraversion and neuroticism on subjective well-being: happy and unhappy people', *Journal of Personality and Social Psychology*, 38, 668–678 (1980)

[3] Argyle, M. *The Psychology of Happiness*. London, Methuen (1987)

Chapter 15
[1] Schachter, S. & Singer, J. 'Cognitive, social and physiological determinants of emotional state', *Psychological Review*, 69, 379–399 (1962)

[2] Marshall, G. D. & Zimbardo, P. G. 'Affective consequences of inadequately explained physiological arousal', *Journal of Personality and Social Psychology*, 37, 970–988 (1979)

Chapter 16
[1] Loftus, E. F. & Palmer, J. C. 'Reconstruction of automobile destruction: An example of the interaction between language and memory', *Journal of Verbal Learning and Verbal Behavior*, 13, 585–589 (1974)

[2] Clifford, B. & Bull, R. *The Psychology of Person Identification*. London, Routledge & Kegan Paul (1978)

Chapter 17
[1] Cherry, E. C. 'Some experiments on the recognition of speech with one and with two ears', *Journal of the Acoustical Society of America*, 25, 975–979 (1953)

[2] Kahneman, D. *Attention and effort*. Englewood Cliffs, N.J., Prentice-Hall (1973)

Chapter 18
[1] Eysenck, M. W. *Human Memory: Theory, Research and Individual Differences*. Oxford, Pergamon (1977)

[2] Tulving, E. 'Cue-dependent forgetting', *American Scientist*, 62, 74–82 (1974)

[3] Tulving, E. & Psotka, J. 'Retroactive inhibition in free recall: Inaccessibility of information available in the memory store', *Journal of Experimental Psychology*, 87, 1–8 (1971)

Chapter 19
[1] Festinger, L. & Carlsmith, J. M. 'Cognitive consequences of forced compliance', *Journal of Abnormal and Social Psychology*, 58, 203–210 (1959)

[2] Wicklund, R. A. & Brehm, J. W. *Perspectives on Cognitive Dissonance*. London, Halstead (1976)

Chapter 20
[1] Gribbin, Mary. 'Granny knows best', *New Scientist*, 84, 350–351 (1979)

[2] Rutter, M., Maughan, Barbara, Mortimer, P. & Ouston, Janet. *Fifteen Thousand Hours*. London, Open Books (1979)

Chapter 21
[1] Eysenck, H. J. 'The development of personality and its relation to learning'. In Murray-Smith S. (Ed.). *Melbourne Studies in Education*, 134–181. Melbourne University Press (1978)

[2] Leith, G. O. 'Individual differences in learning: interactions of personality and teaching methods'. In *Personality and Academic Progress, Conference Proceedings*, 14–25. London, Association of Educational Psychologists (1974)

[3] Trown, E. A. & Leith, G. O. 'Decision rules for teaching strategies in primary schools: Personality-treatment interactions', *British Journal of Educational Psychology*, 45, 130–140 (1975)

Chapter 22
[1] Miller, N. E. 'Learning of visceral and glandular responses', *Science*, 163, 434–445 (1969)

[2] Miller, N. E. & DiCara, L. 'Instrumental learning of heart rate changes in curarized rats: Shaping, and specificity to discriminative stimulus', *Journal of Comparative and Physiological Psychology*, 63, 12–19 (1967)

[3] Seer, P. 'Psychological control of essential hypertension: Review of the literature and methodological critique', *Psychological Bulletin*, 86, 1015–1043 (1979)

Chapter 23
[1] Eysenck, H. J. 'Personality, cancer and cardiovascular disease: a causal analysis', *Personality and Individual Differences*, 5, 535–553 (1985)

[2] Eysenck, H. J. 'The respective importance of personality, cigarette smoking and intervention effects for the genesis of cancer and coronary heart disease', *Personality and Individual Differences*, 9, 453–464 (1988)

[3] Steptoe, A. *Psychological Factors in Cardiovascular Disorders*. New York, Academic Press (1981)

[4] Chincey, M. A. & Rosenman, R. D. (Eds.). *Anger and Hostility in Cardiovascular and Behavioral Disorders*. Washington D.C., Hemisphere (1985)

[5] Booth-Kewley, S. & Friedman, H. 'Psychological predictors of heart disease: a quantitative review', *Psychological Bulletin*, 101, 343–362 (1987)

[6] Price, V. A. *Type A Behavior Pattern*. New York. Academic Press (1982)

[7] Grossarth-Maticek, R., Eysenck, H. J. & Vetter, H. 'Personality type, smoking habits and their interaction as predictor of cancer and coronary heart disease', *Personality and Individual Differences*, 9, 479–495 (1988)

[8] Eysenck, H. J. 'Personality, stress and cancer', *British Journal of Medical Psychology*, 61, 57–75 (1988)

Chapter 24
[1] Maclean, P. D. *A Triune Concept of the Brain and Behaviour*. Toronto, University of Toronto Press (1973)

[2] Eysenck, H. J. *Crime and Personality*. London, Routledge & Kegan Paul (1977)

[3] Solomon, R. L. 'Punishment', *American Psychologist*, 19, 239–253 (1964)

[4] Solomon, R. L., Turner, L. H. & Lessac, H. S. 'Some effects of delay punishment on resistance to temptation in dogs', *Journal of Personality and Social Psychology*, 8, 233–238 (1968)

[5] Ayllon, T. & Azrin, N. *The Token Economy*. New York, Appleton-Century-Crofts (1968)

[6] Sarason, J. G. 'A cognitive social learning approach to juvenile delinquency'. In Hare R. D. & Schalling D. (Eds.). *Psychopathic Behaviour*. London, Wiley (1978)

[7] Stumphauzer, J. S. *Behaviour Therapy with Delinquents*. Springfield, C. C. Thomas (1973)

[8] Stumphauzer, J. S. *Progress in Behaviour Therapy with Delinquents*. Springfield, C. C. Thomas (1973)

[9] Walters, G. C. & Grusec, J. E. *Punishment*. San Francisco, W. H. Freeman (1977)

Chapter 25
[1] Shils, E. 'Authoritarianism: "Right" and "Left"'. In Christie R. & Jahoda M. (Eds.). *Studies in the scope and method of 'The Authoritarian Personality'*. Glencoe (Illinois), The Free Press, 24–49 (1954)

[2] Hayek, F. A. *The Constitution of Liberty*. London, Routledge and Kegan Paul (1960)

[3] Jaensch, E. R. *Der Gegentypus*. Leipzig, J. A. Barth (1938)

[4] Adorno, T. W., Frenkel-Brunswick, E., Levinson, D. J. & Sanford, R. N. *The Authoritarian Personality*. New York, Harper & Row (1950)

[5] Eysenck, H. J. *The Psychology of Politics*. London, Routledge & Kegan Paul (1954)

[6] Eysenck, H. J. & Coulter, T. 'The personality and attitudes of working-class British communists and fascists', *Journal of Social Psychology*, 87, 59–73 (1972)

[7] Eaves, L. & Eysenck, H. J. 'Genetics and the development of social attitudes', *Nature* (London) 249, 288–289 (1974)

[8] Eysenck, H. J. & Wilson, G. D. *The Psychological Basis of Ideology*. Lancaster, Medical & Technical Publishers (1978)

[9] Popper, K. *The Open Society and its Enemies* (2 volumes). London, Routledge & Kegan Paul (1945)

[10] Grossarth-Maticek, R., Eysenck, H. J. & Vetter, H. 'The causes and cures of prejudice: An empirical study of the frustration-aggression hypothesis', *Personality and Individual Differences*, 9 (1988)

Index

PHOTOGRAPHY CREDITS

DAS PHOTO 126
Sally and Richard Greenhill 102, 198, 233
Lesley Hamilton 82
Tom Hanley 32/33, 40
Alan Hutchison 188 right
Susan Kuklin 84, 87 (4), back jacket (bottom left)
Mansell Collection 127
Mary Evans Picture Library 193
Multimedia 11, 20, 21, 28, left and right, 30 top, 34, 38, 42, 48, 59, 85 top, 94 bottom, 103, 113, 123 top, 133 top, 136/137, 147, 149 top, 166, 167, 168 right, 187 (4), 192, 205, 206, 208/209, 217, 221 *Aliza Auerbach* 95 *Yael Braun* 116, 148, 151, 214 *Arnold Desser* 219 *Rudi Geller* 75 *Miki Koren* 14, 23 bottom, 24, 25, 26 right, 30 bottom, 36/37, 50, 51, 57 bottom, 66, 68, 69, 73, 78 bottom, 79, 93, 108 top and bottom, 134, 139, 153, 156 bottom, 164, 168 left, 169, 173, 176/177, 178, 180/181, 183, 185, 186, 188 left, 195, 204, 227, 234/235 *Israel Sun* 15, 16, 13 left and right, 19, 35, 39, 78, top, 80, 85 inset, 98/99, 101, 122, 128, 130, 133 bottom, 140, 142/143, 150, 170, 190/191, 199 top, 201 top and bottom, 218 *Ron Isaak* 18, 27, 56, 60, 119, 147 bottom, 211, 213, 228, 247 *Arnon Orbach* 23 top, 118, 171, 238 *Sergio Trippodo* 70, 71, 144 *Colin Urquhart* 123 bottom, 138, 199 inset, 229, 236
Liza Mackson 57 top, 63, 207, back jacket (top left, top right, bottom right)
Metropolitan Police 160, 239
Stanley Milgram (from the film *Obedience* distributed by New York University Film Library) 44 (3)
R. Milon 100
Pixfeatures 53 top
Rex Features 36, 46, 53 bottom, 111, 119 (Belg-Ingh), 158, 159, (3), 161 (3), 172, 242, 245
David Simson 17, 26 left, 45, 47, 64/65, 94 top, 96, 135, 226
Frank Spooner Pictures 31
Sunday Times Magazine 88
Herbert Terrace 90/91 (5)

ARTWORK CREDITS

Jane Cope 115, 156, 162
John Strange 81, 106, 107, 109, 110, 121, 222, 223, 224, 225, 231, 234, 243, 244, 248

Multimedia Books Limited have endeavoured to observe the legal requirements with regard to the rights of suppliers of photographs and illustrations.

The cartoon on p. 162 is identical to that on page 156, but the question 'what is different. . .' probably misled you into thinking there were differences. Memories are easily distorted by leading questions.